Others

Others

J. Hillis Miller

PRINCETON UNIVERSITY PRESS

PRINCETON AND OXFORD

Copyright © 2001 by Princeton University Press
Published by Princeton University Press, 41 William Street,
Princeton, New Jersey 08540
In the United Kingdom: Princeton University Press,
3 Market Place, Woodstock, Oxfordshire OX20 1SY

Library of Congress Cataloging in Publication Data

Miller, J. Hillis (Joseph Hillis), 1928–
Others / J. Hillis Miller.
p.   cm.
Includes bibliographical references and index.

ISBN 0-691-01224-5 (alk. paper)—
ISBN 0-691-01223-7 (pbk. : alk. paper)

1. European fiction—19th century—History and
criticism.   2. Criticism—Europe—20th century.
3. Difference (Psychology) in literature.   I. Title.
PN3499. M48 2001
809.3'0094—dc21   00-066945

This book has been composed in Sabon

Printed on acid-free paper. ∞

www.pup.princeton.edu

Printed in the United States of America

1 3 5 7 9 10 8 6 4 2

1 3 5 7 9 10 8 6 4 2
(Pbk.)

In memory of Michael Sprinker

———————————

CONTENTS

ACKNOWLEDGMENTS

IN ALMOST ALL this book's chapters, only a portion of the longer essay I originally wrote was published in the various places that I indicate below. The full, often much longer, essays are restored here. All have been more or less elaborately revised for this book. I am grateful to all those who originally invited me to turn my attention to this or that author, text, or topic, and for their kindness in allowing me to reuse this material in a different form and context. I am grateful also to those students who helped me work out these ideas in seminars at the University of California at Irvine.

A portion of chapter 1 was published in a different form in a pamphlet for private circulation as "Friedrich Schlegel and the Anti-Ekphrastic Tradition," *Litteraturkritik & Romantikstudiers Skriftrække* 24 (University of Aarhus, Denmark), 25 pp. This portion has also appeared in a volume dedicated to Murray Krieger and published by the University of California Press.

Chapter 2 was published in an earlier form as "The Topography of Jealousy in *Our Mutual Friend*," in *Dickens Refigured: Bodies, Desires and Other Histories*, ed. John Schad (Manchester: Manchester Press, 1996), 218–35.

A shorter version of chapter 3 was published in a Festschrift for H. M. Daleski as "The Roar on the Other Side of Silence: Otherness in *Middlemarch*," in *Rereading Texts/Rethinking Critical Presuppositions*, ed. Shlomith Rimmon-Kenan, Leona Toker, and Shuli Barzilai (Frankfurt am Main: Peter Lang, 1997), 137–48.

A shorter version of chapter 4 was published as the introduction to Anthony Trollope, *Marion Fay* (London: The Folio Society, 1997), xi–xxix.

Chapter 5 was previously published in a much shorter version as "*Heart of Darkness* Revisited," in Joseph Conrad, *Heart of Darkness* (Boston: Bedford Books, 1996), 206–20. A preliminary version of the chapter as a whole was published as a pamphlet for local circulation in Denmark as "Should We Read *Heart of Darkness*?," *Arbejdspapirer* (Dept. of Comparative Literature, University of Aarhus), 17–98.

An earlier, partial version of chapter 6 was published as "Sharing Secrets," in Joseph Conrad, *The Secret Sharer*, ed. Daniel R. Schwarz (Boston: Bedford Books, 1997), 232–52.

Chapter 7 has been published in a somewhat different form in *Deconstructions*, ed. Nicholas Royle (Houndmills and New York: Palgrave, 2000).

About half of chapter 8 has been published as "Just Reading *Howards End*," in *Howards End*, ed. Alistair M. Duckworth (Boston: St. Martin's Press, 1996), 467–82.

An earlier version of chapter 9 was published in French as " 'Le Mensonge, le Mensonge Parfait': Théories du mensonge chez Proust et Derrida," trans. Yasmine Van den Wijngaert, revue par Chantal Zabus et Cécile Hayez, in *Passions de la littérature,* ed. Michel Lisse (Paris: Galilée, 1996), 405–20.

Part of chapter 10 has been published in *Material Events*, ed. Thomas Cohen et al. (Minneapolis: University of Minnesota Press, 2000).

An earlier, somewhat shorter version of chapter 11 was published as "Derrida's Others," *Applying to Derrida*, ed. John Brannigan, Ruth Robbins, and Julian Wolfreys (New York: St. Martin's Press, 1996), 153–70.

I am grateful to all involved for allowing me to use these essays here in revised form.

The dedication to Michael Sprinker testifies to a long and unclouded friendship with a wonderful scholar and person whose premature death was an irreparable loss to me and to many others.

Others

INTRODUCTION

> . . . l'autre appelle à venir et cela n'arrive qu'à
> plusieurs voix.
> —Jacques Derrida

I BEGIN with this enigmatic epigraph from Derrida's "Psyché: Invention de l'autre" to signal the way this book circles around at the end to try to explain what Derrida means by saying "the other calls [something] to come and that does not happen except in multiple voices."[1]

My title is a reference—to a considerable degree counter, original, spare, strange, ironic—to all those ways the concept of the "other" is used in literary and cultural studies these days. Most such uses mean by "other" the racial, gendered, or ethnic other. The word is used invidiously to name the way a hegemonic culture or gender group views different and subaltern ones as exotic or inferior or just plain alien, and therefore as something it would be a good idea to erase or assimilate by some form, overtly violent or not, of ethnic cleansing. As these essays attempt to make clear, I mean by "others" something different, an element of the "completely other" that inhabits even the most familiar and apparently "same," for example my sense of myself or of my neighbor or my beloved, the "alter ego" within my own home or culture, or my sense of my own culture as such, or my sense of literary and philosophical works that belong to my own culture. Those are, I claim, other to themselves, as well as to "me." They are divided, riven, their unity "blotched out beyond unblotching," as Wallace Stevens puts it in "The Comedian as the Letter C."[2] A self may find its own depths, for example its unconscious, other to itself. Or another person may be other. Or another nation or ethnic group may be other, though not necessarily in a way that sees them as subaltern. Representations of this otherness have had great diversity. Proust's Marcel in *Remembrance of Things Past* finds Albertine's supposed lesbianism bewilderingly, fascinatingly, other. Jacques Lacan, in a celebrated formula, defined the unconscious as "the discourse of the other." The notion of the other has great importance, though with a different meaning in each case, in influential theorists like Jacques Derrida, Emanuel Lévinas, and Jean-François Lyotard. A full repertoire would be more or less interminable.

In all these diverse and conflicting uses of the word "other," as Lévinas and Derrida have argued,[3] two different concepts of otherness govern as the chief alternatives. On the one hand, the other may be another version of the same, in one way or another assimilable, comprehensible, able to be appropriated and understood. On the other hand, the other may be truly and radically other. In the latter case, the other cannot be turned into some version of the same. It cannot be made transparent to the understanding, thereby dominated and controlled. It remains, whatever effort we make to deal with it, irreducibly other. As Jacques Derrida puts this: "Tout autre est tout autre. (Every other is completely other.)"[4]

Just what it might mean to speak of the "completely other" will become clear through the explorations of it in the various chapters that follow. I have from the beginning of my literary study been haunted by the sense of a radical otherness mediated in multiple ways by literary works. In this book I have attempted to come to terms as directly as possible with that "sense." This can only be done, I hold, through "readings," not through abstract or conceptual theorizing. This is because the otherness I seek is not a concept but an elusive feature of specific verbal constructs, different in each case. Though all the authors studied here belong to more or less the same epoch, the period that extends from romanticism to the present day, I am skeptical about attempts to historicize my topic, for example by calling this book "Otherness from Schlegel to Derrida." Of course changes in class, economic structure, and social context during this period can explain a lot about each of the authors treated here, even about the concept of otherness in each case. Nevertheless I hold that the particular way otherness is present in each cannot be predicted from the biography or social position of the authors in question or even by what those authors read of earlier work. If a given literary work were fully explicable in terms of its context, it would not be worth reading. It is worth reading only if it is in some way inaugural, if it is performative in a certain somewhat anomalous speech act sense, that is, if it brings something wholly new into the world, and if reading it gives the reader access to something he or she can reach in no other way. That "something" I am calling the "others."

In one way or another the wholly other is ghostly and takes the form of an apparitional promise. The tout autre is something already there, a revenant from some immemorial past, and yet heralds or invokes or demands a future, for example a better democracy or a better interpersonal situation to come, like that vague promise detected hovering in the air by the narrator at the end of E. M. Forster's *A Passage to India*: " 'No, not yet,' . . . 'No, not there.' "[5] This promise of something better to come is a political or millennial dimension in all these texts that may be a specific historical feature to be associated with revolutionary movements from the end of the eighteenth century on in Europe and the Americas, or even with Marx's "messianic without messianism," as Derrida has called it in *Specters of Marx*.[6]

This book begins and ends with chapters on three theorists of otherness: Friedrich Schlegel, Paul de Man, and Jacques Derrida. I have read these, however, not as the first or last word on the topic of otherness, but as testimonies, each quite different from the other two, of an experience of otherness that is on the same plane of witnessing as that of my various more strictly literary works and authors. These three chapters could have been augmented by chapters on Maurice Blanchot and Emmanuel Lévinas, both of whom have been important for my thinking about the wholly other. I have wanted, however, to let the testimony of the literary works speak for themselves and not be overwhelmed by "theory." In any case Blanchot and Lévinas, like de Man and Derrida, would each have had a different story to tell, nor would the four of them add up to a homogenous theory of the "tout autre."

Literary works in the conventional sense have always more interested me than theoretical works as mediations in various ways, different in each case, offering a glimpse of the wholly other. Each chapter on a literary work in this book attempts to approach my topic through the unique way in which the words on the pages as read serve as mediums, in more than one sense of the word, of the wholly other. The inclusion of chapters on two works by the same author, Conrad, is meant to indicate that it is risky or unwise to generalize for a given author. Individual works, even those by the same author, must each be read as a unique testimony to otherness.

I have used the plural in my title, "others," to avoid the implicit personification in speaking in the singular of "the other," as well as to avoid the assumption that the other is, whether a person or not, necessarily and ascertainably unified, single, whole. When one says "the other" and means the "wholly other," it is almost impossible to avoid thinking of that other as a person or quasi-person, perhaps an old man with a long gray beard, Joyce's mad feary father. Why should we beg the question and assume that the other is "one," and a person to boot? To say "others" disrupts that almost irresistible presumption. It makes of the wholly other possibly a multitudinous murmurous cacophony, like Friedrich Schlegel's "chaos," discussed in my first chapter. This murmur "calls to come" in many overlapping and incompatible voices, such as the voices that speak in the various texts I have read in this book. I have read them with all the respect I could muster for the way the "others" call through them, in a unique voice in each case, for something to come.

This book is the product of a long-term project in teaching, lecturing, and writing that has allowed me to think out further through readings of specific examples the problematics of otherness in literature. Now the disjecta membra of that project are brought together in their completed form, assembled from their dispersal into a more or less shapely whole, just as the parts of Osiris's body were gathered by Isis and reassembled. The wholly other, present everywhere in my various texts and yet absent from any direct encounter, perception, or naming, may be figured as that missing part or member Isis could not find. The other is always there and not there, in a species of ghostly semblance, as my readings will show.

NOTES

1. "Psyché: Invention de l'autre," *Psyché: Inventions de l'autre* (Paris: Galilée, 1987), 61. For an English translation, see "Psyche: Inventions of the Other," trans. Catherine Porter, in *Reading de Man Reading*, ed. Lindsay Waters and Wlad Godzich (Minneapolis: University of Minnesota Press, 1989), 65. I have in this case made my own translation. My version is a little more awkward but also a little closer to the somewhat strange syntax of the original.

2. Wallace Stevens, *Collected Poems* (New York: Knopf, 1954), 28.

3. See Emmanuel Lévinas, "La trace de l'autre," *Tijdschrift voor Philosophie* (Sept. 1963): 605–23; "The Trace of the Other," trans. A. Lingis, in *Deconstruction in Context: Literature and Philosophy*, ed. Mark C. Taylor (Chicago: University of Chicago Press, 1986), 345–59; and Derrida, "Psyché," 11–61, esp. 58–61. I have discussed these two concepts of the other in more detail in *Black Holes* (Stanford: Stanford University Press, 1999).

4. Jacques Derrida, *Aporias*, trans. Thomas Dutoit (Stanford: Stanford University Press, 1993), 22. I have changed Dutoit's "completely" to "wholly."

5. E. M. Forster, *A Passage to India* (New York: Harcourt Brace Jovanovich, 1984), 362.

6. See Jacques Derrida, *Spectres de Marx* (Paris: Galilée, 1993), 96: "messianique sans messianisme"; *Specters of Marx*, trans. Peggy Kamuf (New York: Routledge, 1994), 181. See also Derrida's commentary on his use of this phrase in Jacques Derrida, "Marx & Sons," in *Ghostly Demarcations: A Symposium on Jacques Derrida's "Specters of Marx,"* ed. Michael Sprinker (London: Verso, 1998), 250–51.

Chapter One

FRIEDRICH SCHLEGEL: CATACHRESES FOR CHAOS

... alle Schönheit ist Allegorie. Das Höchste kann
man eben, weil es unaussprechlich ist, nur allegorisch sagen.
—Friedrich Schlegel[1]

"I envy those men who become mythological while
living," Yeats said to Wilde, half in compliment, and
received the reply, "I think a man should invent his
own myth." It was an injunction Yeats would remember
all of his life.
—Richard Ellmann, *Oscar Wilde*

I SHALL APPROACH "otherness" in Friedrich Schlegel by the apparently indirect route of his ideas about mythology. "Myth"—the word alone might give rise to an inexhaustible and interminable historical commentary. Moreover the word "myth" in the various Western languages is tied to a tangle of other key words in our tradition. It would require another interminable commentary, infinity piled on infinity, or deep beneath deep, to sort out those connections. A single contradiction or aporia, however, inhabits all this complexity. It is a true aporia, a dead end in logical thinking. Myth cannot logically be two contradictory things at once. Nevertheless, in our tradition it is two contradictory things at once. On the one hand, "myth" names a story that is human, all too human, a beguiling fiction that may be dangerously untrue. On the other hand, a "myth" is a story about the gods in their relations to human beings. This story embodies a people's deepest insights into its origins and destiny. For Aristotle "muthos" means what in English is usually translated as "plot," one of the six parts of a tragedy, along with character, diction, thought, spectacle, and song. "The plot (muthos)," says Aristotle, "is the imitation (mimesis) of the action:—for by Plot I here mean the arrangement of the incidents" (1450a).[2] Aristotle goes on to say that the plot or structure of the incidents is the most important part of all. Why? Because "tragedy is an imitation, not of men, but of an action and of life, and life consists in action, and its end is a mode of action, not a quality" (1450a; 27). Another way Aristotle puts this is to affirm that the purpose of a tragedy is to arouse and purge pity and fear. The sequence and concatenation of the incidents, leading to the reversal of fortune (*peripeteia*) and the discovery (*anagnorisis*), effects the purgation (*catharsis*). Therefore the plot or muthos—what one might call, following Andrzej Warminski, the syntax of the incidents—is the most important feature. You could have a tragedy without character or spectacle (though it is hard to imagine such a thing), but not without muthos. The muthos, myth, or plot is a purely instrumental arrangement or design intended to produce a certain performative effect.

On the one hand, any story, true or false, will do as long as it produces the desired effect. Performative efficacy, not referential or constative veracity, is what matters. On the other hand, the actual muthoi chosen by the Greek tragedians whom Aristotle discusses are taken from the cycles of stories about families that have, to put it succinctly, got in trouble with the gods: "Now the best tragedies," says Aristotle, "are founded on the story of a few houses,—on the fortunes of Alcmaeon, Oedipus, Orestes, Meleager, Thyestes, Tellephus, and those others who have done or suffered something terrible" (1453a; 47). The archetypal tragedy, for Aristotle, is Sophocles's *Oedipus the King*. Far from being just any sequence of incidents that have the right cathartic arrangement, the plot or muthos of this tragedy leads ultimately to perhaps unanswerable questions involving human destiny as the Greeks understood it: Why has Apollo decided to make Oedipus suffer so? What has Oedipus done that would justify such a terrible fate?

In Plato the same contradictory notion of myth can be observed, though it has in Plato a different structure and a different affective valence. On the one hand, Plato condemns the poets because they tell lying (and obscene) stories about the gods. On the other hand, Plato (or rather Socrates) notoriously uses myths at crucial moments in his own argument. Examples are the myth of the original androgynous human being in *The Symposium* and the myth of Er in *The Republic*. Socrates condemns in one place what he uses in another. Plato has it both ways though he cannot, logically, have it both ways. For example, in *The Republic* he uses double diegesis when he has Socrates condemn double diegesis. Plato plays the role of Socrates condemning Homer for speaking part of the *Odyssey* in Odysseus's name.

A similar doubleness can be identified in each of the chief historical stages in Western uses of the word myth or its concept: in Latin appropriations of Greek myth such as Ovid's *Metamorphoses*, in the revival of Greek and Roman antiquity in fourteenth- and fifteenth-century humanism, in that great turning point in Western intellectual history, the period of romanticism, and in twentieth-century uses of the word "myth." The latter inherit the romantic version of a doubleness that makes a myth both a dangerous fiction and a way of expressing the most profound and enig-matic truths, truths that cannot be expressed conceptually but must be put in narrative form. In our own time, a once influential form of literary theory and literary criticism was called "myth criticism" or "archetypal criticism." This was elaborately developed, for example, by Northrop Frye in *Anatomy of Criticism*.[3] Derived by various relays from romanti-cism and from eighteenth-, nineteenth-, and twentieth-century myth criti-cism and anthropology, such as Frazer's *The Golden Bough*, as well as from Jungian archetypal psychoanalysis, this mode of criticism presup-posed that even apparently "realistic" and historically referential literary works draw their secret power from unostentatiously repeating the con-tours of some universal myth. The story of Dorothea, Casaubon, and Will Ladislaw in George Eliot's *Middlemarch*, for example, can be shown to repeat the story of Ariadne, Theseus, and Bacchus, as discreet refer-ences in the novel indicate.

Nevertheless, the word "myth," particularly in recent years, has taken on a distinctly dyslogistic flavor. Myth has become almost a synonym for ideology or for that ideological element called an ideologeme, that is, for something unconsciously assumed to be true that is actually false. An ideologeme mistakes a linguistic for a material reality. In the United States, for example, we speak of "the myth of upward mobility," or "the myth of supply-side economics," or "the myth of the strong silent man." Roland Barthes's book about the fantasies of consumer culture is called *Mythologies*,[4] while a recent book by Jean-Luc Nancy and Philippe La-coue-Labarthe is called *Le mythe Nazi*.[5]

How could this doubleness occur? How could the same word come to mean both something very good and something very bad? What is the secret connection between the two valences of the word "myth"? How does the one lead to the other, or necessarily imply the other, or never exist without some hint of the other? I shall suggest answers to these questions by interrogating a text that comes at a crucial moment in the historical development I have sketched: Friedrich Schlegel's "Rede über die Mythologie" ("Talk on Mythology") from the *Gespräch über die Poesie* (*Dialogue on Poetry*). The *Dialogue on Poetry* was written in Jena and published in 1800 in the third volume of the *Athenäum*, the journal that Friedrich Schlegel and his brother August Wilhelm founded in 1798.

Though the *Dialogue on Poetry* is distantly modeled on Plato's dia-logues, it lacks the dialectical impetus that leads Socrates, in Plato's dialogues, step by step toward some final conclusion, even though that conclusion, as in the *Protagoras*, may be that we now only know even better than we did when we started what we do not yet know. Therefore we must go on searching for answers to our questions. Schlegel's *Dia-logue on Poetry*, on the contrary, is made up of relatively desultory discussions among a pseudonymous group of intellectuals, including two women. Their conversation is something that might have occurred among the members of the Jena circle when they met at the home of Friedrich's brother, August Wilhelm Schlegel. The give-and-take of dialogue among the participants is interrupted by the presentation of what today we should call "papers" by members of the group. The participants, according to the best guesses of the scholars, are supposed to represent Schelling, Novalis, Tieck, August Wilhelm Schlegel, A. W. Schlegel's wife, Caroline, Friedrich Schlegel himself, and his mistress, Dorothea Veit. The "Talk on Mythology" is spoken by Ludovico, who is supposed to represent Schelling or perhaps Fichte. These guesses by Schlegel scholars can neither be confirmed nor be disconfirmed. Not much is gained, for example, by trying to relate the "Rede über die Mythologie" to Schelling's thought, though Schlegel *is* deeply indebted to Fichte, as Paul de Man (and Hegel before him) has shown. The whole of the *Gespräch über die Poesie* expresses Schlegel's own ideas, in their characteristic self-contradictory profusion. In what sense they are self-contradictory, and necessarily so, I shall explain later.

The *Gespräch über die Poesie* is not so much a dialogue in the Platonic sense as a chain of fragments, in Schlegel's sense of fragment. Like Nietzsche after him, Friedrich Schlegel recognized that the major modern genre, the novel, derived more from Plato's dialogues than from Alexandrine narratives. The seventy-seventh of the Athenäum fragments asserts that "A dialogue is a chain or garland of fragments. An exchange of letters is a dialogue on a larger scale, and memoirs constitute a system of fragments."[6] He might have gone on to say that a novel, which he saw as the characteristic genre of romanticism, is also a chain, garland, or system of fragments. "A novel is a romantic book," Schlegel asserted in the "Letter about the Novel," one of the interpolated essays in the *Dialogue on Poetry*.[7] One of the "Critical Fragments" asserts that "Novels are the Socratic dialogues of our time" (G, 7; E, 3).

The reader will see the paradox in these formulations. If the fragments are really fragments, they cannot be joined together in a chain, garland, or system. However they are assembled, they still remain a contiguous set of incompatibles. It would be a dangerous mistake, for example, to try to use a chain of fragments to anchor a boat. They just cannot be connected to one another in a way that will hold. A chain of fragments is a chain that does not enchain or concatenate. "A fragment," says Schlegel, "like a miniature work of art, has to be entirely isolated from the surrounding world and be complete in itself like a porcupine (in sich selbst vollendet sein wie ein Igel)" (G, 47; E, 45). This completeness, however, consists of bringing together incompatible ideas into such close proximity that they explode into irrationality. "If one becomes infatuated with the absolute and simply can't escape it," asserts one fragment by Schlegel that Novalis included in his *Blütenstaub* (Pollen), "then the only way out is to contradict oneself continually and join opposite extremes together. The principle of contradiction [that says a thing either is or is not so and so; this is the law of the excluded middle] is inevitably doomed, and the only remaining choice is either to assume an attitude of suffering or else ennoble necessity by acknowledging the possibility of free action" (E, 17). This "free action," it seems, takes the form of contradicting oneself continually and joining opposite extremes together. It is an action because it is a speech act, as I shall show. The result of enclosing such contradictions within the prickly, noli me tangere, porcupine-like enclosure of a fragment is defined in another fragment: "Wit is an explosion of confined spirit (Witz ist eine Explosion von gebundnem Geist)" (G, 17; E, 11).

I shall return later to the question of just why it is that Schlegel is unable in principle to write a work that coheres, that does not contradict itself, that obeys Aristotelian or modern principles of organic unity, that is, possesses a shapely form with beginning, middle, end, and underlying logos holding the whole thing together. Along with several other works by Friedrich Schlegel—the three sets of fragments (the *Kritische Fragmente*, the *Athenäums-Fragmente*, and the *Ideen*), the essay "Über die Unverständlichkeit" ("On Incomprehensibility"), and the strange *roman à clef, Lucinde*—the *Dialogue on Poetry* is one of the crucial texts of German romanticism or, more specifically, of Jena romanticism. Within the *Gespräch über die Poesie*, the "Rede über die Mythologie" is one of the most important moments. To understand it in its context of Friedrich Schlegel's other work and the broader intellectual milieu within which it was written would, so it seems, be to go a long way toward understanding German romanticism as one stage in the long Western history of the word "myth." Schlegel's attention to the possibility of *Unverständlichkeit*, incomprehensibility, should, however, give even the most confident reader pause.

Friedrich Schlegel's place in intellectual history is equivocal. On the one hand he is recognized as a key figure in romanticism. An immense secondary work on his writings exists. The twenty-two-volume *Kritische Friedrich-Schlegel-Ausgabe*, under the general editorship of the late Ernst Behler, is a monument of twentieth-century scholarship.[8] On the other hand, if Paul de Man is right, and he usually is in such matters, this enormous effort has been to some degree an unintentional work of covering up what is most threatening and disquieting about Friedrich Schlegel's work.[9] Schlegel's conversion to Catholicism in 1808 and his rewriting of crucial passages in his own earlier work provided the model for this cover-up.

What is so dangerous about Friedrich Schlegel's writings that it would lead sober scholars to turn away from what he says or to make him say something other than what he says? One answer is to recognize that Schlegel was a great theorist and practitioner of irony. The threatening aspects of irony always call forth their repression. Schlegel's fragments are ironical through and through, as are the other key works by him I have mentioned. Many of the fragments, moreover, in one way or another attempt to define irony. Hegel, who understood Schlegel to a considerable extent at least, for example his derivation from Fichte,[10] and detested him, as did Kierkegaard, though for somewhat different reasons, gives a clue. As Kierkegaard says in *The Concept of Irony*, "As soon as Hegel mentions the word 'irony,' he promptly thinks of Schlegel and Tieck, and his style is immediately marked by a certain resentment."[11] Passages denouncing Schlegel appear in Hegel's *Ästhetik*, in the *Grundlinien der Philosophie des Rechts*, in the *Vorlesungen über die Geschichte der Philosophie*, and in "Über 'Solger's nachgelassene Schriften,'" all repeating more or less the same indignant reproaches. In *Elements of the Philosophy of Right*, for example, Schlegel's brand of irony is anathematized as "evil (evil, in fact, of an inherently wholly universal kind) (das Böse, und zwar das in sich ganz allgemeine Böse)."[12] In the essay on his deceased colleague Solger, Hegel speaks of "the wanton disregard of things that are sacred and of the highest excellence such as marks the period of Friedrich von Schlegel's 'Lucinde,'" and of "the most brazen and flourishing period of irony."[13] Kierkegaard's *The Concept of Irony* contains a long section sharply attacking Schlegel's *Lucinde* and his concept of irony generally.[14]

Why is Schlegel's irony so dangerous? Why does it arouse such intellectual violence and resentment? Hegel's remarks about Schlegel in the section of the introduction to the *Ästhetik* entitled "Irony" suggests one answer. Irony is here defined by Hegel as "infinite absolute negativity."[15] This definition is later echoed and used again with a slightly different valence by Kierkegaard in *The Concept of Irony*. Irony is a power of the ego that just says no to everything. In a famous formulation, Schlegel defined irony as "permanente Parekbase" (permanent parabasis).[16] This is itself an ironically self-contradictory definition, since parabasis, the momentary breaking of dramatic illusion when one of the actors in a play comes forward to speak in his own person, must have some fictive illusion to suspend, whereas permanent parabasis would be perpetual suspension with nothing left to suspend. Paul de Man, in "The Concept of Irony," after having said that it is impossible to give a definition of irony or to state its concept, nevertheless ultimately defines irony as follows: "if Schlegel said irony is permanent parabasis, we would say that irony is the permanent parabasis of the allegory of tropes."[17] As Hegel recognizes and as Paul de Man demonstrates in detail, Schlegel's conception of irony derives from Fichte. "[T]he *ego*," says Hegel in the *Ästhetik*, discussing Schlegel's derivation from Fichte,

> can remain lord and master (Herr und Meister) of everything, and in no sphere of morals, law, things human and divine, profane and sacred, is there anything that would not first have to be laid down by the *ego* (nicht durch Ich erst zu setzen wäre), and that therefore could not equally well be destroyed by it. Consequently everything genuinely and independently real becomes only a show (ein Schein), not true and genuine on its own account or through itself, but a mere appearance (ein bloßes Scheinen) due to the *ego* in whose power and caprice (Gewalt und Willkür) and at whose free disposal it remains. . . . [T]he divine irony of genius [is] this concentration of the *ego* into itself, for which all bonds are snapped and which can live only in the bliss of self-enjoyment (nur in der Seligkeit des Selbstgenusses leben mag). This irony was invented by Friedrich von Schlegel and many others have babbled about it or are now babbling about it again. (G, 13:94, 95; E, 1:64–65, 66)

Hegel's scandalized distaste is overtly directed at what he sees as the immorality and obscenity of *Lucinde*, the way it makes light of the marriage bond. *Lucinde* was deplored also by Kierkegaard as an extreme example of the sort of immorality to which unrestrained irony leads.[18]

Somewhat more covertly, however, though it surfaces openly in his remarks on irony in Solger, Hegel's perhaps deeper objection to Schlegel's irony is that it puts a stop to dialectical progress. If irony is infinite absolute negativity, saying no to everything, it is therefore a permanent suspension or parabasis. Once you have got into this state of suspension you cannot get out of it or go on progressing through *Aufhebung* or sublation toward the eventual fulfillment of the absolute Idea. Irony is antithesis without any possibility of synthesis at a higher stage. It is an aporia in the etymological sense: a dead end or blind alley beyond which it is impossible to progress. "To this negativity," says Hegel, "Solger firmly clung, and of course it is *one element* (ein Moment) in the speculative Idea, yet interpreted as this purely dialectical unrest and dissolution of both infinite and finite (als diese bloße dialektische Unruhe und Auflösung des Unendlichen wie des Endlichen gefaßt), only *one element*, and not, as Solger will have it, the *whole* Idea" (G, 13:99; E, 1:68–69).

Kierkegaard's way of putting this was to say that, on the one hand, Socrates's irony came at an appropriate moment. It was the infinite absolute negativity that destroyed Greek culture and made way for the coming of Christ and Christianity. Christ's advent will lead ultimately to the second coming, the last judgment, and the end of history. Schlegel's irony, on the other hand, has come at the wrong time. It is anachronistic. It puts time out of joint. It is a radical danger to Christianity and to its historical progression, since it threatens to stop or suspend that progression. It must therefore be eliminated at all costs. Unfortunately for him, Kierkegaard, Danish parson though he was, had a great gift for irony in the Schlegelian sense. He spent all his life trying unsuccessfully to expunge it from himself by ascribing it to this or that pseudonymous alter ego, for example the "Either" of *Either/Or*. Kierkegaard was a master of double diegesis and therefore subject to what Plato saw as its innate immorality. This immorality is inseparable from the irony intrinsic to double diegesis or, as we should call it today, indirect discourse.

Another reason, however, makes irony dangerous. Paul de Man demonstrates that it is difficult, if not impossible, to state in so many words a "concept of irony," though he ends up doing so nevertheless. Why this difficulty? It is because irony is, in the end, or perhaps even from the beginning, when there is no more than a "touch of irony" in a discourse, unreasonable, incomprehensible. Irony is Unverständlichkeit as such, as Schlegel's essay "Über die Unverständlichkeit" abundantly shows. It shows this in its comic failure to be entirely reasonable and perspicuous about irony. Almost everyone knows that irony is a trap for the unwary or for the naively trusting, such as those government officials who took Defoe's "A Short Way with the Dissenters" seriously and were angry enough to put Defoe in the stocks when they found out he had been being ironic, saying one thing and meaning another. Nothing is more embarrassing, or more enraging, than to be caught out taking an ironic remark seriously or "straight." Irony also, however, and more dangerously, is a trap for the wary. It is particularly dangerous for those who think they understand it, who think they possess a valid "concept of irony" and can therefore protect themselves from it. This includes all the learned scholars, including myself here, who have been so courageous, or so foolish and foolhardy, as to write about irony, that is, to try to make it clear and understandable. Irony cannot be understood. It is the un-understandable as such.

Fragment 108 of the "Critical Fragments" says this with deceptively clear irony. The reader will note that the strategy of the fragment is to assert in various ways that irony is dangerously unreasonable because it consistently defies the principle of contradiction:

> Socratic irony is the only involuntary (unwillkürliche) and yet completely deliberate (besonnene) dissimulation (Verstellung). It is equally impossible to feign (erkünsteln) it or divulge (verraten) it. To a person who hasn't got it, it will remain a riddle even after it is openly confessed (nach dem offensten Geständnis). It is meant to deceive (täuschen) no one except those who consider it a deception and who either take pleasure in the delightful roguery of making fools of the whole world or else become angry when they get an

inkling they themselves might be included. In this sort of irony, everything should be playful and serious, guilelessly open and deeply hidden (verstellt). . . . It is the freest of all licenses, for by its means one transcends oneself; and yet it is also the most lawful, for it is absolutely necessary. It is a very good sign when the harmonious bores (die harmonisch Platten) are at a loss about how they should react to this continuous self-parody, when they fluctuate endlessly until they get dizzy (bis sie schwindlicht werden) and take what is meant as a joke (Scherz) seriously (Ernst) and what is meant seriously as a joke. (G, 20–21; E, 13)

As Georgia Albert, who has written brilliantly on this fragment,[19] observes, "schwindlicht" means "dizzy," all right, but it also has overtones of "swindle" and "lie or deceive." The attempt to master irony leads inevitably to vertigo, as though one had lost one's footing in reason, no longer had "understanding" in the literal sense of something solid to stand on under one's feet. Irony also leads one to feel as if swindled or to become a self-swindler, deceived or a deceiver self-deceived, in an endless unstoppable oscillation or rotation, like being caught in a revolving door. The reader will note that the passage is a tissue of those conceptual oppositions that organize logical thinking about consciousness and morality: involuntary as against deliberate, hidden as against open, deception of others as against self-deception, freedom as against obedience to law or necessity, seriousness as against joking or playfulness. Irony is on both sides of all of these oppositions at once, so one cannot be defined as prior to the other or as the determinate negation of the other. Rather than having the power of dialectical thinking in its orderly progression, the person who confronts irony or gets caught up in it is thrown back and forth from one opposite to the other as each turns into the other in an endless accelerating dizzy fluctuation. The persons most victims of irony are those who think they can master it as a straightforward "deception" (which assumes one knows the truth that is being hidden) and then can use it as a tool to fool others. Such persons are fooled by their attempt to fool others. It is better to be dumb enough or enough of a harmonious bore to be bewildered and to know you are bewildered. Who, however, would want to be a harmonious bore? No wonder Hegel was scandalized. Hegel was not a harmonious bore. He was a great philosopher. Still—one thinks what it must have been like to listen to Hegel's lectures, delivered in a thick Swabian accent. In any case, Hegel was not, so far as I know, invited to the Schlegel salons. He is not present as a pseudonymous personage in the *Dialogue on Poetry*.

Unfortunately the reader of the passage is not exempt from the vertigo it names and mimes. The reader is caught up in the dizzying alternations the text names, led by it not to a masterful understanding of irony but to an experience of Unverständlichkeit. This is the most unsettling aspect of this fragment. If you do not understand the passage you are led to fluctuate endlessly between belief and disbelief. If you understand it you are plunged into dizzy incomprehension by your very act of understanding. Either way you have had it, which is a way of saying that the aporias central to Schlegel's thought are not tame impasses in logic or mere matters of wordplay. As Schlegel observes in "Über die Unverständlichkeit," "Irony is something one simply cannot play games with (Mit der Ironie ist durchaus nicht zu scherzen). It can have incredibly long-lasting after effects (nachwirken)" (G, 370; E, 37). It might be safer to leave irony alone. How can one be sure, however, in a given case, that one is not speaking ironically, without meaning to do so, or that one's interlocutor is not an ironist?

What does Schlegelian irony and its repudiation by most of those who have understood him best have to do with Schlegel's concept of myth? The short answer is to say that mythology is for Schlegel ironic through and through. To understand just what that means, however, it will be necessary to look at a key sequence of formulations in the "Rede über die Mythologie" and read them as carefully as possible. "Mythology" in the passage and in its surrounding context is associated with a set of key words in Schlegel's thought, not only "irony," but also "chaos," "allegory," "hieroglyph," "symbol," "fragment," "the sublime," "arabesque," "imagination," "form," "work," "magic," "play," "wit," "romantic," "nature," "charm," "part," "whole," and so on. Each of these words is related to the others to form the nonsystematic system of Schlegel's thought. Schlegel says in one of the fragments: "It is equally fatal for the mind (den Geist) to have a system and to have none. It will simply have to decide to combine the two" (G, 31; E, 24). That is what I mean when I say Schlegel's thought is a nonsystematic system. His discourse is systematic and violently antisystematic at one and the same time. Each of the words I have listed is twisted anasemically from its usual or expected meaning by its relation to the other words and to the absent and ultimately indefinable center, the "chaos" that governs Friedrich Schlegel's thought, as I shall show, and is his version of the otherness that is the subject of this book. No system in the ordinary sense can exist around a black hole.

The "Talk on Mythology" makes near its beginning one of Friedrich Schlegel's most famous assertions: "Our poetry, I maintain, lacks a focal point, such as mythology was for the ancients; and one could summarize all the essentials in which modern poetry is inferior to the ancient in these words: We have no mythology. But, I add, we are close to obtaining one or, rather, it is time that we earnestly work together to create one"

(G, 497; DP, 81). Schlegel has been sternly reproached, for example, by Wilhelm Dilthey and Friedrich Gundolf,[20] for the absurdity of claiming that a genuine mythology can be deliberately and self-consciously created. I shall later explain the rationale for this apparently implausible idea.

The "Talk on Mythology" defines what the new mythology would be like and works toward attaining it. It is a wonderfully exuberant rhapsody, hyperbolically optimistic about the possibilities of a new burst of poetry. This will be achieved by deliberately creating a new mythology to match the ancient Greek and Roman one: "The new mythology, in contrast, must be forged from the deepest depths of the spirit; it must be the most artful of all works of art, for it must encompass all the others: a new bed and vessel (ein neues Bette und Gefäß) for the ancient, eternal fountainhead (Urquell) of poetry, and even the infinite poem concealing the seeds of all other poems" (G, 497; E, 82). The new mythology, in accordance with one of the deepest paradigms of romanticism, will be progressive, a gradual, dynamic movement toward a far-off goal. It will approach that goal in infinite approximations, as a curve approaches its asymptote. The new vessel will be both bed and vessel, in an odd and contradictory combination. It will be underlying ground or matrix (bed), as in "streambed," and at the same time a container (vessel), in two incompatible forms of synecdoche. The new mythology will be substance in the etymological sense: ground and also encompassing and shaping vehicle or embodiment.

Essential to Schlegel's conception of the new mythology is a combination of universal and individual of which the fragments give many examples. Each of these new poems will be altogether individual, while at the same time expressing the universal fountainhead of poetry: "Everything interpenetrates everything else, and everywhere there is one and the same spirit, only expressed differently (alles greift ineinander, und überall ist ein und derselbe Geist nur anders ausgedrückt)" (G, 497; E, 82).

The "Talk on Mythology" is inhabited by a characteristic romantic image of history, present also in Novalis and in a different way in Hegel. At this moment we are poised between the golden age that was (the Greeks) and the golden age to come. The future golden age is infinitely distant. It is an asymptote that the new poetry will approach in endlessly postponed degrees of approaching. The rhapsodic exuberance of the "Talk on Mythology" anticipates the ironic wildness of later postromantic works like Rimbaud's *Illuminations* or William Carlos Williams's *Kora in Hell*. All three of these are caught within the paradigm of a paradoxical, constantly repeated inaugural moment that must both build on what came before and at the same time destroy it to make way for the wholly new. For Schlegel the new mythology will combine idealism (Kant and Fichte) and realism (Spinoza as mystic pantheist): "Idealism in any form must transcend itself in one way or another, in order to be able to return to itself and remain what it is. Therefore, there must and will arise from the matrix of idealism a new and equally infinite (grenzenloser) realism, and idealism will not only by analogy of its genesis be an example of the new mythology, but it will indirectly become its very source" (G, 499; E, 83–84).

Taking Shakespeare and Cervantes (rather surprisingly if we think of romanticism, in the usual way, as a delimited historical period) as exemplary of "the marvelous wit of romantic poetry which does not manifest itself in individual conceptions but in the structure of the whole," Schlegel says, or has Ludovico say, in the "Talk on Mythology": "Indeed, this artfully ordered confusion (Verwirrung) , this charming symmetry of contradictions (Widersprüchen), this wonderfully perennial alternation of enthusiasm and irony which lives even in the smallest parts of the whole, seem to me to be an indirect mythology" (G, 501; E, 86). What does the word "mythology" mean here? Why is it called "indirect"? Why is it associated not only with enthusiasm but also with irony? Answering these questions presupposes an understanding of all Schlegel's writing. The passage I have cited is, however, one version of that whole. Reading it, in its immediately surrounding context, may give access to that whole. It should be stressed, however, that the presupposition of a part-whole relation in which synecdoche would be true, in the sense that the part would be a cunning miniature of the whole and give full understanding of it, is one of the assumptions Schlegel puts in question. A Schlegelian fragment is neither a part nor a whole. If it were a part then it could be completed and would then no longer be fragmentary. If it were a whole, it would not be a fragment at all. A true fragment is not a whole in itself because it is enigmatically incomplete, but it is also not part of a larger whole. It is rather a catachrestic allegory of that wholly other that Schlegel calls "chaos."[21]

The most economical way to move toward an understanding of what Schlegel means by "an indirect mythology" is to ask what, for Schlegel, is the referent of this mythology. What does an indirect mythology name? To what does it give us access? What does it represent? I have spoken of the way Greek mythology expressed the Greeks' deepest sense of the relation of human beings to the gods. *Oedipus the King*, for example, focuses on the ultimately inscrutable relation of Oedipus to Apollo. In Schlegel's case the new romantic mythology for which he calls and which he sees as already partly accomplished by Shakespeare and Cervantes (and no doubt by his own *Lucinde*) expresses human beings' relation to what he calls "chaos" or "the sublime" (das Höchste).

What do these words mean for Schlegel? The word "chaos" appears often in his fragments. An example is one definition of irony: "Irony is the clear consciousness of eternal agility, of an infinitely teeming chaos" (G, 97; E, 100). A characteristic Schlegelian contradiction inhabits this formulation: how could one have clear consciousness of an infinitely abundant chaos? A nearby fragment says: "Confusion (Verworrenheit) is a chaos only when it can give rise to a new world" (G, 97; E, 100, trans. slightly altered). "Chaos": the word means originally an open, gaping mouth. On the one hand, chaos is a yawning, fathomless abyss, an Abgrund. On the other hand, chaos is a confused plurality, the copresence of the possibility of all "worlds" and of all definite forms, both natural forms and linguistic formulations. Examples of the latter are Schlegel's fragments, or the works of Shakespeare and Cervantes, or any example of what Schlegel calls the new "mythology," for example his own *Lucinde*. Schlegel's special conception of myth and mythology arises from the relation of myth to the chaos out of which any myth arises and which it names, represents, symbolizes, or allegorizes. That is why Schlegel calls the swarm of romantic works, including those by Shakespeare and Cervantes, an *indirect* mythology. It is indirect because no direct expression of chaos is possible. That is also why he emphasizes not the systematic coherence of Greek mythology as the unified expression of a single culture, but its confused abundance. Since what it stands for is the teeming plurality of chaos, it must be itself chaotic and irrational. "For this is the beginning of all poetry," says Ludovico at the end of the sequence in the "Tall on Mythology" I am following, "to cancel (aufzuheben: this is Hegel's famous untranslatable word *aufheben*, which means both lift up and cancel) the progression and laws of rationally thinking reason (der vernünftig denkenden Vernunft), and to transplant us once again into the beautiful confusion (Verwirrung) of imagination, into the original chaos of human nature, for which I know as yet no more beautiful symbol than the motley throng (das bunte Gewimmel) of the ancient gods" (G, 502: DP, 86). Mythological works that do what they are supposed to do are "indirect" because chaos or "the highest" cannot be spoken of directly.

In my own terminology, a terminology Friedrich Schlegel does not use, chaos is the wholly other, or the wholly others, beyond consciousness and beyond any literal naming. As Ludovico puts this, in a formulation that comes in the discussion after the presentation of his "Rede über die Mythologie" and that I have taken as one of my epigraphs: ". . . alle Schönheit ist Allegorie. Das Höchste kann man eben, weil es unaussprechlich ist, nur allegorisch sagen (. . . all beauty is allegory. The sublime, because it is unutterable, can be expressed only allegorically" (G, 505; DP, 89–90). The translation here dares to translate "das Höchste" as "the sublime," whereas the word means "the highest." The normal

German word for "the sublime" is "das Erhabene." My translation in note 1 says "the highest." Ludovico's assertion follows statements by Antonio and Lothario that give one example of the way the key terms I listed above are continuously arranged and rearranged by Schlegel in the series of transformations that make up his fragmentary discourse. "Even in the quite popular genres, for instance in drama (Schauspiel)," says Antonio, "we demand irony; we demand that events, men, in short the play of life (das ganze Spiel des Lebens), be taken as play (auch als Spiel) and be represented as such." To which Lothario responds: "All the sacred plays of art (Alle heiligen Spiele der Kunst) are only a remote imitation of the infinite play of the universe (von dem unendlichen Spiele der Welt), the work of art which eternally creates itself anew" (G, 504–5; DP, 89). Ludovico answers with the sentence I have cited above. To say what you have just said in other words, he asserts, all beauty is allegory. Since the highest (das Höchste) is inexpressible (unaussprechlich), it can therefore only be said allegorically. Allegory, however, as the reader can see, is closely associated with "play" and with irony. The passage plays on different uses of the word "play," "Spiel" in German. We demand irony in popular drama because such dramas must say one thing and mean another, as irony does in its simplest and most canonical definition. Even popular drama must represent events and men, that is, the play of life, *as* play, as something not to be taken seriously in itself. This is necessary because the function of the representation is not to give us access to men and events but to wrest the representation from its realistic referentiality so that it can stand ironically for something other than itself. Ironic undercutting or suspension is essential to this saying one thing but meaning another. Saying one thing and meaning another, however, is also the standard definition of allegory.

Modern definitions of allegory from Schlegel through Ruskin, Pater, Proust, Benjamin, and de Man stress the ironic discrepancy and unlikeness between the allegorical vehicle or vessel and that for which it stands. To give one example: Proust's Marcel asserts that Giotto's Charity in the *Allegory of Virtues and Vices* at Padua looks like a kitchen maid handing a corkscrew up through a grating from the lower kitchen level to the one above. It is a wonderfully ironic and subversive association or figurative displacement on Marcel's part. If this woman were not labeled "Karitas," says Marcel, the spectator would never know that the stout, matronly figure in Giotto's fresco is meant to represent Charity. Another way to put this is to say that allegory is ironic through and through, as Schlegel implicitly asserts in the play of definitions turning on the word "Spiel" that makes up the immediate chain of give and take in this moment of the dialogue.

What Schlegel elsewhere calls "chaos" is given a slightly different definition in Lothario's intervention. "All the sacred plays of art," says Lothario, "are only a remote imitation (nur ferne Nachbildungen) of the infinite play of the universe (dem unendlichen Spiele der Welt), the work of art which eternally creates itself anew (dem ewig sich selbst bildenden Kunstwerk)." The universe as a whole is here defined as an infinite play, with a suggestion of an eternal teeming of transformations, play in the sense of free play or improvisation. That infinite play is defined as already itself a work of art. It is a work of art that has no author. This artwork continually creates itself anew, in an endless process of transformation and substitution, shaping and reshaping itself like the heaving waves of some everlasting sea. Since this strange work of art, the universe as infinite play, cannot be named directly, it is by the "sacred plays of art," that is, by human art as fulfilling its sacred duty of allegory, only remotely imitated, in "ferne Nachbildungen," distant after-images, just as Shakespeare and Cervantes are an indirect mythology (eine indirekte Mythologie).

Just what does it mean to speak allegorically? What Schlegel says about mythology will give the answer. The sequence of formulations Ludovico presents in the central assertions of the "Talk on Mythology" is a little chain or garland of fragments, starting and stopping abruptly, changing terminology from one sentence to another. This chain does not make a sequential or dialectical argument. Each sentence is enclosed in itself, like a porcupine. Each is an explosion of wit thrown out allegorically toward the *unaussprechlich* chaos. If each formulation is an allegorical emblem unlike that for which it stands, the elements in the sequence are not wholly congruent or like one another.

The sequence I shall follow begins with a rhetorical question that is given in a separate paragraph: "And what else is any wonderful mythology but hieroglyphic expression of surrounding nature in this transfigured form of imagination and love (in dieser Verklärung von Phantasie und Liebe)?" (G, 500–501; DP, 85). Ludovico has just been talking about Spinoza's work. He sees the latter as providing a model for romantic poetry in its inspired use of imagination and love. The term "mythology" has not been used in the discussion of Spinoza. It reappears abruptly after two paragraphs about Spinoza. The "gorgeous nonsense" of the hero's rhapsodies in *Lucinde* would perhaps give the best idea of what Schlegel means by imagination and love. He means sexual feeling as it generates stories, that is, a "wonderful mythology." Such stories are hieroglyphic expressions of the sublime or of chaos. Just as any mythology must be indirect, so these mythological stories of imagination and love are transfigured forms that turn love into a hieroglyphic expression of surrounding nature. Like any hieroglyph, they express what they name in a transferred, figurative, and indirect form. "Hieroglyph" and "allegory" are consonant terms. "Nature" here names not only human nature but also physical nature that is the visible emblem of the invisible and inexpressible chaos from which it is derived. A hieroglyphic expression of nature, in the form of stories about human love and imagination that make a "wonderful mythology," is a hieroglyph of a hieroglyph.

Lucinde fits this definition exactly. The "Talk on Mythology," written at more or less the same time as Schlegel was composing *Lucinde*, bears the same relation to *Lucinde* as Aristotle's *Poetics* does to Sophocles's *Oedipus the King*. Schlegel in the "Talk on Mythology" and in the "Letter on the Novel," the last of the interpolated essays in the *Dialogue on Poetry*, serves as his own Aristotle. He presents the theory of poetry, mythology, and the novel that would be appropriate for understanding and justifying *Lucinde*.

Lucinde takes some justifying. It remains in various ways scandalous. Not only is it in places obscene, it is also wildly incoherent in its disobedience of usual novelistic form. There are time shifts, flashbacks, interruptions, abrupt stoppings followed by restartings from a new place that leave the reader bewildered, not entirely sure at any moment just where he or she is. The novel, if novel it can be called, is not a coherent diegesis. It is made of a sequence of detached narrative segments incoherently patched together, with many interpolated philosophical reflections. *Lucinde* presents bits and pieces of storytelling and other forms of discourse that seem to have been detached from their explanatory contexts. This so-called novel is intensely egotistical. It is narcissistic or even onanistic. As Paul de Man has observed, one section, "Eine Reflexion," looks at first like an interpolated philosophical "reflection" not entirely unlike the "Talk on Mythology" or the "Letter on the Novel" in the *Dialogue on Poetry*. Looked at from a slightly different perspective, however, by a species of anamorphosis, the solemn philosophical terminology of "Eine Reflexion" turns out to be the vehicle of a reflection on the physical problems of sexual intercourse as these arise from the differences between male and female physiology.[22] That is materialization of the spiritual with a vengeance! Just what the necessity and significance of such materializations are I shall explain later. *Lucinde*, finally, has the scandalous side attending any *roman à clef*. It is supposed to be a narration, from Friedrich Schlegel's perspective of course, of his liaison with Dorothea Veit, then still a married woman. It is no wonder that Hegel and Kierkegaard were horrified. On the other hand, *Lucinde* does exemplify what Schlegel meant by the creation of a new mythology. For better or worse, it is a major expression of German romanticism. It contains, moreover, passages crucial for an understanding of Schlegel's thought. One of these I shall discuss later.

What it might mean to say that the elements of the new mythology are hieroglyphs of a hieroglyph is made clearer by the next two sentences after the ones quoted above. These also form a separate paragraph. Each new fragment, as the reader encounters it, is another different perspective, or witty contradictory explosive glimpse, or allegorical representation, of that absent center, the wholly others, chaos. Since no hieroglyph can speak directly of the unspeakable, no one hieroglyph has priority or adequacy. Each is replaced as soon as it is spoken or inscribed by a new, different, and incompatible one. Each fragment is like a new bit of data from a black hole, data that gradually give more and more information about what cannot be seen or named directly. "Mythology," says Ludovico, "has one great advantage. What usually escapes our consciousness can here be perceived and held fast through the senses and spirit like the soul in the body surrounding it, through which it shines into our eye and speaks to our ear" (G, 501; E, 85). This fragment, as the reader can see, depends on a metaphorical proportion. As the soul is to the body, so is the aboriginal chaos, das ursprüngliche Chaos, as Schlegel calls it a few sentences later, to the mythology which is its allegorical expression. Just as the soul is invisible and inaudible but can be indirectly seen in the body, its bed and vessel, so the referent of a mythology, of a myth, or of a mytheme, is not something we can see or hear. We can never become directly conscious of it. Just as the body surrounds and holds fast the soul, so a mythology embodies, in the sense of enclosing within itself, what usually escapes our consciousness. A mythology is a way of making us conscious of that of which we are usually not conscious. We are conscious of it, however, indirectly, as we know the soul by way of the body. Since the body is not really like the soul, our knowledge of the soul by way of the body is indirect. The body is the allegorical expression of the soul, just as a mythology is an allegorical expression of "the highest," the unspeakable, the Unaussprechlich. An example is the way Schlegel's *Lucinde* is an allegory of the deepest insights of imagination and love. "Body" in *Lucinde*, the hyperbolic presentation of the intimate details of an illicit love affair, is the indirect expression of "the highest."

Another crucial figure, however, appears in this formulation. Hegel in the *Ästhetik* defined beauty as the "sinnliche Scheinen der Idee," the sensible shining forth of the Idea.[23] *Scheinen* in German means both appear and seem. Schlegel's formulation, both here and in other crucial places where he uses the figure of shining forth or through, for example three

paragraphs later than the citation now being discussed, is a kind of diabolical parody before the fact of Hegel's formula. In Schlegel's case what
shines through (*durchschimmert*) is not the absolute Idea, toward the
fulfillment of which all history moves, as in Hegel, nor the noble soul that
shines through the body, in the figure Schlegel uses, but chaos as allegorically revealed by a mythological work like *Lucinde*. Even though that
chaos is defined as "the highest," it does not have the characteristics of
spiritual clarity and totality associated with Hegel's "Idea." Schlegel's
chaos is the teeming, pullulating copresence of the possibility of everything or anything. It gives no support to ordinary standards of morality
and lawfulness, whereas Hegel's Idea is their transcendent support, or at
any rate Hegel struggled mightily through many weighty volumes and
many courses of solemn lectures to demonstrate that this is the case.

If a passage discussed earlier played on various possibilities of meaning in
the word "play" (*Spiel*), and if the passage just read turns on the double
meaning of "shimmer though" (*durchschimmern*), as both a physical and
an allegorical shining forth, the next self-contradictory fragments turn on
the multiple meanings of a particularly rich family of words in German:
Bild, bilden, Bildung, umbilden, anbilden. Bild means form and is translated as such in the English version. It also means figure and metaphor, as
well as portrait or picture. *Bilden* means to form, but also to educate.
Bildung is formation but also education—formation in the sense of in-
forming submission to a discipline or curriculum. A university education,
for example in Humboldt's idea of it in his plan for the University of
Berlin, is devoted not only to teaching knowledge (*Wissenschaft*), but also
to Bildung, to the formation of citizens of the state. *Anbilden* means con-
form, while *umbilden* means transform.
    Schlegel uses a play on these various words to express a double para-
dox. On the one hand the sublime chaos already has form or has been
given various cultural forms. We should make use of those preexisting
forms in our new mythology. On the other hand chaos is without form.
It is rather a place of constant transformation. The proper way to give
poetic expression to this is to produce a new mythology that is itself in
constant transformation. Moreover, this new mythology must be radically inaugural, innovative, not dependent on any preexisting forms. On
the one hand the new mythology will be constative. It will seek the best
indirect expression of what is always already there but usually escapes
our consciousness and can never be directly expressed. On the other hand
the new mythology will be performative in a radical sense. It will be a
speech act that is a new start. It will invent "the highest" not in the sense
of discovering it but in the sense of casting out new forms that rise out of
the original chaos but are deliberately manipulated transformations of it.

"In regard to the sublime (wegen des Höchsten)," says Ludovico, "we do not entirely depend on our emotions (unser Gemüt)" (G, 501; DP, 85). To translate *das Höchste* as "the sublime" is, as I have said, daring, perhaps even a sublime daring, since the usual German word for the sublime is *das Erhabene*. Schlegel probably just means "the highest" in the sense of the most elevated, the most out of reach, and the most valuable in itself, that unspeakable of which mythologies are allegorical expressions. It is somewhat misleading to bring in all the Kantian, Burkean, and Hegelian associations of the sublime by translating *das Höchste* as "the sublime." To say we do not entirely depend on our emotions in regard to the highest is to say that irrational feelings, love and imagination as manifested in *Lucinde*, for example, are not the only way to get in relation to the highest. The other way is to "take part everywhere in what is already formed (an das Gebildete)" (ibid.). Schlegel goes on to say that this means we should "develop, kindle and nourish the sublime (das Höchste)," in two ways: "through contact with the same in kind, the similar (des Gleichartigen, Ähnlichen), or if of equal stature (bei gleicher Würde) the hostile; in a word, give it form (bilden)" (G, 501; E, 85–86). This is an odd and not entirely perspicuous expression. Its somewhat covert logic seems to be the following: Since the highest is itself a place of contradictions, we should develop, kindle, and nourish it not only by things that seem to be similar to it, but also through appropriately grand things that are hostile to it, such as Schlegel's details about bodily love in *Lucinde*. Just as Schlegel's fragments generate their explosive wit by bringing together in the tight space of a sentence or two logically contradictory expressions, so the highest, since it cannot in any case be spoken of directly or literally, must be spoken of simultaneously in what is like and unlike it. Or rather, nothing is really either like or unlike it in the usual sense. To express it simultaneously in the like and the unlike is to give it form, to shape it, in an act that Schlegel calls *bilden*. Since it does not have fixed form in itself, any form we give it will be both adequate and inadequate.

The notion of "giving form" to the highest, Behler and Struc's translation of *bilden*, is crucial here. The highest does not in itself have a form comprehensible to human consciousness. The function of any mythology, whether that of the Greeks or that of the new romantic mythology that is in the process of being created, is to give form not so much to the formless as to something that is a place of constant transformation. That something has forms, if forms they can be called, that are alien to human consciousness. Schlegel's expression of this necessity is somewhat hyperbolic or even shrill: "If the sublime, however, is incapable of being intentionally created (Ist das Höchste aber wirklich keiner absichtlichen Bildung fähig), then let us give up any claims to a free art of ideas (freie Ideenkunst), for it would be an empty name" (G, 501; E, 86). A free art of ideas would be intentional (*absichtlich*) creation, the Bildung of the new mythology as an allegory of the inexpressible.

What it means to say mythology is a Bildung whose essential trait is constant transformation is indicated in the next paragraph of Ludovico's discourse, as well as in a consonant passage in *Lucinde*. Giving form to the highest is not a single static gesture. It is a perpetual process of performative metamorphosis. This is so because that for which the allegorical myth stands is itself not a fixed unity, such as the Platonic One or the Christian Godhead, three in one, but the locus of constant transformation.

"Mythology," says Ludovico, "is such a work of art created by nature (ist ein solches Kunstwerk der Natur)" (ibid.). The translation here makes a not wholly justified choice by saying "created by nature." Which is it, subjective or objective genitive, in the phrase "Kunstwerk der Natur"? The phrase must contain the possibility of both. The German might mean "work of art created by Nature," or it might mean "natural work of art," or it might mean "artwork representing nature," as when we say, "That is a picture of so and so." The German literally says, "artwork of nature," just that. This point is worth dwelling on because of a fundamental, and highly traditional, ambiguity in Schlegel's use of the word *Natur*. The word, in his usage, means nature as intermediary between human beings and the aboriginal chaos. It also means human nature. It also means, especially given the avowed influence of Spinoza's pantheism on Schlegel's thinking in the "Talk on Mythology," a single continuous realm that includes "the highest" as well as nature in the limited senses of physical nature, and human nature to boot. An "artwork of nature" arises from, represents, and is continuous with nature in this complex sense.

Ludovico goes on to say that in the "texture (Geweb)" of a mythology that is intertwined with nature in this way, "the sublime is really formed (ist das Höchste wirklich gebildet)" (ibid.). The sentence contains undecidable alternative possibilities of meaning. *Gebildet* either may mean the creation of something that was not there at all before the mythology brought it into being, or it may mean that the mythology gives form to the formless chaos that was always already there. The rest of the sentence does not decide one way or the other, but it helps the reader understand why it is impossible to decide. In such a mythology, says Ludovico, "everything is relation (Beziehung) and metamorphosis (Verwandlung), conformed and transformed (angebildet und umgebildet), and this conformation and transformation (Anbilden und Umbilden) is its peculiar process, its inner life and method, if I may say so" (ibid.). Far from being a fixed set of mythological stories, the new mythology will be, like romantic poetry in general in Schlegel's idea of it (the two are more or less synonymous), dynamic, never finished, constantly changing.

A celebrated fragment, fragment 116 of the *Athenaeum Fragments*, is the best expression of this. "Romantic poetry," says Schlegel, "is progressive, universal poetry. . . . Other kinds of poetry are finished (fertig) and are now capable of being fully analyzed. The romantic kind of poetry is still in the state of becoming; that, in fact, is its real essence: that it should forever be becoming and never be perfected. . . . It alone is infinite, just as it alone is free; and it recognizes as its first commandment that the will [in the sense of arbitrary willfulness; the German word is *Willkür*] of the poet can tolerate no law above itself" (G, 38–39; E, 31–32). This refusal to accept any law above itself is one feature of Schlegel's thought that outraged Hegel, but one can see its necessity. If the new mythology is going to be forever becoming and never perfected, it can move toward its infinitely distant goal only by rejecting whatever has come before and working in a radically inaugural way. If it is to progress, it must, in an absolutely free and willful creative gesture, be a new law unto itself. That means rejecting any preexisting law.

This freedom and willfulness must enter into the intimate texture of the new mythology. This means that if, on the one hand, it is characterized by establishing new and hitherto unheard of relations (*Beziehungen*) among the elements that enter into it, on the other hand these relations must not be fixed. They must rather be in a constant state of change. This change takes two forms, as is indicated by the two forms of *bilden* that are employed: *anbilden* and *umbilden*, conformed and transformed. Each new element must be conformed to the one to which it is related, but this process is also a transformation of the new element that is assimilated into the dynamic system.

The alert reader will notice that what Schlegel is describing here is nothing more or less than a tropological system. Metaphor and the other master tropes—synecdoche, metonymy, and prosopopoeia—as they work by substitution, condensation, displacement, naming, and renaming, are the primary linguistic tools whereby the process of giving form by conformation and transformation, in a perpetual metamorphosis, is accomplished.

The consonance of Schlegel's formulations here with an admirably exuberant affirmation of the poet's power in Wordsworth's *Preface* of 1815 will confirm this. Wordsworth is talking about a series of figurative metamorphoses in a passage from one of his own poems, "Resolution and Independence." The passage and its commentary might have been written as an exemplification of what Schlegel says about the way the poet gives the law to himself and continually transforms things in a sovereign

exercise of his tropological power. Wordsworth's phrase "just comparison," however, indicates a sense that the figures he uses are "justified" by
objective similarities, whereas Schlegel does not make such a claim. What
Wordsworth says is a comment on the following passage in "Resolution
and Independence," as he cites it in the *Preface*:

> As a huge stone is sometimes seen to lie
> Couched on the bald top of an eminence,
> Wonder to all who do the same espy
> By what means it could thither come, and whence,
> So that it seems a thing endued with sense,
> Like a sea-beast crawled forth, which on a shelf
> Of rock or sand reposeth, there to sun himself.
>
> Such seemed this Man; not all alive or dead
> Nor all asleep, in his extreme old age.
>
> . . . .
>
> Motionless as a cloud the old Man stood,
> That heareth not the loud winds when they call,
> And moveth altogether if it move at all.
>
> (ll. 57–65; 75–77)

Here is Wordworth's commentary on these lines:

In these images, the conferring, the abstracting, and the modifying powers of
the Imagination, immediately and mediately acting, are all brought into con-
junction. The stone is endowed with something of the power of life to ap-
proximate it to the sea-beast; and the sea-beast stripped of some of its vital
qualities to assimilate it to the stone; which intermediate image is thus
treated for the purpose of bringing the original image, that of the stone, to a
nearer resemblance to the figure and condition of the aged Man; who is
divested of so much of the indications of life and motion as to bring him to
the point where the two objects unite and coalesce in just comparison. After
what has been said, the image of the cloud need not be commented on.[24]

All this aspect of Schlegel's theory of myth seems admirably positive and
optimistic. This is the side that has been most often stressed by those
critics and scholars who approve of Schlegel and who want to affirm his
importance as one of the founders of romanticism or of what we would
today call aesthetic ideology in its modern form. Things are not quite so
simple, nor quite so cheerful, with Friedrich Schlegel, however.

A darker side of the motif of transformation emerges a little later in the
"Talk on Mythology" and in the echoing passage in *Lucinde* to which I
referred earlier. The reader will remember that the function of the new
mythology is to form allegories, indirect expressions, of "the highest," or

of what Schlegel calls "chaos." Works contributing to the formation of the new mythology must be in constant transformation because what they indirectly represent is not fixed but is in constant, senseless metamorphosis, subject to deformations beyond the human power to comprehend. "Senseless" is the key word here, and I must now show why it is justified and why this senselessness gives such a dark tone to Schlegel's notion of mythology.

The paragraph about the way the highest is really formed by a mythology that is a constant process of metamorphosis is followed by the passage I quoted earlier that amalgamates, in an act of transformation and conformation of its own, the "marvelous wit of romantic poetry [meaning Shakespeare and Cervantes], which does not manifest itself in individual conceptions but in the structure of the whole," with mythology. We are now in a better position to understand the sentence: "Indeed, this artfully ordered confusion (diese künstlich geordnete Verwirrung), this charming symmetry of contradictions (Widersprüchen), this wonderfully perennial alternation of enthusiasm (Enthusiasmus) and irony which lives even in the smallest parts of the whole, seem to me to be an indirect mythology themselves" (G, 501; DP, 86). Having said that the wit of romantic poetry lies in the structure of the whole, not in individual parts, Schlegel now says the alternation of enthusiasm and irony is vitally present even in the smallest parts of the whole. It must be both at once, in another example of the symmetry of contradictions of which Schlegel speaks. The wit of romantic poetry is present in the asymmetrical symmetry of the whole, something slightly askew or amiss in the whole structure that makes it explosively witty, as a fragment is witty. Unlike an example of harmonious organic unity, with each part contributing to a whole that hangs together—with nothing in excess, as Aristotle says should be the case with a good tragedy—a work of the new mythology will be made up of parts that mirror the paradoxical witty structure of the whole. It is not simply that one part is not consonant with some other part, though perfectly coherent and self-consistent in itself. Each smallest part is itself riven by the same kind of contradictions that dominate the larger structure. It repeats those contradictions in miniature, as each part of a fractal repeats the pattern of the whole. It is not that one part is enthusiastic and another part ironical, but that even the smallest part is enthusiastic and ironic at once.

The next sentence gives that asymmetrical symmetry a name that has a complex resonance in Schlegel's thought and in that of German romanticism generally.[25] Schlegel says both romantic witty poetry and the new mythology are organized as arabesques: "The organization [of both romantic poetry and mythology] is the same, and certainly the arabesque (die Arabeske) is the oldest and most original form of human imagination (der menschlichen Phantasie)" (ibid.). As other passages in Schlegel show, he thinks, when he says "arabesque," as much of Raphael's arabesques—complex designs of beasts, flowers, and foliage—as of the Muslim designs to which Raphael was alluding. In either case an arabesque is, like the airy flourishes of Corporal Trim's stick in *Tristram Shandy*, a tangle of lines whose interleaved wanderings are governed by a center that is outside the design itself and that is located at infinity. An arabesque is a complex of asymptotic curves.

The words "enthusiasm" and "irony" are not chosen at random. Enthusiasm: the word means "possessed by a god." Insofar as witty romantic poems, poems that are an indirect mythology themselves, are enthusiastic, they contain or are possessed by that "highest" to which they give indirect, allegorical expression. "Irony": we know what that means. It means incomprehensibility, vertigo, a dead end in thought, the permanent suspension or parabasis of dialectical progression. A mythology must be both enthusiastic and ironical at once, in defiance of reason. It must be enthusiastic in order to be inhabited by the highest. Since that highest is also chaotic, however, it can only be adequately allegorized in a mythology that is self-canceling, against reason or alogical. Schlegel's name for this kind of discourse is "irony." This combination is itself contradictory and ironic. How could a person or a discourse be at once enthusiastic and ironic? Each feature would suspend or cancel the other.

The necessity for this impossible combination is made clear in the two sentences that follow. These are the climactic formulations of the whole braided or enchained sequence of assertions I have been following. Both romantic wit and any mythology must be enthusiastic in the precise sense that they allow the highest to shimmer through, according to that figure of *sinnliche Scheinen* used earlier in the sequence. At the same time what shines through must be expressed ironically because it is, like irony, senseless, absurd, mad. It would then fulfill Paul de Man's definition of irony in "The Rhetoric of Temporality": "Irony is unrelieved *vertige*, dizziness to the point of madness."[26] In de Man's witty sentence, "unrelieved" must be taken not only in the sense of unremitting, without relief, but also as an unostentatious translation of the Hegelian term *Aufhebung* as "relief." *Aufhebung* is more or less untranslatable, since it means, simultaneously, "cancel," "preserve," and "lift up." It might, however, be translated as "relief." Unrelieved vertigo would be a dizziness that could be defined as an infinite absolute negativity incapable of dialectical sublation, lifting up, or relief. "Neither this wit nor a mythology can exist," says Schlegel, "without something original and inimitable which is absolutely irreducible (ohne ein erstes Ursprüngliches und Unnachahnliches, was schlecthin unauflöslich ist), and in which after all the transformations (Umbildungen) its original character and creative energy are still dimly visible, where the naive profundity (der naive Tiefsinn) permits the semblance of the absurd and of madness, of simplicity and foolishness (den Schein des Verkehrten und Verrückten oder Einfältigen und Dummen), to shimmer through (durchschimmern läßt)" (G, 501–2; E, 86).

These are strong words—the absurd, madness, simplicity (in the sense of simplemindedness), and foolishness. As Paul de Man observes in "The Concept of Irony" (AI, 180–81), these words sharply undercut any strongly positive, humanistic reading of the passage as a whole, such as might seem to be authorized by what is said earlier about the ability of a mythology to represent the highest allegorically, as well as by many other passages in Schlegel. Such passages seem to give a cheerful allegiance, in accordance with aesthetic ideology generally, to a progressive view of history as moving closer and closer to a union with the highest under the guidance of romantic poetry and the new mythology. The endpoint of the new mythology's insight is, on the contrary, the shimmering through of the madness and stupidity of the aboriginal chaos.

As Paul de Man also observes in the same place, Schlegel rewrote the first version of these phrases to make them even stronger. Originally Schlegel wrote "the strange (das Sonderbare), even the absurd (das Widersinnige), as well as childlike and yet sophisticated (geistreiche) naïveté"; later he substituted "Verkehrten und Verrückten oder des Einfältigen und Dummen" (ibid.). This revision in the direction of a starker confrontation with the senselessness of chaos also gives little support to the assertion by the "many critics," alluded to in Behler and Struc's introduction to the English translation of the Dialogue on Poetry, who "have seen in this demand for a new mythology the first symptom of Schlegel's later conversion to Catholicism" (DP, 27). Catholicism is a broad and catholic religion, but there is no way, I believe, it can be made to jibe, even distantly, with the conception of a chaotic, impersonal, mad "highest" presented in the Dialogue on Poetry. The conversion to Catholicism would have to be seen as a fleeing from this rather than its continuation.

The "something original and inimitable which is absolutely irreducible" is that aboriginal chaos. The words "original," "inimitable," and "irreducible" must be taken in strong or literal senses. This "something" is radically original in the sense of being the transcendent source of everything, not just in the weaker sense that we speak of "poetic originality." It is inimitable not in the sense that Charles Dickens was known as "the inimitable Boz," but in the literal sense that it is impossible to represent it directly in a mimesis. It is "unspeakable" and can only be spoken of indirectly. It is absolutely "irreducible" in the sense that it cannot be reduced

by analysis to its component elements. Though it is the locus of a constant
self-differentiation, it cannot be adequately differentiated, analyzed, or
reduced by human language. Nevertheless, its original character and creative energy still shine dimly through all the formations, conformations,
and transformations that characterize a mythology.

Chaos shines through because this mythology combines, as Schlegel's
oxymoron expresses it, naiveté with profundity. The new mythology is
naively profound, or profoundly naive, like a fairy story. It is profound
without knowing that it is profound. The combination of naiveté and
profundity makes it both enthusiastic and ironical at the same time. What
shines through, however, is not the original absurdity, madness, simplicity, and stupidity of chaos, but only its Schein, that is, both a distant,
indirect gleam of it and its "semblance," as the translation puts it. Probably that is a good thing, since the closer one gets to that original chaos
the closer one gets to absurdity, dizziness to the point of madness. Mythology, it may be, is a protection as well as a means of insight.

Nevertheless, what Schlegel stresses in the final sentence of the enchained sequence I have been following is the irrationality of poetry and
the way it puts us within chaos. The sentence, in its use of the word *aufzuheben*, is a parodic anticipation of Hegelian dialectical sublation. In
Schlegel's case the Aufhebung does not raise us to a higher level in the
endless progression toward the far-off fulfillment of union with absolute
spirit, the Idea, nor does it move toward the achievement of Absolute
Knowledge. It transplants us into a mad chaos. It leads to total non-
knowledge. Hegel was right to be appalled.

As opposed to Paul de Man, who stresses the madness of ironic language in Schlegel, I want to argue that Schlegel's difference from Hegel
arises from a different intuition about what is beyond language, Schlegel's chaos as against Hegel's Idea. Everything follows, I claim, from that
difference. Every feature of Schlegel's nonsystematic system makes sense
(a strange kind of nonsensical sense) when everything he says is seen as
swirling around those "wholly others" he called chaos.

Here is that final sentence, the last link in this nonconcatenated chain.
I quote it again now that we have made our way back to it through the
linked sentences that precede it: "For this is the beginning (Anfang) of all
poetry, to cancel (aufzuheben) the progression (Gang) and laws of rationally thinking reason, and to transplant (zu versetzen) us once again into
the beautiful confusion of imagination (die schöne Verwirrung der Phantasie), into the original (ursprüngliche) chaos of human nature, for which
I know no more beautiful symbol than the motley throng of the ancient
gods" (G, 502; E, 86). About the stuttering repetition of the prefix *Ver-* in
"vernünftig . . . Vernunft" (reasonable reason), in "versetzen," and in

"Verwirrung," already used a few sentences earlier, I shall have more to say later. If *aufzuheben* means not just cancel, but preserve, and raise up, thereby suggesting that poetry is a kind of higher reason, the passage makes clear that this higher reason is not rational, but a confusion. The translation affirms that poetry "transplants" us into that original confusion, but *versetzen* means literally, according to *Cassell's German Dictionary*, "set over, move, transfer; move from one grade to another in school; pawn, hock; reply." The word, in one of its valences, as meaning "transpose," is almost a synonym for *übersetzen*, translate. The prefix *ver-*, as in this verb, is antithetical, both an intensive and a privative. *Versetzen* can mean to put forth or deposit as collateral for a loan, in short, to put in hock, as well as transpose, set across. In Schlegel's usage here, *versetzen* affirms that the words of poetry have a magic power to transpose the reader into the realm of the original chaos, just as if he were being translated into another language home where another mother tongue is spoken. That new language, however, is the language of madness and foolishness.

A passage in *Lucinde* concentrates all the motifs I have been explaining. It will demonstrate that these key terms are present not just in the *Dialogue on Poetry* and in the fragments. The passage comes at the end of the characteristically overheated autobiography of the hero's life and just before a section entitled "Metamorphosis." *Lucinde* seems more dominated by hectic enthusiasm than by irony, unless the irony is so hidden in this naive profundity that it is hard to see. Probably this is the case. Here is the passage:

> Man's spirit (Geist) is his own Proteus: it transforms itself (verwandelt sich) and won't account for itself when it tries to come to grips with itself. In that deepest center of life, the creative will (die schaffende Willkür) produces its magic (ihr Zauberspiel). There are the beginnings and the ends where all the threads of the fabric of spiritual culture (der geistigen Bildung) disappear. Only whatever advances gradually in time and extends in space, only what happens is the subject (Gegenstand: really "object, thing; subject [matter], theme, topic") of history. But the mystery (Geheimnis: secret) of a momentary (augenblicklichen: a starting in the blink of an eye, in an instant; instantaneous) beginning or transformation (Entstehen oder Verwandlung) can only be divined (erraten) and it can only be divined in Allegory.
>
> It's not without reason that the fantastical boy whom I liked best of the four immortal Novels who appeared to me in the dream was playing with a mask. Allegory has crept even into what seems pure description (Darstellung) and fact, and has mixed meaningful lies with beautiful truths. But only

as a spiritual breath (geistiger Hauch) does allegory hover over the whole mass of things, like Wit who plays invisibly with his creation, only a trace of a smile playing on his lips.[27]

In accordance with the intense narcissism and self-enclosure of *Lucinde*, this passage begins an adaptation of the myth of Proteus that turns the encounter with a divine other into an encounter with oneself. The deepest depths of the self are now the locus of the inexpressible other. The spirit of man is his own Proteus. Proteus was a prophetic sea-god in the service of Poseidon who escaped all attempts made by anyone, for example Hercules, to get him to foretell the future. He escaped by turning himself into one creature after another. The drama of Hercules's wrestling with Proteus is here transformed into an unsuccessful struggle to come to terms with oneself. It is unsuccessful because the deepest levels of the self merge with the unknowable and inexpressible place of beginning and end where all the threads of the fabric of spiritual culture disappear.

This transposition of the story of Proteus is a miniature allegory. Allegory here is close to wit, which in turn is close to irony, though in this passage irony is not mentioned. Irony is elsewhere, however, also described by Schlegel as hovering over an entire discourse like an invisible breath, just as wit does here. Irony is in this passage present only covertly in that trace of a smile playing on the lips of Wit. Wit is here personified, as are those "four immortal novels" about which the hero, somewhat bathetically, dreamt. To think of a novel as personified as a handsome boy is more than a little ridiculous. Prosopopoeia is not mentioned overtly in the passages about mythology or allegory discussed so far. Nevertheless, the "motley throng of the ancient gods" would of course be allegorical personifications of "the highest," that is, prosopopoetic catachreses for the inexpressible chaos that can only be expressed indirectly.

Allegory is like wit is like irony because all three say one thing and mean another. They turn, trope, or transform language. The other that they mean, for Schlegel however, is the madness and stupidity of the unattainable beginning or primordial place of transformation, the Chaos for which all allegories are catachreses. It is beginning *or* transformation, Entstehung *oder* Verwandlung. This is because the beginning is already transformation. Here allegory has crept into what seems pure description and fact. "Chaos" is named, ambiguously, "the deepest center of life." I say "ambiguously" because it is impossible to tell whether Schlegel means a subjective center or a center outside man's spirit of which man's protean spirit, with its penchant for transformation (sideways metamorphoses, like Proteus's changes), is an allegory. It is both, since at the "deepest center" one goes outside subjectivity into that place of beginning and ending where all the threads of spiritual culture, geistigen Bildung, disappear. In a somewhat similar way Freud, in a celebrated passage in the *The Interpretation of Dreams*, says each dream is, like a mushroom mycelium, an arabesque-like tangle of lines around an unattainable origin. Each dream leads down to a place that no Traumdeutung can reach.[28]

The figure of the tangled threads of history, a web that advances gradually in time and space from that absent center or chaos, matches the figure of the arabesque and is a gloss on it. History is allegory and for that reason ironic, as de Man hints in "The Concept of Irony" when he says history is very curiously linked to irony (AI, 184). History as a continuous unfolding is opposed to the radically inaugural beginnings that punctuate it as new starts. The latter emerge in primary acts of transformation from the unattainable center. Whatever happens, was geschieht, is like those tangled threads around the unknowable center of the mushroom mycelium in the passage I have cited from Freud. History is therefore an ironical allegory of the madness, at that deepest center, in jener tiefsten Mitte. That center is secret, a mystery, a Geheimnis. It can therefore only be divined, that is, intuited, glimpsed indirectly.

This divining or glimpsing requires a vehicle, a medium, something to carry the thought and keep it from being empty. The name for that is "allegory." Allegory is defined a moment latter in a proto-de Manian way as the use of what seems pure description and fact as figures for that secret. The word "secret" must here be taken in a strong sense. It is a secret that may never be revealed. The secret in question is a true Geheimnis, the secret of an instantaneous beginning or transformation that deflects the onward course of history. This secret is both Entstehung and Verwandlung, both beginning and transformation. This is so because transformation characterizes that infinitesimal beginning or that threshold of beginning. The beginning is already transformation not only because it is continual transformation within itself but also because it cannot begin. It cannot, that is, get over that threshold from the infinitely distant chaos and enter into history without turning itself into something else, troping itself, becoming something open to naming as pure description and fact. The beginning is transformation. All the other metamorphoses or substitutions in the netlike web follow from that first figure. To put this another way, the beginning is already a figure, as for Rousseau the first word is a metaphor. A novel is ironic through and through because under the guise or in the mask of describing facts, history, it actually names the secret beginning and the deepest center of life, though it necessarily names them indirectly. Another (ironic) way to put this, or another way Schlegel puts it, is to say that pure description and fact, in a novel for example, are "beautiful truths" that are mixed with "meaningful lies," "bedeutende Lügen." Beautiful lies are expressions that are not literally true but have allegorical meaning. "Bedeutende Lügen" is an

ironical name for the ironic way of speaking the truth, as Nietzsche was
to argue in "On Truth and Lie in an Extramoral Sense," foreshadowed in
Schlegel's phrase here.

If the closer one approaches to the "deepest center of life" the closer one
approaches to madness and foolishness, this ought either to be evident in
some way in Schlegel's own discourse, or else one would need to conclude
that he is talking about indirect allegory rather than doing it. If the former, Schlegel is not really contributing to the composition of the new
mythology that will give form to the highest. That I have been able to
explicate what Schlegel says, show its reasonableness, the way it all hangs
together and makes sense, would seem to demonstrate that Schlegel is,
even in *Lucinde*, excluded from what he most wants to express. Is there
any way in which "the semblance of the absurd and of madness, of simplicity and foolishness" "shimmers through" what he says? One way is in
the pervasive irony of all Schlegel's major works, the fragments, the *Dialogue on Poetry*, "Über die Unverständlichkeit," and *Lucinde* itself. All
these works combine enthusiasm and irony in an uneasy mix. The reader
can never be sure whether to take Schlegel at his word, or whether he is
setting a trap for the naive reader. "Über die Unverständlichkeit" is a
good example. Schlegel keeps saying that since readers have found his
contributions to the *Athenäum* incomprehensible in part at least because
they are perhaps ironical, he will write for once entirely without irony.
Most readers can see, however, that "On Incomprehensibility" is savagely ironic from beginning to end. It is always impossible to tell whether
Schlegel is being serious or not. He may be or he may not be. The meaning
is suspended in a permanent parabasis.

   Another way that Schlegel's writing is mad and foolish, in consonance
with that of which it talks, is less obvious and more subtle. One effect of
the insistent repetition of a given word and its similars is progressively to
empty the word of meaning and make it sheer sound. Passages I have
discussed contain good examples of this: Spiel, Spiel, Spiel, Spiel; bilden,
Bildung, anbilden, umbilden; all the words using the prefix *Ver-*, including words that mean confusion, madness, and the absurd, that echo
through the passage that has been my focus: Verwandlung, Verfahren,
Verwirrung, Verkehrten, Verrückten, venünftig . . . Vernunft, Verwirrung (again), versetzen, and, of course, Unverständlichkeit in the title of
another essay. Ver-, Ver-, Ver-, Ver-: the prefix calls attention to itself,
especially perhaps to a non-German speaker. It tends toward materializing itself as marks on the page or as empty noise. Ver-, as I have said, is
an antithetical prefix. It serves either as an intensive or as a privative, or
both, as in the notorious example of *versprechen*, promise, and *sich ver-*

sprechen, make a slip of the tongue, perjure oneself.[29] *Verstand*, meaning mind, intellect, brain, becomes *unverständlich*, meaning incomprehensible, becomes *Verkehrten* and *Verrückten*, meaning madness and absurdity, as the ver- approaches nearer and nearer to being mere nonsense noise.

Paul de Man has noticed this feature of Schlegel's style. He calls it "the free play of the signifier" and associates it with irony. He makes this free play the endpoint or climax of his reading of Schlegel. It is the way Schlegel himself becomes dizzy to the point of madness and makes his reader vertiginous too. "Über die Unverständlichkeit," says de Man, "is full of puns, etymological puns in the manner of Nietzsche, in which a great deal is made of plays on *stehen* and *verstehen*, *stellen* and *verstellen*, of *verrücken* (insanity), and so on" (AI, 181). De Man's example is the notorious section of *Lucinde*, "Eine Reflexion," in which solemn philosophical terminology actually describes sexual intercourse. "Words," says de Man, "have a way of saying things which are not at all what you want them to say. You are writing a splendid and coherent philosophical argument but, lo and behold, you are describing sexual intercourse. . . . There is a machine there, a text machine, an implacable determination and a total arbitrariness . . . which inhabits words on the level of the play of the signifier, which undoes any narrative consistency of lines, and which undoes the reflexive and the dialectical model, both of which are, as you know, the basis of any narration" (ibid.). "As you know?" Most people did not know that at all before de Man told them. De Man seems to have caught a little irony here himself, as he certainly has in the sentence turning on "lo and behold." "There is no narration without reflection, no narrative without dialectic," de Man concludes, "and what irony disrupts (according to Friedrich Schlegel) is precisely that dialectic and that reflexivity, the tropes. The reflexive and the dialectical are the tropological system, the Fichtean system, and that is what irony undoes" (ibid.). As the other essays in *Aesthetic Ideology* (all written or presented as lectures later than "The Concept of Irony") confirm, de Man came to define the implacable text machine as exposure of the materiality of the letter, though just what de Man meant by materiality is one of the more enigmatic questions about his late work. I shall return to de Man's materiality in the last essay in this book.

What Friedrich Schlegel meant by a materializing of language that empties it of meaning and makes it just so much lumpish matter is expressed in an exuberantly comic and ironic passage early in "Über die Unverständlichkeit." The passage comes just after Schlegel promises that he is really going to be "comprehensible (verständlich), at least this time" (G, 531).[30] The passage is about "a real language (eine reele Sprache)" (ibid.), something, so Schlegel says, that Kant's genius as a philosopher made possible. This "real language" would be an adequate vocabulary, at last, for talking directly and literally about "the highest." It corresponds to, and perhaps influenced, Walter Benjamin's idea, in "Über die Aufgabe des Übersetzers," of a "reine Sprache," a pure language. Who, among those who have thought about the matter at all, has not dreamed of such a language?

Schlegel's figure for this real language is the promise made by a certain chemist named Girtanner that in the nineteenth century people will be able to fulfill the age-old alchemical dream and make gold of base metals. The simplest kitchen utensils will be made of silver or gold. The real language will be like this universal gold, ruler or measure of everything. Gold is a universal measure understood by all people of all countries. "Among the Chinese, I thought," says Schlegel, in a weird, racist list that accelerates toward the more and more exotic, "among the English, the Russians, in the island of Japan, among the natives of Fez and Morocco, even among the Cossacks, Cheremis, Bashkirs, and Mulattoes, in short, wherever there is even a little enlightenment and education, silver and gold are comprehensible (verständlich) and through them everything else" (G, 532–33; OI, 34). In the same way the real language will be universal. It will be understood and used by all people of all cultures. In it the dream of a lingua franca will come true at last, as English these days is fulfilling that dream in a quite problematic way.

Something strange, however, happens to Schlegel's figure in the course of its development. It gets literalized, materialized, just as does philosophical language in "Eine Reflexion." The figure is thereby made mad and stupid, as well as ironically funny. When gold and silver are so common that kitchen utensils can be made of them, then an artist "will be allowed only to write his works in bas-relief, with gold letters on silver tablets" (G, 533; OI, 34). This sounds splendid, though such books would be a little hard to carry around, just as would a desktop computer today, our present ironic fulfillment of Schlegel's prophecy. His next sentence, however, marks the ironic turn. "Who," asks Schlegel, "would want to reject so beautifully printed a book with the vulgar remark that it doesn't make any sense (sie sei unverständlich)?" (ibid.). The universal verständlichkeit of gold here suddenly reverses into the unverständlichkeit of gold letters that are incomprehensible. The more literature is materialized by being printed on precious metals that serve as the standards and measure of human value, the more senseless it becomes, that is, the more cut off from serving the prime purpose of poetry, which is, as you know, to allegorize the highest, the original and originating chaos. The more precious it becomes, in one sense, the more valueless it becomes, in another sense, until this grandly ambitious poetry becomes no more than dead letters, letters made of gold, no doubt, but signifying nothing, just as that computer on my desktop is, seen from one perspective, no more than a great lump of senseless materiality.

De Man in his commentary on this passage assimilates it to his interest, at that time in his thinking, in the mechanical play of language as sheer grammar and as tropological substitution that escapes human intention and escapes sense too, in a particular form of materialization. De Man stresses the way Schlegel's parodic "reele Sprache" becomes "circulation which is out of hand, not like nature but like money, which is sheer circulation, the sheer circulation or play of the signifier, and which is, as you know, the root of error, madness, stupidity, and all other evil" (AI, 181). Schlegel, however, stresses not only the way gold and silver are universally comprehensible, in all languages and in all cultures, but also how through them everything else is made comprehensible. Everything else is made comprehensible by being defined as worth so much gold or so much silver, as, in Marx's analysis, all labor, raw materials, and the products of labor are reduced to their money's worth, the universal medium of exchange. On the one hand, the more this earthly and material standard of making everything comprehensible, verständlich, is successful, the less will anything produced by its means, even poetry printed in gold letters, have any meaning in relation to the highest. From that perspective, it will be "unverständlich," as Schlegel says. On the other hand, in a further turn of Schlegel's irony, only a poetry that is senseless, unverständlich, stupid can be said to be allowing the madness and foolishness of aboriginal chaos to glimmer through. Its failure is its success. Though it does not give understanding of chaos, since chaos is Unverständlichkeit as such and cannot be understood, it does allow a precious indirect confrontation, at a distance, through a semblance (Schein), of das Höchste.

The ultimate materialization, and the most savage irony of all in Schlegel's ironic essay on irony, comes in the next brief paragraph. Here the materialization I have been following is identified with death and with a cadaver from which the spirit has flown, leaving senseless matter behind. Girtanner, the scientist who promised an immediate golden age is, says Schlegel, "dead and consequently so far removed from being able to make gold that one might extract with all possible artistry only so much iron out of him as might be necessary to immortalize his memory (Andenken) by way of a little medallion" (G, 533; OI, 34). Far from turning to gold, Girtanner's body might by its cremation, in an alchemical process in reverse, yield only a bit of one of those baser metals he promised to transmute. What is the exchange value of a dead body? Almost always nil. The idea of having a little iron medallion (Schaumünze: literally a show coin, a coin minted for display, not for circulation) made out of one's own body is repulsive, to say the least. I certainly hope it does not happen to

me. Such a medallion would be like that book in the collection of the
Boston Athenaeum that was, at the author's request, after his death,
bound in his own skin. In either case, the endpoint is a grotesque materialization, something senseless and absurd, just as the meaningless poetry made of gold letters on a silver tablet devalues gold rather than en-
hancing it.

The figure dominating all these ironic jokes is that of language and its
material base. Since language always requires some kind of material sub-
stratum on which to be inscribed, even the rarefied matter of modulated
sound waves for spoken language, language is always in danger of being
turned back into that base. It is in danger of becoming mere sound or
marks, and so made valueless, like a coin stamped with nonsense words
or with the words rubbed off by use.

This encompassing irony, a kind of ultimate irony of irony, will allow,
finally, understanding, if I dare to use that word, of another recurrent
motif in Schlegel's work. This is the definition of poetry as magic. In the
dialogue leading up to Ludovico's presentation of the "Talk on Mythology," Ludovico asserts that "poetry is the finest branch of magic"
(G, 496; DP, 80). After Ludovico's talk, Lothario (who is sometimes said
to represent Novalis) asserts, apropos of Dante, that "Actually, every
work should be a new revelation (Offenbarung) of nature. Only by being
individual and universal (Eins und Alles) does a work become *the work*
(wird ein Werk zum Werk)" (G, 507; DP, 92). A moment later he stresses
the word again, speaking of the "independence and inner perfection for
which I simply cannot find another word but the work (als das von
Werken)" (ibid.). The word "work" here means primarily a work of art,
of course. Dante's *Divine Comedy* is one example Schlegel gives. The
insistence on the word, however, gives it alchemical or magical overtones.
The great "work," for medieval alchemy, was the transmutation of base
metals into gold. That transmutation was a figure for the transfiguration
of the human spirit by a kind of magic into someone worthy of salvation
or even into a kind of deity. If poetry is the noblest magic, this means that
poetry does not promise or give knowledge. It works performatively to
bring something about, as though it were a magic formula. It is a feature
of magic formulas, however, that they are, at least superficially or to pro-
fane ears and eyes, senseless, stupid: "Abracadabra! Hocus pocus!" says
the magician, and something happens. A pack of cards is turned into a
pigeon. Schlegel's conception of mythology is ultimately performative,
not constative. A work of mythology is a speech act that works through
its senselessness to reveal, in a magic opening up, a gleam of the semblance of chaos. The "of . . . of" in this formula indicates the double

remove. The mythological work thereby works to transform its readers through this revelation. We do not come to know anything through a myth. We are made different, magically. The mythological work works.

The final irony, however, is that since this transformation is brought about not by knowledge but by a magic speech act, there is no way to know, for sure, whether the revelation is a true one, or only a semblance, a Schein. "Hocus pocus" is a slang term for the beguiling procedures of a fraud. The pack of cards is not really turned into a pigeon. It is a sleight of hand. The paradox of all speech acts appears here in a hyperbolic form. It is hyperbolic because the speech act in question deals with the highest destiny of humankind. It is the speech act enabling all other speech acts. The performative side of a speech act is alien to knowledge. It makes something happen, but just how, by just whose authority, and just what happens can never be known for certain. Another way to put this is to say that mythologies are for Schlegel forced and abusive transfers of language, thrown out to name something that has no proper name and that is wholly unknown and unknowable. The rhetorical name for this procedure, as I have said, is catachresis. I therefore call Schlegel's myths catachreses for chaos. For Schlegel, what cannot be known for certain is whether new mythological works create a spurious semblance of the highest out of hocus pocus, language's magic power to project new virtual realities, or whether such works open doors allowing us to glimpse a semblance, a Schein, of that preexisting, perennial, wholly other realm Friedrich Schlegel calls "chaos." Nothing could be more important to know, but we cannot know. We can only believe, and bear witness for, one alternative or the other. This is the way in which Schlegel's assertions about myth and irony embody that doubleness or aporia in the term "myth" I began by identifying. It is also the way they embody the threat to rationality and dialectical thought that made Hegel so indignant.

Notes

1. ". . . all beauty is allegory. One can say the highest only allegorically, since it is unspeakable" (my translation).

2. S. H. Bucher, *Aristotle's Theory of Poetry and Fine Art, with a Critical Text and Translation of The Poetics* (New York: Dover Publications, 1951 [reprint of 1909 ed.]), 25. Further references will be to this edition and translation, preceded by the traditional manuscript numbering.

3. (Princeton: Princeton University Press, 1957).

4. (Paris: Seuil, 1957).

5. (La Tour d'Aigues: Editions de l'Aube, 1991).

6. Friedrich Schlegel, *Kritische Schriften* (Munich: Carl Hanser, 1964), 33, henceforth G; Friedrich Schlegel, *Philosophical Fragments*, trans. Peter Firchow (Minneapolis: University of Minnesota Press, 1991), 27, henceforth E.

7. G, 515; Friedrich Schlegel, *Dialogue on Poetry and Literary Aphorisms*, trans. Ernst Behler and Roman Struc (University Park: The Pennsylvania State University Press, 1968), 101, henceforth DP.

8. Ed. Ernst Behler, Jean-Jacques Anstett, and Hans Eichner (Munich: F. Schöningh, 1958–).

9. See "The Concept of Irony," in *Aesthetic Ideology*, ed. Andrzej Warminski (Minneapolis: University of Minnesota Press, 1996), 182, henceforth AI: "The best critics who have written on Schlegel, who have recognized his importance, have wanted to shelter him from the accusation of frivolity, which was generally made, but in the process they always have to recover the categories of the self, of history, and of dialectic, which are precisely the categories which in Schlegel are disrupted in a radical way." The two examples of this recuperation de Man gives are Peter Szondi and Walter Benjamin, two names to conjure with. To these names may be added the even more august names of Hegel and Kierkegaard. If all these dignitaries got Schlegel wrong, how could we expect to do better?

10. For a brilliant essay on this topic, see Werner Hamacher, "Position Exposed: Friedrich Schlegel's Poetological Transposition of Fichte's Absolute Proposition," in *Premises: Essays on Philosophy and Literature from Kant to Celan*, trans. Peter Fenves (Cambridge: Harvard University Press, 1996), 222–60.

11. Søren Kierkegaard, *The Concept of Irony*, trans. Howard V. Hong and Edna H. Hong (Princeton: Princeton University Press, 1989), 265–66. Lee Capel's translation has "indignation" rather than "resentment." Søren Kierkegaard, *The Concept of Irony*, trans. Lee M. Capel (Bloomington: Indiana University Press, 1968), 283. Friedrich Schlegel makes Hegel indignant.

12. G. W. F. Hegel, *Grundlinien der Philosophie des Rechts*, *Werke* (Frankfurt am Main: Suhrkamp, 1970), 7:279; Hegel, *Elements of the Philosophy of Right*, trans. H. B. Nisbet (Cambridge: Cambridge University Press, 1991), 182.

13. Cited in Kierkegaard, *The Concept of Irony*, trans. Hong and Hong, 547.

14. Ibid., 286–301.

15. "Unendliche absolute Negativität," G. W. F. Hegel, *Vorlesungen über die Ästhetik*, *Werke* (Frankfurt am Main: Suhrkamp, 1981), 13:98, henceforth G; *Aesthetics: Lectures on Fine Art*, trans. T. M. Knox (Oxford: Clarendon Press, 1975), 1:68, henceforth E.

16. Die Ironie ist eine permanente Parekbase,—": Friedrich Schlegel, "Zur Philosophie" (1797), Fragment 668, in *Philosophische Lehrjahre I* (1796–1806), ed. Ernst Behler, *Kritische Friedrich Schlegel-Ausgabe*, 18:85.

17. AI, 179.

18. This is not entirely unlike blaming President Clinton's behavior on deconstruction, as numerous journalists did during Clinton's impeachment hearings.

19. See Georgia Albert, "Understanding Irony: Three *essais* on Friedrich Schlegel," *MLN* (1993): 825–48. The comment on "schwindlicht" is on 845.

20. Cited by Ernst Behler and Roman Struc in their introduction to DP, 28–29.

21. The best discussion of the contradictory, incomprehensible "logic" of the

fragment is Hans-Jost Frey's admirable *Unterbrechungen* (Zürich: Edition Howeg, 1989); *Interruptions*, trans. Georgia Albert (Albany: State University of New York Press, 1996). "Understanding," says Frey, "is precisely the suppression of fragmentariness, since it creates context (Zusammenhang: holding together, cohering) where every relation breaks off. The fragment is neither a whole nor a part. This means that it cannot be understood from the perspective of the whole (Das Verstehen ist geradezu die Unterdrückung des Fragmentarischen, indem es Zusammenhang schafft, wo jeder Bezug abbricht. Das Fragment ist weder ein Ganzes noch ein Teil. Das bedeutet, dass es nicht vom Ganzen her verstehbar ist)" (G, 28; E, 26). Other helpful discussions, from perspectives different from Frey's, of the Schlegelian fragment are Rodolphe Gasché's "Foreword: Ideality in Fragmentation," in Schlegel, *Philosophical Fragments*, vii–xxxii; and Phillipe Lacoue-Labarthe and Jean-Luc Nancy, *L'absolu littéraire* (Paris: Seuil, 1978), esp. 57–178; Lacoue-Labarthe and Nancy, *The Literary Absolute*, trans. Philip Barnard and Cheryl Lester (Albany: State University New York Press, 1988), 39–58. The original French version of the latter book contains French translations of a large number of Friedrich Schlegel's fragments. These are omitted in the English version.

22. See AI, 168.

23. "Das *Schöne* bestimmt sich dadurch als das sinnliche *Scheinen* der Idee." Hegel, *Vorlesungen über die Ästhetik*, 1:151. "Therefore the beautiful is characterized as the pure appearance of the Idea to sense." Hegel, *Äesthetics*, 1:111.

24. William Wordsworth, *Poetical Works*, ed. Thomas Hutchinson and Ernest de Selincourt (London: Oxford University Press, 1966), 754.

25. See Karl Konrad Polheim, *Die Arabeske: Ansichten und Ideen aus Friedrich Schlegels Poetik* (Munich: F. Schöningh, 1966).

26. Paul de Man, "The Rhetoric of Temporality," *Blindness and Insight*, 2d. ed. (Minneapolis: University of Minnesota Press, 1983), 215.

27. Friedrich Schlegel, *Lucinde* (Stuttgart: Reclam, 1973), 78; Schlegel, *"Lucinde" and the Fragments*, trans. Peter Firchow (Minneapolis: University of Minnesota Press, 1971), 104.

28. Sigmund Freud, *The Interpretation of Dreams*, trans. James Strachey, *Standard Edition of the Complete Psychological Works* (London: Hogarth Press, 1953–66), 5:530. Here is Samuel Weber's translation of the passage, with key words from the German inserted: "Even in the best interpreted dreams, there is often a place [*eine Stelle*] that must be left in the dark, because in the process of interpreting one notices a tangle of dream-thoughts arising [*anhebt*] which resists unravelling but has also made no further contribution [*keine weiteren Beiträge*] to the dream-content. This, then, is the navel of the dream, the place where it straddles the unknown [*dem Unerkannten aufsitzt*]. The dream-thoughts, to which interpretation leads one, are necessarily interminable [*ohne Abschluss*] and branch out on all sides into the netlike entanglement [*in die netzartige Verstrickung*] of our world of thought. Out of one of the denser places in this meshwork, the dream-wish rises [*erhebt sich*] like a mushroom out of its mycelium." Samuel Weber, *The Legend of Freud* (Minneapolis: University of Minnesota Press, 1982), 75. Weber's commentary on this passage (75–83) is of great value, particularly in calling attention to the differences in implication between Freud's

German and Strachey's English translation and in its close attention to the figurative rhetoric of what Freud wrote.

29. Notorious because of a passage at the end of Paul de Man's "Promises (*Social Contract*)" that plays on the double meaning of *versprechen*. See *Allegories of Reading* (New Haven: Yale University Press, 1979), 277.

30. For the English: "On Incomprehensibility," in *German Aesthetic and Literary Criticism: The Romantic Ironists and Goethe*, ed. Kathleen Wheeler (Cambridge: Cambridge University Press, 1984), 33, henceforth OI.

Chapter Two

CHARLES DICKENS:
THE OTHER'S OTHER
IN *OUR MUTUAL FRIEND*

ALL NOVELS tend to create a virtual reality in the minds of their readers. Houses, rooms, roads, streets, hills, rivers, and so on get organized in a mental topography that may vary from reader to reader, just as do readers' imaginations of the way the characters look. It might be difficult to study these variations empirically. Investigating such mental mappings is, however, one project of current geographical and anthropological sub-disciplines. Readings of novels can contribute to that investigation. Victorian novels are, among many other things, often powerful verbal mappings of London or of other regions of England. Among Victorian novels, Dickens's have perhaps contributed most to the sense we still have today of what nineteenth-century London was like.

The interior space a novel generates in its reader's mind works as a strong vehicle of meaning. It helps define the way the characters exist in themselves as well as the way they are related to one another. If a given novel is based on a historically existent urban or country topography, as is the case with so many Victorian novels, then the reader's prior sense of the place, the city of London for instance, plays a strong role in determining his or her imaginary mapping. The sense of a "real" place, however, is also, though in a somewhat different way, an imaginary mapping. It is determined, in the case of London, by which parts of the city a given person knows best and by the way he or she is accustomed to travel within the city. My sense of London is strongly influenced by the configuration of the Underground and by the fact that I have lived at different times in Hampstead and in Kensington, while working almost daily at the British Library. My London is almost as skewed as that famous *New Yorker* cover that shows New York City in detail, but everything beyond the Hudson River all the way to the Pacific as foreshortened and distorted. My London is also strongly influenced by the great series of Victorian and early twentieth-century novels that presume knowledge of London: from *Oliver Twist* to *Our Mutual Friend* and *Edwin Drood* in Dickens's case, but including also many of Trollope's novels, for example *Ayala's Angel*, and, later, much of Henry James's work, for example *The Wings of the Dove* and *The Golden Bowl*.

Victorian novels were written for readers who for the most part knew London or even lived there. This meant that the mention of specific streets or regions had an immediate resonance. Such place names served as a shorthand code for the social and economic status of the inhabitants. The carefully noted itineraries through East London the Artful Dodger follows with Oliver in *Oliver Twist* are one Dickensian example. The social placement of Ayala and her sister, in Trollope's *Ayala's Angel*, as they move from their father's little "bijou" of a house in South Kensington to the houses of their two aunts, one a grand house in Queens Gate, the other a small one in Notting Hill, is a good Trollopeian example. The walk Densher, in James's *The Wings of the Dove*, takes on Christmas Day from "his own small quarters" first to Sir Luke's house, then to Mrs. Lowder's in Lancaster Gate, then through Hyde Park to the Brompton Oratory, and finally down to Kate Croy's father's house in Chelsea, forms the climax of that novel. All these novels presume that their readers already know London. For an American reader, a good Victorian map of London, or at least a modern *A to Z Atlas of London and Suburbs*, is an essential ancillary tool in reading. Even such a map, however, does not give the social meaning of the various localities. In some cases, an author has provided a map of the imaginary geography on which his novels depend, for example Faulkner's map of his invented Yoknapatawpha County in Mississippi, or Hardy's maps of the Wessex country. Those maps, however, are only an aid to the mapping activity the novels themselves generate as they are read. Each novel creates its own unique imaginary topography, even when it is based on a real place.[1]

Dickens's *Our Mutual Friend* is a cardinal example of the creation out of words of such a singular mental topography. It differs slightly but in significant ways from Dickens's earlier great London novels, for example *Bleak House*. In *Our Mutual Friend*, as in *Bleak House*, the self-enclosed idiosyncrasy of the characters is signaled by their enclosure in domestic interiors that mirror their individuality and oddness. Krook's rag and bottle shop and the basement room of Grandfather and Grandmother Smallweed, in *Bleak House*, correspond, as examples of this, to Boffin's Bower, Venus's shop, the Veneering mansion, or the pub called the Six Jolly Fellowship Porters in *Our Mutual Friend*. The difference between the two novels is a difference of nuance, but it is an important nuance. *Bleak House* emphasizes much more overtly the way all these apparently dispersed and unlike people, each hermetically sealed in his or her uniqueness, are nevertheless connected to one another, responsible for one another. This is elaborately worked out on the level of plot. In *Bleak House* everybody turns out to be involved in one way or another with Esther

Summerson's story or with the Jarndyce case in Chancery. As Inspector Bucket says, "the whole bileing of people was mixed up in the same business, and no other."[2] This interconnection is also worked out on the topographical level in the stress on the way you can get from one of these strange interiors to any of the others. The itineraries are often carefully given. The omniscient narrator of *Bleak House* expresses this interconnectedness in the form of questions the novel answers by way of the revelation of the central mystery of Esther's parentage:

> What connexion can there be, between the place in Lincolnshire, the house in town, the Mercury in powder, and the whereabout of Jo the outlaw with the broom, who had that distant ray of light upon him when he swept the churchyard-step? What connexion can there have been between many people in the innumerable histories of this world, who, from opposite sides of great gulfs, have, nevertheless, been very curiously brought together! (BH, 256)

As I say, it is a matter of nuance, but the result, at least in my own mental mapping, is that I have a much clearer image of the relation of places to one another, as of the relation of the characters and plots, for *Bleak House* than for *Our Mutual Friend*. This might be exemplified by a juxtaposition of the famous opening of *Bleak House* with an episode set in a London fog in the middle of *Our Mutual Friend*. In the opening of *Bleak House*, "fog [is] everywhere" (BH, 13). Dickens, as every reader of that novel knows, gives a long list of the places where it is foggy: up the river, down the river, everywhere in London, finally zooming in, as one might say, on the Court of Chancery, where the fog is densest. The fog in *Bleak House*, however, more joins people together than it separates them, just as the case of Jarndyce and Jarndyce makes everyone in the novel interconnected.

The fog in *Our Mutual Friend*, at the opening of Book Three, on the contrary, more separates people than joins them, or it joins them in the common fate of death as the ultimate separation. The fog in *Our Mutual Friend* is a great sea that drowns everything and everybody. This could be seen, the narrator tells the reader, from a perspective outside London on high ground. The ubiquitous motif of drowning in *Our Mutual Friend* is in this passage universalized as the condition of all those who live in London. Londoners are already figuratively drowned even before some of them are literally drowned. The fog separates each person from his or her neighbor. It puts each in a condition likened to death by drowning. The fog at the same time joins them in that all are drowning in the fog and all are coughing and choking with the same gigantic head cold. Though all Londoners are cut off from one another, the fog and the catarrh are the mutual friends, so to speak, of each. They are joined by what separates them:

> From any point of the high ridge of land northward, it might have been discerned that the loftiest buildings made an occasional struggle to get their heads above the foggy sea, and especially that the great dome of Saint Paul's seemed to die hard; but this was not perceivable in the streets at their feet, where the whole metropolis was a heap of vapour charged with muffled sound of wheels, and enfolding a gigantic catarrh.[3]

In the next paragraph after the passage just cited, Riah makes his way from Pubsey and Co. in Saint Mary Axe to Fascination Fledgeby's chambers in the Albany by an itinerary that is exactly named. Like so many of the itineraries in *Our Mutual Friend*, it could be followed today on a street map or on foot in the real London, "by Cornhill, Cheapside, Fleet Street, and the Strand, to Piccadilly and the Albany" (480). Nevertheless, what Dickens here emphasizes is the way each of these locations is separated from the others by the dense fog: "Almost in the act of coming out at the door, Riah went into the fog, and was lost to the eyes of Saint Mary Axe" (480). Though Fledgeby is himself "Pubsey and Co.," the difference between Riah's shabby office in Saint Mary Axe and Fledgeby's luxurious flat in the Albany works to hide the connection. Riah, with his long staff and skirt, seems to those who see him to appear out of the fog and then disappear into it, as if he must be an apparition—strange, ghostly, or uncanny. The fog makes Riah a species of Baudelairean revenant, like those seven identical old men who appear on a foggy day in Paris, in Baudelaire's "Les sept veillards": "Fourmillante cité, cité plein de rêves, / Où le spectre en plein jour raccroche le passant! (Swarming city, city full of dreams, / Where the ghost in broad daylight accosts the bypasser!)."[4] Londoners, however, have more a habit of rationalizing or suppressing uncanny urban apparitions than does the Baudelairean persona: "Thither he went at his grave and measured pace, staff in hand, skirt at heel; and more than one head, turning back to look at his venerable figure already lost in the mist, supposed it to be some ordinary figure indistinctly seen, which fancy and the fog had worked into that passing likeness" (480). In *Our Mutual Friend*, moreover, in spite of many passages that give an exact description of the movement by one of the characters from one interior to another, street by street,[5] and in spite of the fact that, as in *Bleak House*, all of the grotesque "minor" characters are involved in one way or another in the larger plots, there are nevertheless some hints of the extreme difficulty of mapping a way to get from any one of these places to at least some of the others. Dickens, in spite of the sovereign command of London's geography he himself had (and ascribes to his narrator), is in *Our Mutual Friend* sometimes a little unusually vague, for him, about how to get there from here. Dickens emphasizes repeatedly, for example, the difficulty of finding the Six Jolly Fellowship Porters and its waterside milieu. When in the third chapter Charlie Hexam takes Mortimer Lightwood and Eugene Wrayburn from the Veneering mansion first to Charlie's father's house and then to the nearby police station where they view the dead body that is presumed to be John Harmon's, the narrator specifies the route taken by the carriage, but not so exactly that the reader might easily find these locations on a map:

> The wheels rolled on, and rolled down by the Monument and by the Tower, and by the Docks; down by Ratcliffe, and by Rotherhithe; down where the accumulated scum of humanity seemed to be washed from higher grounds, like so much moral sewage, and to be pausing until its own weight forced it over the bank and sunk it in the river. In and out among vessels that seemed to have got ashore, and houses that seemed to have got afloat—among bowsprits staring into windows, and windows staring into ships—the wheels rolled on, until they stopped at a dark corner, river-washed and otherwise not washed at all, where the boy alighted and opened the door.
> "You must walk the rest, sir; it's not many yards." . . .
> "This is a confoundedly out-of-the-way place," said Mortimer, slipping over the stones and refuse on the shore, as the boy turned the corner sharp. (63)

Much later on in the novel, Riah and Jenny Wren, the dolls' dressmaker, have considerable difficulty finding the Six Jolly Fellowship Porters: "When they had plodded on for some time nigh the river, Riah asked the way to a certain tavern called the Six Jolly Fellowship Porters. Following the directions he received, they arrived, after two or three puzzled stoppages for consideration. and some uncertain looking about them, at the door of Miss Abbey Potterson's dominions" (496).

The most elaborate and extended account of this relative failure in mapping, however, is John Harmon's unsuccessful attempt to reconstruct just what happened to him, and where, when he was drugged and then thrown into the river to drown: "Perhaps I might recall, if it were any good to try, the way by which I went to it [Limehouse Church] alone from the river; but how we two went from it to Riderhood's shop, I don't know—any more than I know what turns we took and doubles we made, after we left it. The way was purposely confused, no doubt" (424); "As to this hour I cannot understand that side of the river where I recovered the shore, being the opposite side to that on which I was ensnared, I shall never understand it now" (427). Harmon's plunge into the Thames to emerge first as Julius Handford and then, when he changes his name again, as John Rokesmith echoes the many drownings or near drownings that precede and follow it in the novel: those of his double George

Radfoot (who is drowned in his place), of Gaffer Hexam, Rogue Rider-hood (twice drowned, once to be recovered, once to drown for good), Eugene Wrayburn, and Bradley Headstone, not to speak of metaphorical drownings like Wegg's being pitched head foremost into a scavenger's cart, "with a prodigious splash" (862), or Fascination Fledgeby, after he has been thrashed by Alfred Lammle and has had pepper put on the plasters Jenny Wren applies, "plunging and gambolling all over his bed, like a porpoise or dolphin in its native element" (793).

All those drownings, near-drownings, or metaphorical drownings in a manner of speaking confound the rationalities of cognitive mapping. Scattered everywhere, all over the map, though especially anywhere on the river that winds its sinuous way from up-country through the city and down to the sea, are places that may allow a momentary or permanent entry into a region of otherness and anonymity, a region where one ceases to be oneself and may (or may not) emerge transformed. Even though the entry spots into this realm of otherness may often be located, they all lead to the same place, a ubiquitous underwater locus of metamorphosis. These entryways are different places and yet they lead to the same place. As is suggested by John Harmon's inability to reconstruct just what ways he went to enter and escape from the Thames, the transition from the mappable spot where a drowning took place to and from the unplaceable place beneath where one may die or be changed cannot be rationally traced.

Another form of the missing transition is the way Dickens in *Our Mutual Friend* leaps from one enclosed location to another even more abruptly and with less explanation than in *Bleak House*. The sign of these transitions is most often the blank between the end of one chapter and the beginning of the next. Even though the all-knowing and all-seeing narrator might have been able to provide detailed itineraries showing how to get from one of these places to the other, he often chooses not to do so. He juxtaposes without any intervening mark but the blank space on the page two incommensurate locales. The result is to suggest that London exists as an unimaginably large conglomeration of self-enclosed and idiosyncratic milieux, each to some degree cut off from all the others and heterogeneous to them, even though a knowing topographer might be able to find a way from one to another. The river in chapter 1, for example, is replaced without transition or explanation by the Veneerings' mansion in chapter 2. These unbridged discontinuities of milieu between one chapter and another are even more pronounced in *Our Mutual Friend* than in *Bleak House*. The reader is left more on his or her own to try in retrospect, after finishing the novel, to put all these dispersed locales together in a unified topography. *Our Mutual Friend* lacks the continuities provided in *Bleak House* by Esther Summerson's narrative and, in a different way, by Inspector Bucket's detective unifications or by the omniscient narrator's ruminations about how all persons and places are connected.

The different threads of the stories, moreover, are less neatly unraveled in the dénouement of *Our Mutual Friend* than in *Bleak House*. Wegg's seriocomic punishment, that of Fledgeby, the death of Bradley Headstone, the resurrection and transformation of Eugene Wrayburn, the smashup of the Lammles, the revelation that Noddy Boffin is not a miser after all, the happy marriage of John Harmon and Bella Wilfer—these are a little dispersed. The novel ends by shifting from one climax to another, not by tying them all together. The different plots are bound together by analogy, by all having, as one might say, as mutual friend the central motif of drowning or near-drowning and resurrection, but they are not, as in *Bleak House*, quite so systematically intertwined at the level of plot. This was made evident in the concluding scene of the recent BBC film of *Our Mutual Friend*. That scene shows a frieze of the different happy couples on the grassy riverbank, side by side in a row but not interacting.

The mediated similarity of characters and plots, in *Our Mutual Friend*, is not, I am claiming, quite the same thing as the demonstration, in *Bleak House*, that everything and everybody is interconnected and interdependent. One further way to talk about this nuance of difference between *Bleak House* and *Our Mutual Friend* is by identifying the significance of the latter's title. If in *Bleak House* "the whole bileing of people was mixed up in the same business, and no other," in *Our Mutual Friend* this sharing of stories is considerably more mediated and indirect. The title names that mediation. Strictly speaking, the phrase "our mutual friend," as any dictionary will tell you, is a solecism, an incorrect usage, but it is one so common that many usage experts now allow it to pass. "Mutual" means "shared," "held in common," as in "mutual affection" used to name the love two people have for one another. "Mutual" can be used to name a friend we share only by a kind of illicit but significant extension of its literal meaning. A certain person is my friend. He or she is also your friend. Though we may not know one another at all and therefore have no mutual feelings of friendship or antipathy, we share a feeling of friendship for the same person. Our friendship for the third who links us is "mutual." We are related to one another, have mutual feelings after all, by way of a third person, though we may not know one another directly at all. The words "our mutual friend" are used in the novel by the uneducated Mr. Boffin, which may excuse Dickens for the mistake. Boffin uses the phrase to name John Rokesmith, alias John Harmon. Rokesmith is Mr. Boffin's secretary and also the Wilfers's lodger, so Mr. Boffin says to Mrs. Wilfer: "I may call him Our Mutual Friend" (157).

The use of the phrase as the title for the whole novel, however, suggests a wider reference. This reference extends even beyond the centrality of

John Harmon to the novel's melodramatic intrigue, beyond, that is, the way John Harmon is mutual friend of all the characters. The novel is full of situations in which one person is related to another not directly but by way of a third person whom both know. This motif of mutual friendship, as it might be called, is closely associated with the motif of doubling, with its overtones of homosexual desire or at any rate of homosociality. This motif is ubiquitous in the novel, most often as chains of doublings in which one character doubles another and is doubled in his[6] turn by yet another. The melodramatic plot depends on the similarity in appearance of George Radfoot and John Harmon, but Harmon later on doubles and redoubles himself by becoming first Julius Handford and then John Rokesmith. Rogue Riderhood is a kind of double, in appearance and profession, of Gaffer Hexam, but Bradley Headstone later dresses as the double of Rogue Riderhood. He does this in order to put the blame for his planned murder of Eugene Wrayburn on Riderhood. Headstone and Riderhood drown locked in one another's arms. Wrayburn and Headstone are doubles in their rival loves for Lizzie Hexam. Mortimer Lightwood so models himself on his idol, Eugene Wrayburn, that they are in a manner of speaking doubles. Boffin becomes his own antithetical double when he pretends to become miserly.

The brotherly doubling of Wegg and Venus in their "friendly move" to cheat Mr. Boffin is a hilarious comic version of the motif of doubling. The scenes presenting this are at the highest level of Dickens's admirable pantomimic notations and wild verbal imagination. In the scene in which Wegg and Venus wrestle on the floor in an ecstasy of quasi-sexual greed, the homosexual component in such doubling is almost scandalously explicit. As Wegg reads to Mr. Boffin stories of misers who have buried fortunes up chimneys or in dungheaps ("One of Mr Dancer's richest escretoires was found to be a dungheap in the cowhouse" [544]), Wegg's wooden leg rises spontaneously in the air and he falls against Venus who is sitting beside him on the settle:

> (Here Mr Wegg's wooden leg started forward under the table, and slowly elevated itself as he read on.)
>
> . . . On the way to this crisis Mr Wegg's wooden leg had gradually elevated itself more and more, and he had nudged Mr Venus with his opposite elbow deeper and deeper, until at length the preservation of his balance became incompatible with the two actions, and he now dropped over sideways upon that gentleman, squeezing him against the settle's edge. Nor did either of the two, for some few seconds, make any effort to recover himself; both remaining in a kind of pecuniary swoon. (544–45)

Later the same evening, after they have spied on Boffin taking a Dutch bottle from its hiding place in the mounds, Venus has forcibly to restrain

Wegg from chasing after Boffin. At a slightly earlier stage, when Boffin has just left, "Wegg clutched Venus with both hands." Venus responds by "clutching him with both hands, so that they stood interlocked like a couple of preposterous gladiators" (548). After Boffin leaves with the Dutch bottle, their embrace rises to a sort of climax: "As in his wildness he [Wegg] was making a strong struggle for it [to free himself so he can chase after Boffin], Mr Venus deemed it expedient to lift him, throw him, and fall with him; well knowing that, once down, he would not be up again easily with his wooden leg. So they both rolled on the floor, and, as they did so, Mr Boffin shut the gate" (553). The doubling relation between Wegg and Venus is mediated by their mutual greed for the treasures supposedly buried in Harmon's dustmounds. The dustmounds are analogous to the depths of the Thames both in the way what they hide may be anywhere under their surface and in the way they serve as a link between persons not otherwise related. Wegg and Venus desire one another by way of their greed and curiosity about what the mounds may hide.

The most extreme form of a doubling mutual friendship is the relation of Bradley Headstone and Eugene Wrayburn. They are joined in that both love Lizzie Hexam. "Our mutual friend"—it is almost a recipe for jealousy. A is a friend of B. C is a friend of B. A and C are related by way of their mutual friend, B. But if I am A, how do I know if B is the same for me as he or she is for C? Does B love C better? There is no direct connection between me and C, only by way of B. It is not the case that the friend of my friend is my friend. Quite the contrary. Almost certainly I am jealous if my friend has another friend, perhaps ragingly jealous if I suspect that my friend is sexually betraying me with his or her other friend, or even, as in the case of what Bradley Headstone suspects of Lizzie, no more than secretly prefers the other friend to me. I have used abstract letters rather than names both to indicate the universality of this pattern and to suggest that anyone who is trapped within its irresistible force loses his or her independent selfhood. Such a person becomes a mere node in a pattern of irresistible and potentially lethal affective forces, forced to adopt a "subject position" determined by the triangular relationships.

Jealousy is a way of being tormentedly related to the wholly other by way of curiosity about the other's other. Let me try to explain this somewhat gnomic formulation by way of Bradley Headstone's jealousy of Eugene Wrayburn. Or does one say his jealousy of Lizzie? We are jealous both of the beloved and of the beloved's supposed beloved, the other's other. The English word jealousy comes from the Greek word *zélos*, meaning emulation, zeal, jealousy. All the meanings given in the *Oxford English Dictionary* stress the way jealousy is first and foremost a strong affect. Jealousy, according to the *OED*, has two now obsolete meanings:

"1. Zeal or vehemence of feeling against some person or thing; anger, wrath, indignation. *Obs.*"; "2. Zeal or vehemence of feeling in favour of a person or thing; devotion, eagerness, anxiety to serve. *Obs..*" Jealousy may be either wrath or devotion, either against or for, but in either case it is primarily a vehemence of feeling. It is by way of both these now obsolete meanings that the King James Bible translates Exodus 20:5, the commandment against idolatrous worship of graven images: "Thou shalt not bow down thyself to them, nor serve them: for I the Lord thy God am a jealous God." The fourth meaning in the *OED* defines amorous jealousy. It is only one form of jealousy among others: "4. The state of mind arising from the suspicion, apprehension, or knowledge of rivalry: a. in love, etc.: Fear of being supplanted in the affection, or distrust of the fidelity, of a beloved person, esp. a wife, husband, or lover." Amorous jealousy is a "state of mind," an exceedingly unpleasant one. It is not necessary to know that the beloved is unfaithful in order to be jealous.

In fact, if Marcel Proust is right, it is impossible ever to know. The furor of jealousy comes from a desire to know what in principle can never be known. "Suspicion," "apprehension," "fear," "distrust"—these are enough to make the lover violently and perhaps even murderously jealous, as in the cases of Shakespeare's Othello and Dickens's Bradley Headstone. The result of jealous suspicion is that every least thing seen may be a sign of the beloved's infidelity. Therefore everything must be remembered as a possible clue. As Alain Robbe-Grillet puts this: "Jealousy is a passion for which nothing ever effaces itself: everything seen, even the most innocent, remains inscribed there [in the jealous passion] once and for all."[7] Proust's admirable extended treatment in *À la recherche du temps perdu* of Marcel's jealousy of Albertine, a jealousy that lasts even beyond her death, shows how this desire to know whether or not the beloved is betraying me cannot ever be satisfied, even though it generates an obsessive inspection and scrutinizing of everything she or he says and does. The least gesture or slip of the tongue may be a clue. I discuss Marcel's jealousy of Albertine in chapter 9 of this book.

Jealous curiosity cannot be satisfied because the vehemence of jealousy puts the lover in what may be called a performative rather than cognitive situation. Everything the beloved says is turned by jealousy into a potential sign by a strange species of speech act on the part of the lover that posits significances that may or may not be there. This means that it becomes impossible ever to find out for sure whether the beloved is lying or not. Contrary to what most people assume, a lie is a speech act, not a false cognitive statement, or, to be more precise, it has a strong performative component that keeps it from being verified as true or false. A lie is a performative utterance because it can, if it is believed, bring about the condition it names. An example is the way Marcel's lying assertion that he does not love Albertine and wants her to leave brings about her departure. A lie belongs to the regime of witnessing, not to the regime of true or false statements. Marcel's inability to understand this sad truth or to accept it when he has glimpses of it (though Marcel as later narrator understands it) causes him intense suffering. It also generates the ironic comedy of a large part of the *Recherche*, since so much of it has to do with Marcel's relation to Albertine.

For Bradley Headstone, too, everything he sees becomes a potential sign inscribed permanently on his jealous passion. He follows Eugene Wrayburn everywhere, spying on him night after night, on the false assumption that he may thereby get confirmation of his jealous suspicion that Lizzie has refused him (Bradley) because she loves Eugene. Whatever he sees, however, remains just that, a sign inscribed on his jealousy. It does not contain in itself the rules for its interpretation or for the verification of an interpretation. The meaning Bradley gives such a sign is performatively posited by him, not intrinsic to the sign itself. As a result, the reading of each such sign, however he reads it, only exacerbates his jealousy. The reading of each such sign is something for which the jealous Bradley Headstone is responsible, or rather the autonomously working mechanism of his jealousy that works against his will to destroy him is responsible. His reading is itself a performative speech act, a blind, unverifiable positing, not a verifiable epistemological interpretation, just as in the case of Marcel's conflicting hypotheses about Albertine's supposed lies. Bradley's error, like Othello's or Marcel's, is to assume that he can get solid, irrefutable evidence that will justify action. Bradley's attempted murder of Eugene Wrayburn parallels Othello's murder of Desdemona and Marcel's decision to separate from Albertine (at the very moment she takes matters into her own hands and leaves him). These are desperate and self-destructive attempts to break the intolerable impasse. Nothing external, however, can justify such actions. They are unjust, an unauthorized taking of the law into one's own hands.

Dickens in his presentation of Bradley Headstone stresses, however, another feature of jealousy. This is the way the inevitably frustrated rage to know the other person wholly and to know the other's relation to the other's others, the beloved's supposed secret lovers, leads also to an encounter with the other within oneself. The jealous suspicion that the beloved is betraying me springs from an impossible desire to know and possess the other wholly. This desire is wonderfully mimed in those scenes in Proust in which Marcel watches the sleeping Albertine. He thinks she cannot betray him while she is no more than innocent, unconscious, sleeping flesh, though she is at that moment farthest from him and most inaccessible. What is permanently unknowable in the other is the other's participation in something wholly other, that other to which Jacques Derrida refers when he says in *Apories*: "Tout autre est tout autre (Every other is completely other)."[8] This anonymous and ubiquitous otherness is expressed, in *Our Mutual Friend*, in the figure of the river's dark depths. Anyone who enters those depths at whatever point on the topographical surface goes into the same place. My own selfhood, however clear and distinct it may seem to me in my self-consciousness, floats on the same dark depths that are the forever hidden regions of the beloved person and reaches down to them. John Harmon, in the passage in which he attempts to reconstruct what happened to him when he was drugged and thrown into the Thames, stresses the loss of his "I" or ego in that experience: "This is still correct? Still correct, with the exception that I cannot possibly express it to myself without using the word I. But it was not I. There was no such thing as I, within my knowledge" (426).The rage of jealousy, which may be defined as wrath born of the impossibility of knowing the other's other, may stir up dark depths of otherness within my own selfhood and bring me to destroy myself.

The scene in which Bradley Headstone proposes to Lizzie Hexam is one of the high points of Dickensian melodrama. Bradley says all the wrong things, the things least likely to persuade her to love him. As he says, his love for her is so violent that it leads him to say things he does not mean to say. He ceases to be himself and becomes a spokesperson for his ungovernable passion:

> "It seems egotistical to begin by saying so much about myself," he resumed, "but whatever I say to you seems, even in my own ears, below what I want to say, and different from what I want to say. I can't help it. So it is. You are the ruin of me." . . . "Yes! you are the ruin—the ruin—the ruin—of me. I have no resources in myself, I have no confidence in myself, I have no government of myself when you are near me or in my thoughts. And you are always in my thoughts now. I have never been quit of you since I first saw you. Oh, that was a wretched day for me! That was a wretched, miserable day!" (452)

This is not the sort of thing that is likely to be the stuff of successful wooing, but worse is to come:

> "You draw me to you. If I were shut up in a strong prison, you would draw me out. I should break through the wall to come to you. If I were lying on a sick bed, you would draw me up—to stagger to your feet and fall there."
>
> The wild energy of the man, now quite let loose, was absolutely terrible. He stopped and laid his hand upon a piece of the coping of the burial-ground enclosure, as if he would have dislodged the stone.

"No man knows till the time comes, what depths are within him. To some men it never comes; let them rest and be thankful! To me, you brought it; on me, you forced it; and the bottom of this raging sea," striking himself upon the breast, "has been heaved up ever since." (454)

As this scene makes clear, the words about the depths of the raging sea are not a metaphorical transfer from the literal naming of the river Thames, in all the scenes of drowning or near-drowning, including Headstone's drowning proleptically foreshadowed in this passage. It is the other way around. The anonymous and unnamable energy within each person is the literal of which the river's black depths are the figurative transfer. This scene ends with Headstone, after Lizzie's refusal, repeating obsessively the name "Mr Eugene Wrayburn," after "bringing his clenched hand down upon the stone with a force that laid the knuckles raw and bleeding" and exclaiming, "then I hope that I may never kill him!" (456). The empty name is a prosopopoetic catachresis for what he has a rage to know but can never know, the otherness of the other, the other's other. This is personified here for him as Lizzie's secret feelings about Eugene Wrayburn and so is embodied in the name "Mr Eugene Wrayburn."

Eugene Wrayburn himself is drawn to Lizzie just as Headstone is. He too must, when Headstone savagely beats him and leaves him for dead in the river, enter watery depths that stand for internal depths that are the same for each person. In Eugene's case, however, his near death is the occasion of a transformation that brings him back a changed man, worthy now to break class barriers, marry Lizzie, and live happily ever after, just as John Harmon is changed by his near drowning, while Headstone plunges into the water at Plashwater Weir Mill Lock to carry his double, the undrownable[9] Rogue Riderhood, to a joint death, locked in an embrace that expresses their unity and similarity.

The word "energy," used by the narrator about Headstone ("The wild energy of the man . . . was absolutely terrible" [454]), names an impersonal power in which all the novel's characters participate. This energy is the inner depth of each. It is a power both for good and for evil, both for death and for life. This energy is Dickens's version of the wholly other. It serves as what one might call a mutual friend for all the characters, male and female alike. It links them across class and gender barriers as well as across barriers of good and evil.[10] Jealousy is one way, though by no means the only way, to break through to a confrontation with an impersonal power alien to the ordinary world of everyday life. This power underlies each person and, for Dickens, is present everywhere in nature too. This ubiquitous force resists rational mapping. It interferes with the reader's efforts to locate every person and every milieu in *Our Mutual*

Friend in some place that might be identified according to familiar spatial coordinates.

As Northrop Frye says, this hidden energy is both destructive and creative, both Thanatos and Eros. It provides the drive for behavior on the surface, but that behavior rapidly becomes mechanical and sterile unless there is a periodic reimmersion in anarchic depths. The wild comic surface and mad linguistic verve of Venus, Wegg, Podsnap, and Mrs. Wilfer are the indirect manifestations of an energy that appears more directly in Headstone's insane jealousy. Dickens's comedy and his melodrama arise from the same sources and are fueled by the same fire. As Frye saw, surface behavior is likely gradually to become more and more cut off from the energy that gives it force. This detachment makes people from both high and low in society behave and speak by rote, like unconscious automatons.

Frye's word "humours" makes it sound a little as if these forms of behavior and speech are primarily psychological quirks. It can easily be shown, however, that they are ideologically motivated. The characters of *Our Mutual Friend* are trapped within Victorian assumptions about class and gender. Victorian ideology and the damage it does to those of both sexes in all levels of society are Dickens's main targets in *Our Mutual Friend*. Bella, who has been forced into a gender mold and left to John Harmon in old Harmon's will, "like a dozen of spoons" (81), is as much a victim of this ideology as is Eugene Wrayburn. Wrayburn's father's wealth has given him an inability to turn seriously to his profession and an unwillingness to consider marrying Lizzie, since she is the daughter of a man who makes his living by finding dead bodies in the Thames. Wegg's mind too is a crazy jumble of received ideas, in this case lower-class ones governed by the clichés of popular culture. This victimization by Victorian ideology is as much the source of the crazy imitation of genteel speech in Mrs. Wilfer as of the inane nationalist stupidities of Mr. Podsnap or the calculated upper-class pretenses of the Veneerings and Lammles. Bella's conviction that she cares only for "money, money, money, and what money can make of life" (520) has the same source. It is equally out of touch with the energy that lies behind her charming self-deceptions. Her reformation can come only when her response to Boffin's pretense that he has become a selfish miser puts her more directly in touch with the depths of feeling within her.

Another example of this unconscious detachment from underlying "reality" is the admirable comedy of the zany conversations between Wegg and Venus. A superb example is the scene in which Wegg comes to try to buy his own leg and foot bones back from Venus. Venus has bought them from the hospital to add to his collection of human bones waiting to be articulated. "I can't work you into a miscellaneous one [skeleton], no how," says Mr. Venus. "Do what I will, you can't be got to fit. Anybody with a passable knowledge would pick you out at a look, and say,—'No go! Don't match!' . . . No, I don't know how it is, but so it is. You have got a twist in that bone, to the best of my belief. *I never saw the likes of you*" (124). Wegg's response is to ask Venus, "What will you take for me?" As he explains, "I have a prospect of getting on in life and elevating myself by my own independent exertions, . . . and I shouldn't like—I tell you openly I should *not* like—under such circumstances, to be what I may call dispersed, a part of me here, and a part of me there, but should wish to collect myself like a genteel person" (126–27). No one except perhaps the Marx Brothers can match Dickens at inventing this kind of wild slapstick and verbal inventiveness.

Wegg's habit of working verses from popular songs and ballads in altered form into his conversation is a brilliant dramatization of Dickens's insight into the way the formulas of popular culture insinuate themselves into our unconscious presuppositions and have political force there. One example among many is Wegg's adaptation of "Home, Sweet Home" to describe Venus "floating his powerful mind in tea" in his bone-articulating and taxidermy shop:

"A exile from home splendour dazzles in vain,
O give you your lowly Preparations again,
The birds stuffed so sweetly that can't be expected to come at your call,
Give you with these the peace of mind dearer than all.
Home. Home, Home, sweet Home!"

—Be it ever," added Mr Wegg in prose as he glanced about the shop, "ever so ghastly, all things considered there's no place like it." (562)

Now it might be thought that the superficiality, inanity, and lack of self-awareness in the comic characters as well as the destructive violence of melodramatic characters like Headstone might be set against some form of direct, sincere speech in the good characters or in the narrator. This is not the case. The narrator expresses his deepest insights not in commentary but by playing the roles of the comic and melodramatic characters, in that extraordinary imaginary theatrical performance each great Dickens novel is. Moreover, there are repeated examples of the way the good characters can express their feelings for one another only through a self-conscious artifice that is another form of role-playing. The most conspicuous examples of this are the way both Jenny Wren and Bella Wilfer express their love for their fathers by treating them as their children. Jenny also expresses her relation to Riah by calling him her fairy godmother, with herself as Little Red Ridinghood. The narrator uses such self-conscious figurative language too. Examples are his account of the marriage of John Harmon and Bella Wilfer by way of the imagined perspective of a Greenwich pensioner he names "Gruff and Glum" (731–32), and his extended use of a metaphor calling the Veneerings's retainer the "Analytical Chemist," "always seeming to say, after 'Chablis, sir?'— 'You wouldn't if you knew what it's made of'" (52).

A formal rhetorical way of putting this is to say that no direct, sincere, literal expression of the impersonal underlying otherness exists. It cannot be named directly. Each expression of it is another inadequate catachresis. The difference is that some of these catachreses, for example Bella's loving playacting with her father, are directly motivated by the anonymous energy and may work for good, while others have long since been cut off from it and go on insanely repeating themselves automatically. An example is Mrs. Wilfer's stately nonsense, some of which I cannot forbear to quote:

> "I may feel—nay know—that I have been deluded and deceived. I may feel—nay, know—that I have been set aside and passed over. I may feel—nay, know—that after having so far overcome my repugnance towards Mr and Mrs Boffin as to receive them under this roof, and to consent to your daughter Bella's," here turning to her husband, "residing under theirs, it were well if your daughter Bella," again turning to her husband, "had profited in a worldly point of view by a connection so distasteful, so disreputable. I may feel—nay, know—that in uniting herself to Mr Rokesmith she has united herself to one who is, in spite of shallow sophistry, a Mendicant. And I may feel well assured that your daughter Bella," again turning to her husband, "does not exalt her family by becoming a Mendicant's bride. But I suppress what I feel, and say nothing of it." (743)

Dickens's extreme relish for inventing and inventing again such speeches for Mrs. Wilfer, as for inventing the crazy dialogues between Venus and Wegg, will be recognized by any reader. This inimitable and inexhaustible linguistic exuberance is the chief greatness of *Our Mutual Friend,* as of Dickens's other works. Since it is chiefly, though not exclusively, a comic exuberance, and since comedy is extremely difficult to talk about intelligently (one's solemn comments seem always somehow off the mark), criticism of Dickens often seems to be talking about peripheral rather than about essential qualities. Critics often discuss, for example, overall form, but that may be less important than the constantly renewed dazzling hyperbolic theatrical inventiveness that makes up most of the substance of Dickens's novels. This exuberance exceeds its incorporation in large-scale plot or in the repetitions that make for thematic coherences. Dickens at the beginning of his career found a way to express in a figure this inexhaustibly renewed comic inventiveness. In the Announcement at the conclusion of Part Ten of *Pickwick Papers,* Dickens says there will be ten more monthly numbers of the novel, "if the Author be permitted to retain his health and spirits." Citing what "the late eminent Mr John Richardson, of Horsemonger Lane Southwark, and the Yellow Caravan with the Brass Knocker, always said on behalf of himself and company, at the close of every performance," he promises "that we shall keep perpetually going on beginning again, regularly, until the end of the fair."[11] Dickens's inventiveness too can be defined as an inexhaustible ability to begin again with something new, a new character speaking a new wild idiom, a new situation or confrontation for characters already invented.

If Dickens's comic hyperbole depends on showing characters irrevocably trapped within ideological matrices of which they cannot be aware, and if they are in any case granted precious little self-consciousness of any sort, how can Dickens plausibly round off his novel with a happy ending, or rather with several juxtaposed happy endings—the marriages of Bella and John, of Eugene and Lizzie, the foreshadowed marriage of Jenny Wren and Sloppy, and the justice done to all the villains? What makes these happy endings plausible? One answer has already been suggested. Those characters, like Jenny Wren and Bella, who can self-consciously transform their situations by living them according to extended playacting metaphors can make a virtual escape from those situations. This also gives them a perspective on their lives that unconscious comedians like Wegg or Mrs. Wilfer can never attain. This difference corresponds to the distinction Baudelaire makes in "De l'essence du rire" between the inadvertently comic, as when a man slips, falls, and we laugh at him, and "le comique absolu (the absolute comic)" in which the same person is both the object of laughter and the spectator who laughs. "The man who trips," says Baudelaire, "would be the last to laugh at his own fall, unless he happened to be a philosopher, one who had acquired by habit a power of rapid self-division (la force de se dédoubler rapidement) and thus of assisting as a disinterested spectator at the phenomena of his own ego (de son *moi*)." Such comedians, Baudelaire says at the conclusion of his essay, "indicate the existence of a permanent dualism in the human being—that is, the power of being oneself and someone else at one and the same time (la puissance d'être à la fois soi et un autre)."[12]

The power of self-doubling playacting that Bella Wilfer and Jenny Wren have transforms their situations without really providing an escape from them. *Our Mutual Friend* shows the possibility of the latter in all those characters who descend into the depths of an anonymous otherness and return transformed. Some can go down and return as a new person, as Eugene does and as John Harmon does. Some return without being changed, like Rogue Riderhood when he nearly drowns but is resuscitated. Some descend without returning, like George Radfoot, like Rogue Riderhood the second time, when he really drowns, and like Bradley

Headstone. The only chance for even a local change in the bad condition of society is some extreme event that breaks up petrified class institutions and begins again after immersion in that impersonal energy, in a rhythm of interruption that the novel repeatedly mimes or enacts. This interruption is extremely dangerous. Some do not come back. John Harmon and Eugene Wrayburn were in mortal danger when they were thrown into the Thames.

Moreover, this breakup of mechanized behavior must be repeated ceaselessly. Society must be renewed again and again at different locations on its topographical surface or it becomes ossified, frozen in unjust class and gender configurations. No single descent and return will work as a symbolic transformation of the whole society, as happens in more traditional works like Greek or Renaissance tragedy. Oedipus's punishment or Hamlet's death, for example, purges a whole society, or is claimed to do so. For Dickens the change works only for the person in question. Bella must be tested and transformed by Boffin's pretense of becoming miserly and treating John Rokesmith cruelly. She has to make her own version of the descent and return. No one else can do that for her. In no other novel by Dickens are so many different characters reformed. The novel nevertheless ends with a final return to a Veneering dinner party that shows the "voice of society" still obstinately stuck in its class prejudices and still united in condemning Eugene's marriage to Lizzie.

The solitary exception is poor little Mr. Twemlow. Twemlow for once speaks up to express his sense that being a lady or a gentleman transcends class distinctions: " 'I say,' resumes Twemlow, 'if such feelings on the part of this gentleman, induced this gentleman to marry this lady, I think he is the greater gentleman for the action, and makes her the greater lady. I beg to say, that when I use the word, gentleman, I use it in the sense in which the degree may be attained by any man. The feelings of a gentleman I hold sacred, and I confess I am not comfortable when they are made the subject of sport or general discussion' " (891–92). Thus speaks Twemlow, but the Veneerings, the Podsnaps, Lady Tippins, Buffer, Boots, Brewer, and the rest disagree. They are by no means changed by the changes that have made Bella, John, and Eugene into new persons. Dickens definitely does not see the transformation of a single person as a synecdoche for the possible transformation of a whole society. Though Little Dorrit and Arthus Clennam, at the end of *Little Dorrit*, are saved for a happy marriage, the world as a whole goes on much as it always has: "They went quietly down into the roaring streets, inseparable and blessed; and as they passed along in sunshine and in shade, the noisy and the eager, and the arrogant and the froward and the vain, fretted, and chafed, and made their usual uproar."[13]

The person who plays all of the roles, those of the good and bad alike, in one gigantic internal theater, is Dickens himself. Baudelaire's formulas about the philosopher who can be comic and the spectator of his own comedy and about the existence of a permanent dualism in the human being are meant to apply primarily to the great comic artists, those persons, as Baudelaire puts it, "who have made a business of developing in themselves their feeling for the comic, and of dispensing it for the amusement of their fellows."[14] Dickens mimes within himself for our benefit many different ways of being related to prevailing Victorian ideological assumptions and many different ways of being related to the underlying impersonal otherness that gives energy to these ways of being. The novel as a whole enacts one large, complex rhythm of descent and return, like a great wave made of many smaller waves that collaborate to a single end.

Here I must disagree with Frye's formulations. He says, in the passage cited in note 10, "The hidden world is thus, once again in literature, the world of an invincible Eros, the power strong enough to force a happy ending on the story in defiance of all probability." Later he asserts that "Dickens's nature is a human nature which is the same kind of thing as the power that creates art, a designing and shaping power." This grants, in my view, too happy a providential design to that anarchic underlying energy. I should rather hold that the designing and shaping power forcing a happy ending in defiance of all probability is Dickens's own histrionic invention in response to the demand made on him by the realm of otherness that, within the fiction, drives all his characters and, in the "real world," drives him to create them. What Dickens does is authorized by that demand but not determined by it in the shape it takes. For what he does, the writing of *Our Mutual Friend*, he is responsible, and he must accept that responsibility. He cannot blame it, as Bradley Headstone tries to blame what he does, on the impersonal force that works through him.

Dickens has put two examples of his own benign, life-giving theatrical creativity in the novel: Bella's transformation of her relation to her father and Jenny Wren's similar ability to live her life as though it were a fairy story. In her profession of dolls' dressmaker, Jenny may be taken as an allegorical expression of Dickens's own profession of making imaginary puppets: Wegg, Venus, Boffin, Bella, and the rest. These come alive for the reader through the power of his creating word, just as Jenny's dolls do for the children who come to own them. *Our Mutual Friend* as a whole is a single, gigantic transformation of the Victorian world in which Dickens lived into a masterpiece of comedy in the Baudelairean sense.

This Dickens theater will not, however, come alive without the reader's collaboration. The reader's activity is analogous to that of Bella, Jenny Wren, or Dickens himself. The reader's bringing to life of the dead words

on the page, as a kind of resurrection or raising of ghosts, must be renewed again and again in what are always unique and singular acts of
reading. No one can let another read for him or her. Each must read for
himself or herself. If Dickens must take responsibility for what he makes
of Victorian London, so must each reader take responsibility for what he
or she makes of *Our Mutual Friend*, as it is reenacted on the scene of that
person's own imaginary topography.

NOTES

1. I have explored some of these imaginary mappings in detail in *Topogra-
phies* (Stanford: Stanford University Press, 1995). See especially the chapter on
Hardy's *The Return of the Native*.

2. Charles Dickens, *Bleak House*, ed. Nicola Bradbury (London: Penguin,
1996), 908; henceforth BH.

3. Charles Dickens, *Our Mutual Friend*, ed. Stephen Gill (Harmondsworth:
Penguin, 1971), 479. Further references will be to this edition.

4. Charles Baudelaire, *Oeuvres complètes*, ed. Y.-G. le Dantec, Bibliothèque
de la Pléiade (Paris: Gallimard, 1956), 159, my translation.

5. One example among many is the account of the route Bradley Headstone
and Charley Hexam take to get from Headstone's school ("The schools—for they
were twofold, as the sexes—were down in that district of the flat country tending
to the Thames, where Kent and Surrey meet, and where the railways still bestride
the market-gardens that will soon die under them" [267]), to Jenny Wren's house:
"Bradley Headstone and Charley Hexam duly got to the Surrey side of Westmin-
ster Bridge, and crossed the bridge, and made along the Middlesex shore toward
Millbank. In this region are a certain little street called Church Street, and a certain little blind square, called Smith Square, in the centre of which last retreat is
a very hideous church with four towers at the four corners, generally resembling
some petrified monster, frightful and gigantic, on its back with its legs in the
air. . . . [T]hey stopped at the point where the street and the square joined, and
where there were some little quiet houses in a row. To these Charley Hexam
finally led the way, and at one of these stopped" (270–71). A footnote in the
Penguin edition tells the reader that the church Dickens finds so ugly is "the
Church of St John the Evangelist built in 1728" (903). It is located at 2E 77 in my
London A to Z.

6. The doubles are all men.

7. Alain Robbe-Grillet, *La jalousie*, ed. Germaine Brée and Eric Schoenfeld
(Prospect Heights, Ill.: Waveland Press, 1990), 3, my translation. I owe this citation to Erin Ferris.

8. Jacques Derrida, *Apories* (Paris: Galilée, 1996), 49; *Aporias*, trans. Thomas
Dutoit (Stanford: Stanford University Press, 1993), 22. See also Jacques Derrida,
Donner la mort (Paris: Galilée, 1999), 114–57; *The Gift of Death*, trans. David
Wills (Chicago: University of Chicago Press, 1995), 82–115.

9. Riderhood has been resuscitated once from nearly drowning in the Thames

at London, and he accepts the folk belief that a man who has escaped from drowning can never be drowned.

10.   Northrop Frye, in one of the most brilliant essays ever written about Dickens, was right on the mark in his formulation of the way this energy works in Dickens. This is true in spite of his use in talking about Dickens of what seems now a quaint language about humors and archetypes and transhistorical genres, language drawn from the vocabulary of Frye's own *The Anatomy of Criticism*. Frye's way of reading Dickens is so original and so close to my own conclusions here (reached before I had thought to return to his essay again after not reading it for many years) that I want to quote substantial extracts from it, in homage to his greatness as a practical critic. That greatness consists in going beyond theoretical presuppositions by way of the insights born of active reading. A full mastery of Frye's theories would by no means enable anyone to anticipate or match what Frye sees in Dickens. This once more shows how reading, "real" reading, an active and interventionist reading that responds to the demand made on the reader by the text, may perhaps be enabled by theory but always goes beyond it and at least partially disqualifies it:

> There is a hidden and private world of dream and death, out of which all the energy of human life comes. The primary manifestation of this world, in experience, is in acts of destructive violence and passion. It is the source of war, cruelty, arrogance, lust, and grinding the faces of the poor. . . . It is not so much better or worse than the ordinary world of experience, as a world in which good and evil appear as much stronger and less disguised forces. . . . Humours are, so to speak, petrified by-products of the kind of energy that melodrama expresses more directly. Even the most contemptible humours, the miserly Fledgeby or the hypocritical Heep, are exuberantly miserly and hypocritical: their vices express an energy that possesses them because they cannot possess it. The world they operate in, so far as it is a peaceable and law-abiding world, is a world of very imperfectly suppressed violence. They never escape from the shadow of a power which is at once Eros and Thanatos, and are bound to a passion that is never satisfied by its rationalized objects, but is ultimately self-destructive. . . . [T]he effect is to give an Andromeda pattern to the heroine's situation, and suggest a demonic ferocity behind the domestic foreground. The same principle of construction causes the stock-response humours like Podsnap or Gradgrind to take on a peculiar importance. They represent the fact that an entire society can become mechanized like a humour, or fossilized into its institutions. . . . The obstructing humours cannot escape from the ritual habits that they have set up to deal with this disconcerting energy that has turned them into mechanical puppets. The heroes and heroines, however, along with some of the more amiable humours, have the power to plunge into the hidden world of dreams and death, and, though narrowly escaping death in the process, gain from it a renewed life and energy. . . . *Our Mutual Friend* has a complex pattern of resurrection imagery connected with dredging the Thames, reviving from drowning, finding treasure buried in dust-heaps, and the like. . . . The hidden world is thus, once again in literature, the world of an invincible Eros, the

power strong enough to force a happy ending on the story in defiance of all probability, pushing the obstructing humours out of the way, or killing them if they will not get out of the way, getting the attractive young people disentangled from their brothers and sisters and headed for the right beds. . . . Dickens's Eros world is, above all, a designing and manipulating power. . . . Dickens's nature is a human nature which is the same kind of thing as the power that creates art, a designing and shaping power. . . . For all its domestic and sentimental Victorian setting, there is a revolutionary, almost a nihilistic, quality in Dickens's melodrama that is post-Romantic, has inherited the experience of the French Revolution, and looks forward to the world of Freud, Marx, and the existentialist thriller. . . . In literature it is design, the forming and shaping power, that is absurd." (Northrop Frye, "Dickens and the Comedy of Humours," in *Experience in the Novel*, ed. Roy Harvey Pearce, Selected Papers from the English Institute [New York: Columbia University Press, 1968], 75–80)

I would not myself bring in so cavalierly in talking about Dickens the French Revolution, Freud, Marx, and the existentialist thriller, though these are provocative analogies. My own way of naming what Frye saw would use a significantly different terminology. Nevertheless, all that Frye says in the extracts I have cited is admirably on the mark, though I differ from him on one or two important points, to be specified later.

11. Charles Dickens, *Pickwick Papers*, ed. Robert Patten (Harmondsworth: Penguin, 1972), 902–3.

12. Charles Baudelaire, "De l'essence du rire," in *Oeuvres complètes*, ed. le Dantec, 717, 728; Baudelaire, "On the Essence of Laughter," in *The Mirror of Art*, trans. Jonathan Mayne (Garden City, N.Y.: Doubleday Anchor, 1956), 140, 152.

13. Charles Dickens, *Little Dorrit*, ed. John Halloway (Harmondsworth: Penguin, 1967), 895.

14. Baudelaire, "On the Essence of Laughter," 152.

Chapter Three

GEORGE ELIOT:
THE ROAR ON THE OTHER SIDE
OF SILENCE

ANTHONY TROLLOPE, George Eliot, and Robert Musil are novelists whose most firm presupposition, so at first it seems, is the presence of consciousness to itself. All three excel in presenting in words a semblance of that self-consciousness that conveys it to a reader. Nevertheless, the reader discovers that for all three, though in different ways in each case, the ground of the self is so alien to self-consciousness that no direct access to it is possible, even though that other self within the self is the basis of ethical decision. The other self within the self ought also to be the glue that holds together the various forms the self takes through time. In a different way in the work of each, for Trollope, Eliot, and Musil that glue is missing, for example in Musil's imagination of the hero of *Der Mann ohne Eigenschaften* (The Man without Qualities).[1]

What testimony do novelists give about the access not to that other self within the self, but to the other other, to other persons, or to what we assume are other persons like ourselves? In novels this other person is most often, but not always, the "significant other," the other of amorous desire, though sometimes the other of rivalry or emulation. The problematic of this other other is quite different from that of the other within the self, even though the other within the self may be the discourse of the other or the introjection of the other's phantom in the work of mourning. I confront the other person in everyday social intercourse, within the general field of other phenomena open to the senses. The other is a body endowed with speech, capable of making gestures that are also signs, capable of giving me gifts, touching me, talking to me on the telephone, sending me letters, telegrams, faxes, e-mail.

A large philosophical literature has confronted the problem of the other person, for example analytical philosophy in the wake of Wittgenstein or phenomenology in its various avatars. For Edmund Husserl, in the fifth Cartesian meditation, for example, the ego has direct access to itself in an act of totalizing self-consciousness, whereas the other ego is in principle inaccessible, except indirectly. For Husserl the other person is an irreducible alterity that cannot by any means be known as I can know myself. It can only be known by an "analogical appresentation." Husserl left at his death many unpublished pages exploring the problem of how we know others. This problem was also an inexhaustible stimulus to Wittgenstein's meditations, for example in all he had to say about the question of whether I can know the pain of another. The problem of our response to the face of the other is a central feature of Emmanuel Lévinas's work. Confronting another person, face to face, is, for Lévinas, an irreducibly inaugural beginning of all ethically responsible thought, decision, and behavior.

For many novelists, however, so it seems at least, the other is not an inassimilable strangeness but another me like me that can be known. This likeness allows in principle for true knowledge of the other person. Surely we have today, after so many generations, gone beyond the naiveté of Rousseau's primitive man who, in his first encounter with another man, out of fear called him a giant and so invented the first metaphor, the archetrope on the ground of which all the airy fabric of language has been constructed, in an endless series of displacements from that first erroneous figure? We now know, so we think, that the other person is another person like ourselves. This other person is in principle able to be known through and through, able to be assimilated in a circuit of identification returning the same to the same. This sameness, it could be argued, is the indispensable basis of any viable and just community, with laws, institutions, and customs that apply to all men and women equally because they are all created equal and therefore can all know one another.

The novel, as all now know, is a genre that developed in the West along with the rise of capitalist democracies. It is not a timeless literary category, but a form of literature conditioned through and through by history. One of the novel's major social functions, it could be argued, is to demonstrate and reinforce, perhaps to generate, the assumption that the other is another person like me. However it may be in real life, first-person novels, on the one hand, allow the narrator to speak directly to the reader out of his or her self-consciousness. The convention of the omniscient narrator, on the other hand, gives the reader of novels using that convention the pleasure of being able, in a fiction at least, to enter into the mind and feelings, even, by an imaginative leap, into the body, of other persons. Through that sympathetic identification the reader can experience a total knowledge of another person, from the inside. This knowledge is born of the virtual coincidence of self and other. Nor is this total knowledge always limited to the narrator or, vicariously, to the reader. Anthony Trollope often ascribes to his characters an intuitive knowledge of what the other person is thinking and feeling. In *The Last Chronicle of Barset* (1867), for example, the reader coincides totally, by way of the narrator's knowledge and verbalization of that knowledge, with the Reverend Crawley's sufferings as he sits day after day brooding angrily over his plight. Trollope also assigns to Crawley's wife a sympathetic understanding of her husband's thoughts and feelings. The reader has knowledge of her knowledge of her husband. Just as both Crawley and his wife are transparent to the reader by way of the narrator's words, so Crawley is more or less transparent to his wife. Many other examples of this transparency can be adduced from one end to the other of Trollope's fictions, though that "more or less" in the previous sentence is not a trivial reservation. A long analysis would be necessary to explore this "more or less."

Things are not always so simple, however, even in Trollope's novels, much less in Jane Austen's, in George Eliot's, or in Marcel Proust's. Trollope, even in so early a novel as *The Warden* (1855), finds the deepest self hidden from the conscious self. Examples in this and other Trollope novels would be the unavailability of the moment when Ayala fell in love with Jonathan Stubbs, in *Ayala's Angel* (1881), or the impossibility of knowing on what grounds Septimus Harding decided to resign the wardenship, in *The Warden*, or Louis Trevelyan's noncoincidence with himself, in *He Knew He Was Right* (1869). *The Last Chronicle of Barset*, to give another example, turns on Crawley's inability to remember how he came by a twenty-pound note. He suffers from a radical lapse in memory. A part of himself is hidden from himself and therefore from the narrator, from his wife, and from the reader. The whole community of Barset circles in fascinated attention around that one area of opacity in their general transparency to one another, to the narrator, and thereby to the reader.

Other novelists find access to the other person even more of a problem. The wonderful comedy of Jane Austen's novels is most often generated by the way an intelligent and sensitive young woman radically misunderstands even those others whom she has the greatest stake in understanding. For George Eliot and for Marcel Proust, finally, knowledge of the other is so problematic that their work tends to focus on just that issue. How is this expressed in George Eliot's work?

Eliot's novels do not at first seem a promising field for encountering the irreducible otherness of others. Her work turns on an opposition between egoism and sympathy. She inherits these concepts from eighteenth- and early nineteenth-century empiricism in literature and philosophy, as present for example in Keats's opposition between the egotistical sublime and the sympathetic imagination, or in the concept of sympathy in Adam Smith and in many other eighteenth-century thinkers both in England and on the continent. Egoism is imprisonment within the narrow bounds of one's own selfish consciousness. This imprisonment cuts one off from other people. Sympathy, as the word implies, is a "feeling with" other people. It allows a person to put himself or herself in the other's place.

Sympathy leads to tolerance and love for my neighbor. These are the basis of good interpersonal relations—happy marriages, for example. They are also the basis of good communities and nations. Chapter 17 of *Adam Bede* (1859) is George Eliot's fullest expression of these presuppositions. They lead to a defense of the novel, her novels in particular, as socially useful. Reading novels breaks down egoism and develops sympathy. It does this because novels present a virtual or imaginary community made of fictive persons with whom the reader is invited to sympathize.

This, at least at the time of *Adam Bede*, is what George Eliot says she believed about real and fictive persons in their intersubjective relations. By the time of *Middlemarch* (1871–72), however, in spite of many apparent continuities between her early work and the later, George Eliot has a quite different conception of the relation between self and other. The plight of even the naturally good and at least potentially sympathetic characters in *Middlemarch* is to fail to have intuitive understanding of other persons. The other is encountered as a text to be read, almost inevitably to be misread. *Middlemarch* is full of notations of this situation. If words can be taken as paradigmatic of other signs, misreading our neighbors is so universal an event in *Middlemarch* that one could justly say that for George Eliot our relation to the other person is a linguistic predicament.

For George Eliot the phenomenal world in general is a complex array of signs to be read, but within that array the face, gestures, behavior, and speech of each other person form a radiant node of signs that all those around him or her are invited to interpret. Once you learn to read, it is extremely difficult not to read. A literate person confronted with a cereal box at the breakfast table will most likely automatically read what is printed on it. "Reading" the signs proffered by other persons is habitual in a similar way, though immensely more is at stake. Lydgate, the luckless country doctor in *Middlemarch*, is an example of the way any member of a community "may be puffed and belauded, envied, ridiculed, counted upon as a tool and fallen in love with, or at least selected as a future husband, and yet remain virtually unknown—known merely as a cluster of signs for his neighbors' false suppositions."[2]

What is the source of these "false suppositions"? Why do we always read our neighbors wrong, even those neighbors whom we have the greatest interest in reading right, for example those with whom we have fallen in love? George Eliot gives two chief reasons for this penchant toward misreading.

One is the universal human habit of thinking by analogy, that is, by figurative displacements. These lead us to see one person as like some other person and then to literalize that similarity. "[W]e all of us, grave or light," says the narrator of *Middlemarch*, who is much given to absolute generalization, "get our thoughts entangled in metaphors, and act fatally on the strength of them" (111). George Eliot's use of the universalizing "we," and my catching of that habit in my own commentary, is, it may be, a dangerous procedure. It tends to assume that each of us is in the same boat with all the others, and therefore like the others. This begs just the question I am trying to raise. In any case, for Eliot the misreading of another person is a salient example of the fatal and fateful mistake of literalizing metaphors. To act on the strength of a metaphor is inevitably to act fatally, that is, both in a way that is fated, coerced, and in a way that causes much grief, perhaps mortal grief.

Poor Edward Casaubon in *Middlemarch*, Dorothea's cold, pedantic, and priggish husband, is a splendid comic example of this. In one place Casaubon is said to think of feelings as kept in a reservoir where they may be stored up indefinitely, kept fresh and ready for use. "Hence," when "he determined to abandon himself to the stream of feeling," he "perhaps was surprised to find what an exceedingly shallow rill it was. As in droughty regions baptism by immersion could only be performed symbolically, so Mr. Casaubon found that a sprinkling was the utmost approach to a plunge which his stream would afford him" (87). In another place Casaubon thinks of his emotions as like money in the bank, multiplying through time if they are not used: "Poor Mr. Casaubon had imagined that his long studious bachelorhood had stored up for him a compound interest of enjoyment, and that large drafts on his affections would not fail to be honored" (111). Though this may be George Eliot's delicate way of telling the reader Casaubon was sexually impotent, this physical impotence, so the passage suggests, is the concomitant of a fatal disability in his understanding of language.

The other reason "we" always misread our neighbors is that our egoism organizes everything around us, including other people, according to our desires and needs. In a celebrated passage George Eliot's narrator proposes an extended metaphor of her own (or his own, since the narrator is at least nominally masculine) for this. This passage is perhaps an invitation to the reader to get his or her thoughts entangled in metaphors and act fatally on the strength of them. The metaphor figures the phenomenal world as like a pier-glass, that is, as like a mirror made of polished metal marked all over with minute scratches. The egoism of a given person is like a candle that apparently organizes those scratches into neat concentric circles:

> Your pier-glass or extensive surface of polished steel made to be rubbed by a housemaid, will be minutely and multitudinously scratched in all directions; but place now against it a lighted candle as a centre of illumination, and lo! the scratches will seem to arrange themselves in a fine series of

concentric circles round that little sun. It is demonstrable that the scratches are going everywhere impartially, and it is only your candle which produces the flattering illusion of a concentric arrangement, its light falling with an exclusive optical selection. These things are a parable. The scratches are events, and the candle is the egoism of any person now absent. (297)

By far the most important "events," for George Eliot's characters, are encounters with those clusters of signs that are other people. What is misleading about the parable of the pier-glass, however, what may lead the critic to a fatal error in reading, is the possible implication that what is at stake in encounters with other people is a matter of seeing right. We must try to figure out what sort of object it is we see from the visual data. Understanding our neighbor is a phenomenological or epistemological problem. In fact, as many other passages in *Middlemarch* make clear, figuring out our neighbor is a matter of reading right, not a matter of seeing right. Moreover, reading right, it may be, is difficult, if not impossible.[3] The key word in this citation is "parable." A parable, like an allegory, speaks otherwise. It says one thing but means another, or it says one thing by means of naming another thing. In the parable of the sower in Matthew, Jesus speaks of the kingdom of heaven by talking about the sowing of seed. In the case of George Eliot's parable of the pier-glass, a linguistic predicament (reading or rather misreading according to our own egoistic predilections the signs our neighbor proffers) is figured as an epistemological predicament (the necessity of seeing the random scratches as arranged in concentric circles). This passage must be read to be understood, which means reading it otherwise, grasping that one thing stands for another thing, not making the mistake of reading literally. What key of interpretation will confirm that we have read the parable right? As Jesus's parable of the sower affirms, understanding a parable involves a performative leap that cannot be taught to another. It is not a matter of verifiable cognition.

Parable

Dorothea Brooke's error in choosing to marry Mr. Casaubon is the most salient example in *Middlemarch* of the destined misreading of the sign-cluster each neighbor presents. George Eliot's account of this in the first book of *Middlemarch* brilliantly dramatizes the gravely comic spectacle of a good and loving person making a terrible error in the choice of a marriage partner. Dorothea is both "ardent" and "theoretic," that is, she has two qualities that lead to illusion and consequent suffering. She has the strong feeling that transfigures things and people, as love notoriously does, according to that Proustian formula whereby "loving is like an evil spell in a fairy-story against which one is powerless until the enchantment has passed."[4] Dorothea also sees things according to theoretical presuppositions, that is, according to blind ideological categories that see things and people as embodiments of abstract conceptions they only superficially resemble, if at all. This unfortunate combination— unfortunate in the sense that it destines Dorothea to much suffering— endows her with a "joyous imaginative activity which fashions events according to desire" (267). Her belief that Casaubon will make a good husband is the result of this fashioning. Such fashioning takes the form of limitlessly expansive extrapolation, the product of a sublime synecdoche. "Signs," says George Eliot," are small measurable things, but interpretations are illimitable, and in girls of sweet, ardent nature, every sign is apt to conjure up wonder, hope, belief, vast as a sky, and colored by a diffused thimbleful of matter in the shape of knowledge" (47). Casaubon is for Dorothea a text to be read, or rather misread, since, like a book, he has a fatal susceptibility to multiple interpretations. A book itself does not explicitly confirm or disallow any of the ways we may read it. It passively abides our readings and misreadings, though it would not be wise to count too confidently on the passivity of the texts we read, since they may have unforeseen power over us. No measure exists to distinguish correct and incorrect readings, even though a given text strongly calls us or demands of us that we read it. Casaubon has a fatal susceptibility to multiple interpretations. In this he is like the Bible, or like *Hamlet*, or perhaps even like *Middlemarch* itself: "the text, whether of prophet or of poet, expands for whatever we can put into it, and even his bad grammar is sublime" (74).

Dorothea's exemplification of this sad law of misreading is defined in terms borrowed from the Protestant theological terminology of her day. The narrator's reading of Dorothea's misreading shows that George Eliot, for example through her work in translating Feuerbach and Strauss, had assimilated the vocabulary of contemporary German hermeneutic theory, as it dismantled the two-thousand-year tradition of reading the Bible as a single coherent whole dictated by God. The narrator gives the Evangelical Christianity that was replaced by Higher Criticism in George Eliot's own intellectual itinerary much of the blame for making Dorothea such a bad reader of Casaubon: "His efforts at exact courtesy and formal tenderness had no defect for her. She filled up all blanks with unmanifested perfections, interpreting him as she interpreted the works of Providence, and accounting for seeming discords by her own deafness to the higher harmonies. And there are many blanks left in the weeks of courtship, which a loving faith fills with happy assurance" (100). Love is like religious faith. It transfigures mean reality by seeing it as the signs of an all-powerful, transfiguring, transcendental source of radiant meaning. It assumes that that there must be a master reality that validates the referential meaning the lover projects into signs, just as the religious believer has faith in God.

Dorothea's misreading of Casaubon not only exemplifies the way we misinterpret signs by projecting on them a coherence born of our own egoistic desires. It also shows the way we get our thoughts entangled in metaphors and act fatally on the strength of them. Casaubon reminds Dorothea of John Frederick Oberlin, of Milton, after his blindness came on, and of Pascal. She then takes this figurative similarity as an identity: "Everyday-things with us would mean the greatest things. It would be like marrying Pascal" (51). That Dorothea should literalize metaphor by making the mistake of seeing her life with Casaubon as a parable in which each everyday thing stands for a higher and greater thing may be a little disquieting if the reader remembers how he or she is building a reading of *Middlemarch*, with some coaching from the narrator, by expanding to apply to the whole novel a parabolic reading of the passage about the pier-glass, taking an everyday thing to mean one of the "greatest things."

Nevertheless, there seems little room for a conception of the absolutely other in George Eliot's serio-comic presentation of Dorothea's misreading of Casaubon. The other person may be a cluster of signs making a species of text that I inevitably misread, but that does not mean the signs are not the outer manifestation, however misleading, of an inner self that could in principle be known, known because it is like my own self. The omniscient narrator of *Middlemarch* is the evidence and guarantee of this accessibility of the other by way of a similarity that crosses class, gender, and national lines. The narrator can and does enter at will into the intimate interior of each character's thoughts and feelings. This solidarity makes us a "we." It makes us all members of one great human community of suffering and solitude.

In one notable moment in *Middlemarch*, after a prolonged immersion in Dorothea's thoughts and feelings, the narrator shifts abruptly from presenting Dorothea's subjectivity to presenting Casaubon's, justifying this displacement by the claim that they are similar and similarly open to the narrator's clairvoyance:

> One morning, some weeks after her arrival at Lowick, Dorothea—but why always Dorothea? Was her point of view the only possible one with regard to this marriage? I protest against all our interest, all our effort at understanding being given to the young skins that look blooming in spite of trouble. . . . In spite of the blinking eyes and white moles objectionable to Celia, and the want of muscular curve which was morally painful to Sir James, Mr. Casaubon had an intense consciousness within him, and was spiritually a-hungered like the rest of us. (312)

If I take seriously the implications of what the narrator says about the situation of the characters in relation to one another, I would need to say that *Middlemarch* is built on a contradiction. On the one hand, the narrator can enter sympathetically into the inner lives of all the characters. On the other hand, for George Eliot other people are no more than a constellation of signs that we are doomed to misread, since no way exists to verify the accuracy of a reading. Even though we might by accident, so to speak, sometimes stumble on the truth, it would be impossible to know that. Such a situation implies a possible absolute singularity in each person. This singularity is as much or more hidden and traduced by outward signs as revealed by them. No sympathetic intuition allowing us to enter into the interiority of another person exists. The clairvoyance of George Eliot's narrator, his ability to get inside all of the characters at will and tell the reader what is going on there, is a commodious linguistic convention making the third-person novel as a genre possible. It is made possible, however, as a fictitious and factitious knowledge of our fellows that is impossible in real life, on the testimony of the novel itself.

An even more radical conception of the alterity of the other person is, however, presupposed in *Middlemarch*. A series of striking passages assert that what underlies the array of signs with which we are presented, including those singular clusters of signs we call other persons, is not any sort of order or coherence. It is a disorderly and meaningless multitudinousness, a loud but inaudible susurrus, a "chaos," in the literal sense of an uncreated confusion,[5] in short, something wholly other.

A number of parabolic figures for this underlying disorder, a disorder without origin, goal, tendency, or reason, are given at certain climactic moments in *Middlemarch*. This chaos is figured as the disorder of the random scratches on the pier-glass. It is figured as the ruins of Rome, layer on layer, that Dorothea confronts on her honeymoon as the reflex of her internal confusion, the ruin of her illusions about Casaubon. It is imaged as the labyrinthine disorder of Casaubon's notes for the "Key to All Mythologies." These notes proliferate in excess of the pigeon-holes he devises to keep them in order. The chaos in question is also figured as the "ruins" Rosamond briefly confronts when her illusory inner world of mistaken interpretation is momentarily demolished by Will Ladislaw's declaration of his love for Dorothea. When the interpreting, ordering candle goes out, Rosamond is left face to face with fragments. She confronts an inner chaos that is to be defined, within the logic of the pier-glass parable, not as a glimpse of the random scratches. These are on principle invisible; they are George Eliot's version of an underlying non-phenomenal materiality, base of all language and other signs. Rosamond's inner chaos is confronted rather as what one might call bits of disconnected arcs, once making neat circles around a single center: "The poor thing had no force to fling out any passion in return; the terrible collapse of the illusion toward which all her hope had been strained was a stroke which had too thoroughly shaken her: her little world was in ruins, and she felt herself tottering in the midst of a lonely bewildered consciousness" (837). Rosamond usually has a strong ego, strong enough to ruin her husband's career as a doctor. Here she momentarily becomes depersonalized, a "thing," like the dead Lucy in Wordsworth's "A Slumber Did My Spirit Seal." Her "I" depends on her "force," her power of sustaining a metaphorical system. That system and the impersonal energy behind it hold her ego together but also mean it is so fragile that it may be ruined in a moment.

It is risky to make a generalization about this analogous to George Eliot's own sweeping generalizations. Such a formulation, however, would assert that the self for George Eliot is the "force" to make a coherent system of metaphors, circles imposed on the scratches, and then stick to that. When the system collapses into ruins, the self vanishes too, or its factitiousness is revealed. The self becomes a "lonely bewildered consciousness," no longer a forceful, ordering ego. In defining the self as a force or as a site of conflicting forces, rather than as a center of cognition, George Eliot is, as in many other of her formulations, closer to Nietzsche than to Hegel or even to Fichte.

If the self is a force, a power to create coherent fictional metaphorical systems, that force also seems to have a fatal tendency, sooner or later, to dismantle the airy aberrant structures it has built. It thereby also deconstitutes the self that is a vulnerable correlate of the structure, since the self is also a construct of conflicting forces. The structure as a whole self-destructs. It reduces itself to ruins. It seems as if it must have secretly incorporated the "underlying" chaos into itself. Perhaps the "force" that sustains the self and its fictions is no more than another name for the roar on the other side of silence.

That roar is named in a striking passage that few readers of *Middlemarch* have failed to notice. The passage comes as part of the magisterial description of Dorothea's association of the ruins of Rome with her inner "confusion" during the first months of her marriage. This confusion is "heightened" by "the very force of her nature." The force must go somewhere. It can now no longer be used to maintain the systematic structure of her illusions, illusions no less unfounded than Rosamond's, though more generously motivated. Therefore it functions to exacerbate her painful confusion. This is a revolt of Dorothea's force against its normal function, even though "permanent rebellion, the disorder of a life without some loving reverent resolve, was not possible to her" (226–27). At the moment, however, her inner world is in disorder. This is so usual an event for a young woman in the first weeks of marriage, says the narrator, that he does not expect his readers to view it as tragic or to be deeply moved by it. Then comes one of those shifts to a universal generalization that are so important a part of *Middlemarch*'s rhetoric, as of Proust's rhetoric in *À la recherche du temps perdu*:

> That element of tragedy which lies in the very fact of frequency, has not yet wrought itself into the coarse emotion of mankind; and perhaps our frames could hardly bear much of it. If we had a keen vision and feeling of all ordinary human life, it would be like hearing the grass grow and the squirrel's heart beat, and we should die of that roar which lies on the other side of silence. As it is, the quickest of us walk about well wadded with stupidity. (226)

George Eliot's extraordinary story "The Lifted Veil" (published in 1878, though written in 1859) shows what a catastrophe it would be for someone actually to have this kind of clairvoyant insight. A strange, ironic light is shed on this demonstration, however, by the fact that the narrator of *Middlemarch* has precisely "a keen vision and feeling of all ordinary human life" and can deploy such vision at will. The narrator has the same kind of keen vision that destroys the protagonist of "The Lifted Veil." It is just such vision that the narrator of *Middlemarch* in the passage just quoted says we are lucky not to have. Nevertheless, in spite of that, *Middlemarch* proposes to pass on to the reader as much of that vision as George Eliot thinks the reader can bear. "Human kind/Cannot bear very much reality."[6] The "reality" in question for George Eliot is not that terrifying, transcendent religious otherness of which her twentieth-century namesake speaks. It is something rather closer to the "X which remains inaccessible and undefinable for us" of Nietzsche's early essay, "On Truth and Lie in an Extramoral Sense."[7] It is the invisible, inaudible, imperceptible "roar" that can only be given in catachrestic figures and that has always already been turned into figures whenever it is encountered or named.

Two sorts of figures are exemplified in the citation. The aural images of growing grass and of the squirrel's heartbeat are of actual noises too soft to be heard. They function as parabolic or catachrestic figures for the inaccessible X, the roar on the other side of silence. Even the word "roar" is in this case a figure, since sound here is of course a parabolic metaphor for all the obscure human pain that seems less than tragic because it is so common. The other sort of figure names the cushioning of stupidity that luckily lies between us and the roar. That protective wadding is the barrier of coarse emotions and coarse vision that incarnates itself in the system of illusory metaphors according to which each man or woman lives. It is like that shield Freud speaks of that protects us from the barrage of sense impressions.[8] This wall of error, for George Eliot, as for Freud or for Nietzsche, in their different ways, is absolutely necessary to human life. Not only does it give order, purpose, and resolve, so that constructive existence can continue. It also hides from us the annihilating roar, the chaos that is "really there," imperceptible to our coarse feeling and to our coarse vision. Beyond our everyday concerns is a zone of "silence," that is, a region from which no sound reaches us because we are well-wadded with stupidity, as though our ears were stuffed, like Odysseus's ears to protect him from the Sirens' song. There is noise there, but we cannot hear it. Beyond that silence, on the other side of the impenetrable wall this deceptive silence keeps up all around us, is the roar.

This roar is a chaos of cacophonous sound. Chaos cannot be described literally. Genuine disorder cannot be imagined. As Conrad's Marlow says in *Heart of Darkness*, "The inner truth is hidden—luckily, luckily."[9] True formlessness is unthinkable, unnamable except in negatives. It is the absolutely other. As soon as it is thought or named it takes some figurative form. It becomes a labyrinth, a network, a stream, a face, concentric circles, or ruins, to give some of George Eliot's figures for this "it" in *Middlemarch*. Or it becomes the negation of some such form of perceptible order or disorder. The sensed data are taken as signs standing for something other than what they are. They are read as emblem, as parable.

The word "chaos" does not have meaning in the same way as the word "web" has meaning. It is possible to have a mental image or a direct perception of something that looks like a web, never of chaos as such. Chaos is like those black holes astronomers hypothesize without ever being able to see them, in order to account for phenomena they *can* see. The multitudinous scratches are initially seen as concentric circles. Their actual lack of order can only be named in terms of the fact that they are not this particular order or that. They seem, for example, to be concentric circles, but they are not. Rosamond's momentary glimpse beyond her illusions, to give another example, cannot be named directly. It can only be defined as the ruin of those illusions.

If what each person at bottom is, even for himself or herself at certain traumatic moments, is an unknown and unknowable alterity, the roar on the other side of silence, then one person cannot in principle know another. The other person is a cluster of signs held together as a fictitious order by the force of the other's ego. Those signs are projected wittingly or unwittingly from the other's ego. The signs are then misread by me on the basis of my own egoistic structuring of myself and my surroundings. The other person is included as part of my ambience. What is "really there" at the heart of the other person is doubly hidden. It is hidden by the factitious order of signs the other has assembled on the surface by body language, behavior, and speech. It is hidden by my propensity to use others in my creation of a factitious order of my own, as Dorothea creates a Casaubon who never existed, makes him up out of her own generous imagination, and as both Rosamond Vincy and Tertius Lydgate create a fictitious personage in place of the real person each is about to marry.

If this is so, how can George Eliot plausibly end *Middlemarch* with Dorothea's happy marriage to Will Ladislaw and Mary Garth's happy marriage to Fred Vincy? That ending's happiness is qualified by the somber qualifications and resolute resistance of the "Finale" to any totalizing judgment, but still it is recognizably a happy ending. The melancholy cadences of the celebrated last paragraph sum up Dorothea's life by insisting on the impossibility of identifying and summarizing its nature and effect. These are "incalculably diffusive," with an implied invitation to the reader to put stress on "incalculably." Dorothea's effects are "unhistoric," not open to the sort of knowledge we think we have of historical events. Therefore they are literally "incalculable." They are not open to measuring, numbering, naming, or accounting for, except in those catachreses the reader has seen the narrator employing. He exemplifies these again here in an image drawn from Herodotus, the image of "that river of which Cyrus broke the strength":

> Her finely-touched spirit had still its fine issues, though they were not widely visible. Her full nature, like that river of which Cyrus broke the strength, spent itself in channels which had no great name on the earth. But the effect of her being on those around her was incalculably diffusive: for the growing good of the world is partly dependent on unhistoric acts; and that things are not so ill with you and me as they might have been, is half owing to the number who lived faithfully a hidden life, and rest in unvisited tombs. (896)

What is the ground of the happy ending of *Middlemarch*? The answer lies in the word "force" used to describe the "glue" that has, for example, fueled Dorothea's mistakes about Casaubon or held Rosamond's fabricated inner life together, leaving her when it fails momentarily face to face with "ruins." For George Eliot the coherence of the self and the coherence of the signs it proffers for other selves' misreading is the effect of an anonymous inaugurating power all persons share. This force is properly performative, or rather what Werner Hamacher calls "afformative,"[10] a preperformative, a deposing positing. This force works by putting forth words or other signs in the baseless fiat of a speech act. It builds airy, orderly structures of signs over a chaos that cannot be counted on to hold up anything. Some of these structures are on the whole bad in their effect, such as Dorothea's misreading of Casaubon. Some are on the whole good in their effect, such as her Ariadne-like[11] commitment to Will Ladislaw at the end of the novel: "'Oh, I cannot bear it—my heart will break,' said

Dorothea, starting from her seat, the flood of her young passion bearing down all the obstructions which had kept her silent—the great tears rising and falling in an instant" (870). Later she ratifies this commitment in properly performative terms when she declares to her sister her promise and her intention to keep that promise: "But this is what I am going to do. I have promised to marry Mr Ladislaw; and I am going to marry him" (880).

Dorothea's saying yes to Will Ladislaw is, in Nietzsche's phrase, her "ungeheure unbegrentzte ja," her prodigious limitless yes. This yes, however, is not based, any more than is her initial commitment of herself to Casaubon, on a verifiable knowledge of the other. It is an ungrounded speech act, not a cognitive insight. As Dorothea gently tells her sister when the latter asks her to explain how it came about that she is to marry Ladislaw: "No, dear, you would have to feel with me, else you would never know" (880). Feeling that leads to performative commitment takes precedence here over knowing. The novel has abundantly demonstrated the severe limitations of this "feeling with." The commitment of Dorothea and Will to one another does not give either of them insight into the inner self of the other. That remains an irreducible alterity, a "ruin," "chaos," or inarticulate "roar" hidden even from the consciousness of the person himself or herself. What that reciprocal commitment does is to create out of signs the shared fabric of their life together, with its beneficent but incalculable effects:

> No life would have been possible to Dorothea which was not filled with emotion, and she had now a life filled also with a beneficent activity which she had not the doubtful pains of discovering and marking out for herself. Will became an ardent public man, working well in those times when reforms were begun with a young hopefulness of immediate good which has been much checked in our days, and getting at last returned to Parliament by a constituency who paid his expenses. (894)

In the broadening out of this marriage based on ardent commitment to a growing social good, the reader can glimpse George Eliot's conception of community. It is a community based on difference and on an irremediable ignorance of the other that no stratagems of sympathetic knowledge can vanquish. *Middlemarch* itself is not so much realism, verisimilar representation, as a vast extended speech act that brings into existence a virtual or imaginary community, analogous to real ones. This performative effect might be thought of as a raising of imaginary specters. (But are not all specters imaginary? Are not all ghosts phantasms?) These figures, the characters in Eliot novels that seem so much like "real people," give the reader good and bad examples of how to act in such a community. For George Eliot, the other, at its deepest level, remains to the end wholly other. Nevertheless, a community based on innumerable inaugurating speech acts of love and resolve can be created and sustained over the unapproachable darkness of that roar on the other side of silence.

A word in conclusion about the relation of this chapter to earlier essays on *Middlemarch* I have published may help to indicate its implications for a more complete reading of the novel.[12] The notion of totality, as, for example, it is worked out in relation to the appeal to history in the oldest of these essays, "Narrative and History," had as its distorted face in the mirror the failure of totalization, some form of fragmentation, the breakdown of wholeness. What I missed then was the significance of the detail in a passage I quoted from Nietzsche that says history has no goal, but we can posit a goal for it. The opposition is not between totality and fragmentation but between two views of history. On the one hand, history is seen as a cognitive totalization that has organic unity. It is coherently organized, with a definite beginning, middle, end. It makes a system about which generalizations can be made, because it is all forms of the same, little waves and big waves alike. On the other hand, history is seen, by Nietzsche and by Eliot, in their somewhat different ways, as drawing such coherence as it has from an inaugural positing that makes heterogeneous fragments into a whole by positing a goal for them. Such an inaugural positing is always blind. It escapes or obscures cognition. This is true even though it is the case that all performatives have a cognitive side, for example in the way they are defined sooner or later by institutional contexts of rules and protocols that they may themselves establish. The lack of cognitive certainty, however, does not mean that such positings are necessarily bad. Far from it. The United States Declaration of Independence was one such positing, as are all such revolutionary enunciations.

George Eliot in *Middlemarch* is not just putting in question the use of history as model for works of literature. She is also implicitly proposing another, performative model. This alternative paradigm is characterized by the presence of the ahistorical, the unhistorical. For her, a large part of what happens in individual life and in society is not open to being narrated on the model of historical bringing into the open (however much Eliot's own narration seems to flourish under the law of truth-telling clarity). Much that happens is unhistorical not just because it does not happen to have found its historian, but because it is in principle not open to historical narration.

What is the character of that nonhistorical element in human life? One name for it is that roar on the other side of silence, all the obscure suffering that is an intervention or interruption by the wholly other, or by what I call, to signal its incoherent multiplicity, the "others." This manifold otherness is inassimilable to narration, to its generalizations and clarities, even negative ones such as what George Eliot says about how the power to generalize is the power to make mistakes. The end of *Middlemarch*'s "Finale" not only undermines its own status as finale and the presumption that the novel has an "ending" in the ordinary sense of a goal toward which all the action is oriented. It also names what it is that forbids such closure. Much of what Dorothea and the others did comes under the category of "unhistoric acts," "hidden life," a life or lives "incalculably diffusive." The stress is on "incalculably." Such hidden lives are not able to be reduced to clarity by the calculating reason, such as the reason that is normally or normatively thought to govern history-writing, certainly history-writing of what Nietzsche called the "monumental" kind.

Something of the same sort puts in question what I said in "Optic and Semiotic" about figurative language in *Middlemarch*. I was correct to make a parallel with the scientific method of Eliot's day and correct to see an example of that in her assumption of a correspondence between small scale and large scale: "The little waves make the large ones and are of the same pattern" (501). This correspondence supports the systole and diastole of inquiry she praises. My error was to take too much for granted a traditional distinction between figurative and literal language. Here, I assumed, is the "realistic" world of *Middlemarch*, on one side, literally present, at least in imagination, and there, on the other side, is the "model" that the narrator constructs of this through recurrent metaphors comparing the "world" of *Middlemarch*, its characters, their circumambient contexts, to a web, to flowing water, to some external object to be identified in perception, to a text, and so on. In fact these figures, in their incoherence, are all literal, since no "real world" of Middlemarch exists anywhere outside the text. The domain of *Middlemarch* really is whatever the narrator calls it: a web, or something flowing, or a text, just as Lydgate builds his theory on a literal word, "tissue." The body is woven of tissues. We still use that word not as the figurative substitution for some other more literal word but as the correct term. These apparently metaphorical words are catachreses. They are improper, but they do not substitute for some other literal realistic language George Eliot might have used. They are not just adornment, nor are they interpretative rhetoric, superimposed on a literal ground, as I tended to assume. As catachreses, forced and abusive transfers, they are constitutive, not descriptive. They are performative positings that are essential to bringing the "world" of *Middlemarch* into existence through language.

Another way to put this is to say that the linguistic tissue of the novel is parabolic throughout, not just intermittently so. To say Eliot wants to unravel the tissue of *Middlemarch* society, a fabric each part of which is "not the sample of an even web" (890), is congruent with the rhetorical strategy of saying that the pier glass stands for the egoism of any person not present. My essay on money in *Middlemarch* already understood that, since, as it showed, money for George Eliot is a figure for the intrinsically parabolic nature of realistic narration. By the addition of ciphers you can make anything stand for anything.[13] This chapter has attempted to go beyond my earlier essays by defining the parabolic in George Eliot as the fabrication of catachreses for that radical otherness she calls the roar on the other side of silence.

NOTES

1. Robert Musil, *The Man without Qualities*, trans. Sophie Wilkinson, ed. consultant Burton Pike, 2 vols. (New York: Knopf, 1995).

2. George Eliot, *Middlemarch*, ed. W. J. Harvey (Harmondsworth: Penguin, 1965), 171. Further references will be to this edition.

3. I have discussed this opposition and have argued for the priority in *Middlemarch* of reading over seeing in "Optic and Semiotic in *Middlemarch*," in *The Worlds of Victorian Fiction*, ed. Jerome H. Buckley, *Harvard English Studies* 6 (Cambridge: Harvard University Press, 1975): 125–45.

4. Marcel Proust, "Time Regained," trans. Andreas Mayor, in *Remembrance of Things Past* (New York: Vintage, 1982), 3:725.

5. *Webster's New Collegiate Dictionary* defines chaos as "the confused state of primordial matter before the creation of orderly forms."

6. T. S. Eliot, "Burnt Norton," in *The Complete Poems and Plays: 1909–1950* (New York: Harcourt, Brace, 1952), 118.

7. *Philosophy and Truth: Selections from Nietzsche's Notebooks of the Early 1870's*, trans. Daniel Brazeale (Atlantic Highlands, N.J.: Humanities Press, 1979), 83. For the German, see F. Nietzsche, *Werke*, ed. Karl Schlecta, III (Munich: Carl Hanser Verlag, 1966), 313: "ein für uns unzugängliches und undefinierbares X."

8. See especially chapter 4 of *Beyond the Pleasure Principle*, trans. James Strachey, *Works*, standard ed. (London: Hogarth Press, 1955), 18:24–33. See also *The Interpretation of Dreams*, trans. James Strachey, *Works*, 5:588–609, and "A Note upon the 'Mystic Writing Pad,'" trans. James Strachey, *Collected Papers* (New York: Basic Books, 1959), 5:175–80.

9. Joseph Conrad, *Heart of Darkness*, ed. Ross C. Murfin, Bedford Case Studies, 2d ed. (Boston: Bedford Books of St. Martin's Press, 1966), 50. See chapter 5, note 3, below for my reasons for citing this edition.

10. See Werner Hamacher, "Afformative, Strike," *Cardozo Law Review* 13, 4 (December 1991): 1133–57.

11. A more or less covert allegorical parallel between Dorothea and Ariadne, with Will Ladislaw as Dionysus and Casaubon either as Theseus or as the Minotaur who devours innocent youths, runs all through the Dorothea part of *Middlemarch*.

12. These include "Optic and Semiotic in *Middlemarch*," plus "Narrative and

History," *ELH* 41, 3 (Fall 1974): 455–73, "*Middlemarch*, Chapter 85," *Nineteenth-Century Fiction* 35, 3 (December 1980): 441–48; and "Teaching *Middlemarch*: Close Reading and Theory," *Approaches to Teaching Eliot's 'Middlemarch'*, ed. Kathleen Blake (New York: Modern Language Association, 1990), 51–63.

13. See "Teaching *Middlemarch*."

Chapter Four

ANTHONY TROLLOPE:
IDEOLOGY AS OTHER IN *MARION FAY*

LITERARY STUDY, like cultural studies and anthropology, often presumes the ultimate transparency and intelligibility of what is studied, however difficult that making intelligible may be. In the case of literary study it is literary texts, not cultures as a whole, for which an accounting must be given, though the one may require the other or help achieve it. All these disciplines tend to assume that what is studied can be accounted for, made to a considerable degree reasonable, comprehensible. That is what research universities are for, to render everything reasonable, according to the Leibnizian principle that says everything has its sufficient reason.[1]

One version of this hypothesis of transparency and accountability is the assumption that we can relatively easily feel our way, through acts of interpretation, to a full understanding of literary texts from the past or from other cultures. This presumption seems particularly cogent with relatively recent texts written in our own dominant language, such as Victorian novels as read, taught, and written about by United States scholars today. These, we may tend to assume, or used until recently to assume, are more or less part of our own immediate heritage. I say "until recently" because much recent work by feminists and cultural critics has focused on an exposure of the unjust presuppositions of "Victorian ideology." Even so, the genuine strangeness or "otherness" of Victorian ideological assumptions may still be obscured by transfers from our own presuppositions, including the assumption that everything can be made reasonable and given its accounting.

If Louis Althusser is right, ideology is a set of imaginary, mistaken assumptions so taken for granted as to seem natural, not culturally determined.[2] One function of literary study is to help identify the more subtle nuances of ideological assumptions as they are represented by a given text. This work of reading will not free us from our own possible participation in the ideology in question or even give us knowledge of its genesis and ramifications, its roots in its "context." Althusser is right about that. Althusser's "A Letter on Art in Reply to André Daspre" put this as follows, making a subtle distinction between "perceiving" and "knowing":

> The problem of the relations between art and ideology is a very complicated and difficult one. . . . I believe that the peculiarity of art is to "make us see,"

"make us perceive," "make us feel" something which *alludes* to reality. If we
take the case of the novel, Balzac or Solzhenitsyn, . . . they make us *see*,
perceive (but not know) something which alludes to reality (ils nous donnent
quelque chose à *voir*, à *percevoir* (et *non à connaître*) qui fait *allusion* à la
réalité).[3]

Seeing and perceiving are here set against knowing. "Alluding" is here
implicitly contrasted to a true representation. To know would presumably mean knowing the way an imaginary ideological relation alludes to
"reality," presumably meaning by "reality" material reality, the actual
conditions of individuals' existence. "Alludes" would name the twisted,
veiling, imaginary representation. An allusion is indirect. It requires decoding, demystification. Only a Marxist analysis, Althusser apparently
assumes, can give that kind of knowledge. Nevertheless, for him, even
knowledge of that analytical, dialectical kind is not enough to bring liber-
ation from the chains of ideology.

Trollope would agree with that. In a characteristically clear and succinct formulation in *Marion Fay*, Trollope's narrator says, "A man cannot rid himself of a prejudice because he knows or believes it to be a
prejudice."[4] A change in social structure, not knowledge, is necessary to
bring about a change in ideology, since the latter is the automatic reflex
of the former. How a change in social structure can be brought about if
everyone within it is bewitched by the ideology that corresponds to that
structure is a knotty question. Marxist analysis has of course given much
attention to this question. I shall suggest my own answers in this chapter.

Whether writing and reading novels can contribute to social change by
being a "critique of ideology," whether it is really the case that art is
powerless in the way Althusser says it is, should also perhaps remain an
open question. That question is one horizon of my investigation here. The
beginning of an answer might be to note that "perception," "seeing,"
"knowledge" are all on the side of the "constative," that is, representative
accuracy or the lack of it. It may be that writing novels and reading them
have also a "performative" side. Novels, that is, may not just give information but may also be a way of doing things with words. That performative dimension may conceivably be more than just "policing," that is,
more than just a reinforcement of the reigning ideology. It is conceivable
that writing or reading a given novel might be an "event" that would
intervene in the materiality of actual history, history considered as material events, to change it, even to change it for the better by moving it
somewhat closer to that possible/impossible horizon of "the democracy
to come." This might happen, for example, if the novel works to expose
hitherto hidden fissures or contradictions in the reigning ideology or to
indicate features of it that are unintelligible.

The phrase "the materiality of actual history" is an echo of Paul de Man.[5] Just what de Man might have meant by the materiality of historical events will be interrogated in the chapter on his work in this book. It can be confidently said now, nevertheless, that "material conditions of existence" should not simply be opposed to "ideology" as the "real" to the "unreal," or as the reality represented or "alluded to" is opposed to the false representation. As Paul de Man says, "no one in his right mind will try to grow grapes by the luminosity of the word 'day,' but it is very difficult not to conceive the pattern of one's past and future existence as in accordance with temporal and spatial schemes that belong to fictional narratives and not to the world. This does not mean that fictional narratives are not part of the world and of reality; their impact upon the world may well be all too strong for comfort."[6] Materiality and ideology are inextricably imbricated in one another, just as "cloth speaks" for Marx and just as that famous table in Marx's *Capital* is not just so much wood but gets wild ideas and is made to dance on its four wooden legs by its participation in a human economy.[7]

I propose to read a relatively obscure novel by Anthony Trollope, *Marion Fay*, to explore in one text the way an ideology may resist full bringing to light, may resist full accountability, may remain other to our reason, though not quite for the reasons Althusser adduces. It may be, I shall suggest, this irreducible obscurity that gives this work (or other works) performative potential, even the possibility of resisting the ideology it seems to affirm and celebrate. It might thereby intervene in "the materiality of history" or come to generate the materiality of history.

Marion Fay is a late novel by Trollope. It was published in 1882, in the last year of Trollope's life. The novel has received relatively little attention. It was not even included in the old Oxford World's Classics editions of Trollope's novels. Nevertheless, it is a characteristic work of Trollope's genius. Things can be learned from *Marion Fay* about Trollope's vision of life that can be learned in no other novel by him. The plots of all Trollope's novels, as well as the plots and subplots within a given multiplotted one, exhibit what might be called fractal self-similarity. It is, however, self-similarity of the kind where an element of unpredictable difference has been introduced. Each part of the whole repeats the pattern of the whole, but in a different way, just as all the leaves on a given tree are similar but not identical, and just as each branch is a version, but with a difference, of the pattern of the whole tree. This means that each and every Trollope novel, short story, or work of nonfiction, each subplot within the main plots, adds something irreplaceable to our understanding of his work.

Michael Sadleir, in a note on the "publishing history, rarity, and value" of *Marion Fay* in *Trollope: A Bibliography*, says this novel is "the only one which was written with languor and in disjointed installments."[8] In spite of my respect for Sadleir, I think he is plain wrong in this case. *Marion Fay*, pace Sadleir, has characteristic Trollopean force and originality, even, in this case, a disturbing and troubling originality. The "disjointed" writing was in part caused by the need to finish other work in the interim, as was the case years earlier, for example, when the writing of *Castle Richmond* was interrupted by the writing of *Framley Parsonage*. *Marion Fay* was first planned in the last weeks of 1878. The original notes for the novel are in the Bodleian Library at Oxford. They show that the main plots and most of the proper names and place names were settled before the writing began. Four chapters were soon written. Trollope then set the novel aside in order to write *Dr. Wortle's School*. A large part of *Marion Fay* was completed during the summer of 1879, from August 6 to September 28, when Trollope was on vacation in the Vosges, the Swiss Alps, and the Black Forest. He wrote away at the novel on all but ten of those days with his usual regularity, writing a chapter a day. That was his idea of a vacation! The novel was published in weekly installments from December 3, 1881, to June 3, 1882 (omitting March 25) in the *Graphic*, a handsomely illustrated weekly magazine in competition with the *Illustrated London News*. *Marion Fay* was illustrated for the *Graphic* by William Small, with one illustration for each installment of the serial. The originals were seven by nine inches in size. A three-volume edition of *Marion Fay* was published by Chapman and Hall about May 15, 1882, without the illustrations. A one-volume "cheap" edition came out in May 1884, over two years after Trollope's death on December 6, 1882. The manuscript of *Marion Fay* is, or was, owned by Robert H. Taylor of Princeton, New Jersey. As R. H. Super has shown in his 1982 edition of *Marion Fay* (which follows the 1884 edition), many discrepancies exist between the early printed editions and the manuscript. Super restored "some 500 substantive readings from the manuscript" "as probably having been altered in error" (xxvi).

Another and deeper reason than "languor" (a most un-Trollopean mood in any case) may have caused Trollope to put aside *Marion Fay* and then pick it up again. More than any other of his novels, it confronts almost directly what was surely one of the most painful parts of Trollope's own life, the death by tuberculosis of so many of his siblings—two brothers and two sisters. Tuberculosis in Victorian England was like AIDS today all over the world. Once you were touched by it, sooner or later, in most cases, you died, and the disease was transmitted from mother to children. The most terrible of all these deaths to Anthony Trollope may have been that of his sister Cecilia. Cecilia lived longer than the others, married Trollope's best friend at the post office, John Tilley, and then died at thirty-two, having borne five children, all but one of whom died of consumption in infancy. Trollope felt to some degree responsible for this catastrophe, since he had introduced his friend to his sister. "I sometimes feel that I led you into more sorrow than happiness in taking you to Hadley," he wrote to John after Cecilia's death.[9]

Marion Fay takes these facts and twists them into a kind of wish-fulfillment in the double plot. The novel focuses on the question of marriage in the political and social context of late Victorian England. Characteristically, Trollope begins *Marion Fay* with a detailed setting out of the family heritage through three generations of the two main aristocratic characters, Lord Hampstead and his sister, Lady Frances. Their grandfather was a conservative marquis, but their father stood for Parliament as "an advanced Radical" (1), much to the disgust of the grandfather. Though the father now is in turn a marquis and has kept his Radical politics, still "Liberal as he was, [he thought] his own blood possessed a peculiar ichor" (4): "Wrong though it might be that there should be a Marquis and a ploughboy so far severed by the injustice of Fate, there had been a comfort to him in feeling that Fate had made him the Marquis, and had made some one else the ploughboy. He knew what it was to be a Marquis down to the last inch of aristocratic admeasurement" (4). This might be an example of what Althusser means by "donner à voir." The passage in miming in indirect discourse the rationale for class feeling makes the reader feel its plausibility with a virtual or imaginary intimacy. The son of this marquis, Lord Hampstead, is even more Radical. He introduces his friend George Roden, a post office clerk he has met at "a small political debating society" (34), to his sister. That meeting ultimately leads to a happy marriage, just the reverse of what happened in real life when Trollope introduced his post office friend to his sister. Lord Hampstead, however, meets through Roden Marion Fay, a Quaker, the daughter of a City clerk. Marion is fatally marked with the dread disease of tuberculosis. I suggest it was not "languor" but a resistance to remembering and working through painful memories that may have delayed the writing of *Marion Fay* and that gives the novel part of its undeniable force. I, at any rate, find both plots of the novel, both the happy one and the sad one, extremely moving and even disturbing, though for different reasons in each case.

"Hadley," in Trollope's letter to John Tilley, is Hadley Cross, a village north of London where Trollope's mother was living when his sister Emily died. *Marion Fay* is full of place names and proper names associated with the north of London: "Hampstead" and "Highgate" are in the novel names of titles in the Kingsbury family, though of course names of suburbs north of London in the real world. Calling the hero Lord

Hampstead is a mild joke, like calling his stepmother's sister's husband, the Secretary of State, "Lord Persiflage." Holloway, also to the north of London, is the location of important parts of the novel's action. Lord Hampstead's house in Hendon is only a few miles from Hadley Cross. "Roden," the name of Lord Hampstead's post office friend in the novel, is also the name of a real street in Holloway, as David Skilton has informed me. All these names are clues to the way Trollope associated the novel with the regions just north of London and with the most painful part of his life.

One of the presuppositions of Trollope's novels most difficult for an American reader to grasp is the taboo against marriage between members of different classes. This is the main subject of both plots of *Marion Fay*. It is not that the United States is a classless society. Our class structure, however, is organized differently and not so strongly marked, for example by the appellations of nobility, of which so much is made in *Marion Fay*. Class in the United States is for the most part a matter of how much money or income you have or the race or ethnic nationality to which you happen to belong. It is somewhat easier in the United States than in England to cross the barriers of class, for example by way of a university education.

Lord Hampstead in *Marion Fay*, however, remains inalterably Lord Hampstead. Even if he were "to call [himself] Snooks" (188), as he momentarily thinks of doing, he would still be Lord Hampstead. His noble birth is an ineradicable part of his essential selfhood, just as George Roden cannot help being the Duca di Crinola even though he stubbornly goes on calling himself George Roden even when he finds that he is an Italian duke. The taboo against interracial marriage we Americans understand very well. It is, or was, stronger even than the taboo against incest that anthropologists tell us is universal in all human cultures worldwide, so breaking down the distinction between nature and culture. "So it's the miscegenation, not the incest, which you cant [sic] bear," says Charles Bon to his half-brother Henry Sutpen in William Faulkner's *Absalom, Absalom!*[10] For *Marion Fay* this might be rephrased, a little hyperbolically, by saying "It's interclass marriage not incest that cannot be borne." It would be all right for Lord Hampstead to marry his stepmother's sister's daughter (hardly incest in the literal sense, though still marriage to a cousin by marriage), but it is abominable, at least to his stepmother, Lady Kingsbury, for him to consider marriage to the daughter of a Quaker "clerk at Pogson and Littlebird's" who lives in Paradise Row, Holloway, a working-class or lower-middle-class neighborhood (190). In the same way, it is abominable for Lord Hampstead's sister, Lady Frances, to accept a proposal of marriage from George Roden the post office clerk, though that marriage becomes acceptable when Roden turns out to be a bona fide Italian duke. All this seems to an American as strange and as cruelly arbitrary, as much requiring an act of imagination to understand, as the kinship rules and laws of exogamy and endogamy that operated among the Kwakiutls or Trobriand Islanders when the anthropologists first invaded their villages.

To read Trollope, however, is a way of coming to "see" the strange marriage rules of Victorian society, at least as one major novelist presented them. Trollope is a great anthropologist of Victorian middle- and upper-class society. Or, to put this another way, just as the stories and myths told by the Kwakiutls or Trobriand Islanders function to reinforce and sometimes to put in question rules about marriage, so Victorian novels served for their first readers as a way of reinforcing and sometimes putting in question Victorian class ideology.[11] As *Marion Fay* makes clear, the period of the novel, that is, the 1870s, was a time when rigid class lines and the hegemony of the hereditary aristocracy were beginning to break down, as was the notion that a proper woman should go in innocence to her marriage bed. This disintegration had by the time, for example, of Henry James's *The Awkward Age* (1899) progressed much further, but Trollope's *Marion Fay* marks a specific historical moment in a process. The narrator in one place registers Lady Frances's sense of this: "She could see that there had been changes in the ways of the world during the last century, during the last half century,—changes continued from year to year. Rank was not so high as it used to be,—and in consequence those without rank not so low. The Queen's daughter had married a subject. Lords John and Lords Thomas were, every day, going into this and the other business" (29). When a class structure of privilege and sharp distinction is endangered, it is likely to be most vehemently defended as part of nature, not culture, and as something the disappearance of which would "bring civilization as we know it to an end." Lady Kingsbury vehemently, absurdly, and destructively represents that view in *Marion Fay*. "Aristocratic dogmas," the narrator says, "were a religion to the Marchioness" (27).

The American reader is aided in coming to "perceive" this ideology of class by one passage in *Marion Fay* where an explicit parallel is made between interracial marriage and interclass marriage. Trollope's racism in this passage is so straightforward and so taken for granted (by him) that some readers may not even pause to reflect on it, but it is obnoxious nevertheless. The passage comes early in the novel. It is one of those characteristic sequences of indirect discourse in Trollope where the narrator presents in the third-person past tense what were originally first-person present-tense musings in the mind of the character. Reflecting on his

success in persuading Lady Frances to promise to marry him, George
Roden thinks to himself:

> Was it not certain that he would give rise to misery rather than to happiness
> by what had occurred between him and Lady Frances? Was it not probable
> that he had embittered for her all the life of the lady whom he loved? He had
> assumed an assured face and a confident smile while declaring to his mother
> that no power on earth should stand between him and his promised wife,—
> that she would be able to walk out from her father's hall and marry him as
> certainly as might the housemaid or the ploughman's daughter go to her
> lover. But what would be achieved by that if she were to walk out only to
> encounter misery? The country was so constituted that he and these Traf-
> fords were in truth of a different race,—as much so as the negro is different
> from the white man. The Post Office clerk may indeed possibly become a
> Duke; whereas the negro's skin cannot be washed white. But while he and
> Lady Frances were as they were, the distance between them was so great that
> no approach could be made between them without disruption. The world
> might be wrong in this. To his thinking the world was wrong. But while the
> facts existed they were too strong to be set aside. (52–53)

This passage is an excellent example of one of the three ways Trollope
gives the reader, even the American reader of today, an inward perception
of Victorian ideology. I have called Trollope an anthropologist of the
Victorian middle and upper classes. An anthropologist often works by
the transcription of interviews. Trollope's methods are more inward and
intimate than that. He constantly presents, by way of the "indirect discourse" the passage just cited illustrates, the inner speech and, by way of
that, the inner thoughts and feelings of the characters. The narrator is
able to enter into the minds and hearts of all the characters and speak
eloquently and lucidly for what is going on there. His speech makes the
characters' attitudes plausible to the reader or at least gives him the power
to see how someone might come to hold them. Trollope excels in that
"donner à voir" that Althusser praises in novels. Trollope's gift of speaking for the characters crosses class and gender lines. It erases the distinctions between good and bad characters. This ability to make the characters transparent to the reader is quite extraordinary. It constitutes one of
the distinctive, and most pleasurable, traits of Trollope's narratives.

If the characters are made transparent to the reader through indirect
discourse, however, they are also made transparent to one another not
only by the intuitive grasp of what the other person is thinking and feeling
that Trollope grants most of his characters, but also by a second distinctive feature of his narrative: the admirable ease, clarity, and eloquence
with which his characters make themselves understood to one another in
dialogue. What Trollope's characters want to convey to one another they

find a way to say, with Mozartian lucidity, simplicity, and succinctness. If the pleasures of penetrating within another mind through indirect discourse are one source of delight in reading Trollope, the pleasures of his mastery of dialogue are another. These are his two chief formal resources.

The intuitive understanding of what the other person is thinking and feeling, granted through language, strikes me as one of the most "unrealistic" aspects of Trollope's novels. Edmund Husserl in our century, as I mentioned in chapter 3, spent virtually endless hours and covered virtually endless pages with notes trying more or less unsuccessfully to work out to his satisfaction how one could go beyond the uncertainties, indirections, and contingencies of "analogical appresentation" in coming to know other minds. For Trollope this is no problem. The mind and feelings of the other characters are in most cases transparent to any given character. This extraordinary capacity almost makes Trollope's novels a species of science fiction, certainly a wish-fulfillment in the guise of realistic representation.

A final form of limpid transparency of the characters to one another and of the whole community to the reader is less noticeable, since it is used less often, but it is important nevertheless. Trollope does not write epistolary novels. Nevertheless, all his novels include letters exchanged among the characters, usually cited verbatim. If Trollope's characters can make themselves understood face to face, they also have an extraordinary ability to write clear and eloquent letters. These letters have their own Mozartian or Trollopean melody about them. They convey to their recipients exactly what they want to convey, as well as conveying to the reader in this third way an understanding of the exact flavor of a given imaginary personality. One charming example of this in *Marion Fay* is the letter Lady Frances writes to her supposedly commoner lover while she is being imprisoned by her stepmother at her father's German estate at Königsgraaf, in the futile hope that she will abandon her love (62).

Trollope for many years worked for the British Post Office. His work there, as his *An Autobiography* makes clear, made him especially sensitive to the ways an efficient postal system puts distant people in communication and expands community feeling beyond those who can meet daily face to face. In *An Autobiography* Trollope tells how he was charged for two years (1851–53) with the job of creating in the rural west of England "a postal net-work which would catch all recipients of letters." "It is amusing," he wrote, "to watch how a passion will grow upon a man. During those two years it was the ambition of my life to cover the country with rural Letter Carriers."[12] Just as today it is the ambition of those in charge of the Internet, the World Wide Web, and the "Information Superhighway" to "wire" everyone in the world so everyone may be put in instantaneous touch with everyone else, so in Victorian England

the postal system was one of the most powerful means for creating national unity as well as for expanding and holding together the British
Empire. Trollope's trips to the West Indies, South Africa, Australia, New
Zealand, and North America, all of which resulted in travel books, were
at least to some degree official. They were undertaken in part on behalf of
the British Post Office by an official or sometime official of it. Trollope's
interest was in expanding the postal system and making it more efficient
as a way of organizing the British Empire. The British Empire was a concomitant of the postal system and the telegraph, just as the new regime of
transnational telecommunications is today weakening the sovereignty of
nation states. Letter-writing can be added to dialogue and indirect discourse as the third of Trollope's salient narrative techniques in aid of
transparency.

If Trollope's characters are transparent to one another and made transparent to the reader by the narrator in the ways I have described, if all the
characters share a single ideology or at least recognize its irresistible
force, what possible source of narrative conflict or interest can there be in
Trollope's novels or in *Marion Fay* as a representative example of them?
How could such novels be anything other than a blind reinforcement of
the ideology already so strongly in place and so decisive in determining
the lives of Trollope's readers?

Any hereditary aristocracy is almost certain to have as its primary collective goal the preservation of its own power and privilege from generation to generation. It can do this through such devices as primogeniture
and the strict control of marriages. Titles and property are redistributed
through marriage, that is, to put it starkly, through the distribution of
women. Such a society therefore has to watch with anxious solicitude
every marriage, such as those marriages Lord Hampstead and his sister
Lady Frances might make in *Marion Fay*. Much more is at stake in each
such marriage than is the case with most marriages in the United States.
With us, marriages are usually a more private matter, of interest only to
the immediate families of those getting married. Only the marriages of
our media celebrities interest us, in addition to our own marriages and
those of our immediate family members.

Nevertheless, just as in traditional societies, for example that of Old
Testament Judaism, a certain amount of exogamy is necessary in order to
prevent too much inbreeding, so in Trollope's England marriages between aristocrats and commoners were, as Lady Frances thinks to herself
in a passage already cited from *Marion Fay*, happening more often. If the
Book of Ruth in the Old Testament is the story of one such marriage in
ancient Judea, Trollope's novels frequently take up the question of cross-
class marriages. Why and when are they justified? Notable examples,

among many others, are to be found in *Lady Anna, The Duke's Children*, and of course *Marion Fay.*

It is just here that a conflict or cleft within Victorian ideology appears. This fissure is brought into visibility by the story Trollope tells. Marriages in a traditional society like that of upper caste Brahmins in present-day Katmandu are still "arranged." The bride has no choice in the matter, beyond the freedom to refuse the arranged marriage and thereby become an "old maid." This is the lowest level in that extremely hierarchical community. In Victorian England, as Trollope presents it, the woman did have a choice. Her just prerogative to say no or yes, to refuse proposals that are approved by all her family and clan, and to accept proposals that were opposed by family and clan, was generally recognized. The woman's choice or, more properly, acquiescence was therefore decisive. She had to utter a performative "yes" for the whole exchange to take place. These "yes's" were decisive both in determining the way society renewed itself from generation to generation and in measuring the integrity of the persons involved. Marriage to someone you do not love with your whole heart is the cardinal sin in Trollope's world. The people in Trollope's novels, along with the narrator himself, focus anxiously on the marriage choices the young women make. It is as though the high value given by the Protestant tradition to personal responsibility, conscientious ethical choice, and private independent decision were in conflict with the need to arrange marriages so that property, titles, and privileges might remain in the hands of the hegemonic class.

On just what basis does the young marriageable woman decide? On what basis ought she to decide? The answer is that she decides because she decides, or rather because something "other" within her, a self deeper than the self, decides for her. This is one remnant of a deep fissure within Christianity itself that remains active in Victorian society as Trollope represents it. This remnant is incompatible with the rational choice of the mate that will best keep bloodlines pure and secure the passing on of aristocratic privilege and property. On the one hand, Christianity authorizes specific codes of ethics, most notably in the Ten Commandments: "Honor thy father and thy mother"; "Thou shalt not bear false witness against thy neighbor" (Exodus 20:12, 16), and so on. We know all those "thou shalt nots" that were carved on the tablets Moses brought down from Mount Sinai. On the other hand, even the Old Testament, for example in the story of Abraham and Isaac, contains proleptically another incompatible or contradictory strand in Christianity. Abraham is forced by an intransigent obligation to obey a secret command from God, to break all ethical laws, and to determine to sacrifice the son he loves without ever justifying himself to his wife or to Isaac, only to God: "God did tempt Abraham, and said unto him, Abraham: and he said, Behold, Here I am"

(Genesis 22:1). Abraham keeps the secret of his compact with God, just as Lady Frances can give no rational accounting of why and how she has come to commit herself to George Roden the post office clerk. From the point of view of a rational ethics the New Testament is even worse than the Old, as in Jesus's terrible commandment to hate one's family and follow Him: "If any one comes to me and does not hate his own father and mother and his wife and children and brothers and sisters, yes, and even his own life, he cannot be my disciple" (Luke 14:26).

A reader might say that Lady Frances can tell a nobleman when she sees one, however much he is disguised as a post office clerk. Lady Frances instinctively chooses someone worthy of her, so it is inevitable that George Roden should turn out to be the Duca di Crinola. The novel, however, says no such thing, any more than the Bible says that Abraham knew God was only testing him when he raised his knife to slay his only son. In both cases, the point of the story is that Lady Frances or Abraham is blindly obeying a command that comes from something violently other to all the normal ties of kinship and propriety. Abraham could only justify his behavior by saying, "God commanded me to do it," just as Lady Frances could only say, "I love him because I love him." The command from the wholly other manifests itself as an irresistible and even violent or excessive emotion impelling the self to act in one way or another. This emotion is, properly speaking, afformative, that is, prior to any explicit speech act.[13] It nevertheless leads to or seeks embodiment in words or other gestures that are performatively felicitous. They work. They make something happen, as when the young woman says "yes" to the man who has proposed to her, or as when Abraham says "Here I am" in response to Jehovah's uttering of his name.[14]

An analogous contemporary version of this split between the ethical and the religious, to keep Kierkegaard's distinction, may be seen in the present-day ideology of "globalization." On the one hand, globalization is a matter of rational calculation governed by economic imperialism and by desire on the part of developed countries to get richer and richer, more and more economically dominant. The radical worldwide transformations we call globalization, moreover, are being brought about as a concomitant of technological developments, primarily the "new regime of telecommunications." These technological innovations are "material," just as were the conditions of production and distribution that made high capitalism possible in the nineteenth and early twentieth centuries, along with the relations between the sexes and classes that Trollope dramatizes in *Marion Fay*. On the other hand, "globalization" or, as the French prefer to call it, "mondialisation," "worldifying," would be impossible without ideologemes that are remnants of the more radical side of Western

Christianity and Judaism. These ideologemes are not just aspects of economic calculation but often even opposed to them. The concept of totality we call "the world" is inseparable from Judeo-Christianity. The notion of "globalization" has its roots in the assumption that there is or might be "one world" that could be brought into economic and cultural unity. Jesus's apostles, in *Acts*, disperse to convert the whole world. They are granted the "gift of tongues," allowing them to transcend the divisions of the world's different languages. Today this is accomplished by making English more and more the universal language, the lingua franca, just as Latin was in medieval and Renaissance Europe. As Jacques Derrida has been showing in recent seminars on perjury and pardon (1999), without Christian-Hegelian assumptions about the role of confession and reconciliation in world history, the worldwide appearance these days of acts of confession, followed by requests for forgiveness and reconciliation, would have been impossible. Examples are the confession by the Pope of Catholic complicity in Nazi atrocities, or the acknowledgment by Swiss banks that they had unjustly retained funds deposited by Jews murdered by the Nazis in the Shoah, or the extraordinary testimonies before the Truth and Reconciliation Commission in South Africa in the wake of apartheid, or Bill Clinton's asking for pardon from the whole country and the whole world for his liaison with Monica Lewinsky. Globalization seems to have called forth these acts of confession and these requests for forgiveness addressed to a transnational community, but they are remnants of the solitary religious response that led Abraham, for example, to say "Here I am" to Jehovah's call. Something similar is present when all those young women in Victorian novels say yes or no to a proposal of marriage.

The moment when the unmarried Englishwoman decides, on her own, to give herself or not to give herself to this or that man is a crucial moment within Victorian society as Trollope describes it. It is an inaugural or originary moment. In this moment something new is begun, something that cannot be certainly predicted beforehand and that cannot be rationally explained or justified. Falling in love is for Trollope, in *Marion Fay* as in his novels generally, unaccountable, irrational. It just happens—or does not happen. Henry James correctly said in an admirable formulation that Trollope made the English girl his special province: "Trollope settled down steadily to the English girl; he took possession of her, and turned her inside out."[15] What characterizes the best of Trollope's girls, in novel after novel, is the extraordinary stubbornness with which they stick to a marriage commitment or love promise once they have made it, or stick to a refusal once they have made it, even though the acceptance or refusal can be justified according to no grounds of prudence or obedience to mother and father. If, in the two bad counterexamples given in *Marion Fay*, Lady Amaldina, the daughter of Lady Persiflage, accepts the bald Lord Llwddythlw out of pure calculation, kissing him "as she might have kissed her grandfather" (136), and if Clara Demijohn shifts back and forth, out of an incurable superficiality, from Tribbledale to Crocker, the two central women in *Marion Fay* are resolutely stubborn once they know where their love lies. Their decisions determine the outcomes of the two plots. Lady Frances, once she has decided to accept the proposal of George Roden the post office clerk, resists all attempts by her family to make her change her mind. "You are not to suppose that I would give him up," she tells her brother, Lord Hampstead. "I shall never do that. I shall go on and wait. When a girl has once brought herself to tell a man that she loves him, according to my idea she cannot give him up. There are things which cannot be changed" (69). When her family takes her abroad to get her to forget George Roden, the narrator tells the reader: "Lady Frances had her own ideas, as to this going away and living abroad, very strongly developed in her mind. They intended to persecute her until she should change her purpose. She intended to persecute them till they should change theirs. She knew herself too well, she thought, to have any fear as to her own persistency" (27). When her father tells her that it is impossible she should marry a post office clerk, she says quietly, "But I shall, papa" (65). And she does marry him. Her stubbornness makes possible the happy ending of one plot.

A woman's stubborn decisiveness also determines the sad ending of the other plot, the one that gives the novel its name. Marion Fay, the Quaker's daughter, persistently refuses to marry Lord Hampstead, though she knows he loves her truly and though she loves him passionately and steadfastly in return. She refuses him for two quite different reasons, though the reasons become metaphors for one another. She believes that it would be unfit for a lower-middle-class girl like herself to marry the great Lord Hampstead. She also knows that she is going to die soon of consumption and that any children they might have would likely die of consumption too. Like Septimus Harding in Trollope's *The Warden*, who appeals to his "conscience," "an inward and an unguided conviction of my own,"[16] as the basis for his decision to resign the Wardenship, so Marion Fay depends on her conscience alone in her refusal to marry Lord Hampstead: "She could not argue the matter out with him, but he was wrong in it all. She was not bound to listen to any other voice but that of her own conscience. She was bound not to subject him to the sorrows which would attend him were he to become her husband" (390). And she does die, as she foresees, leaving Lord Hampstead desolate and resolved never to marry, so that the Marquisate will pass to the children of his half brothers by his father's second marriage.

The prohibition against a marriage between Lord Hampstead and Marion Fay depends not only on an implied equation between interclass marriage and interracial marriage, as in the passage already cited, but also on an implied equation between such taboos and the taboo against marrying someone mortally ill. Just what is meant by the word "conscience" as used by Trollope? It is a key term in his ethical vocabulary. It is Trollope's name, a thoroughly Christian one, for the relation within the self between the conscious and rational ego and depths of the self that are the substance of the self. Those depths are the self's substance in the sense of being what stands beneath the self as what it is truly made of as well as what supports it as its ground. At the same time these depths are wholly other to that rational level, a gulf more than a solid ground. That is what justifies Septimus Harding in saying his decision is not only "inward" but "unguided." The depths of conscience issue implacable demands that the daylight self act in one way or another, even when that behavior seems against all common sense. Obeying the command of conscience, just as Abraham obeyed Jehovah, is the only source of true personal integrity.

This feature of Christianity persisted within English culture, as Trollope's novels show, even beyond its explicit theological grounding into the work of a more or less secularized writer like Trollope. It was a deeply embedded assumption about selfhood and about the basis of justified personal choice. It is possible to see this of course as just another ideologeme, something actually cultural that is taken as natural, God-given.[17] It is an ideologeme, moreover, that Trollope's novels reinforce just as powerfully as they reinforce the ideologemes of class and gender difference.

That, however, supports just the point I am making. The ideology of the British middle and upper classes in the late Victorian period, as registered in Trollope's novels, was riven by a deep cleft between what Kierkegaard calls the "ethical" and what he calls the "religious," just as Christianity itself is. On the one hand was the rational and codified ethical code: honor thy father and mother; thou shalt not steal; and so on. On the other hand was the appeal to a wholly other within the self, the still small voice of conscience that speaks secretly and with absolute authority to Abraham or to Lady Frances. The exigence and absolute demand enforced by this voice cannot be communicated to others. It goes counter to the ethical goods and obligations one has to one's family and to one's class. To other people, for example to one's parents, or to one's family generally, what the voice of conscience commands sounds like immorality, even like madness. The instant of decision, says Kierkegaard somewhere, is madness.[18] Nevertheless, the voice of the other within the self is absolutely coercive. Its demand is irresistible, at least to anyone who has personal integrity.

Though all the innumerable cases where young unmarried women respond to the secret voice of conscience and decide to accept or refuse an offer of marriage are necessary to keep English society going, to allow it to renew itself in the marriages that redistribute privilege and property, the decisions are not made, and must not be made, with the aim of conserving the status quo. They are the agents of gradual or even fairly abrupt change, such as the change that was breaking down aristocratic hegemony in Trollope's day. As I have said, Lady Frances makes her decision to marry George Roden without knowing he is really the Duca di Crinola. The dénouement that reveals he is a duke may be called a conservative ideological cover-up of what is genuinely radical and threatening to the status quo in *Marion Fay*.

In this cover-up of a subversive religious dimension, the dimension of an appeal to a wholly other, the happy ending of Lady Frances's story is just the opposite of Sophocles's *Oedipus the King* as interpreted by Freud. For Freud the religious dimension of *Oedipus* (the unfathomable question of why Apollo punishes Oedipus so cruelly) is a cover for the real meaning, which is the "Oedipus complex," Oedipus's hatred of his father and incestuous love for his mother.[19] In *Marion Fay* the conservative social meaning is a cover for the true "religious" meaning, the meaning that says the right decision is made in response to an inner voice that is the wholly other within the self.

Trollope notoriously defined himself as "an advanced but still a conservative Liberal."[20] He strongly supported Gladstone. The outcome of *Marion Fay*'s two plots, however, might be said to lean toward the conservative side. It turns out, against all probability, that George Roden the post office clerk is really the Duca di Crinola. He is, therefore, from the perspective of her aristocratic family, a fit husband for Lady Frances. The purity of her aristocratic bloodline is not contaminated after all by marriage to a commoner. Lord Hampstead, for all his Republican views and for all his steadfast love of Marion, is prevented from marrying beneath his rank by Marion's resolute refusal of him and by her death. If he sticks to his resolve never to marry, his father's title of Marquis of Kingsbury will pass to the eldest son of the more or less odious Lady Kingsbury, his stepmother. The aristocracy survives intact.

Nevertheless, in the demonstrations of the aristocracy's fragility, its vulnerability, and especially in showing that its persistence depends absolutely on the private and unpredictable decisions of the weakest and most helplessly dependent members of all classes, "English maidens," whose decisions potentially may bring radical changes in social structure, *Marion Fay* certainly does not unequivocally take Lady Kingsbury's part. The novel shows that the handwriting was on the wall forecasting the weakening and dilution of the hereditary aristocracy. To put this another way: *Marion Fay* is itself the handwriting on the wall, in spite of the conservative outcomes of the two stories.

Did *Marion Fay* work to bring about the breakdown of the British class system? Yes and no. The question is like asking whether Nadine Gordimer's *July's People*, which in 1981 imagined what the end of apartheid would be like, actually contributed to bringing about the end of apartheid. The performative effect of *Marion Fay* obviously depended to some degree on its readers. Even those naïve readers, however, who took the novel "straight" and accepted its ending as a demonstration that the class system is natural, since Lady Frances "naturally" fell in love with a man who turns out to be a duke, were nevertheless exposed until the "happy ending" to the possibility that Lady Frances, by following the private inclinations of her heart, would be marrying beneath her station and that this marriage would be a good thing. Other readers might have been astute enough to see the discovery that George Roden is the Duca di Crinola as an ironic parody of a common motif in popular fiction, as an unrealistic and extremely unlikely absurdity, like Roden's Italian name, a conservative wish-fulfillment. In any case, an Italian duke is not quite the same thing as an English one, as all those impecunious Italian aristocrats in Henry James's fiction, most notably Prince Amerigo in *The Golden Bowl*, demonstrate.

It is not all that easy to get empirical evidence about how a novel was read by its first readers. Contemporary reviews are usually the closest one can come, unless there are comments in letters or memoirs. The four short, unsigned reviews of *Marion Fay* collected by Donald Smalley in *The Critical Heritage* volume of early reviews and essays on Trollope's work cover just the spectrum of response I have been hypothesizing.[21] The one in the *Athenaeum* does not mention Lady Frances's love for George Roden at all but praises instead the love story of Lord Hampstead and Marion Fay. The two sentences in the New York *Critic* find the novel "very, very tiresome and unnatural": "He not only resorts to the old-fashioned device of having his young plebian prove to be a duke, but he indulges in an excess of feeble sentiment which makes the whole thing ridiculous" (495). It is surely significant that only the American reviewer is enough outside the British class system as to see it as "unnatural." The other two English reviews more or less accept the conservative reading, though with differences in nuance. The *Saturday Review* reviewer observes that "there are many chapters expended on the question whether the post office clerk whom we know as George Roden should or should not call himself by the Italian title which it turns out was his father's before him. These young democrats, however, do not get much beyond the fact of their opinions, and the inconvenience they cause to their friends; they do not even begin to regenerate the world" (494). The implication is that if the characters within the imaginary world of the novel do not even begin to regenerate that world, neither will the novel, though it is perhaps implicitly recognized that the novel might conceivably intervene to move the English world toward a more democratic form. The fourth review, that in the *Spectator*, rather straddles the fence: "We cannot help being rather disappointed that Mrs. Roden's [that is, George Roden's mother's] unknown husband should turn out to be a somebody, and that in consequence George's marriage with Lady Frances should be made more palatable to her big relations. This conclusion leaves on the mind rather an impression of incompleteness and want of art. . . . [M]any readers will probably prefer the end as it is; for it has the merit of shocking no one's prejudices, is a happy compromise of principles, and makes it more probable that Mr. George and Lady Frances Roden will live happily ever after" (496). The reviewer would, it appears, rather prefer that George Roden should not turn out to be a duke, but he recognizes that most readers will think it more likely that the marriage will be a happy one if George Roden is a duke.

Insofar as *Marion Fay* has a performative dimension, that is, insofar as it has worked on its readers, then or now, as a way of doing things with words, it has, as one distinct possibility, functioned, even on such a reader as the *Spectator* reviewer, to encourage approval of private and extra-social or even antisocial decisions based on the appeal of a wholly other other within the self. Such decisions are a danger to the status quo and to the class, race, and gender ideology the novel otherwise seems so blithely to confirm and reinforce. They move toward the distant horizon of a more perfect democracy to come.

NOTES

1. Leibniz expresses this as follows in paragraph 32 of *The Monadology*: "there can be no fact real or existing, no statement true, unless there be a sufficient reason why it should be so and not otherwise" (Gottfried Wilhelm Leibniz, *The Monadology and Other Philosophical Writings*, trans. Robert Latta [New York: Garland, 1985], 235; this translation was originally published in 1898). Leibniz, it should be remembered (and often is not remembered), goes on to add: "although these reasons usually cannot be known by us" (ibid.).

2. "Ideology," says Althusser, "is a 'representation' of the imaginary relationship of individuals to their real conditions of existence" (Louis Althusser, "Ideology and Ideological State Apparatuses (Notes toward an Investigation)," in *Lenin and Philosophy and Other Essays*, trans. Ben Brewster (New York: Monthly Review Press, 1972), 163.

3. "Réponse de Louis Althusser," *La nouvelle critique*, no. 175 (1966): 141–42; Louis Althusser, "A Letter on Art in Reply to André Daspre," in *Lenin and Philosophy*, 221–22.

4. Anthony Trollope, *Marion Fay*, ed. R. H. Super (Ann Arbor: University of Michigan Press, 1982), 11. Further citations will be to this edition.

5. For this phrase, see Paul de Man, "Anthropomorphism and Trope in the Lyric," in *The Rhetoric of Romanticism* (New York: Columbia University Press, 1984), 262. In the essay "Kant and Schiller," de Man speaks of "an *occurrence*, which has the materiality of something that actually happens, that actually occurs." On the next page he says that in his model, "history is not thought of as a progression or a regression, but is thought of as an event, as an occurrence. There is history from the moment that words such as 'power' and 'battle' and so on emerge on the scene. At that moment things *happen*, there is *occurrence*, there is *event*." See Paul de Man, "Kant and Schiller," in *Aesthetic Ideology*, ed. Andrzej Warminski (Minneapolis: University of Minnesota Press, 1996), 132, 133. This passage is discussed in chapter 10.

6. Paul de Man, *The Resistance to Theory* (Minneapolis: University of Minnesota Press, 1986), 11.

7. Cloth speaks in section 3 on "The Form of Value or Exchange-Value" in the opening chapter of *Capital*, and the fetish-table (Fetisch-Tisch) stands on its legs and head, as well as dancing, in the chapter on "The Fetishism of Commodities and the Secret Thereof." See Karl Marx, *Capital*, ed. Frederick Engels, trans. Samuel Moore and Edward Aveling (New York: International Publishers, 1974), 1:52, 71. Here are these two quite extraordinary passages of prosopopoeia in Marx: "We see, then, all that our analysis of the value of commodities has already told us, is told by the linen itself, so soon as it comes into communication with another commodity, the coat. Only it betrays its thoughts in that language with which alone it is familiar, the language of commodities" (52). "The form of wood, for instance, is altered by making a table out of it. Yet, for all that, the table continues to be that common, every-day thing, wood. But, so soon as it steps forth as a commodity, it is changed into something transcendent. It not only stands with its feet on the ground, but, in relation to all other commodities, it stands on its head, and evolves out of its wooden brain grotesque ideas, far more wonderful than 'table-turning' ever was" (71). For a discussion of this speaking cloth and this dancing table, see Werner Hamacher's admirable "Lingua Amissa: The Messianism of Commodity-Language and Derrida's *Specters of Marx*," in *Ghostly Demarcations: A Symposium on Jacques Derrida's "Specters of Marx,"* ed. Michael Sprinker (London: Verso, 1998).

8. Michael Sadleir, *Trollope: A Bibliography* (London: Constable, 1928), 314.

9. Anthony Trollope, *The Letters*, ed. N. John Hall (Stanford: Stanford University Press, 1983), 1:19.

10. William Faulkner, *Absalom, Absalom!* (New York: Vintage, 1972), 356.

11. Another example would be the oral narratives about marriage negotiations that circulate today among upper-caste Brahman families in Kathmandu, Nepal. These stories both enforce the rigid rules about marriage in that group and at the same time put them in question by at least hinting that they are arbitrary,

cruel, and unjust. See Sarah E. Miller, "Twice-born Tales from Kathmandu: Stories that Tell People," Ph.D. dissertation, Cornell University, 1992.

12. Anthony Trollope, *An Autobiography*, ed. David Skilton (London: Penguin, 1996), 62. Further references will be to this edition, the first to be scrupulously edited in light of the original manuscript. According to Skilton, it "follows the manuscript as closely as possible" (xxv).

13. See chapter 3, note 10.

14. For a celebrated reading of the episode of Abraham and Isaac in *Exodus*, see Søren Kierkegaard, *Fear and Trembling*, trans. Walter Lowrie (Garden City, N.Y.: Doubleday Anchor, 1954), 21–132; and for a reading of both *Exodus* and Kierkegaard on Abraham's sacrifice of Isaac, see Jacques Derrida, "A qui donner (savoir ne pas savoir)," and "Tout autre est tout autre," the third and fourth sections of his *Donner la mort* (Paris: Galilée, 1999), 79–157; Jacques Derrida, "Whom to Give to (Knowing Not to Know)," and "Tout Autre Est Tout Autre," in *The Gift of Death*, trans. David Wills (Chicago: University of Chicago Press, 1995), 53–115.

15. Henry James, "Anthony Trollope," in *Literary Criticism: Essays on Literature; American Writers; English Writers*, ed. Leon Edel and Mark Wilson (New York: The Library of America, 1984), 1349–50. What James says about Trollope's treatment of "the English girl" is so generous and so right on the mark that I allow myself to quote more of it:

> he bestowed upon her [the English girl] the most serious, the most patient, the most tender, the most copious consideration. He is evidently always more or less in love with her, and it is a wonder how under these circumstances he could make her so objective, plant her so well on her feet. But, as I have said, if he was a lover, he was a paternal lover; as competent as a father who has had fifty daughters. He has presented the British maiden under innumerable names, in every station and in every emergency in life, and with every combination of moral and physical qualities. She is always definite and natural. She plays her part most properly. She has always health in her cheek and gratitude in her eye. She has not a touch of the morbid, and is delightfully tender, modest and fresh. Trollope's heroines have a strong family likeness, but it is a wonder how finely he discriminates between them. One feels, as one reads him, like a man with "sets" of female cousins. Such a person is inclined at first to lump each group together; but presently he finds that even in the groups there are subtle differences. Trollope's girls, for that matter, would make delightful cousins. (1350)

16. Anthony Trollope, *The Warden*, ed. David Skilton, World's Classics ed. (Oxford: Oxford University Press, 1991), 253.

17. It is worth remembering that J. L. Austin, in *How to Do Things with Words*, makes an explicit attack on the Christian notion that the efficacy of a performative utterance, for example saying "I do" in a marriage ceremony, depends on the inner disposition of the one uttering the performative. This assumption, Austin argues, actually leads to immorality and to the breakdown of contractual commitments, since anyone can excuse himself or herself from a commitment by saying, "I said that, but I didn't really mean it." Since the inner dispo-

sition of the other is unknowable, Austin argues, it is better to say "My word is my bond" and to hold people to commitments they make verbally or in writing, whatever they may have been thinking or feeling at the time. A performative must be public, attestable. Since inner disposition cannot be certainly known, it had better be left out of the account:

> For one who says "promising is not merely a matter of uttering words! It is an inward and spiritual act!" is apt to appear as a solid moralist standing out against a generation of superficial theorizers: we see him as he sees himself, surveying the invisible depths of ethical space, with all the distinction of a specialist in the *sui generis*. Yet he provides Hippolytus with a let-out [when he says, in Euripides's play *Hippolytus*, as Austin translates the Greek: "my tongue swore to, but my heart (or mind or other backstage artiste) did not"; the Greek word is *phren*], the bigamist with an excuse for his "I do" and the welsher with a defence for his "I bet." Accuracy and morality alike are on the side of the plain saying that *our word is our bond*. (J. L. Austin, *How to Do Things with Words*, ed. J. O. Urmson and Marina Sbisà, 2d ed. [Oxford: Oxford University Press, 1980], 9–10)

In other places, however, Austin makes "sincerity" one of the conditions of a felicious performative. We must, after all, really mean what we say, be of sound mind, not drunk, insane, or coerced, for a performative utterance to be efficacious (e.g., 21). This contradiction lies at the center of Austin's theory of speech acts, as I demonstrate in more detail in the chapter on Austin in *Speech Acts in Literature* (Stanford: Stanford University Press, 2001).

18. Quoted in Derrida, *The Gift of Death*, 65; *Donner la mort*, 66.

19. As I have argued in *Reading Narrative* (Norman: University of Oklahoma Press, 1998), 14–17, I think Freud is wrong. If you subtract the religious dimension from *Oedipus the King*, hardly anything is left. Religious issues are woven inextricably in the text. *Oedipus the King*, pace Freud, is about the unanswerable question of why Apollo is so appallingly cruel and unjust to Oedipus.

20. Trollope, *An Autobiography*, 186.

21. *Trollope: The Critical Heritage*, ed. Donald Smalley (London: Routledge & Kegan Paul; New York: Barnes & Noble, 1969), 493–96.

Chapter Five

JOSEPH CONRAD:
SHOULD WE READ
HEART OF DARKNESS?

The inaccessible incites from its place of hiding.
—Jacques Derrida

SHOULD WE READ *Heart of Darkness*? May we read it? Must we read it? Or, on the contrary, ought we not to read it or allow our students and the public in general to read it? Should every copy be taken from all the shelves and burned? What or who gives us the authority to make a decision about that? Who is this "we" in whose name I speak? What community forms that "we"? Nothing could be more problematic than the bland appeal to some homogeneous authoritative body, say professors of English literature everywhere, capable of deciding collectively whether "we" should read *Heart of Darkness*. By "read" I mean not just run the words passively through the mind's ear, but perform a reading in the strong sense, an active responsible response that renders justice to a book by generating more language in its turn, the language of attestation, even though that language may remain silent or implicit. Such a response testifies that the one who responds has been changed by the reading. Part of the problem, as you can see, is that it is impossible to decide authoritatively whether or not we should read *Heart of Darkness* without reading it in that strong sense. By then it is too late. I have already read it, been affected by it, and passed my judgment, perhaps recorded that judgment for others to read. Which of us, however, would or should want to take someone else's word for what is in a book? Each must read again in his or her turn and bear witness to that reading in his or her turn. In that aphorism about which Jacques Derrida has had so much to say, Paul Celan says, "Niemand / zeugt für den / Zeugen (Nobody / bears witness for the / witness)."[1] This might be altered to say, "No one can do your reading for you." Each must read for himself or herself and testify anew.

This structure is inscribed in *Heart of Darkness* itself. The primary narrator bears witness through exact citation to what he heard Marlow say one night on the deck of the cruising yawl *Nellie*, as he and the other men, the Lawyer, the Accountant, the Director of Companies, representatives of advanced capitalism and imperialism, waited for the tide to turn so they could float down the Thames and out to sea, presumably on a pleasure cruise.[2] They have enough wealth and leisure to take time off to do as an aesthetic end in itself what Marlow has done for pay as a professional seaman. The profession of the primary, framing narrator is never specified. He cites with what the reader is led to believe is conscientious and meticulous accuracy just what Marlow said. What Marlow said, put within quotation marks throughout, is a story, the recounting of and accounting for what he calls an "experience" that "seemed somehow to throw a kind of light on everything about me—and into my thoughts. It was sombre enough too—and pitiful—not extraordinary in any way— not very clear either. No, not very clear, and yet it seemed to throw a kind of light."[3] That recounting and accounting centers on an attempt to "render justice," as Marlow puts it (94), to Kurtz, the man he meets at "the farthest point of navigation and the culminating point of my experience" (22). What Marlow says at the beginning is also an implicit promise to his listeners and to us as readers. He promises that he will pass on to them and to us the illumination he has received.

The observant reader will note that the language Conrad gives Marlow mixes constative and performative dimensions. On the one hand, Marlow's experience shed a kind of light on everything. It made him "see" in the double meaning Conrad habitually gives to "see," as does everyday language: see as visual seeing and see as understanding, acquiring new knowledge. On the other hand, Marlow's experience conferred an obligation that can only be fulfilled by performative language, by "rendering justice" (94) or "remaining loyal" (88). The performative and constative dimensions of any "accounting" or "recounting" are, necessarily, intertwined, as they are in any speech act. *Heart of Darkness*, however, is unusually explicit in its emphasis on the performative side of Marlow's language, the way it is a specific kind of speech act, namely, an attestation. "I have remained loyal to Kurtz," says Marlow, "to the last, and even beyond" (88). "I did not betray Mr. Kurtz—it was ordered I should never betray him—it was written I should be loyal to the nightmare of my choice" (81). Who did the "ordering" or the "writing" here is not said explicitly. Presumably Marlow means it was written down in the book of his Fate, a sufficiently vague notion. It was because it was to be. Actually it was written down in the book Conrad made up about Marlow, as the reader may happen to reflect. Or rather, as Marlow confesses in his account of the last episode, his visit to Kurtz's "Intended" (after Kurtz has died on the journey back down the African river and Marlow has returned to the city that "always makes [him] think of a whited sepulcre" [24]), he has by telling his lie to the Intended failed to render full justice to Kurtz: "It seemed to me that the house would collapse before I could escape, that the heavens would fall upon my head. But nothing happened. The heavens do not fall for such a trifle. Would they have fallen, I wonder, if I had rendered Kurtz that justice which was his due? Hadn't he said he wanted only justice?" (94). Kurtz had indeed said to Marlow just that: "I want no more than justice" (91).

Earlier Marlow had said, "I laid the ghost of his gifts at last with a lie" (64). Marlow's lie was to tell the Intended, with her soul as pure as a cliff of crystal, with her candid brow, that Kurtz's last words were her name, whereas his actual last words were, in "a cry that was no more than a breath," "The horror! The horror!" (86). Is Marlow's lie justified? Can we exonerate Marlow for it? Was this lie in any sense a way of rendering Kurtz justice? Marlow has told us he abhors lies, that they have a taint of mortality about them: "You know I hate, detest, and can't bear a lie," he says, "not because I am straighter than the rest of us, but simply because it appalls me. There is a taint of death, a flavor of mortality in lies—which is exactly what I hate and detest in the world—what I want to forget. It makes me miserable and sick, like biting something rotten would do" (42). To say a lie has a taint of death is odd. It suggests that only by telling the truth can we hold off death, though Marlow says just the reverse concerning his lie. It has laid the ghost of Kurtz's gifts, the greatest of which was the gift of speech, "the gift of expression, the bewildering, the illuminating, the most exalted and the most contemptible, the pulsating stream of light, or the deceitful flow from the heart of an impenetrable darkness" (63).

A lie puts us in complicity with death, at the mercy of death. A lie lets death into the human community. This is a somewhat hyperbolic version of the repudiation of the right to lie in Immanuel Kant's opuscule, "On the Presumed Right to Lie Out of Love for Humanity." A lie is never justified, says Kant, even to save someone's life, since any lie radically threatens human society. The latter depends on strict truth-telling in every circumstance, even the most extreme. "Truth" is a key word, though an exceedingly ambiguous one, in Marlow's narration in *Heart of Darkness*. His whole story is put under the aegis of giving a true account of his experience. That obligation is passed on to the primary narrator and then on to you and me as readers. The promise to give faithful testimony is, like promises in general, always messianic. It has to do with death and the last days, with the sort of promise an Apocalypse makes. Even so routine a promise as the one made by the signatory of a mortgage note invokes death, as the etymology of "mortgage" indicates. To sign a mortgage note is to engage one's life unto death, to put one's death on the line. The great exemplary apocalypse in our tradition, the last book of the Christian Bible, *Revelations*, ends with the promise and invocation of an imminent unveiling that always remains future, never quite yet here and now: "He which testifieth these things saith, Surely I come quickly. Amen. Even so, come, Lord Jesus" (Rev. 22:20).

Marlow is in the position of someone who survives the death of another. In Kurtz's end, death and the consequent responsibilities of the survivor enter as central issues in the novel. As Marlow says, "I was to have the care of his memory" (66), just as the Intended's first words to Marlow about Kurtz are "I have survived" (91). Surely the first obligation of the survivor is to tell the truth about the dead. What is peculiar about Marlow's survival of Kurtz is that Kurtz is presented when Marlow finally encounters him as already the survivor of his own death. Kurtz is already the ghost of himself. In that sense he cannot die. This is testified to in the way he survives in Marlow's narration and in the way the dusk still whispers his last words when Marlow returns to Europe and visits Kurtz's "Intended." It is hardly the case that Marlow has laid the ghost of Kurtz's gifts with a lie, since the ghost still walks, even in the room where Marlow tells his lie to the Intended. That ghost, far from being laid, is resurrected, invoked, conjured up, each time *Heart of Darkness* is read.

Perhaps Marlow means no more than that he appeased the Intended's desire to keep Kurtz's eloquence alive by lying about what that eloquence really said and what its source was. It is not Kurtz the spectral survivor and revenant who is buried when Kurtz "dies," but his mere bodily envelope or cadaver: "But I am of course aware that next day the pilgrims buried something in a muddy hole" (87). The chain of obligation begins with Kurtz, who has passed judgment in those words "The horror! The horror!" He "had pronounced a judgment upon the adventures of his soul on this earth. . . . He had summed up—he had judged. 'The horror!' He was a remarkable man. After all, this was the expression of some sort of belief; it had candour, it had conviction, it had a vibrating note of revolt in its whisper, it had the appalling face of a glimpsed truth—the strange commingling of desire and hate" (87). The chain then goes to Marlow, who testifies as survivor for Kurtz, keeping Kurtz alive in his narration, and telling to his auditors on the *Nellie* the truth he had withheld from the Intended. The primary narrator in his turns bears witness to what Marlow said by citing it exactly and by placing it in an exegetical context that is implicitly a reading.

Exact citation, prior to any interpretation, is one of the most important ways to testify or to render justice, as in my citations from Conrad's *Heart of Darkness* here. Each quotation is accompanied by an implicit oath: "I swear to you this is what Conrad really wrote, or at least what Conrad's most authoritative editors attest he wrote."[4] The obligation to render justice is then passed from Conrad's primary narrator to any reader, each one of whom nowadays is Conrad's survivor. From each reader it is demanded once again to do justice to Conrad and to *Heart of*

Darkness, to attest to what happens when the book is read—telling the truth, the whole truth, and nothing but the truth.

Bearing witness in an interpretation or reading, for example of *Heart of Darkness*, is a performative speech act, but of a peculiar and even anomalous kind. This kind is not accounted for by J. L. Austin's speech act theory in *How to Do Things with Words*.[5] A performative interpretation transforms what it interprets. It therefore cannot be fully justified by constative, verifiable evidence, any more than can acts of bearing witness in general. No one bears witness for the witness. That the witness saw what he or she says he or she saw, or that he or she responded in a certain way in an act of reading, has to be taken on faith. That is why, in murder cases in the United States for example, the jury is asked to decide not whether the defendant is guilty but whether they believe "beyond a reasonable doubt" that the defendant is guilty. As Jacques Derrida and Werner Hamacher have in different ways affirmed, interpretation in this performative sense, an interpretation that is inaugural, that intervenes to change what is read and to initiate something new, fulfills in a paradoxical way the eleventh of Marx's Theses on Feuerbach: "The philosophers have only *interpreted* the world in various ways; the point, however, is to *change* it."[6] In this case, the interpretation does the changing. It changes the world, in however small a way, by changing once and for all an element of that world that has power to make things happen, in this case a literary text, *Heart of Darkness*.

Nor have Conrad's readers failed to respond to this demand for interpretation. A large secondary literature has sprung up around *Heart of Darkness*. These essays and books of course have a constative dimension. They often provide precious information about Conrad's life, about his experiences in Africa, about late nineteenth-century imperialism, especially about that terrible murderous devastation wrought by King Leopold of Belgium in the Belgian Congo, as it was then called, about the supposed "originals" of characters in *Heart of Darkness*, and so on. This secondary literature, however, often also has an explicit performative dimension. Conrad's novel is brought before the bar of justice, arraigned, tried, and judged. The critic acts as witness of his or her reading, also as interrogator, prosecuting attorney, jury, and presiding judge. The critic passes judgment and renders justice.

Heart of Darkness has often received a heavy sentence from its critics. It has been condemned, often in angry terms, as racist or sexist, sometimes as both in the same essay. Examples are the influential essay of 1975 by the distinguished Nigerian novelist, Chinua Achebe ("Conrad was a bloody racist"), or an essay of 1989 by Bette London: "Dependent upon unexamined assumptions, themselves culturally suspect, the novel, in its representations of sex and gender, supports dubious cultural claims; it participates in and promotes a racial as well as gender ideology that the narrative represents as transparent and 'self-evident.'"[7] Edward Said's judgment in *Culture and Imperialism*, though giving Conrad his due as a critic of imperialism and recognizing the complexity of doing justice to *Heart of Darkness*, is in the end equally severe in his summing up: "The cultural and ideological evidence that Conrad was wrong in his Eurocentric way is both impressive and rich."[8] These are powerful indictments. If what they say renders justice to *Heart of Darkness*, if their witness may be trusted, it might seem inevitably to follow that the novel should not be read, taught, or written about, except perhaps as an example of something detestable. Nevertheless, according to the paradox I have already mentioned, you could only be sure about this by reading the novel yourself, thereby putting yourself, if these critics are right, in danger of becoming sexist, racist, and Eurocentric yourself. Even so, no one bears witness for the witness, and no one else can do your reading for you.

To pass judgment anew, it is necessary to take the risk and read *Heart of Darkness* for yourself. I shall now try to do that. First, however, I must ask a final question. Suppose I or any other reader or community of readers were to decide that Conrad, or rather *Heart of Darkness*, is indeed racist and sexist. Would it be possible, after passing that verdict, to pardon Conrad or the novel he wrote, to exonerate *Heart of Darkness* in some way, and get him set free, so to speak? To put this another way, would truth in this case lead to reconciliation? To be reconciled is to be able to say, as the Truth and Reconciliation Commission in South Africa has hoped would happen, "I forgive you. I am reconciled with you, though I now know you tortured and murdered my father or mother, husband or wife, brother or sister, or my neighbor, my friend." Though the slaves were emancipated in the United States 130 years ago and women given the vote 80 years ago, the United States is still in many ways a racist and sexist country. The sins of the fathers are visited on the children even unto the third generation. One might add that those sins are visited also on the children and the children's children of those whom the fathers have wronged. The United States, like all of Africa in different ways, will take many more generations to become reconciled to its history, to reach anything like the horizon of a more perfect democracy. This is that democracy that is always, as Jacques Derrida says, "to come." Thomas Mann, in "Death in Venice," cites a French proverb, "Tout comprendre c'est tout pardonner. [To understand everything is to forgive everything.]"[9] "Death in Venice" powerfully ironizes or puts in question that cheerful enlightenment confidence in the exonerating power of comprehension. It may be that the more knowledge we have the less able we are to pardon, or that pardoning, a speech act of the most exemplary and sovereign kind, has to occur, if it occurs, in the teeth of knowledge. On the one hand, to understand everything is, it may be, to find it almost impossible to forgive. Certainly that is the case with the critics I have mentioned. On the other hand, perhaps a true pardon is only of the unforgivable, as Derrida has been arguing in his recent seminars on "Pardon and Perjury." If it is forgivable it does not need forgiveness. Only the unforgivable requires forgiveness.

The question of forgiveness is inscribed within *Heart of Darkness* in the way Marlow's narrative is an implicit appeal to his listeners on the *Nellie*, and indirectly also to us as readers, to forgive him for his choice of nightmares, for his loyalty to Kurtz. We are also asked, paradoxically, to forgive him for his perjury, for the lie he tells the Intended, an act of disloyalty to Kurtz. Marlow's narrative is a species of confession. A confession is always a demand or prayer for forgiveness. It often reveals more that needs forgiveness than the confessor knows. In this case that might be the presumed racism and sexism of which Marlow (or Conrad) seems unaware. In his confession Marlow makes up for his lie by telling the truth, unless, in a final irony, "The horror!" and the Intended's name (just what that is the reader never learns) come to the same thing, so that Marlow uttered the truth after all, even the first time. That, however, it might be argued, is no excuse, even if for those in the know. Marlow, it could be said, tells the truth obliquely, but the result of his lie is that the Intended lives out the rest of her life within the shadowy confines of an illusion, that is, within a "horror" that she does not even know is a horror. Marlow's lie, "white lie" though it is, is performatively effective because it is believed. Kant would have condemned it for unraveling the social fabric.

Nothing is said about the response of those on board the *Nellie* to Marlow's story. We do not know whether or not they forgive him his lie. The Director of Companies, after Marlow finishes his story, says no more than "We have lost the first of the ebb" (95), meaning that Marlow's story has kept them from leaving when they ought. The primary narrator ends his account by making an observation that might seem to be evidence of the effect of Marlow's story on his way of seeing: "the tranquil waterway leading to the uttermost ends of the earth flowed sombre under an overcast sky—seemed to lead into the heart of an immense darkness" (95). Any further or more explicit passing of judgment is left to the reader. It is up to us—or rather up to me, since reading and bearing witness to what happens in reading are always solitary, lonely acts. This is the case however much such judgments may be performed within the coercive and determining context of codes, conventions, and protocols of reading. Historically and geographically determined ideologies also speak through the solitary reader when he or she sums up and passes judgment, as Kurtz did when he said "The horror! The horror!" or as Marlow did when he said of Kurtz, "He had summed up—he had judged.

'The horror!' He was a remarkable man" (87), or as Achebe did when he said "Conrad was a bloody racist." Nevertheless, each person who passes judgment must take personal responsibility for doing so. He or she must also take responsibility for whatever further consequences that act of reading may have.

The first thing to say in passing judgment on *Heart of Darkness* is that it is a literary work, not history, not a travel book, a memoir, an autobiography, or any other genre but some form of literature. It is a literary work, moreover, belonging to a particular historical time and place. It is, that is, a work of English literature written at the moment of high capitalism and imperialism. This may seem obvious enough, but much criticism forgets this fact or elides it. An example is what the editor of the Norton Critical Edition, Robert Kimbrough, says about the "Backgrounds and Sources" section of the volume. The first part of this, says Kimbrough, "sets the story within its historical context." The second "offers all that Conrad ever biographically recorded concerning his Congo experience, the artistic projection of which is *Heart of Darkness.*" The third "reminds us that, autobiographical though it may be, the story was to Conrad a significant, but objective work of art" (N, 84). Kimbrough, the reader can see, wants to have it several ways at once. *Heart of Darkness* is an objective work of art (whatever that means), but it is at the same time embedded in a historical context, the "projection" (whatever that means) of Conrad's "biographical" experience, and it is, after all, "autobiographical." These "backgrounds and sources" invite the reader to measure the novel by its referential accuracy. It is an almost irresistible temptation to do so, especially once you know these background "facts." An example of such yielding is talking about the place where the main events occur as the Congo or about the sepulchral city where Marlow gets his job as Brussels, whereas neither the Congo nor Brussels is anywhere named as such in the novel, while the Thames is named in the third sentence. At the very least such reticence needs to be recognized as a symptom. More radically, it is a signal that the only way to enter the countries where the events of *Heart of Darkness* occur is by reading the novel, not by visiting Belgium or what is now again called the Congo.

Conrad fought a lifelong battle in his letters, prefaces, essays, and overtly autobiographical writing, such as *The Mirror of the Sea* (1906), *A Personal Record* (1912), and *Notes on Life and Letters* (1921), to get his readers and critics to accept that his work is literature, not thinly disguised autobiography or travel literature. I give two examples out of a large number. Arthur Symons, in *Notes on Joseph Conrad: With Some Unpublished Letters* (1925), cites a letter to him from Conrad in which the latter rejects Symons's identification of Conrad with his fictive character, Kurtz: "For the rest I may say that there are certain passages in your article which have surprised me. I did not know that I had 'a heart of darkness' and 'an unlawful soul.' Mr. Kurtz had—and I have not treated him with easy nonchalance" (N, 153). A letter of July 14, 1923, to Richard Curle, responding to Curle's *Times Literary Supplement* review of the recently published Dent Uniform Edition of Conrad's works, complains bitterly of the way Curle has perpetuated the falsehood that he, Conrad, is no more than a writer of sea stories. "I was in hopes," writes Conrad,

> that on a general survey it could also be made an opportunity for me to get freed from that infernal tale of ships, and that obsession of my sea life which has about as much bearing on my literary existence, on my quality as a writer, as the enumeration of the drawing-rooms which Thackeray frequented could have had on his gift as a great novelist. After all, I may have been a seaman, but I am a writer of prose. Indeed the nature of my writing runs the risk of being obscured by the nature of my material. . . . That the connection of my ships with my writings stands, with my concurrence I admit, recorded in your book is, of course, a fact. But that was a biographical matter, not literary. (N, 152)

What is the difference between biography and literature? Conrad goes on in his letter to Curle to specify the difference in a striking figure. Almost all his "art," says Conrad, consists "in my unconventional grouping and perspective" (N, 153). Artistic grouping of what? Of the apparently referential or historical material of the story that is placed within the grouping and lighting. This material is necessary to the illuminating grouping and to its artistic effect in the same way that invisible radio waves require sending and receiving apparatuses to be detected, even though what is important is the invisible waves, not the apparatus: "Of course the plastic matter of this grouping and of those lights has its importance, since without it the actuality of that grouping and that lighting could not be made evident any more than Marconi's electric waves could be made evident without the sending-out and receiving instruments" (N, 153). The referential, mimetic, or representational aspect of his works, Conrad is saying, is all for the sake of providing a necessary material base for bringing something invisible into visibility through an artful arrangement of that material. This figure is consonant with the often-cited passage within *Heart of Darkness* itself about the peculiar nature of Marlow's stories as opposed to the usual stories seamen tell. I shall return to that passage.

Much Conrad criticism recognizes tacitly that *Heart of Darkness* is literature but then talks about it as if it were something else. Indeed it is almost impossible to avoid making this elementary error, since every text invites a referential or what Derrida calls, following Sartre, a "transcendent" reading, that is, a reading going beyond the work's language toward the exterior world to which it presumably refers.[10] To put this another way, to call *Heart of Darkness* a literary work, as I just have, is a speech act that responds to certain possibilities in the text. I have implicitly said, "I declare *Heart of Darkness* is literature." It would be equally possible to declare that *Heart of Darkness* is history, or memoir, or autobiography. To do this would be in one way or another to label the novel a straightforwardly mimetic or referential work that deserves to be judged by its truth value, its accuracy of representation. Many critics have done just that. No distinguishing marks certainly identify a given text as literary or as nonliterary, in spite of the many conventional codes that ordinarily indicate a text is literature or not literature. This uncertainty results from the way each may present itself in the guise of the other. A page from a telephone book can be taken as literature. One can imagine a fictitious telephone book that would look exactly like a real one, though the numbers would not work if you were to try to use them to call someone.

If taking *Heart of Darkness* as literature or as not literature is a speech act, an act of belief or of bearing witness, not a constative statement, this means that whoever declares it to be one or the other must take responsibility for his or her declaration. He or she must say, "I did it. I have declared that *Heart of Darkness* is literature (or, on the contrary, is history or autobiography). I accept responsibility for the consequences of saying that." I hereby do that now for my claim that *Heart of Darkness* belongs to literature. To say *Heart of Darkness* is a literary work, I hasten to add, by no means exonerates Conrad from responsibility for what is said within it, but it does change the terms and conditions of that responsibility. Just how?

Literature as an institution in the West is of relatively recent date. It began more or less in the Renaissance. "Literature" as we Westerners know it is a radically overdetermined historical product belonging only to Western societies. Greek tragedy is not literature in the modern Western sense, nor is classical Chinese poetry, however much these may look like more or less the same thing as our literature. Greek tragedy was a species of quasi-religious ritual, and Chinese poetry had class and institutional functions, not to speak of a texture of political or historical allusions, that were not quite like anything in the West. Whether United States so-called literature or South African Anglophone so-called literature is literature in the same sense that Conrad's *Heart of Darkness* is literature is a subtle and difficult question, a question whose answer must by no means be taken for granted. I suspect the nature and social function of United States and South African literature are significantly different from those of British literature. Certainly it is difficult, for example, to apply (without distorting them) to Melville, Hawthorne, or Dickinson paradigms developed for English Victorian literature, though they are contemporary with it.

Literature in the modern Western sense is a concomitant of democracy with its precious right to free speech, of the modern nation-state, of European worldwide economic and political imperialist hegemony, of print culture, of modern notions of authorship, of copyright laws, and of post-Cartesian notions of subjectivity and of the subject/object dichotomy. Democratic freedom of speech, as guaranteed by a particular nation state, is, as Jacques Derrida has cogently argued in the prefatory interview in *Acts of Literature*, essential to literature in the modern European sense. Since it would be difficult to convict Derrida of either racism or sexism (though attempts have been made), his testimony may be valuable here in working out how to pass judgment on *Heart of Darkness*. Though of course free speech always has its limits and is never more than imperfectly achieved, always something yet to come, nevertheless in principle it makes literature possible by making it permissible to say anything and, in a certain specific sense, to disclaim responsibility for it by saying, "That is not me speaking but an imaginary character. I am exercising my right to free speech in the name of a higher responsibility."[11]

All these features I have named (democratic free speech, the nation state, European hegemony, print culture, copyright laws, Cartesian notions of the ego), make a heterogeneous system, of which literature in the modern Western sense is only one element. If one element is changed, the whole system is changed, including any member of it. Several of these intertwined elements are in our time being radically altered. We hear on all sides these days of the decline of the nation state. Cartesian or Hegelian notions of subjectivity are no longer taken for granted, to say the least. Print culture is being rapidly replaced by a new regime of telecommunications: television, cinema, videotapes, faxes, e-mail, computer databases, the Internet with its unimaginable and incoherent multiplicity of data, including literature (that is being transformed by this new medium) and literary scholarship—all floating freely in global cyberspace. Among all that chaotic wealth I discovered, for example, a hypercard version of *Heart of Darkness* and downloaded it into my computer. It was prepared partly in Florida, partly in Norway, though the e-mail address is Dartmouth College in New Hampshire. Reading *Heart of Darkness* in this version is different in many hard-to-define ways from reading it in a printed book. We live in a postcolonial world in which Europe and even the United States are less and less dominant, as, for example, East Asian economies challenge the hegemony of Western ones in size and global power. Freedom of speech on the Internet does not mean the same thing as freedom of speech in face-to-face encounters in an old-fashioned New England town meeting, or freedom of speech as exercised in a printed text. The result of these changes may be that we are coming to the end of Western-style literature as it extended from Shakespeare to Conrad and his European contemporaries. The study of this literature was institutionalized in departments of national literatures in Western-style universities all over the world. Those universities are part of the legacy of imperialism and colonialism.

Literature in the modern Western sense is, it may be, already a thing of the past. It is now an object of historical investigation and imaginative, spectral resurrection, not something that is or could be currently produced, since the enabling conditions have changed so radically. Misreadings of *Heart of Darkness* as though it were a straightforwardly historical, referential, or autobiographical document may be evidence that literature can no longer easily be understood in terms of older protocols, codes, and conventions of reading, though of course such mimetic misreadings of literature have always been current. They too are part of our legacy from the now-vanishing regime of print culture. As I have said, a fictional telephone book can always be taken as a real one. The need for the ritual disclaimer (often a manifestly lying one) saying "any resemblance to real persons, living or dead, is purely coincidental" testifies to the ubiquity of the confusion and the need to try to ward it off.

In just what way does *Heart of Darkness* invite reading as literature rather than, say, as a historical account or as an autobiography? The most obvious way is in the displacement from Conrad to two imaginary narrators, neither of whom is to be identified with Conrad, any more than Socrates, in the Platonic dialogues, is to be identified with Plato. The reader who says Conrad speaks directly for himself either in the words of the frame narrator or in Marlow's words does so at his or her peril and in defiance of the most elementary literary conventions. Whatever the frame narrator or Marlow says is ironized or suspended, presented implicitly in parabasis, by being given as the speech of an imaginary character.

Conrad's way of talking about Marlow's origin, nature, and relation to his creator is peculiar, evasive. It is a little like the response "R.," presumably Rousseau himself, though this is not confirmed, gives, in the second preface to Rousseau's *La nouvelle Héloïse*, when he is asked by "N." whether the letters that make up the novel are real letters or fictive ones. "R." says he does not know and, when pressed by "N.," says he is afraid of lying if he answers definitely one way or the other.[12] In the "Author's Note" of 1917 to *Youth*, the volume that contains *Heart of Darkness*, as well as "Youth" (in which Marlow first appeared) and "The End of the Tether," Conrad responds to "some literary speculation" about Marlow's "origins." "One would think that I am the proper person to throw a light on the matter;" says Conrad, "but in truth I find that it isn't so easy" (N, 155). Marlow, he goes on to say, "was supposed to be all sorts of things: a clever screen, a mere device, a 'personator,' a familiar spirit, a whispering 'daemon.' I myself have been suspected of a meditated plan for his capture" (ibid.). Conrad continues to talk ironically and ambiguously about Marlow as if he were a real not a fictive person. Or rather he speaks of Marlow as a fictive person whose existence is nevertheless inseparable from that of Conrad himself in the sense that neither would "care" to survive the other:

> That is not so. I made no plans [to "capture" him]. The man Marlow and I came together in the casual manner of those health-resort acquaintances which sometimes ripen into friendships. This one has ripened. For all his assertiveness in matters of opinion he is not an intrusive person. He haunts my hours of solitude, when, in silence, we lay our heads together in great comfort and harmony; but as we part at the end of a tale I am never sure that it may not be for the last time. Yet I don't think that either of us would care much to survive the other. In his case, at any rate, his occupation would be gone and he would suffer from that extinction, because I suspect him of some vanity. (Ibid.)

By denying that he had made premeditated plans for Marlow's capture, Conrad means to deny, I assume, that Marlow was the product of a calculated literary artifice. He just appeared, spontaneously, like a ghostly double or like that "secret sharer" who appears on the protagonist's ship in "The Secret Sharer," subject of the next chapter of this book. Marlow appears to "haunt" Conrad's hours of solitude, that is, the hours he does his writing. They then "part at the end of a tale." A ghost, especially one's own specter, is both the same as oneself and yet different. This one has his own assertive opinions. These are not, Conrad implies, Conrad's own opinions, any more than Kurtz's opinions are the same as Marlow's. Just as Conrad is "haunted" by Marlow, so Marlow is haunted by Kurtz, who is spoken of repeatedly as a ghost. Marlow speaks of "the shade of Mr. Kurtz," "this initiated wraith from the back of Nowhere" (65–66), of Kurtz as an "apparition" (76), a "shadow" or "Shadow" (81, 82), "like a vapour exhaled by the earth" (82), again as a "shade" (85), as "an eloquent phantom" (94), as a "disinterred body" (64). A ghost does not, cannot, die. It returns, as a revenant, just as Marlow hears Kurtz's voice still whispering his last words when he visits the Intended back in Europe: "The dusk was repeating them in a persistent whisper all around us" (94).

Heart of Darkness is made of a chain of these ambiguous doublings and hauntings: of Marlow by Kurtz, of the primary narrator by Marlow, of Conrad by Marlow, of the Intended by the African woman who is presumably Kurtz's mistress, and of the reader by the whole series. The reader is haunted by the tale, made to feel a "faint uneasiness" by it just as the frame narrator is by Marlow's story (43). The reader pores over and over the text trying to come to terms with it so it can be dismissed and forgotten.

A second way *Heart of Darkness* presents itself as literature is in the elaborate tissue of figures and other rhetorical devices that make up, as one might put it, the texture of the text. The simplest and most obvious of these devices is the use of similes, signaled by "like" or "as." These similes displace things that are named by one or the other of the narrators. They assert that this (whatever it is) is like something else. This something else forms through recurrence a consistent subtext. This subtext functions as a counterpoint defining everything that can be seen as a veil hiding something more truthful or essential behind.

The first of many uses of the figure naming things veils that are lifted to reveal more veils behind comes when the frame narrator, describing the evening scene just before sunset, when the sky is "a benign immensity of unstained light" (N, 4), as it looks from the *Nellie* at anchor in the Thames estuary, says: "the very mist on the Essex marshes was *like* [my emphasis] a gauzy and radiant fabric, hung from the wooded rises inland, and draping the low shores in diaphanous folds" (18). Such recurrent figures establish a structure that is apocalyptic in the etymological sense of "unveiling," as well as in the sense of having to do with death, judgment, and other last things.

These similes, as they follow in a line punctuating the text at rhythmic intervals, are not casual or fortuitous. They form a system, a powerful undertext beneath the first-level descriptive language. They invite the reader to see whatever either of the narrators sees and names on the first level of narration as a veil or screen hiding something invisible or not yet visible behind it. When each veil is lifted, however, it uncovers only another veil, according to a paradox essential to the genre of the apocalypse. Apocalypse: the word means "unveiling" in Greek. If one had to name the genre to which *Heart of Darkness* belongs, the answer would be that it is a failed apocalypse, or, strictly speaking, since all apocalypses ultimately fail to lift the last veil, it is just that, a member of the genre apocalypse. The film modeled on *Heart of Darkness*, *Apocalypse Now*, was brilliantly and accurately named, except for that word "now." Apocalypse is never now. It is always to come, a thing of the future, both infinitely distant and immediately imminent.

In *Heart of Darkness* it is, to borrow Conrad's own words, as if each episode were "some sordid farce acted in front of a sinister back-cloth" (28). The novel is structured as a long series of episodes. Each appears with extreme vividness before the reader's imaginary vision, brought there by Conrad's remarkable descriptive power. It then vanishes, to be replaced by the next episode, as though a figured screen had been lifted to reveal yet another figured screen behind it. The darkness lies behind them all, like that "sinister back-cloth" Marlow names. The misty Essex shore in the opening frame episode is, in the passage already cited, "like a gauzy and radiant fabric" (18). The fog that obscures the shore just before Marlow's ship is attacked is said to have "lifted as a shutter lifts" and then to have come down again, "smoothly, as if sliding in greased grooves" (55). The change that comes over Kurtz's features just before he utters his judgment is "as though a veil had been rent" (86), in an explicit reference to the figure of apocalypse as unveiling, revelation, as well as to the rending of the Temple veil at the time of Christ's crucifixion.

Heart of Darkness is structured by this trope of successive revelations. These unveilings unveil not so much the truth behind as the act of unveiling itself, since no "bottom" to the series is reached, no ultimate revelation given. Each scene is in a sense just as close and just as far away from the unnamable "truth" behind it as any other. Marlow's journey in *Heart of Darkness* and that of the reader as he or she gets deeper and deeper into the book is a movement in place. The scene on the *Nellie* is replaced by the scenes in the offices of the trading company in the sepulchral city: the two old women in black at the entrance, knitting and knitting, like two Fates; the doctor who measures Marlow's head and says "the changes take place inside, you know" (26). These scenes give place to the sequence of brief episodes that makes up the central story, as Marlow makes his way deeper and deeper into the heart of darkness: the French ship firing pointlessly into the bush ("Pop, would go one of the six-inch guns; a small flame would dart and vanish, a little white smoke would disappear, a tiny projectile would give a feeble screech—and nothing happened. Nothing could happen" [29]); the dying "workers" in the grove of death; the starched and scented accountant, keeping perfect records in the midst of pointless confusion; the corpse with a bullet-hole in its forehead Marlow "absolutely stumble[s]"(35) upon during his two-hundred-mile trek to reach the beginning of inland navigation on the river, where he finds his ship has been wrecked; his encounter with the skeleton of his predecessor, who has been killed in an absurd dispute over two chickens; the storage shed at the Central Station that suddenly bursts into flames in the middle of the night; the macabre dance on the tinpot steamer's deck performed by Marlow and the chief mechanic to celebrate their expectation that rivets will come; the Eldorado Exploring Expedition, with its "absurd air of disorderly flight with the loot of innumerable outfit shops and provision stores," which vanishes "into the patient wilderness, that closed upon it as the sea closes over a diver" (46, 49); the finding of the book about seamanship, Towson's *Inquiry*, annotated in what Marlow takes to be cipher; the death of Marlow's African helmsman as the ship approaches Kurtz's station and is attacked from the shore; the encounter at the station with the Russian dressed like a harlequin; the appearance through Marlow's telescope of those "symbolic" heads on stakes; Marlow's rescue of Kurtz when the latter tries to crawl back to join the Africans he has commanded and bewitched, so that they worship him; the apparition on the shore of what the reader supposes is Kurtz's African mistress; Kurtz's death and summing up, "in a whisper at some image, at some vision—. . . 'The horror! The horror!' " (86); the echo or repetition of the African woman's gesture of raising her arms in the final episode of Marlow's encounter back in Europe with Kurtz's "Intended," when he tells his lie; the return in the final brief paragraph to the deck of the *Nellie* where Marlow has been telling his story and to the concluding vision of the Thames as a "tranquil waterway leading to the uttermost ends of the earth [that] flowed sombre under an overcast sky—seemed to lead into the heart of an immense darkness" (95).

You may say that of course any narrative consists of a sequence of episodes that give place to one another. *Heart of Darkness* is nothing special in doing that. The difference, however, is in the way the materials and personages of each episode vanish, never to return again except in Marlow's memory. A novel roughly contemporary with *Heart of Darkness*, Henry James's *The Wings of the Dove*, for example, consists of a series of episodes all right, but the same characters are returned to again and again in a slow rotation of encounters that advances the action. In *Heart of Darkness* each episode is like a separate sinister farce enacted before a black backcloth. The whole is like a sequence of dream visions, each with little connection to the ones before and after. Each vanishes for good, as though a veil had been lifted to reveal yet another such scene behind it that vanishes in its turn, in a rhythm of ironic undercutting and displacement that punctuates Marlow's journey. He journeys deeper and deeper toward the fulfillment of an implicit promise, the promise to make or find a final revelation or unveiling. That promise, it hardly needs saying, is never kept. It cannot be kept. Just why that is so and just what that nonfulfillment means remain to be seen.

A third distinctively literary feature of *Heart of Darkness* has already been named in passing. The novel is ironic through and through. The reader might wish this were not the case. We may deplore Conrad's radical irony, but there it is, an indubitable fact. *Heart of Darkness* is a masterwork of irony, as when the eloquent idealism of Kurtz's pamphlet on "The Suppression of Savage Customs" is undercut by the phrase scrawled at the bottom: "Exterminate all the brutes!" (66), or as when the dying Africans in the grove of death are called "helpers" in the great "work" of civilizing the continent (32). Marlow's narrative in particular is steeped in irony throughout. The problem is that it is impossible to be certain just how to take that irony. Irony is, as Hegel and Kierkegaard said, "infinite absolute negativity," or, as Friedrich Schlegel said, a "permanent parabasis," a continuous suspension of clearly identifiable meaning. It is a principle of unintelligibility, or, in Schlegel's word, *Unverständlichkeit*.[13] Irony is a constant local feature of Marlow's narrative style. He says one thing and means another, as when the Europeans at the Central Station engaged in the terrible work of imperialist conquest, the "merry dance of death and trade" (29), are said to be, in yet another simile, like "pilgrims": "They wandered here and there with their absurd long staves in their hands, like a lot of faithless pilgrims bewitched inside a rotten fence" (38).

This stylistic undercutting is mimed in that larger structure of the replacement of each episode by the next, so that each is undermined by the reader's knowledge that it is only a temporary appearance, not some ultimate goal of revelation attained. Each is certain to vanish and be replaced by the next scene to be enacted before that sinister backcloth.

A fourth ostentatious literary feature of *Heart of Darkness* is the use of recurrent prosopopoeias. The personification of the darkness (whatever *that* word means here) begins in the title, which gives the darkness a "heart." Prosopopoeia is the ascription of a name, a face, or a voice to the absent, the inanimate, or the dead. By a speech act, a performative utterance, prosopopoeia creates the fiction of a personality where in reality there is none. Or is there? Once the personifications are in place, it seems as if the personality had been there all along, waiting to be recognized by a name. All prosopopoeias are also catachreses. They move the verbal fiction of a personality over to name something unknown and unknowable. The "something" is, therefore, strictly speaking, unnamable in any literal language. It is something radically other than human personality: something absent, inanimate, or dead. It is no accident that so many traditional examples of catachresis are also personifications: "headland," "face of a mountain," "tongue of land," "table leg." The phrase "heart of darkness" is such a catachrestic prosopopoeia, to give it its barbarous-sounding Greek rhetorical name. We project our own bodies on the landscape and on surrounding artifacts. In *Heart of Darkness* the prosopopoeias are a chief means of naming by indirection what Conrad calls, in a misleading and inadequate metaphor, "the darkness," or, "the wilderness," or, most simply and perhaps most truthfully, "it."

More than a dozen explicit personifications of this "it" rhythmically punctuate *Heart of Darkness*, like a recurring leitmotif. The darkness is not really a person, but an "it," asexual or transsexual, impersonal, indifferent, though to Marlow it seems like a person. The wilderness surrounding the Central Station, says Marlow, "struck me as something great and invincible, like evil or truth, waiting patiently for the passing away of this fantastic invasion" (38). A little later Marlow says "the silence of the land went home to one's very heart—its mystery, its greatness, the amazing reality of its concealed life" (41). Of that silent, nocturnal wilderness Marlow asserts, "All this was great, expectant, mute, while the man [one of the agents at the station] jabbered about himself. I wondered whether the stillness on the face of the immensity looking at us two were meant as an appeal or as a menace. . . . Could we handle that dumb thing, or would it handle us? I felt how big, how confoundedly big, was that thing that couldn't talk and perhaps was deaf as well" (42). "It was the stillness of an implacable force brooding over an inscrutable intention. It looked at you with a vengeful aspect. . . . I felt often its mysterious stillness watching me at my monkey-tricks, just as it watches you fellows [his listeners on the *Nellie*] performing on your respective tightropes for—what is it? half a crown a tumble—" (49, 50). The wilderness destroys Kurtz by a kind of diabolical seduction: "The wilderness had patted him on the head, and, behold, it was like a ball—an ivory ball; it had caressed him, and—lo!—he had withered; it had taken him, loved him, embraced him, got into his veins, consumed his flesh, and sealed his soul to its own by the inconceivable ceremonies of some devilish initiation. He was its spoiled and pampered favourite" (64). The Africans at Kurtz's Inner Station vanish "without any perceptible movement of retreat, as if the forest that had ejected these beings so suddenly had drawn them in again as the breath is drawn in a long aspiration" (76).

This last citation indicates another and not unpredictable feature of the prosopopoeias in *Heart of Darkness*. The personification of the wilderness is matched by a corresponding transformation of the African people who intervene between Marlow and the "it." Just as, in Thomas Hardy's *The Return of the Native*, the extravagant personification of the nighttime heath that opens the novel leads to the assertion that Eustacia Vye, who rises from a mound on the heath to stand outlined in the darkness, is, so to speak, the personification of the personification, its exposure or visible embodiment, so, in *Heart of Darkness*, all the Africans Marlow meets are visible representatives and symbols of the "it." Though it may be racist for Marlow (who is not necessarily Conrad, the reader should remember) to see the Africans as an inscrutably "other," as simple "savages" or "primitives," when their culture is older than any European one and just as complex or sophisticated, if not more so, this otherness is stressed for the primary purpose of making the Africans visible embodiments and proofs that the "it," the darkness, is a person.

This personification of personification is an underlying feature of all Marlow's prosopopoeias, but it is made most explicit in the scene where the woman the reader may presume is Kurtz's African mistress appears on the shore:

> She was savage and superb, wild-eyed and magnificent; there was something ominous and stately in her deliberate progress. And in the hush that had fallen suddenly upon the whole sorrowful land, the immense wilderness, the colossal body of the fecund and mysterious life seemed to look at her, pensive, as though it had been looking at the image of its own tenebrous and passionate soul. . . . She stood looking at us without a stir, and like the wilderness itself, with an air of brooding over an inscrutable purpose. (77)

This passage, like the one describing the way the wilderness has seduced Kurtz, seems to indicate that this "it" is after all gendered. It is female, a colossal body of fecund and mysterious life. Since the wilderness is supposed to represent a mysterious knowledge, "like evil or truth," this personification does not jibe very well with the "sexist" assertions Marlow makes about the way women in general, for example Marlow's aunt or Kurtz's Intended, are "out of it," invincibly innocent and ignorant. At the least one would have to say that two contradictory sexist myths about women are ascribed to Marlow. One is the European male's tendency to personify the earth as a great mother, full of an immemorial, seductive wisdom. The other is the European male's tendency to condescend to women as innately incapable of seeing into things as well as men can.

Strong hints of homosexual or at least homosocial relations complicate the sexual politics of *Heart of Darkness*. Other critics have seen this in Conrad's work. Those businessmen gathered on the *Nellie* for a weekend away from any women are a splendid example of what Eve Sedgwick means by male homosociality. The pleasure yacht is suggestively, though of course also conventionally, given a familiar woman's name. Most of the doublings that organize the novel are of male by male, in that long chain I have identified. The most important of these is Marlow's infatuation with Kurtz, his extravagant fidelity to him, even beyond the grave. I have scrupulously in this chapter referred to the reader as "he or she." A moment's reflection, however, will show that men and women are unlikely to read the novel in just the same way or to feel just the same kind of obligation to account for it, to render it justice. Both genders will have that obligation, but each in a different way.

The final scene pits Marlow's intimacy with Kurtz against the Intended's. "Intimacy grows quickly out there," Marlow tells the Intended. "I knew him as well as it is possible for one man to know another" (92). A strong suggestion is made that Marlow is jealous of the Intended, as a man who loves another man is jealous of that man's heterosexual loves. Marcel Proust, however, who presumably knew about this, has Marcel in À *la recherche du temps perdu* claim that the Baron de Charlus was only jealous of his lovers' other male lovers, not at all of their heterosexual partners. In any case, to the other doublings I have listed would need to be added the way Marlow doubles the particolored Russian in his fascination with Kurtz. Again hints are given that Marlow envies the Russian his intimacy with Kurtz. He wants to have Kurtz all to himself, to be Kurtz's sole survivor, so to speak, the sole keeper of his memory. The only overt reference to homosexuality occurs in an interchange between Marlow and the Russian: "We talked of everything,' he [the Russian] said, quite transported at the recollection. 'I forgot there was such a thing as sleep. The night did not seem to last an hour. Everything! Everything! . . . Of love too.' 'Ah, he talked to you of love!' I said, much amused. 'It isn't what you think,' he cried, almost passionately. 'It was in general. He made me see things—things'" (71–72).

Conrad's invention of Marlow at once embodies, reveals, and ironically puts in question the complex system of Western imperialist and capitalist ideology. I mean "invention" here in both senses—as finding and as making up. Among the ingredients of this system are not just a certain "sexist" vision of women but also a strand of homosociality or even homosexuality. This was certainly an important feature of English society in Conrad's day. It has also been shown to be a feature of the imperialist enterprise generally, for example in the European presentation of non-European men as exotic, often even, in an obvious wish-fulfillment, as sexually perverse.

All four of the stylistic features I have identified—the use of fictional narrators, of recurrent tropes, of irony, and of personification—constitute a demand that *Heart of Darkness* be read as literature, as opposed to being taken as a straightforwardly mimetic or referential work that would allow the reader to hold Conrad himself directly responsible for what is said as though he were a journalist or a travel writer. Of course any of these features can be used in a nonliterary work, but taken all together as they are intertwined in *Heart of Darkness*, they invite the reader to declare, "This is literature."

In the name of what higher responsibility does Conrad justify all this "literary" indirection and ironic undercutting, all this suspending or redirecting of his novel's straightforwardly mimetic aspect? In the name of what higher obligation is everything that is referentially named in a pseudo-historical or mimetic way displaced by these ubiquitous rhetorical devices and made into a sign for something else? If *Heart of Darkness* is a literary work rather than history or autobiography, just what kind of literary work is it? Just what kind of apocalypse, if it is an apocalypse? What lies behind that veil? The frame narrator, in a passage often cited and commented on, gives the reader a precious clue to an answer to these questions, though it is left to the reader to make use of the clue in his or her reading:

> The yarns of seamen have a direct simplicity, the whole meaning of which lies within the shell of a cracked nut. But Marlow was not typical (if his propensity to spin yarns be excepted), and to him the meaning of an episode was not inside like a kernel but outside [the ms has "outside in the unseen"], enveloping the tale which brought it out only as a glow brings out a haze, in the likeness of one of those misty halos that sometimes are made visible by the spectral illumination of moonshine. (20)

"To spin yarns" is a cliché for narration. To tell a story is to join many threads together to make a continuous line leading from here to there. Of that yarn cloth may be woven, the whole cloth of the truth as opposed to a lie that, as the proverbial saying has it, is "made up out of whole cloth." The lie as cloth makes a web, screen, or veil covering a truth that remains hidden behind or within. This inside/outside opposition governs the narrator's distinction between two kinds of tales. On the one hand, the first kind is the sort of seaman's yarn it has been assumed by many reader's and critics Conrad was telling in his stories and novels. The meaning of such a tale lies within, like the kernel within the shell of a cracked nut. I take it this names a realistic, mimetic, referential tale with an obvious point and moral. Marlow's tales, on the other hand, and by implication this one by Conrad, since so much of it is made up of Marlow's narration, have a different way of making meaning. All the visible, representational elements, all that the tale makes you *see*, according to that famous claim by Conrad in the preface to *The Nigger of the "Narcissus"*, that his goal was "before all, to make you *see*,"[14] are there not for their own sakes, as mimetically valuable and verifiable, for example for the sake of giving the reader information about imperialism in the Belgian Congo. Those elements have as their function to make something else visible, what the manuscript calls the "unseen,"[15] perhaps even the unseeable, as the dark matter of the universe or the putative black holes at the center of galaxies can in principle never be seen, only inferred.

Conrad's figure is a different one from those black holes about which he could not have known, though his trope is still astronomical. It is an example of that peculiar sort of figure that can be called a figure of figure or a figure of figuration. Just as the mist on a dark night is invisible except when it is made visible as a circular halo around moonlight, light already secondary and reflected from the sun, and just as the mimetic elements of Marlow's tale are secondary to the putatively real things they represent at one remove, so the meaning of Marlow's yarns is invisible in itself and is never named directly. It is not inside the tale but outside. It is "brought out" indirectly by the things that *are* named and recounted, thereby made visible, just as, for example, Marlow when he visits the Intended hears Kurtz's last words breathed in a whisper by the dusk: "The dusk was repeating them in a persistent whisper all around us, in a whisper that seemed to swell menacingly like the first whisper of a rising wind. 'The horror! The horror!'" (94). The reader will note the way the whispered sound is onomatopoetically echoed here in the repetition three times of the word "whisper," with its aspirant and sibilant "whuh" and "isp" sounds. The illumination provided by the tale is "spectral," like a liminal, ghostly sound. It turns everything into a phantom, that is, into something that has come back from the dead, something that cannot die, something that will always, sooner or later, just when we least expect it, come again.

The miniature lesson in aesthetic theory the frame narrator presents here is an admirably succinct expression of the distinction between mimetic literature and apocalyptic, parabolic, or allegorical literature. In the latter, everything named, with however much verisimilitude, stands for something else that is not named directly, that cannot be named directly. It can only be inferred by those that have eyes to see and ears to hear and understand, as Jesus puts it in explaining the parable of the sower in Matthew 13. All these genres have to do with promising, with death, with the truly secret, and with last things, "things," as Jesus says, "which have been kept secret from the foundation of the world" (Matt. 13:35).

It is not so absurd as it might seem to claim that *Heart of Darkness* is a secular version of what are, originally at least, intertwined religious or sacred genres: apocalypse, parable, and allegory. Conrad himself spoke of the "piety" of his approach to writing and of his motive as quasi-religious. "One thing that I am certain of," he wrote in that letter to Symons already quoted, "is that I have approached the object of my task, things human, in a spirit of piety. The earth is a temple where there is going on a mystery play childish and poignant, ridiculous and awful enough in all conscience. Once in I've tried to behave decently. I have not degraded the quasi religious sentiment by tears and groans: and if I've been amused and indifferent, I've neither grinned nor gnashed my teeth" (N, 154).

In the case of *Heart of Darkness*, just what is that "something else" for the revelation of which the whole story is written? The clear answer is that the something else is the "it" that Marlow's narration so persistently personifies and that Kurtz passes judgment on when he says "The horror!" All details in the story, all the mimetic and verisimilar elements, are presented for the sake of bringing out a glimpse of that "it." The revelation of this "it" is promised by the frame narrator when he defines the characteristic indirection of meaning in Marlow's yarns. Many critics of *Heart of Darkness* have made the fundamental mistake of taking the story as an example of the first kind of seaman's yarn. Those critics, like F. R. Leavis, who have noticed all the language about the unspeakable and "inscrutable" "it" have almost universally condemned it as so much moonshine interfering with Conrad's gift for making you *see* the material world, his gift for descriptive vividness and verisimilitude. At least such critics have taken the trouble to read carefully and have noticed that there are important verbal elements in the text that must be accounted for somehow and that do not fit the straightforward mimetic, descriptive paradigm.

Is the "something," the "it," ever revealed, ever brought into the open where it may be seen and judged? The clear answer is that it is not. The "it" remains to the end unnamable, inscrutable, unspeakable. The "it" is Conrad's particular version, in *Heart of Darkness* at least, of those "others" that are the subject of this book. The "it" is falsely, or at any rate unprovably, personified by Marlow's rhetoric as having consciousness and intention. It is named only indirectly and inadequately by all those similes and figures of veils being lifted. How could something be revealed that can only be encountered directly by those who have crossed over the threshold of death? The reader is told that "it" is "The horror!" but just what that means is never explained except in hints and indirections. Nothing definite can be said of the "it" except that it is not nothing, that it *is*, though even that is not certain, since it may be a projection, not a solicitation, call, or demand from something wholly other. Of the "it" one must say what Wallace Stevens says of the "primitive like an orb," "at the center on the horizon": "It is and it/Is not and, therefore, is."[16] If "it" is wholly other it is wholly other. Nothing more can be said of it except by signs that confess in their proffering to their inadequacy. Each veil lifts to reveal another veil behind.

The structure of *Heart of Darkness* is a self-perpetuating system of an endlessly deferred promise. This is the implicit promise that Marlow makes at the beginning of his tale when he says that though his meeting with Kurtz, "the farthest point of navigation and the culminating point of my experience," was "not very clear," nevertheless "it seemed to throw a kind of light" (7). This illumination he implicitly promises to pass on to his hearers. The primary narrator passes it on to us, the readers. The fulfillment of this promise to reveal, however, remains always future, something yet to come, eschatological or messianic rather than teleological. It is an end that can never come within the series of episodes that reaches out toward it as life reaches toward death. In this *Heart of Darkness* works in a deferral analogous to the way *Revelations* promises an imminent messianic coming that always remains future, to come, beyond the last in the series, across the threshold into another realm and another regime. It is in the name of this unrevealed and unrevealable secret, out of obligation to it, in response to the demand it makes, though it still remains secret and inaccessible, that all *Heart of Darkness* is written. The presence within the novel of an inaccessible secret, a secret that nevertheless incites to narration, is what makes it appropriate to speak of *Heart of Darkness* as literature.

The place where this ultimate failure of revelation is made most explicit is Marlow's comment on the difference between Kurtz, who summed up at the moment of his death, giving words to "the appalling face of a glimpsed truth" (87), and Marlow's own illness that took him to the brink of death and then back into life again, therefore not quite far enough to see what Kurtz saw:

> And it is not my own extremity I remember best—a vision of greyness without form filled with physical pain, and a careless contempt for the evanescence of all things—even of this pain itself. No! It is his extremity that I seemed to have lived through. True, he had made that last stride, he had stepped over the edge, while I had been permitted to draw back my hesitating foot. And perhaps in this is the whole difference; perhaps all the wisdom, and all truth, and all sincerity, are just compressed into that inappreciable moment of time in which we step over the threshold of the invisible. Perhaps! (87–88)

How would one know without crossing that bourne from which no traveler returns? You cannot "live through" another's death. The other must die his or her own death; you must die yours—both in incommunicable solitude. To "know" you must die first. If you know, you are, necessarily, no longer around to tell the tale. Even knowing this remains, necessarily, a matter of "perhaps." It is, nevertheless, in the name of this nonrevelation, this indirect glimpse, as the moon spectrally illuminates a ring of mist, that Marlow's judgment of imperialism is made. The "it" is the sinister backcloth before which all the seriocomic antics of those carrying on the merry dance of death and trade, including their racism and sexism, are ironically suspended, made to appear both horrible and futile at once. The ubiquity of the "it" allows Marlow to imply the identity between the African woman and Kurtz's Intended that is so crucial to the story. This ubiquity also allows him to assert an all-important identity between the early Roman conquerors of Britain, present-day British commerce as represented by the Director of Companies, the Lawyer, and the Accountant, and the enterprise of imperialism in Africa. Of the El-dorado Exploring Expedition, Marlow says, "To tear treasure out of the bowels of the land was their desire, with no more moral purpose at the back of it than there is in burglars breaking into a safe" (46). Something similar, however, is said about the Romans near the beginning of Mar-low's narration. It is said in a way that gives it universal application: "The conquest of the earth, which mostly means the taking it away from those who have a different complexion or slightly flatter noses than ourselves, is not a pretty thing when you look into it too much" (21). *Heart of Darkness* looks into it. Early readers saw the novel as an unequivocal condemnation of Leopold II and of Belgian imperialism in the Congo. I note in passing that now (2000), when a new regime has taken over in the Congo, transnational companies are fighting for the rights to exploit min-eral deposits there, for example copper. This new global economy is not all that different from the imperialism of Conrad's day. Of course the novel represents, in Marlow, Eurocentric views. It was written by a Euro-pean with the apparent intent of evaluating such views by embodying them in a narrator. Of course it represents sexist views. It was written to dramatize what might be said by an imaginary character, Marlow, a white male of Conrad's class and time, just as Conrad's critics today rep-resent their times, races, sexes, and nations, however superior, more just, their judgments may be. I claim, however, that by being displaced into Marlow as narrator and by being measured against the "it," these Euro-centric views are radically criticized and shown as what they are, that is, as elements in a deadly and unjust ideology.

What of Kurtz, however? Is he not different from the other agents of imperialism? The latter are possessed by "a flabby, pretending, weak-eyed devil of a rapacious and pitiless folly" (31). They have no insight into the way they are victims of the imperialist ideology as well as victim-izers of those it exploits. Kurtz, on the other hand, "was a remarkable man," as Marlow himself repeatedly asserts, in a phrase he picks up from one of the agents. Kurtz was a kind of universal genius: a painter, a musi-cian, a poet (he recites his own poetry to the Russian), spectacularly suc-cessful in getting ivory, an extremely gifted journalist, a brilliantly power-ful speaker, a forceful writer, the author of a stirring pamphlet, his report to "the International Society for the Suppression of Savage Customs": " 'By the simple exercise of our will we can exert a power for good practi-cally unbounded,' etc. etc. From that point he soared and took me with him. The peroration was magnificent, though difficult to remember, you know. It gave me the notion of an exotic Immensity ruled by an august Benevolence. It made me tingle with enthusiasm. This was the unbounded power of eloquence—of words—of burning noble words" (66). Kurtz was potentially a great politician, as the journalist Marlow meets back in Europe after Kurtz's death assures him: "'but Heavens! how that man could talk! He electrified large meetings. He had faith—don't you see—he had the faith. He could get himself to believe anything—anything. He would have been a splendid leader of an extreme party. 'What party?' I asked. 'Any party,' answered the other. 'He was an—an—extremist'" (89). The famous scrawled note at the end of the pamphlet's manuscript, "Exterminate all the brutes!" (66), says with brutal candor the truth, that the suppression of savage customs culminates in the suppression of the "savages" themselves. That footnote scrawled "in an unsteady hand" testifies to Kurtz's remarkable understanding of the imperialist, philanthropic, and missionary enterprise.

Just what goes wrong with Kurtz? His case is obviously of greater interest than that of any of the others Marlow meets or even than that of Marlow himself. The latter has survived and speaks as a sane man, "one of us," in the voice of ironic, European, enlightened rationality. Or rather he could be said to speak in that voice except for his fascination with Kurtz and with that "it" that solicits him to speech. What he says of the Russian's infatuation with Kurtz could be said of his own fascination: "He had not meditated over it. It came to him, and he accepted it with a sort of eager fatalism. I must say that to me it appeared about the most dangerous thing in every way he had come upon so far" (71). Marlow gives the reader his diagnosis of Kurtz's "madness." Speaking of those heads on stakes, Marlow says:

> there was nothing exactly profitable in these heads being there. They only showed that Mr. Kurtz lacked restraint in the gratification of his various lusts, that there was something wanting in him—some small matter which, when the pressing need arose, could not be found under his magnificent eloquence. Whether he knew of this deficiency himself I can't say. I think the knowledge came to him at last—only at the very last! [The ms originally added here: If so, then justice was done.] But the wilderness had found him out early, and had taken on him a terrible vengeance for the fantastic invasion. I think that it whispered to him things about himself which he did not know, things of which he had no conception till he took counsel with this great solitude—and the whisper had proved irresistibly fascinating. It echoed loudly within him because he was hollow at the core. (58–59)

On the one hand, the story of Kurtz's degradation is an example of the familiar narrative cliché of the European who "goes native." Kurtz, like Lingard in *The Rescue*, like Lord Jim in *Lord Jim*, and like Charles Gould in *Nostromo*, crosses over a border and ceases to be wholly European. Kurtz sets himself up as a sort of king in the alien land, thereby anticipating the destiny of most colonies to become ultimately independent nations. In doing so, they thereby betray in one way or another the ideals, the ethos, the laws and conventions of the colonizing country. The United States did that in 1776. The somewhat hysterical fear that this will happen, or that it will necessarily be a disaster if it does happen, has haunted the colonial enterprise from the beginning. On the other hand, Kurtz never completely makes that break. After all, he allows Marlow to rescue him when he has crawled back ashore in his attempt to join the Africans who have become his subjects. He dies oriented toward Europe and toward the desire that he will "have kings meet him at railway stations on his return from some ghastly Nowhere, where he intended to accomplish great things" (85).

What goes wrong with Kurtz? How might he, or another person, Marlow for example, protect himself from the corrupting whisper of the wilderness? Just here Marlow's rhetoric, or Conrad's rhetoric as ascribed to Marlow, is contradictory. It is contradictory in an interesting and symptomatic way. Marlow names several different ways to protect oneself from the threat of counterinvasion by the "it" that has entered Kurtz because he is "hollow at the core" (74).

One way is blind insensitivity: "Of course a fool, what with sheer fright and fine sentiments, is always safe" (52). That includes most of the "pilgrims," the agents of imperialism.

Another way to protect oneself from the darkness is through devotion to hard but routine physical or mental work, what Conrad calls "the devotion to efficiency" (21). This he identifies as a fundamental feature of the capitalist and imperialist ethos. Indeed it still is a feature of our ideology in the United States. The stated mission of the University of California, for example, is to "help make California competitive in the global economy." University "downsizing" for efficiency's sake matches corporate downsizing for profit's sake. The starched and scented accountant in *Heart of Darkness* is protected by his fanatical devotion to keeping his books accurate and neat. Marlow, so he tells the reader, is saved from succumbing to the darkness through his focus on getting his wrecked steamer back in working order and then getting it safely up the river: "Fine sentiments be hanged. I had no time. I had to mess about with white-lead and strips of woollen blanket helping to put bandages on those leaky steam-pipes—I tell you. I had to watch the steering, and circumvent those snags, and get the tin-pot along by hook or by crook. There was surface-truth enough in these things to save a wiser man" (52).

The third way to protect oneself seems clear enough. It turns out, however, to be the most equivocal. This is indicated by changes and omissions in the manuscript. Just after saying "the conquest of the earth . . . is not a pretty thing when you look into it too much," Marlow goes on to add:

"What redeems it is the idea only. An idea at the back of it; not a senti-mental [ms: mouthing] pretence but an idea; and an unselfish belief in the idea—something you can set up, and bow down before, and offer a sacri-fice to" (21). The ironic religious language at the end here sounds a little ominous. More or less the same thing, however, with much less evident irony is asserted much later in the story when Marlow is talking about the appeal made to him by the dancing, shouting Africans on the shore: "Let the fool gape and shudder—the man knows, and can look on without a wink. But he must meet that truth [the truth of the "prehistoric" men's dancing that is closer to the origin of mankind: certainly a familiar racist cliché there, since modern African cultures are no closer to the origins of mankind than modern European ones are] with his own true stuff—with his own inborn strength. Principles? Principles won't do. Acquisitions, clothes, pretty rags—rags that would fly off at the first good shake. No; you want a deliberate belief. An appeal to me in this fiendish row—is there? Very well; I hear; I admit, but I have a voice too, and for good or evil mine is the speech that cannot be silenced" (52).

The contradiction here is a double one. In an excised passage from the early place where, apropos of the Roman invasion of Britain, Marlow says the idea redeems it, he says that he admires the Roman conquerors just because they did not have any redeeming idea but were just robbers and murderers on a grand scale: "The best of them is they didn't get up pretty fictions about it. Was there, I wonder, an association on a philan-thropic basis to develop Britain, with some third rate king for a president and solemn old senators discoursing about it approvingly and philoso-phers with uncombed beards praising it, and men in market places crying it up. Not much! And that's what I like!" (from the ms, cited N, 7). No doubt this was cut in part because it was too overt an attack on King Leopold, but it is also in direct contradiction to Marlow's claim a mo-ment later in the published version, just after where the cut passage would have gone, that "what redeems it [imperialism whether Roman or mod-ern] is the idea only. An idea at the back of it; . . . and an unselfish belief in the idea" (21).

The other contradiction, however, lies in that phrase "deliberate be-lief" and in the way Kurtz is defined as an adept at deliberate belief: "He could get himself to believe anything—anything" (89). A deliberate be-lief is a contradiction in terms, an oxymoron. You either believe or do not believe. A deliberate belief is a pretense to believe even though you know the belief is a fictional confidence in something that does not exist or that you do not really believe exists, in this case a solid base for the philanthropic ideals that justify imperialism. To say "I declare I believe so and so" or "I will myself deliberately to believe so and so" is a paradig-matic speech act of a kind not envisioned by Austin. It is an anomalous performative, in the strong sense of anomalous: outside the law. This sort of performative creates its own ground out of whole cloth. It lifts itself by its own bootstraps. A deliberate belief, praised so unreservedly here by Marlow, is, however, what makes Kurtz hollow at the core and so vulnerable to invasion by the "wilderness." You must believe and not believe. Such a belief undoes itself in the act of affirming itself. It is hollow at the core. Belief in what? In the capitalist idea, but in that idea as promise, as the promise of an ultimate messianic revelation and an ultimate millennial reign of peace and prosperity for the whole world. This is that "exotic Immensity ruled by an august Benevolence" that Kurtz's pamphlet promises is to come. This promise is still being made today on behalf of the new global economy and the new universal regime of scientifico-bio-techno-tele-mediatic communications.

The reader will perhaps have foreseen the conclusion toward which my evidence is drawing me. The complex contradictory system of Kurtz's imperialist ideology matches exactly the ideology that proposes a literary work as the apocalyptic promise of a never-quite-yet-occurring revelation. It would not be a promise if it were not possible that the promise might not be kept. The literary promise of an always postponed revelation is strikingly exemplified not only by Marlow's narration but also by *Heart of Darkness* as a whole. Conrad's novel, not just Marlow's fictive account, fits this paradigm. The novel is made up of a chain of spectral duplications that is reinforced by formal and figural features I have described.

Just how does Kurtz's ideology repeat that of Marlow and of Conrad? The literary work, for example *Heart of Darkness* or Marlow's narration within it, is governed by what Derrida calls "the exemplary secret of literature,"[17] This secret makes it possible for the work to be the endlessly deferred promise of a definitive revelation that never occurs. This pattern is not only literary but also linguistic. It depends on the way a work of literature is made of language and not of any other material or substance. Marlow stresses over and over that though Kurtz was a universal genius, an artist, musician, journalist, politician, and so on, his chief characteristic was his gift of language: "A voice! a voice! It was grave, profound, vibrating, while the man did not seem capable of a whisper. . . . Kurtz discoursed. A voice! a voice! It rang deep to the very last. It survived his strength to hide in the magnificent folds of eloquence the barren darkness of his heart" (77, 85). Kurtz, in short (a pun there on Kurtz's name, which means "short" in German; Marlow makes a similar joke [76]), has a magnificent mastery of language that is similar to Marlow's own, or to Conrad's. "An appeal to me in this fiendish row—is there? Very well; I hear;

I admit, but I have a voice too, and for good or evil mine is the speech that cannot be silenced" (52).

What does Kurtz talk or write about? The reader is told of the lofty idealism of the pamphlet on the Suppression of Savage Customs. Kurtz has bewitched the particolored Russian, as Marlow ironically attests, by "splendid monologues on, what was it? on love, justice, conduct of life— or what not" (75). Most of all, however, Kurtz's discourse is dominated by unfulfilled and perhaps unfulfillable promises made to the whole world on behalf of Eurocentric imperialist capitalism and in support of his role own as its embodiment: "All Europe contributed to the making of Kurtz" (66). Kurtz is like a John the Baptist announcing the new capitalist messiah, or perhaps is himself that self-proclaimed messiah. That his betrothed is called "the Intended" is the emblem of this future-oriented, proleptic feature of Kurtz's eloquence. "I had immense plans," he "mutters," when Marlow is trying to persuade him come back to the boat. "I was on the threshold of great things" (82). Later, as he lies dying on the ship that is taking him back toward Europe, his "discourse" is all future-oriented, all promises of great things to come: "The wastes of his weary brain were haunted by shadowy images now—images of wealth and fame revolving obsequiously round his unextinguishable gift of noble and lofty expression. My Intended, my station, my career, my ideas—these were the subjects for the occasional utterances of elevated sentiments" (85).

The fulfillment of these promises is cut short by a death that seals a secret or "mystery" that Kurtz carries with him to the grave. This secret is the necessary accompaniment of his grandiose promises. In being inhabited by this mystery, Kurtz is the embodiment not just of European capitalist imperialism's ideology but also of its dark shadow, a ghost that cannot be laid, the "it" that is the inevitable accompaniment of imperialism. Marlow identifies this "it," in figure, both with Kurtz and with the "wilderness" that has invaded his soul. Since Kurtz embodies the darkness, when it has invaded his hollowness, it is logical that he himself should become the "god" that the Africans worship and crawl before. This strikingly anticipates the fascist or violent authoritarian possibilities within capitalist imperialism. Kurtz's soul, like the "it," is "an inconceivable mystery" (83). He has "a smile of indefinable meaning" (84). "His was an impenetrable darkness" (86). Marlow's allegiance to Kurtz and through Kurtz to the wilderness makes him feel as if he too were "buried in a vast grave full of unspeakable secrets" (79), just as the African woman matches the wilderness in having "an air of brooding over an inscrutable purpose" (77). The forest has an "air of hidden knowledge, of patient expectation, of unapproachable silence" (72). It was "the stillness of an implacable force brooding over an inscrutable intention" (49).

These words—"unspeakable," "inscrutable," "unapproachable"—must be taken literally. Kurtz in his actions and words is no more able to remove the last veil in an ultimate revelation than Marlow or Conrad can in their narrations. In all three cases a promise is made whose fulfillment or definitive nonfulfillment always remains yet to come.

What can one say to explain this contradiction: that Kurtz's magnificent idealistic eloquence is at the same time inhabited by an impenetrable darkness? Both Marlow's narration and Kurtz's eloquence, since both are based on that special speech act called a promise, are subject to two ineluctable features of any promise: (1) A promise would not be a promise but rather a constative statement of foreknowledge if it were not possible that the promise will not be kept. A possible nonfulfillment is an inalienable structural feature of any promise, whether made in literature or in politics. (2) Any promise is an invocation of an unknown and unknowable future, of a secret other that remains secret and is invited to come into the hollow uncertainty of the promise.

In the case of Marlow's narration, which I claim is an exemplary literary work, what enters the narration is all that talk of the inscrutable, the impenetrable mystery, the unspeakable secret, and so on, that has so offended some of Conrad's readers. In Kurtz's case the millennial promise made by imperialist capitalism, since it is hollow at the core, cannot be separated from the possibility, or perhaps even the necessity, of invasion by the "it," what Conrad calls the "heart of darkness." Kurtz's case is exemplary of that. It is a parable or allegory of this necessity. No imperialist capitalism without the darkness. They go together. Nor has that spectral accompaniment of capitalism's millennial promise of worldwide peace, prosperity, and universal democracy by any means disappeared today. Today the imperialist exploitation of Conrad's day and its accompanying philanthropic idealism have been replaced, as I have said, by the utopian promises made for the new global economy and the new regime of telecommunications, but injustice, inequality, poverty, and bloody ethnic conflicts continue all over the world.

As Jacques Derrida and Werner Hamacher have recognized, the political left and the political right are consonant in the promises they make. The promise of universal prosperity made for the new economy dominated by science and transformative communications techniques echoes the messianic promise, a messianism without messiah, of classical Marxism. It also echoes the promises made by right-wing ideologies, even the most unspeakably brutal, for example the Nazi promise of a thousand-year Reich. We are inundated, swamped, and engulfed every day by the present form of those promises—in newspapers and magazines, on television, in advertising, on the Internet, in political and policy pronouncements. All these promise that everything will get bigger, faster, better, more "user-friendly," and lead to worldwide prosperity. These promises are all made by language or other signs, "the gift of expression, the bewildering, the illuminating, the most exalted and the most contemptible, the pulsating stream of light, or the deceitful flow from the heart of an impenetrable darkness" (63).

I return to my beginning. Should we, ought we to, read *Heart of Darkness*? Each reader must decide that for himself or herself. There are certainly ways to read *Heart of Darkness* that might do harm. If it is read, however, as I believe it should be read, that is, as a powerful exemplary revelation of the ideology of capitalist imperialism, including its racism and sexism, as that ideology is consonant with a certain definition of literature that is its concomitant, including the presence in both capitalism and literature of a nonrevelatory revelation or the invocation of a nonrevealable secret, then, I declare, *Heart of Darkness* should be read. It ought to be read. There is an obligation to do so.

NOTES

1. Paul Celan, "Aschenglorie (Ashglory)," in *Breathturn*, trans. Pierre Joris, bilingual ed. (Los Angeles: Sun & Moon Press, 1995), 178–79.

2. The "original" (but what is more problematic than this concept of an original base for a fictional work?) of the framing scene was, if Ford Madox Ford is to be believed, Conrad's residence in Stamford-le-Hope in Essex from September 1896 to September 1898. There he knew various businessmen who did indeed take weekend cruises on a yawl. "[H]e was still quivering," says Ford, "with his attempt, with the aid of the Director, the Lawyer, and the Accountant, to float a diamond mine in South Africa. For Conrad had his adventures of that sort, too— adventures ending naturally in frustration. . . . while waiting for that financial flotation to mature, he floated physically during week-ends in the company of those financiers on the bosom of that tranquil waterway [the Thames]" (Joseph Conrad, *Heart of Darkness: An Authoritative Text; Backgrounds and Sources; Essays in Criticism*, ed. Robert Kimbrough, Norton critical ed. [New York: Norton, 1963], 127, henceforth cited as N). "To float a diamond mine in South Africa"! Nothing is said about this in the story itself, and Marlow, the reader must always remember, must be kept strictly separate from Conrad himself, as separate as the narrator of "The Secret Sharer" must be kept from his ghostly double. Ford's testimony, however, shows that Conrad himself was complicit, or wanted to be complicit, if he could have raised the money for it, in an exploitative imperialist enterprise that is not so different from Leopold II's merciless and murderous exploitation of the Congo or from Kurtz's raiding the country for ivory. He appears momentarily to have fancied himself a miniature Cecil Rhodes.

3. Joseph Conrad, *Heart of Darkness*, ed. Ross C. Murfin, Bedford Case Studies, 2d ed. (Boston: Bedford Books of St. Martin's Press, 1966), 22, henceforth cited by page number in the text. I have cited this edition because it is easily available and contains other useful material. It reprints *Heart of Darkness* from

the 1921 Heinemann edition of Conrad's *Collected Works*, the last version of the text that had Conrad's approval.

4. The original manuscript is in the Beinecke Library at Yale University. The Norton Critical Edition cites some important manuscript passages omitted from the printed version. I shall cite from the Norton edition a few of these in my turn, trusting the Norton editor to have cited accurately.

5. J. L. Austin, *How to Do Things with Words*, ed. J. O. Urmson and Marina Sbisà, 2d ed. (Oxford: Oxford University Press, 1980).

6. See Werner Hamacher, "Lingua Amissa: The Messianism of Commodity-Language and Derrida's *Specters of Marx*," in *Ghostly Demarcations: A Symposium on Jacques Derrida's "Specters of Marx,"* ed. Michael Sprinker (London: Verso, 1998), 189–91; Jacques Derrida, *Spectres de Marx* (Paris: Galilée, 1993), 89; *Specters of Marx*, trans. Peggy Kamuf (New York: Routledge, 1994), 51. Derrida speaks here of "performative interpretation, that is, of an interpretation that transforms the very thing it interprets," and he observes that this definition of the performative does not fit Austin's definition of a speech act, any more than it fits the orthodox understanding of Marx's eleventh thesis on Feuerbach.

7. These citations are from the "Critical History" section in Conrad, *Heart of Darkness*, ed. Murfin, 107, 109.

8. Edward Said, *Culture and Imperialism* (New York: Vintage Books, 1994), 30.

9. Thomas Mann, "Death in Venice," in *Death in Venice and Seven Other Stories* (New York: Vintage, 1956), 13.

10. See Jacques Derrida, *Acts of Literature*, ed. Derek Attridge (New York: Routledge, 1992), 44: "'Transcend' here means going beyond interest for the signifier, the form, the language (note that I do not say 'text') in the direction of the meaning or referent (this is Sartre's rather simple but convenient definition of prose)."

11. See ibid., 37–38.

12. Jean-Jacques Rousseau, *La nouvelle Héloïse, Oeuvres complètes*, ed. Bernard Gagnebin and Marcel Raymond, Pléiade ed., 4 vols. (Paris: Gallimard, 1964), 2:27–29.

13. I discussed Schlegelian irony in detail in chapter 1.

14. Joseph Conrad, *The Nigger of the "Narcissus"* (London: Penguin, 1989), xlix: "My task which I am trying to achieve is, by the power of the written word, to make you hear, to make you feel—it is, before all, to make you *see*."

15. Chapter 8 will show the importance of the word "unseen" in E. M. Forster's *Howards End*.

16. Wallace Stevens, "A Primitive Like an Orb," in *The Collected Poems* (New York: Knopf, 1954), 440–43, ll. 87, 13–14.

17. Jacques Derrida, "Passions," trans. David Wood, in *On the Name*, ed. Thomas Dutoit (Stanford: Stanford University Press, 1995), 29.

Chapter Six

CONRAD'S SECRET

The moment of decision is a madness.
—Kierkegaard

IN A STATEMENT already quoted in chapter 5, Conrad said, "My task which I am trying to achieve is, by the power of the written word, to make you hear, to make you feel—it is, before all, to make you *see*."[1] What most immediately strikes the reader of "The Secret Sharer" is Conrad's extraordinary descriptive power. Conrad excels in what might be called a force not so much of representation as of presentation. He can use words to make things present. From the opening depiction of the Gulf of Siam as seen from a ship anchored at sunset off the mouth of the Meinam River all the way through to the climactic account of the ship's agonizingly slow reversal of direction just before it goes aground on Koh-ring Island, the reader is almost made to feel that he or she has been there and has had these experiences. The fact that the topographical names are of real places reinforces this verisimilitude.

This representational vividness is not limited to the outward appearances of sea, sky, and the details of seafaring. Conrad succeeds also in making the reader feel as if he or she had been, so to speak, inside the narrator's skin and had experienced all his subjective feelings as well as seen what he saw. The reader becomes the sharer of the narrator's secret feelings, just as the narrator says he was able to put himself inside Leggatt's feelings and thoughts when he told how he killed an insolent seaman: "I did not think of asking him for details, and he told me the story roughly in brusque, disconnected sentences. I needed no more. I saw it all going on as though I were myself inside the other sleeping suit."[2]

"To make you *see*," as you can see, has a double meaning. It can refer to physical seeing or to seeing in the sense of having an intimate understanding, as when someone says, "Now I see." Seeing names not just detached, external vision. It also names a penetrating vision that gets inside what might be thought of as impenetrably hidden within the other person. Narration as the sharing of secrets—that might be an alternative way to express what Conrad means by saying he wants "to make you see." If Leggatt shares his secret with the narrator, the narrator shares the secret again, along with his own secrets, at least some of them, with the reader. This happens, in the case of the narrator's understanding of Leggatt, to a considerable degree by a wordless telepathy that has its uncanny side. The reader in turn is asked to understand things that, as in most works of fiction, are only implied, not fully spelled out. We are invited to have the kind of telepathic understanding of the narrator that the narrator has of Leggatt.

Just what it might mean to share a secret or what kind of secret it is that can be shared remains to be seen. It would seem that to keep a secret secret it would need to be kept jealously secret. An "open secret" is not really a secret, as the ironic oxymoron of the phrase implies. Nevertheless, "The Secret Sharer" depends on the assumption that some secrets can be shared without ceasing to be secret.

The story suggests, moreover, that such sharing is more than the imparting of knowledge. It also lays on the one who receives the secret an obligation, a responsibility to judge, to decide, to act. The narrator of "The Secret Sharer," for example, must decide whether to hide the fugitive Leggatt or to turn him over to the law as embodied in the captain of the *Sephora*, Leggatt's ship.[3] Moreover, he must do this instantaneously, precipitously, as is often the case with ethical decision. He does not have time to think it all out and weigh the pros and cons. Once he has decided and has hidden Leggatt in his cabin, he cannot go back on his decision, since to do so would be to admit his own guilt, his complicity in Leggatt's crime.[4] Even if he had infinite leisure to think over what he should do, his final decision would be precipitate, an interruption, irruptive, since a just ethical decision can never be clearly made on the basis of preexisting rules or laws. It is a leap in the dark, always at least implicitly violent, like Leggatt's murderous attack on the mutinous seaman, or like his spontaneous decision to leap into the water off the deck of the *Sephora*: "Then a sudden temptation came over me. I kicked off my slippers and was in the water before I had made up my mind fairly (36)."[5] Or it is like the narrator's decision to hide Leggatt. We must, therefore, pass judgment not only on Leggatt but also on the narrator. Did he do right or wrong in hiding the fugitive murderer Leggatt? On what basis did he make that decision? On what basis should we judge him?

What should *we* do, if anything, when we have read "The Secret Sharer"? Reading the story is a little like having our privacy intruded on in the same way as Leggatt suddenly and unexpectedly enters the narrator's life. It puts on us an obligation to act in some way, but act how? What should we do? Or, rather, what should *I* do, since the act of reading is a personal, individual, and secret event. Others can see that I hold the book in my hands and am running my eyes from line to line, but what is going on inside my mind and feelings is hidden, unless I choose to make it public, to bring it out into the open. Even then I am unlikely to be able to communicate my feelings clearly. In the same way, the episode in the narrator's life recounted in "The Secret Sharer" would have remained secret if he had not chosen to write it down and publish it so all the world might read it. Conrad's idea for this story would also have remained secret if he had not written the story. In this it would have been like all that host of unwritten novels we are told swarmed in Dostoevsky's mind. My reading of "The Secret Sharer" would also remain secret unless I were to decide to talk about my reading, to teach the story, or to write an essay about it, such as this one. I have then told my own secret and have submitted my judgment of the story to the judgment of others. Literature, particularly story-telling in literature, as well as teaching and writing about literature, seems to have something essentially to do with the sharing of secrets.

To apply that to this specific case, however, raises some puzzling questions. To whom is the narrator of "The Secret Sharer" speaking, or to whom or for whom is he writing? In other works by Conrad, for example *Lord Jim* or *Heart of Darkness*, an elaborate fiction gives the narrator a name (Marlow) and a distinct individuality. These novels also put the narrator in a described situation. They show him telling the story to specified auditors, motivated to do so by a particular demand for narration. All that specificity is missing in "The Secret Sharer." The story just begins. It starts with an abrupt sentence in the first person, past tense. This sentence transports the reader to a place and to an event that took place at some unidentified time in the past, though we are told later in the story that it was years earlier: "On my right hand there were lines of fishing-stakes resembling a mysterious system of half-submerged bamboo fences" (24). To whom is the narrator addressing these words? Are we to imagine him as speaking or as writing? Where? When?

Since no time, no situation of narration, no specific auditors are given, it might even be possible to imagine that the narrator is talking to himself. The verbs are in the past tense. The speaker or writer may be remembering these events in an inward musing reminiscence that we as readers have magically been given the power to overhear. It might be said that "The Secret Sharer," in its lack of a circumstantial accounting for its coming into existence, exposes by negation the dependence of any confession on some external, technological device, some means of recording or inscription. A confession I make to myself is not a confession, though in the tradition of religious confession the confession might be made inwardly to God. St. Augustine's *Confessions*, for example, purport to be addressed to a God who knows it all already. We as readers are just overhearing a confession that is addressed to a divine other. Unless "The Secret Sharer" had been written down and published by a relay of handwriting or typewriting, typesetting, and printing, it would have remained secret. It needs also to be remembered that *The Secret Sharer* is a fictive confession, a story that Conrad has made up. The only access to the secrets the story tells is by way of the story itself. If all copies of the story were to vanish, so too would vanish any means of reaching the secret it tells, or perhaps does not tell. That remains to be seen.

The narrator's confession, moreover, is curiously incomplete. Neither the narrator nor the ship he commands is given a name. Those names are kept secret, whereas the name of the man the narrator hides in his cabin, "Leggatt," is given, along with the name of his ship, the *Sephora,* and a possible name for its captain, "Archbold." The name is ironically inappropriate, since Archbold is anything but bold. He is certainly not an original or "arch" model of boldness. The carefully guarded namelessness of the narrator and of his ship means that the narrator has confessed without confessing. We can hardly hold him publicly responsible or hail him before the law if we do not even know his name, not to speak of the exact date of the events, the name of his ship, and so on. Such details would have been obtained first of all from a witness testifying in a court of law.

Nor will it do to assume that the story is straightforwardly autobiographical. We cannot take it for granted that the name of the narrator is the same as the name of the author on the title page: Joseph Conrad. We know from external biographical evidence that the events narrated in "The Secret Sharer" did not, so far as anyone knows, happen to Conrad, though they were based in part on real events that happened to other people.[6] But Conrad has apparently made up the central episode, the hiding of the fugitive. To put this another way, absolutely no verification of this one way or the other exists. It is an impenetrable secret. Who knows? Maybe something of the sort did happen to Conrad back in the 1880s and he had kept it secret all those years, until he wrote the story in 1910. The story itself is the only evidence we have, and that is no evidence one way or the other, since a work of fiction proves nothing about the historical existence of the things it names.

It may be, however, that the best self-portrait is the portrait of another. An author is always revealing secrets about himself, even when he tells the stories of people most unlike himself. This would parallel the way the narrator of "The Secret Sharer," in spite of strongly identifying himself with Leggatt as his secret self, his double, his alter ego, nevertheless insists that "[h]e was not a bit like me, really" (34). In any case, the narrator of "The Secret Sharer" jealously preserves the situation of isolation from human judgment he describes at the beginning of the tale: "In this breathless pause at the threshold of a long passage we [he and his ship] seemed to be measuring our fitness for a long and arduous enterprise, the appointed task of both our existences to be carried out, far from all human eyes, with only sky and sea for spectators and for judges" (25). The narrator will be judged only by the sky and sea, or he wants only to be judged by them. In the same way, Leggatt refuses to be judged by the appointed civil authorities. "But you don't see me coming back to explain such things to an old fellow in a wig and twelve respectable tradesmen, do you?" he scornfully asks. "What can they know whether I am guilty or not—or of *what* I am guilty, either?" (52). The narrator at no point asks for an exonerating judgment from the reader. He says he wants only sky and sea for spectators and judges. Even so, by telling the story, he breaks that isolation, "far from all human eyes," though he does not tell us his name or the name of his ship. Even if the reader is only by accident, so to speak, overhearing the narrator musing to himself, that means we have been made stand-ins for the sea and sky, which are the real spectators and judges. The narrator, like Leggatt, has sidestepped the officially empowered legal authorities. He has gone over their heads to appeal first to the sky and sea and then indirectly, perhaps even inadvertently, to us the readers, or rather to me as reader, since my reading and judgment are, at least initially, solitary and remain solitary unless I choose to reveal it to others.

"The Secret Sharer," you can see, is a curious form of testimony, witness, or deposition. The reader is implicitly put in the position of judge or jury. The phrase saying only the sea and sky are spectators and judges invites the reader to think of his or her duty as going beyond spectatorship to judgment. We must pass judgment on Leggatt. Was he justified in strangling the mutinous crewman or was it unjustified manslaughter, voluntary or involuntary? What should his punishment be? We must also pass judgment on the narrator. Did he do right or wrong in harboring the fugitive murderer, Leggatt? Did he pass the test qualifying him as fit for the command of a ship on a long and arduous voyage? An anxiety about that is a primary motif in the story, as in other stories and novels by Conrad, for example "The Shadow Line," "Typhoon," and *The Nigger of the "Narcissus."* The narrator tells us that he was "untried as yet by a position of the fullest responsibility," and he says, "I wondered how far I should turn out faithful to that ideal conception of one's own personality every man sets up for himself secretly" (26).[7] Here is another form of doubling, not that of the narrator by Leggatt, but an internal doubling whereby the narrator is doubled by his ideal image of himself. That other self presides over his evaluation of himself, not any external code. It may be that Leggatt is, for the narrator, no more than a fortuitous external representation of that hidden secret self, that ideal conception of himself to which he must be faithful.

The narrator keeps emphasizing the solitude of a ship captain's situation. The captain represents the law on board ship. He must make the

ultimate decisions and take the final responsibility, as in the last episode
of "The Secret Sharer," when the narrator brings the ship dangerously
close to the shore before bringing the ship about. In doing this he is
guided only by what he calls his "conscience" (56), though just what he
means by that is not wholly clear. I shall return to this question. Just as
the crew cannot challenge his commands, though they think he is irre-
sponsible, drunk, or mad, so no other member of the ship's crew would
have the legal right to judge him for secretly harboring a murderer in his
cabin. As he says, "Of course, theoretically, I could do what I liked, with
no one to say nay to me within the whole circle of the horizon" (39). In
practice, he is constrained by an immense set of rules and conventions for
a captain's behavior. He transgresses these rules and conventions at his
peril, as when, against all custom, he takes an anchor watch himself or
when he takes the ship too close to shore.[8] The first of these transgressions brings Leggatt, as if by magic, before him as a demand for an immediate, isolated, decision.

All that I have said so far presupposes that "The Secret Sharer" is a challenge to any reader's tact and perception as a reader. Like all good works
of literature, it puts the reader on trial, so to speak. If the primary aim of
"The Secret Sharer" is to make the reader *see*, hardly any reader can
avoid feeling that at the same time it must have another meaning besides
the manifest one of telling a good story, making us see it. Certainly the
story has traditionally been read as having some further purport. "The
Secret Sharer," almost all its readers have assumed, must have a more
esoteric or secret significance in which "this" (some realistic detail in the
story) stands for "that" (some symbolic or allegorical meaning). Like
many other works by Conrad, "The Secret Sharer" seems as if it must be
some kind of parable, allegory, or fable. It must have some deeper meaning. This the reader ought by appropriate decoding to be able to identify,
just as the parables of Jesus in the New Testament, though they are stories
about everyday life in ancient Judea, stories about farming, fishing, and
household life, nevertheless have parabolic meanings about the kingdom
of heaven and how to get there. We know this because Jesus tells the
disciples just what those meanings are, in so many words, for example in
the parable of the sower in the Gospel of Matthew: "But he that received
the seed into stony places, the same is he that heareth the word, and anon
with joy receiveth it; Yet hath he not root in himself, but dureth for a
while: for when tribulation or persecution ariseth because of the word, by
and by he is offended" (Matt. 13:20–21), and so on. More generally the
Gospel of Matthew affirms that Jesus spoke to the multitude in parables
"that it might be fulfilled which was spoken by the prophet, saying, I will
open my mouth in parables; I will utter things which have been kept se-

cret from the foundation of the world" (Matt. 13:35). The parables of Jesus are a way of revealing secrets, sharing them with all the world, while at the same time keeping them secret, since, as Jesus says, most of his auditors will not understand them.

The problem of course is that "The Secret Sharer," if it is a parable, is a secular one. It does not have the large context of centuries of biblical interpretation and of institutionalized Christianity that helps with the parables of Jesus, even though Conrad's other work, modernist fiction, English literature as a whole, and an enormous contradictory tradition of modern literary theory and criticism form a context establishing a horizon of expectations about what sort of allegorical meanings might be plausible in a story like this. Nevertheless, "The Secret Sharer" itself nowhere in so many words tells the reader just what the second level of meaning is. In spite of that, readers have not failed to rise to the bait, so to speak. No careful reader can doubt that any good reading of the story would need to take account of the way it has to do with the narrator's relation to himself, with his relation to other persons, especially Leggatt, and with important social questions of law, justice, and authority.

Many different interpretations have been proposed on the assumption that "The Secret Sharer" must have some further meaning beyond the manifest one of telling a good story. It would be a long business to recapitulate these in their diversity. "The Secret Sharer" has been interpreted as a disguised autobiography, by way of its relation to the events of Conrad's life as a seaman. It has been interpreted as a story about homosexuality, as a version of the widespread motif of the *Doppelgänger*, as a story about the role of the test in establishing the fitness of males to be members of the elite group of leaders during the period of British imperialism, and so on, in somewhat incoherent profusion. One could imagine plausible interpretations in terms of Freud's "uncanny" or of Lacan's notion that the unconscious is the discourse of the other. All these explanations take the form of explicitly or implicitly saying: "All the others have got it wrong, but I can tell you what 'The Secret Sharer' is *really* about." They claim to have found out the story's secret meaning.

A distinction may be made at this point between all such interpretations, which may be called "hermeneutic," and another way of approaching the story that may be called "rhetorical reading." This distinction corresponds to one made by the primary narrator in Conrad's *Heart of Darkness*. That narrator, you will remember from the previous chapter, distinguishes between two kinds of stories: those whose meaning is separate and identifiable, like a nut in a nutshell, and those whose meaning the story brings out through its own verbal activity, as the moon makes visible an otherwise invisible haze in the night air. The distinction I am making parallels this one. It sets "interpretation" against "reading." The

former interprets the story by way of its relation to something distinct
from the words. The latter interrogates the words themselves in their
interplay. A hermeneutic interpretation is guaranteed by the reference of
the words to something distinct from them, as the kernel of the nut is
distinct from the nutshell. The "something distinct" may be the life of the
author, or historical facts, either general or specific, or some external
code of interpretation—religious, Freudian, Lacanian, feminist, new his-
toricist, postcolonial, or whatever—some interpretative procedure that
knows what it is going to find and can therefore always find what it seeks.
Such a procedure knows how to crack the nut and find the kernel, or, to
vary the metaphor, it knows how to crack the code and decipher anything
written in that code. A Freudian version of such an interpretation, for
example, might read the narrator's exclamation when he first sees Leggatt's naked body in the water beside the ship ("A headless corpse!" [29])
and say, "Ah ha! Decapitation. That means castration."

Freud himself, of course, was usually not so mechanical in his readings,
conspicuously not so in the essay called "Das 'Unheimlich'" (The "Uncanny"). Freud's "Das 'Unheimlich'" is itself an uncanny text in its repetitions, contradictions, revisions, apologies, and doublings. It is uncanny
also in being the site of a battle between hermeneutic and rhetorical procedures. As such, it is not a dictionary of symbolic equivalences that can
be used to translate details in a "this for that" (e.g., "headless corpse =
castration"), but a text that must itself be rhetorically read in a way similar to the way we read a literary work. I am not saying that Freud's essay
is a work of literature, only that it has to be read as carefully as if it were
a work of literature and to some degree by the same procedures.

What I am calling a rhetorical reading of "The Secret Sharer" might
even ultimately come to the same conclusion about that headless corpse
(that it has something to do with castration), but only on the basis of a
more or less elaborate internal reading. A rhetorical reading starts with
the words and stays with them, paying close attention to subtle nuances
of suggestion in figures of speech, in recurrences of words and nuances of
wordplay. It presumes that the meaning of the tale is generated or constituted by the words of the tale, or brought out into the open out of the
"unseen" by them and by them alone, like the mist by the moon, rather
than being something that preexists them, something to which they refer.
In the case of "The Secret Sharer," as with literary works in general, every
detail, every figure of speech, every word or phrase and variation on those
when they recur, counts. This means that a full reading of the story would
require a virtually interminable accounting, something impossible to give
in reasonable compass. What can be given here is the outline of a full
reading and some exemplary readings of details.

Take, for example, the hat the narrator gives to Leggatt that then appears in the water just in the nick of time to help the narrator bring the ship about before it goes aground. Few readers will have failed to notice that hat and to see that it comes at a turning point in the story, in more ways than one. It must have some "symbolic" meaning. If beheading means castration, a hat, as a covering for the head, must be a phallic symbol. A hat fetishist displaces his anxiety about a part of his body, the phallus, to a fascination with an article of clothing that protects a different part of the body, a part that is a displaced representative of the phallus. Does the hat in "The Secret Sharer" work this way? Is it a symbol of the bond between the narrator and Leggatt, the manhood the narrator shares with Leggatt? He gives Leggatt his hat at the last minute before Leggatt prepares to dive into the water and swim ashore to confront whatever strange destiny awaits him there. He is motivated by his sense of identity with Leggatt, by a foresuffering of what Leggatt is likely to have to endure in his wanderings. He gives Leggatt his own hat in a silent, semicomic pantomime: "A sudden thought struck me. I saw myself wandering barefooted, bareheaded, the sun beating on my dark poll. I snatched off my floppy hat and tried hurriedly in the dark to ram it on my other self. He dodged and fended off silently. I wonder what he thought had come to me before he understood and suddenly desisted" (56). The giving of the hat is presented as a curiously violent, quasi-sexual event, almost like a kind of rape. Their groping, lingering handshake, the most overt sign of homosexual affection between them, follows. To give another person your own hat is certainly a mark of intimacy and affection. For Leggatt to wear the narrator's hat is a sign of their doubling identity. To say all this would be an example of hermeneutic interpretation, relating the signs to an external code that gives you meanings, in this case Freud's system of phallic or genital symbols. A shoe usually means the female genitals, in whatever dream it is encountered. A hat usually means the phallus. Loss of hat equals loss of head equals loss of penis. To take off your hat to someone is symbolically to disarm and unman yourself momentarily. The king's subjects usually may not wear their hats in the presence of the king. As a special privilege, those who hold doctorates from the University of Zaragosa are allowed to wear their academic hats in the presence of the king of Spain. They (the male ones, that is) are allowed to retain the symbols of their manhood even before the king.

This all seems plausible enough, and clearly applicable to an interpretation of "The Secret Sharer," but the hat does not quite work that way in the story. Leggatt leaves the hat behind in the water. He thereby repudiates whatever identity with the narrator wearing the narrator's hat would symbolize. This leaving behind of the hat is the moment of definitive division of Leggatt and the narrator. They go their separate ways. The narrator is freed of the burden of responsibility for his double and can take up his command of his ship and the men on her, as well as his affectionate intimacy with the ship, consistently seen as feminine throughout the story. When Leggatt swims away and the ship turns, the narrator turns from a homosexual to a heterosexual orientation. But this turning is made possible by a new meaning given by the narrator to the hat. This new meaning is an example of a rhetorical reading by the captain, not a hermeneutic interpretation:

> Was she moving? What I needed was something easily seen, a piece of paper, which I could throw overboard and watch. I had nothing on me. To run down for it I didn't dare. There was no time. All at once my strained, yearning stare distinguished a white object floating within a yard of the ship's side. White on the black water. . . . I recognized my own floppy hat. It must have fallen off his head . . . and he didn't bother. Now I had what I wanted—the saving mark for my eyes. . . . It had been meant to save his homeless head from the dangers of the sun. And now—behold—it was saving the ship, by serving me for a mark to help out the ignorance of my strangeness. Ha! It was drifting forward, warning me just in time that the ship had gathered sternway. (59)

The hat has now become just a hat, white on the black water. Anything discernible would have done as well, as the narrator says, a piece of blank paper, for example, the paper in that case playing the role of the sign rather than the matrix for receiving signs, white on black rather than black on white. Whatever meaning the hat may have had as something shared between Leggatt and the captain is now forgotten, erased. The hat now becomes a neutral marker, in itself indifferent, like a blank bit of paper on which anything can be inscribed. You can write anything you like on it. It is up to you. You have to read it, but the reading is an active intervention. Reading now becomes a kind of writing or positing. The captain reads the hat as evidence that the ship is moving backward, so he can come about, shift the sails, and save the ship from going aground. The hat gives him the cue for the command: "Shift the helm" (59). The hat passes from the captain to Leggatt and back again, or back again to the neutral space between them, the space that now divides them. The hat now becomes the marker of the narrator's turning away from Leggatt to sail off alone, a proud sailor confronting his new destiny, just as the narrator defines Leggatt, in the last sentence of the story, as "a free man, a proud swimmer striking out for a new destiny" (60). Leggatt is free of the tie to the narrator that keeping the latter's hat would have signified.

A rhetorical reading may begin with tropes, for example the sexual meanings attributed to the hat, but it ends with performative positing.

Such positing characteristically involves some element of irony as the undermining of clear knowledge. The irony here lies in the difference between the narrator's understanding of the story and Conrad's or the reader's, as well as in the lingering doubt the reader may have about the way we should judge the narrator's action and the grounds for that judgment. That white hat stands out against the unfathomable darkness of the sea as a catachrestic name covers over the unknowability of what it names. I shall return to this perhaps obscure formulation.

What I am calling rhetorical reading and have exemplified in the meaning the captain gives to the hat does not deny the referential force of words. The Gulf of Siam, the River Meinam, and the pagoda really exist and are named by the story. Conrad accurately reports the details of seafaring and shiphandling. The story does have the immense and overdetermined context of Conrad's life, modern European history, and the history of Western imperialism. These must be presumed in any reading. The more we know about them the better. A rhetorical reading shows, however, that the story appropriates and reworks the referential force of the words for its own performative purposes. The meaning of the story is not exhausted by its historical references. In the case of the hermeneutic interpretation, the meaning, as the word "hermeneutic"[9] suggests, is a preexisting secret outside the words of the story, to which those words refer, and that proper procedures of interrogation may discover. It is a secret, but it may be made manifest. It may be known. A rhetorical reading hypothesizes that the story appropriates those referential meanings and makes of them a new meaning generated performatively by the words. The secret, if there is one, is all in the words, not behind them or in some other ascertainable realm, even though the words seem to be a response to another kind of secret, a secret not reachable at any sort of hermeneutic depth but rather absolutely unpresentable by any direct means. The unseen is unseen.

A complication in my distinction between interpretation and reading must, however, at this point be noted. This further twist is already present in Conrad's distinction between two kinds of stories. Both sorts of meaning, after all, are outside the words of the story, even though the distinction is clear between a seaman's story that can be summarized "in a nutshell," as we say, and a story like one of Marlow's whose meaning is insubstantial, a ghostly implication, "a misty halo," as Conrad puts it, "made visible by the spectral illumination of moonshine." In both cases, nevertheless, the meaning is distinct from the story, though in a quite different way for each. A story whose meaning is like the nut in the nutshell is controlled by its reference to something that preexists it and that could be reached by other means. We do not need "The Secret Sharer" to tell us that beheading stands for castration. Freud already told us that.

The historical and biographical facts to which "The Secret Sharer" refers can be known in other ways, by reading history books about British imperialism or by reading Conrad's biography. That misty halo, however, though it is outside the story, can only be made visible by just this story, by just these words in just this order. The words of the story bring the meaning into the open, though it seems, after that exposure, to have been there all along waiting to be revealed. The story seems to be a response to a demand by that meaning to get itself told, narrated, revealed, just as the invisible mist is there waiting to be made visible by the illumination of moonshine. The story is a speech act, a performative. It is constitutive, inaugural. It makes something happen. It is a way of doing things with words. Nevertheless, the meaning it reveals always seems to have been there already, waiting to be revealed, like that invisible mist. Jacques Derrida expresses succinctly the way a work of literature as a singular speech act is both the inauguration of the new and at the same time a strange act of memory: "Reading as much as it writes, deciphering or citing as much as it inscribes, this act is also an act of memory (the other is already there, irreducibly), this act enacts [cet acte prend acte]."[10]

These two ways of deciphering, and some variants, are, it happens, embodied more or less covertly in "The Secret Sharer" itself. The chief mate, with his "terrible growth of whisker" and his habitual ejaculation, "Bless my soul, sir! You don't say so!" (25–26) is a comic embodiment of the hermeneutic approach. As the narrator tells us, "He was of a painstaking turn of mind. As he used to say, he 'liked to account to himself' for practically everything that came his way" (26). He says, "Bless my soul" to protect himself from the possibly malign or devilish influence of a scandalous piece of information, just as we say "God bless you" when someone sneezes, to prevent the devil from rushing in during the brief moment when the sneezer has expelled his soul by sneezing and the place where the soul was is empty.[11] If the devil got in, it might be a case of possession by one's diabolical double or devilish other. Until the first mate has found a rational, lawful explanation or "accounting" for everything that seems anomalous, unaccountable, he fears not so much for his sanity as for his salvation, his soul's health.

The comic example the narrator gives of this has an emblematic, allegorical force. The first mate, says the narrator, wanted painstakingly to explain everything, "down to a miserable scorpion he had found in his cabin a week before. The why and the wherefore of that scorpion—how it got on board and came to select his room rather than the pantry (which was a dark place and more what a scorpion would be partial to), and how on earth it managed to drown itself in the inkwell of his writing desk—

had exercised him infinitely" (26). This is a good example of the way small, apparently insignificant details or locutions in "The Secret Sharer" count, must be scrutinized, and may have a covert meaning beyond the obvious literal one. That miserable scorpion surely corresponds to Leggatt who, like the scorpion, has mysteriously come aboard the ship. As an outlaw Leggatt is a scorpion-like danger to all the crew and their orderly life. Later in the story, after the captain of the *Sephora* has visited the narrator's ship looking for Leggatt, the chief mate quotes the crew's scandalized rejection of the idea that he might be on board: "As if we would harbor a thing like that" (46). It is not, moreover, without significance that the scorpion has drowned itself in an inkwell, in a manner of speaking contaminating or poisoning the ink, just as the ink with which the narrator (or Conrad himself) writes down the story accounting for Leggatt has been adulterated by the presence of that particular scorpion, though Leggatt does not in the end drown himself[12] but plunges into the sea to swim away toward shore and vanish, a free man ready to begin his new life.

The chief mate applies his hermeneutic technique of accounting to explain with careful reasoning and to his own satisfaction just what it means that another ship is anchored behind an island nearby: "She was, he doubted not, a ship from home lately arrived. Probably she drew too much water to cross the bar except at the top of spring tides. Therefore she went into that natural harbor to wait for a few days in preference to remaining in an open roadstead" (26). The second mate confirms that the chief mate has interpreted the signs correctly and drawn the correct logical conclusions, that he is a good hermeneut: "That's so. . . . She draws over twenty feet. She's the Liverpool ship *Sephora* with a cargo of coal. Hundred and twenty-three days from Cardiff" (26). How does the second mate come by these facts? The tugboat skipper has told him. If the chief mate represents the hermeneutic method as a deductive accounting by way of a rational interpretation of signs, the second mate represents the confirmation of such an interpretation by external historical facts. The latter would parallel an interpretation of "The Secret Sharer" such as Norman Sherry presents in *Conrad's Eastern World* by giving us the results of his historical research into the background facts on which Conrad based the tale. It would also be confirmed by what Conrad himself says about "The Secret Sharer."[13] In the "Author's Note" of 1920, Conrad says, "The basic fact of the tale I had in my possession for a good many years. It was in truth the common possession of the whole fleet of merchant ships trading to India, China, and Australia." He goes on to say he had learned of the episode even before it got into the newspapers: "I had heard of it before, as it were privately, among the officers of the great

wool fleet in which my first years in deep water were served." The episode happened on a ship called the *Cutty Sark*, belonging to a certain
Mr. Willis, "a notable ship-owner in his day."[14] What Conrad calls the
"basic fact," however, is apparently not the central motif of his story, the
hiding by the narrator of the fugitive murderer, but the murder itself, if it
is a murder. That is up to us to decide.

The problem with a hermeneutic interpretation of "The Secret Sharer"
is that the events presented in the story lend themselves neither to the
logical and deductive accounting represented by the chief mate nor to the
historical confirmation represented by the second mate. The narrator of
"The Secret Sharer" represents the alternative of a rhetorical reading of
those events as they are manifested by signs. His procedures of reading
involve (1) a respect for what is mysterious and perhaps ultimately unaccountable in those signs; (2) an exacting attention to those signs in all
their detail, in their materiality; (3) a procedure of displacement whereby
the signs are in the act of narration displaced sideways in one way or
another into other figurative signs; (4) an implicit recognition that reading, like the tropological change that says "this is like that," in one way
or another is a performative speech act that reads signs by proffering new
signs that can never be rationally authorized by the text but have another
kind of authorizing. Such an act of reading is never a mere impersonal
"accounting for." Reading is an active, transformative intervention, not
a passive reception. The narrator's procedures of reading also involve
(5) an acceptance of the fact that the one who performs such a speech act
must take responsibility for it and for its effects on others, in a shifting
from rational accounting to performative engagement and obligation;
and, finally, (6) recognition that such a retelling is a response to a demand
made by some "other" that leads to a new form of understanding, understanding not as rational accounting but as an inaugural repetition or
doubling, as what the narrator does obscurely doubles what Leggatt has
done and must do so if he is to be able to say "I understand" in response
to Leggatt's "I understand."[15] The reader, in turn, is called upon not just
to understand rationally but to take his or her place in a chain of inheritance imposing a legacy of responsibility. Just how this might happen
remains to be shown.

It is not certain beforehand what is the best way to read "The Secret
Sharer." Only an actual reading will tell, one that starts, as always should
be the case, with questions.

Let me begin at the beginning, with the title. It seems transparent
enough, but just what does it mean? To whom or to what in the story
does it refer? Like all titles, it functions as a clue. It is, the reader assumes,

a synecdochic summing up whereby the part stands for the whole and is presumably like the whole. A reader asks himself or herself, "Why did he call it this?" A title is both outside what it names, an alien or stranger to the text that may conceivably be related to it only ironically, and at the same time part of the text, a member of the family of terms we use to understand it. A title is outside and inside at once. In the case of "The Secret Sharer," though not of course with all titles, the title is actually repeated inside the story, not just something outside it that gives it a name. The phrase is used more than once to define Leggatt when the narrator of the story is hiding him in his cabin. He calls Leggatt early in the story "the secret sharer of my life" (40), then, soon after, "the secret sharer of my cabin" (43), and in the story's last sentence, "the secret sharer of my cabin and of my thoughts" (60).

What is a secret sharer? A secret *sharer*? A *secret* sharer? A different meaning arises depending on which word is stressed. If "sharer" is stressed, "secret" is an adjective modifying "sharer." Leggatt secretly shares the narrator's cabin, lives there with him, shares his thoughts, though no one else knows. If "secret" is stressed, "secret" is a noun and "sharer" is another noun. Leggatt is someone who shares a secret or secrets. But does the title name only Leggatt? Its use as a title that sums up the whole story invites the reader to look for a wider reference. Does the narrator not, as I have already suggested, share Leggatt's secret when Leggatt tells his story, and then share it again with the reader in telling his story? Just what is a secret, if there is such a thing? If there is such a thing, can it be shared? Does it remain a secret when it has been shared? Is there such a thing as a shared secret? Does it not cease to be secret when it is shared? What does it mean to speak of a secret as "shared"? Divided, cut in two? As when we speak of a shared meal? All these questions are raised by an attempt to decide the exact force of the title. "Shared" is related in meaning and etymology to "sheared," as a ploughshare cuts the furrow, dividing the earth. To share something usually means to cut it into at least two pieces, though it can also mean "to have in common," as when we say "They shared a bed." A secret, it would seem, cannot be cut in two in this way. It is an indivisible whole, is it not, like a single person? It is incapable of being doubled. When a secret becomes an open secret, shared promiscuously, it is hardly a secret any longer. Anyone with some small experience of life knows that when you say "I'll tell you a secret, if you promise to keep it," you might as well be shouting it from the housetops or printing it on the front page of *The New York Times*.

As Jacques Derrida has demonstrated (in *Donner le temps: 1. La fausse monnaie*,[16] in *Passions*,[17] and in a series of admirable seminars given some years ago now, prior to those books), a true secret, if there is such a thing, cannot be revealed. If it can be revealed it is not really a secret, or, to put this another way, one must distinguish between those quasi-secrets that can be revealed, such as state secrets or secret recipes, and another kind of more secret secret that cannot by any means be revealed. Does "The Secret Sharer" hide a secret of that sort? What would the traces or marks of such a secret be? Even if it is an unpresentable and unrevealable secret, we would not know of its existence unless it manifested itself in indirect signs of some sort announcing its hidden existence. Something must say, "There is a secret there." That would give another reading of the title. To share a secret might not mean to share it with another person, but to participate in the secret, to be subject to its force, even though the secret as such cannot be revealed. What would then be passed on from Leggatt to the narrator is not some identifiable secret that might be revealed, but subjection to the irresistible force of a secret that cannot be revealed as such but that nevertheless imposes a pitiless obligation on those who come to be subject to it, to share in it.[18] That may be, but, after all, there seems little we would like to know about "The Secret Sharer" that we cannot know. It seems as if the narrator tells all. He shares all the secrets with the reader. What remains still secret at the end of the story?

Jacques Derrida has, in the various works just referred to, seen an essential relation between literature and the secret. Literature keeps its secret. A work of literature is all on the surface, all there in the words on the page, imprinted on a surface that cannot be gone behind. This means that there are certain secrets or enigmas in a work of literature that cannot by any means be penetrated, though answers to the questions they pose may be essential to a reading of the work. We cannot know, for example, whether Leggatt is telling the truth in his version of the murder. He is in this like a witness in the witness box. We have only his word for it. Nor can we know how the narrator came to be captain of this ship. He refrains openly from telling us: "In consequence of certain events of no particular significance, except to myself, I had been appointed to the command only a fortnight before" (26). When someone talks like that, it is reasonable to think he may be hiding something. What that something may be we shall never know. Nor is the reader told what was the name of the captain of the Sephora. Archbold? Maybe, but the narrator cannot remember, or says he cannot remember: "It was something like Archbold—but at this distance of years I hardly am sure" (41). Archbold would, as I said earlier, certainly be an ironically inappropriate name for him, since the narrator says he was a shy man whose "main characteristic" was "a spiritless tenacity." He gives his ship's name and other particulars "in the manner of a criminal making a reluctant and doleful confession" (41). This makes him an ironic double of Leggatt and the narrator, both of whom make confessions. Conrad's figure puts in the readers' minds the topic of confession. It reminds us that we are reading a confession about a confession, neither of which is either reluctant or doleful.

Or are they? The narrator's testimony is incomplete. He seems reluctant to tell us everything. If I were a lawyer for the prosecution I would have a few questions to ask him, beyond asking him to tell me his name, the name of his ship, and a few more particulars in the way of dates and facts. For example, the reader can never know just what was the version of the murder given by the captain of the *Sephora*, since the narrator explicitly refuses to give that other version: "he had to raise his voice to give me his tale. It is not worth while to record that version" (42). Why not? One would have thought the captain would have been a valuable additional witness. Certainly he would have been called upon in a court of law to tell his story. The narrator seems so certain that Leggatt told the truth that he discounts any other version. In doing so, he does keep a secret from the reader, a secret the reader therefore has no way of ever knowing.

As a matter of fact, the narrator gives the reader the essence of the *Sephora*'s captain's interpretation of what happened. Captain Archbold, if that is really his name, sees the events as evidence of God's providence, not, as Leggatt sees them, as evidence of his (Leggatt's) bravery in setting the reefed foresail in the midst of a terrible storm. "God's own hand in it," says the captain of the *Sephora*. "Nothing less could have done it. I don't mind telling you that I hardly dared give the order" (43). Leggatt insists that the captain gave no such order, that he, Leggatt, acted on his own and saved the ship, just as he (according to him) justifiably took the law into his own hands when he killed the mutinous crewman. The latter was an "ill-conditioned snarling cur" (31). It might be noted that a few lines later Leggatt himself becomes in retrospect doglike when he tells how he took the crewman by the neck and "[shook] him like a rat" (32). This doubling is redoubled much later when the narrator shakes the chief mate to get him to go forward to tend to the head-sheets when they are about to go aground: "'You go forward'—shake—'and stop there'—shake—'and hold your noise'—shake—'and see these head-sheets properly overhauled'—shake, shake—shake" (58). Leggatt obscurely doubles the rebellious crewman, as the narrator doubles Leggatt. Like the crewman, both Leggatt and the narrator transgress against convention or law. The covert similarity is hidden by the narrator's strong endorsement of Leggatt's judgment that the crewman was one of those "miserable devils that have no business to live at all. He wouldn't do his duty and wouldn't let anybody else do theirs" (31). The narrator agrees. He tells the reader, "I knew well enough the pestiferous danger of such a character where there are no means of legal repression" (31). Readers of *The Nigger of the*

"Narcissus" (1897) will remember in that novel the sullen, resentful, and mean-spirited character Donkin as another Conradian character who malingers, complains, and refuses to do his duty.

What the narrator says of the crewman Leggatt kills in "The Secret Sharer" would seem to give support to a reading of Conrad as an arch-conservative spokesperson for British ideas of hierarchy, duty, fidelity, imperial responsibility, the white man's burden, and so on, with the overtones of sexism and racism that are associated with such allegiances. Conrad's narrator asserts that on board ship "there are no means of legal repression" (31). To preserve the laws of duty, obedience, and so on, someone must act against the law, outside the law, in a strange kind of unlawful law-preserving or law-establishing violence.[19] "The Secret Sharer," in its confrontation of this disquieting aspect of the law, in particular law on board ship, is analogous to Herman Melville's *Billy Budd*. To read them side by side would be instructive.

It is not exactly the case, however, that on board ship "there are no means of legal repression," as the captain of the *Sephora* indicates when he says to Leggatt, "I represent the law here" (35). A ship captain is not the law, but he represents the law. This, however, is also the case on shore. The law is never present in person, but only in its representatives: the police, a lawyer, a judge, a jury. The whole apparatus of the law is not the law but a representation of the absent law. The way the captain represents the law makes the narrator's claim that there are no means of legal repression of an insubordinate crewman seem strangely problematic. The captain of the *Sephora*, for example, does not hesitate to "arrest" Leggatt and keep him locked in his cabin.

Captain Archbold, as against the narrator's judgment and as against Leggatt's self-evaluation, sees Leggatt as without question a murderer. He must be turned over "to the law" (43) as soon as he can be got ashore. In fact the captain is morbidly concerned with his responsibility for doing that: "His obscure tenacity on that point had in it something incomprehensible and a little awful; something, as it were, mystical. . . . Seven-and-thirty virtuous years at sea . . . seemed to have laid him under some pitiless obligation" (43). Why is this sense of obligation "incomprehensible," "awful," "mystical"? Perhaps because it is a sense of justice that leads beyond itself to injustice. It uses an appeal to law to justify the unjustified and unjustifiable. In any case, neither Leggatt nor the narrator feels that pitiless obligation. Their obligation is rather to another force of law, to one that may be equally incomprehensible, awful, even mystical, whatever Conrad may mean by such portentous terms. Which obligation should we credit? Which behavior should we approve of and imitate?

Moral life is full of situations not entirely unlike Leggatt's situation or the narrator's. What would I have done in Leggatt's situation or in the narrator's? What *should* I have done, and on the basis of what moral and public law, or secret and private one?

It might seem that by the end all that is of importance in "The Secret Sharer" has been laid open, all secrets revealed, so that they are not secret any more. The fact of the murder was known to everyone in the whole merchant fleet in that area. The narrator tells us the whole story, at least his version of it. Nothing of importance seems to remain hidden. Nevertheless, nagging questions remain as to the grounds for Leggatt's act and its doubling in what the narrator does. The narrator speaks of Leggatt as "the secret sharer of my life." That seems to limit the title to naming Leggatt as the secret presence hidden from all the others on board the ship, but who nevertheless shares the narrator's life, eats his food, sleeps in his bed in his sleeping suit, uses his bathroom, sees him in the most intimate acts, for example taking a bath. We cannot even be sure that they may not share the captain's bed, after that first night, when the narrator tells us that he spent the night on his couch. On the question of whether or not they slept together in the same bed the narrator gives no information. It is an impenetrable secret, though the reader would like to know. A good bit of affection exists between them, in any case, as well as a strong sense of identity, most overtly in their farewell handshake as they crawl on hands and knees in the dark sail locker: "Our hands met gropingly, lingered united in a steady, motionless clasp for a second. . . . No word was breathed by either of us when they separated" (56).

Leggatt, as the story tells the reader again and again, is the narrator's hidden double, his other self, as intimately known and understood as his own self. The narrator lies for Leggatt, for example by persuading the captain of the *Sephora* that Leggatt is not there. How can we be sure he is not lying to us or withholding some important secret in the guise of telling all? Apparently complete openness, as Poe's "The Purloined Letter" notoriously shows, is the best way to hide something. The narrator is also a secret sharer in another way. He shares his secret with us, or with me as reader. Even if I think of him as talking to himself, reminiscing, his secret thoughts have in some miraculous way been exposed, so that I can read his mind, just as the narrator says he can read Leggatt's mind. The reader, I as reader, become the secret sharer of a secret. My sharing is secret because reading is secret. What it does to me, as I have said, is silent, leaves no mark. "The Secret Sharer," as one can see, is made of a whole series of secret sharers, in both senses, *secret* sharers and secret *sharers* who are also doubles of one another: Leggatt, the narrator, the

reader, even Captain "Archbold," anyone who writes an essay about the
story and so passes the secret and the responsibility for the secret on to
another person, anyone who reads that essay, this one for example, and
thereby becomes a secret sharer, a sharer of the secret.

To try to formulate more exactly just what that secret might be, I turn
now to the first paragraph of the story. This paragraph is a striking example of the way the narrator's tale is not just objective description but
at every turn a figurative transformation and an active intervention, as
what I would call "rhetorical reading" must always be. The narrator's
way with language gives the reader a model for his or her own activity.
    Along with the wonderfully vivid scene-setting that the opening para-
graph has as its apparent main goal, it also unostentatiously sets up several other horizons of expectation that are crucial to the meaning of the
narration that begins after the scene has been set. (1) The first paragraph
introduces the motif of doubling and redoubling. (2) It initiates the reader
into a process whereby one thing stands for another or is like another. In
this it is a primer or introductory handbook about how to read paraboli-
cally. (3) It gives the reader the first example of something that is mysterious, incomprehensible, something not open to rational knowing.
    The very first sentence does all three of these things at once, besides
being effective at making us *see*: "On my right hand there were lines of
fishing stakes resembling a mysterious system of half-submerged bamboo
fences, incomprehensible in its division of the domain of tropical fishes,
and crazy of aspect as if abandoned forever by some nomad tribe of fishermen now gone to the other end of the ocean, for there was no sign of
human habitation as far as the eye could reach" (24). This is an accurate
description of a real place in the real world. It tells the reader that the
water is quite shallow off the mouth of the River Meinam at the head of
what used to be called the Gulf of Siam. It tells us, moreover, that there
were bamboo fish weirs there, that is, fenced enclosures with a narrow
opening that traps schools of small fish when they swim in the opening
and cannot find their way out again. Such fish weirs, though not of bamboo, are still used in the shallow waters around Deer Isle, Maine, where
I spend my summers. I have (in December 1994) seen such weirs, probably in this case of bamboo, in the shallow water on the western side of
Taiwan, south of the city of Kaohsiung, much closer geographically to the
ones Conrad describes than Deer Isle, Maine.
    Though Conrad knew they were fish weirs, since he calls them "fishing
stakes," nevertheless he chose to describe them, in a way that is characteristic of his art of description throughout his work, as if he did not quite
understand them, as if they were "mysterious," "incomprehensible."
They look like "half-submerged bamboo fences" whose purpose is in-

scrutable. Just as words can become strange, uncanny, when they are repeated over and over, so, looked at in a certain way, even ordinary things can seem to harbor some unfathomable secret, as the life of the fishermen who made these "crazy" (in the sense of "dilapidated," but also with a hint of "insane") fish weirs is unknown. In a similar way, much later in the story, the narrator stresses what is mysterious about the human life on the islands where Leggatt is put ashore: "Unknown to trade, to travel, almost to geography, the manner of life they harbor is an unsolved secret" (53).[20]

The first sentence also unostentatiously introduces the theme of division, sharing, or doubling. The system of bamboo fences is incomprehensible in its *division* of the domain of tropical fishes. A little later in the paragraph, "two small clumps of trees, one on each side" (24) of the river mouth, are a small-scale doubling like that introduced later when the narrator tells us that in the cuddy (that is, the room on the ship used as the officers' dining room), "Two bunches of bananas hung from the beam symmetrically, one on each side of the rudder casing" (33). The next sentence makes explicit the parallel between the bananas and the doubling of the narrator by Leggatt: "two of [the] captain's sleeping suits were simultaneously in use" (33). The name Leggatt, though it may be modeled on "legate" and pronounced the same, contains, as I have noted, two sets of doubled consonants. These are a material inscription of Leggatt's connection with doubling.

Later in the first paragraph, to return to that, the entire scene is divided and then subdivided in a mirroring that anticipates and universalizes that of the two main characters. The narrator sees "the straight line of the flat shore joined to the stable sea, edge to edge, with a perfect and unmarked closeness" (24). The doubling of shore and sea in its unmarked intimacy is like the intimate doubling of the narrator and Leggatt. What happens to the one seems almost to happen to the other. The narrator often feels he is outside himself and dwelling inside the skin or inside the sleeping suit of the other man: "I was constantly watching myself, my secret self, as dependent on my actions as my own personality" (40); "The mental feeling of being in two places at once affected me physically as if the mood of secrecy had penetrated my very soul" (48). The doubling of sea and shore, however, that so distinctly anticipates the relation between the narrator and Leggatt, preparing the reader unawares for it, is doubled once more in the description of the whole expanse of the earth, sea and sky together. The great dome of the evening sky, an elemental and sublime[21] spectacle, doubles the sea and shore: "one levelled floor half brown, half blue under the enormous dome of the sky" (24).

Conrad's phrasing in this last quotation, however, exemplifies one more of the chief stylistic features of this opening paragraph. It is a feature

also present in Kant's celebrated example in *The Critique of Judgment* of
the arching sky over the sea as in its inhuman materiality a correlate of
sublime feelings. In Conrad, as in Kant, the sea and shore together become a "levelled floor" and the sky becomes a "dome." The whole scene
becomes one gigantic architectural construction. It is as though it is not
possible to confront directly a scene representing sublime feelings and
then name it without turning its alien otherness into something more familiar and human, in this case a manmade dwelling. "Floor" and "dome"
are examples of those original catachreses whereby we give names to
what has no proper name and cover over what is wholly other by giving
it familiar labels that make it seem something within which we can be
at home.

This transformation of inhuman nature into a humanized architectural
construction is already present earlier in the paragraph when the narrator
sees the "group of barren islets" as something "suggesting ruins of stone
walls, towers, and blockhouses" (24). The paragraph is a tissue of such
comparisons. The fish weirs look "as if abandoned forever by some
nomad tribe of fishermen" (24). The curving river inland is intermittently
visible in "gleams as of a few scattered pieces of silver" (25), and the tug
winding up that river eventually disappears "as though the impassive
earth had swallowed her up without an effort, without a tremor" (25).
All these "as ifs," the reader can see, are humanizations of the inhuman
nature they serve to name. The sky is like a dome, the sea and shore a
floor. The islets are ruined buildings, the river is like silver coins, the earth
is a huge beast that can swallow whole tugboats at a gulp. An imaginary
narrative about nomad fishermen is invented to account for the crazy
aspect of those fish weirs.

These figures show that the first paragraph, far from being, as I began
by saying, just wonderfully vivid description that makes the reader feel he
or she had been there, is the site of a strong verbal will to power on
Conrad's part (or the narrator's part). This will to mastery describes
things by transforming them into something they are not. What might at
first appear to be neutral description is a series of performative speech
acts. These do not just describe. They posit. They do this on their own
independent, unauthorized say-so. In this they fulfill Aristotle's remark in
the *Poetics* that a gift for metaphor is a mark of genius in a poet, the one
thing the poet cannot learn from another.[22] It is as if the narrator were
saying, "let these barren islets be seen as ruined towers, walls, and blockhouses," and so on. If "The Secret Sharer" is obliquely the story of how
the narrator grew up to the point where he was worthy of the solitude and
independent responsibility of command, the verbal mastery of the first
paragraph is evidence that he has long since achieved that right to command. He has command over words. He can use words performatively to

change what is there before him into something else—the sky into a dome, rocky islets into ruined cities, the sea and shore into a floor, the fish weirs into abandoned fences, the whole natural inhuman landscape into a humanized architectural scene of abandonment and desolation. What it might mean to say that these speech-act transformations are unauthorized or only secretly authorized and how that might correspond to other unauthorized acts in the story remains to be seen.

One way to investigate this further is to recognize that the story throughout turns on a series of key words and word clusters that gain a peculiar meaning and force through their repetition. Objections have been made, by Marvin Mudrick and other critics, to these repetitions as a notable characteristic of Conrad's style. They are said to be tedious and obvious. Such critics have missed the point. "Double," "stranger," "secret," "ghostly," "mysterious," "conscience" "understand"—the repetition of these words, and their variants, calls attention to them, singles them out by using them over and over in somewhat different surrounding verbal contexts. They thereby become strange and even progressively emptied of meaning, as any word does when it is repeated many times. A word's materiality, what gives it force, begins to show through its immaterial meaning if it is repeated often enough. It becomes senseless sound or marks on the page.

The most salient examples of this are the manifold repetitions of the word "double," though the same thing could be demonstrated with all the other words I listed above: "In a moment he had concealed his damp body in a sleeping suit of the same grey-stripe pattern as the one I was wearing and followed me like my double" (30); "murmured my double distinctly" (31); "My double gave me an inkling of his thoughts" (31); "my double there was no homicidal ruffian" (31); "he would think he was seeing double" (33); "My double followed my movements" (33); "anybody bold enough to open [the door] stealthily would have been treated to the uncanny sight of a double captain busy talking in whispers to his other self" (34); "My double breathed into my very ear, anxiously" (37); "I took a peep at my double" (39), and so on and on, double and after double, through many more doublings.

The careful reader will note that the word "double" appears first as an explicit trope, a simile. Dressed in a striped sleeping suit like the one the narrator is wearing, Leggatt follows the narrator "*like* [his] double" (my italics). The first-time reader cannot tell at this point whether this is important or only a passing figure inserted for vividness. From then on, however, the simile, weakest of tropes, becomes a literal assertion. Leggatt is "my double," just that, and said over and over to be so, as if the verbal similitude had had the power to materialize itself. It is as though a simile could be a speech act, a way of doing things with words. It makes happen as literal fact what it initially names as an "as if." The insistent repetition matches the opening tropological transformations. It is another curious version of the performative will to power over words or the will to make use of words in acts of power.

The will in question is not that of a subjective ego in full possession of its free power of volition. The words seem rather to act on their own, or they promise to do so. Such word use is a process creating the self. The narrator of "The Secret Sharer" ceases to be a stranger to himself and becomes worthy of command through his response to the demand made on him by Leggatt. That response operates through the narrative trans- formations that make up the verbal texture of "The Secret Sharer." The story does what it talks about.

Words repeated insistently, as Conrad does in this story, become de- tached, enigmatic. They seem to harbor a secret. The repetition of the key words makes them somehow uncanny. They become intruders into the sentences in which they are used so that they stand out rather than being fully assimilated into a local meaning.[23] In this they are like Leggatt himself, the ghostly guest who invades the narrator's ship as an alien presence. Such words in their repetition work as repetitive speech acts: "secret"; secret"; "secret"; "secret"; "double"; "double" "double"; "double," etc., in a mad and maddening refrain that has annoyed some readers. They have not seen how the repetition mimes the story's central theme. The narrator himself more than once says that his sense of being double and living within two minds and bodies was almost a form of insanity: "all the time the dual working of my mind distracted me almost to the point of insanity" (40); "I think I had come creeping quietly as near insanity as any man who has not actually gone over the border" (51). To be of two minds, to be subject to a doubling repetition, is to be on the brink of insanity.

The collective force of this cluster of words as they are repeated again and again in different combinations is to make of the story as a whole a large-scale version of the kind of transformation effected by the perfor- mative tropes of the first paragraph. In the latter, the scene of sea, sky, islets, and shore is turned into a sublimely desolate architectural construc- tion. In the former, the literal story of the harboring by the narrator of a fugitive murderer is changed by the narrator's language into an uncanny story of doubling and repetition. The narrator's performative positings turn objective description into a testimony or confession addressed to me as reader. The episode becomes what it was not in itself, without the nar- rator's intervention, namely, a narrative of the invasion of a safe domicile by a ghostly stranger who upsets the familiar economy of that home and puts a terrible burden of responsibility on its inhabitant. This is the traditional mission of such ghostly invaders in older similar narratives, for example "Sir Gawain and the Green Knight."

The usual pattern of the *Doppelgänger* story, however, is given a significant variation in Conrad's telling of it. Or perhaps it would be better to say that "The Secret Sharer" makes explicit an implicit feature of the *Doppelgänger* story. Here the one who is haunted by a strange double is already, as he tells us, a stranger on the ship. The rest of the crew have all been together for a year and a half, while the captain has quite recently joined the ship as its new and untried captain. Moreover, he is also, as he tells us, a stranger to himself. By this he appears to mean that he does not yet know whether he will be able to measure up to the demands of command or whether he will measure up to his own secret conception of himself: "All these people had been together for eighteen months or so, and my position was that of the only stranger on board. . . . But what I felt most was my being a stranger to the ship; and if all the truth must be told, I was somewhat of a stranger to myself" (26). The invasion of the captain's life by an even stranger stranger, Leggatt, the double of the captain's strangeness, is explicitly said to be brought about by the captain's own strangeness. It is the captain's decision to transgress the "established routine of duties" (28) on the ship that with seemingly magic promptness brings Leggatt into his life as the objective embodiment of his own strangeness: "I felt painfully that I—a stranger—was doing something unusual when I directed [the mate] to let all hands turn in without setting an anchor watch" (27).

Sigmund Freud, citing Schelling, defines "uncanny" (*unheimlich*) as "the name for everything that ought to have remained . . . hidden and secret and has become visible."[24] As I said earlier, Freud's essay is inexhaustibly rich and complex, not least in its contradictions. This is not the place to try to read it in detail. Conrad's story in one place, already cited, uses the word "uncanny": anyone coming into the captain's cabin "would have been treated to the uncanny sight of a double captain busy talking in whispers with his other self." In many ways, moreover, the story corresponds to key aspects of Freud's examples of the uncanny. Not only is doubling in itself uncanny, according to Freud, as are other forms of repetition, but Freud also stresses the gruesome aspects of the uncanny and their relation to sexual mutilation, as well as to ghost effects and to the invasion of the home by a spooky personage who represents something familiar that ought to be kept secret.

Leggatt appears first, in a passage I have quoted, as a headless corpse. In the water he is "ghastly, silvery, fishlike" (29). Once he is hidden in the narrator's cabin he becomes a phantom presence there, attired "in the ghostly grey of [his] sleeping suit" (31). That doubling presence makes "a

scene of weird witchcraft, the strange captain having a quiet confabula-
tion with his own gray ghost" (33). At one point, the narrator says, "an
irresistible doubt of his bodily existence flitted through my mind. Can it
be, I asked myself, that he is not visible to other eyes than mine? It was
like being haunted" (51). The narrator's success in keeping Leggatt hidden raises the question of whether others can see him at all, whether he is
not the narrator's personal ghost.

The English word "uncanny" does not of course fully translate the
German word *unheimlich*. Both, however, are double or antithetical
words. "Uncanny" comes from "can," to know how, be able. "Canny"
means not only shrewd but "susceptible of human understanding; explicable; natural," while uncanny is the opposite: "exciting wonder and
fear: inexplicable; strange, as in 'an uncanny laugh.'" The second meaning of "uncanny," however, shows that it is not so much the opposite of
"canny" as it is canny knowledge and insight carried to that hyperbolic
point where it reverses itself and becomes uncanny: "so keen and perceptive as to seem preternatural, as in 'uncanny insight.'"[25] In the same way,
as any reader of Freud's essay knows, what is uncanny about the word
unheimlich is that it too reverses itself and comes to mean not something
alien to the home, unhomey, but precisely something familiar to the
home, a home secret that ought to have been kept hidden, but has come
out of the closet, so to speak. "Thus 'heimlich,'" says Freud, "is a word
the meaning of which develops towards an ambivalence, until it finally
coincides with its opposite, 'unheimlich.' 'Unheimlich' is in some way or
other a sub-species of 'heimlich'" (30).

Understanding the uncanny, the reader can see, means comprehending
the incomprehensible, since the uncanny is by definition strange, inexplicable. If the reader has "The Secret Sharer" in mind, he or she will remember both the emphasis on what is mysterious and indescribable about
Leggatt for the narrator and the counterstress on the total understanding
that the narrator and Leggatt have of one another. Of Leggatt's telling of
his story the narrator says: "There was something that made comment
impossible in his narrative, or perhaps in himself, a sort of feeling, a quality, which I can't find a name for" (36). Naming is here opposed to feeling
and wordless understanding. Though he cannot name it, he can understand it, as their ultimate exchange of affirmations asserts: "I understand"; "I only hope I have understood, too"; "You have. From first to
last" (55).

The "individual instances" of the *unheimlich* Freud examines in large
part depend on a resource of the German word not present in the English
one. "Heim" means "home" in German. The group of "heim" words,
including *unheimlich*, is associated with family relationships and with the
domestic economy of the house and its grounds—its division into sepa-

rate rooms devoted to different uses; its doors, windows, closets, walls, and gates. The English word "uncanny" does not so overtly have such associations. Freud's discussion of E. T. A. Hoffmann's "The Sandman" is the most extended of his investigations of uncanny literary works. Hoffmann's story involves the invasion of a home and family enclosure. Conrad's story is also an admirable exploitation of the relation of the uncanny to the home and to the opposition between belonging to the home, being a familiar there, and being a stranger. A ship is like a large home with many rooms. The crew is in a manner of speaking one big family. The narrator stresses how they all know one another. He is the only stranger. He is an alien guest who nevertheless dwells within the heart of the home, the captain's quarters, and has a right to be there. Leggatt enters the captain's quarters as the double of the narrator's strangeness, an inner strangeness within what is already strange.

Much of the meaning of "The Secret Sharer" is carried unostentatiously by the careful attention to the exact layout of the captain's quarters and to the way the narrator lives there and manages to keep Leggatt hidden. If the captain's quarters are deep within the ship, in a protected place near the stern, those quarters are themselves further divided and subdivided within, so that there are insides of the insides, outside insides and inside insides. The cabin itself is L-shaped, the narrator tells us, with the door opening into a public inside, so to speak, where the captain's desk and couch can be seen from the door. Around the corner, invisible from the door, an inside of the inside, is the long leg of the L, where the captain's "bed place," as he somewhat curiously calls it, is located. This bed place is a raised bunk with drawers beneath and curtains that may be drawn to protect its privacy, making it an inside of the inside of the inside. Beyond that, at the end of the ell, are coats hung on hooks, behind which Leggatt part of the time hides crouching on a camp stool. In that ell is also the door to the captain's bathroom, another inside of the inside of the inside, where Leggatt spends most of his time, since it is the most hidden and private place of all. Nevertheless, just as there are portholes in the bed-place giving the farthest inside direct access to what is outside the whole ship, exterior to its labyrinthine or *mise en abyme* domestic structure, so there is another doo: in the bathroom leading back into the saloon (the name for a common sitting area on board ship). That door is never used, except by the steward when he enters to clean the bathroom, but it is another example of the way the most inside and private nevertheless leads to the public and outside.

This whole configuration is an admirable materialization of the narrator's relation to Leggatt and to the ship's crew. The trick is to make the whole area appear public, for example to give normal access to it for the steward who cleans the rooms, keeps them in order, and brings the captain his morning coffee, as well as for the chief mate and for the captain of the *Sephora* when the latter comes aboard looking for Leggatt, while at the same time keeping Leggatt invisibly hidden there, giving him a bed to sleep in, feeding him, and so on. This part of the story is a wonderfully concrete externalization of the fear of having one's most secret and even shameful privacies invaded and exposed to public view.

Just what is the uncanny secret that is as familiar as one's own private part of the house? It must be a secret that is in danger of being exposed, or rather that *is* apparently exposed by the captain's narration though it ought to remain hidden, or perhaps still does remain hidden after all the narrator's confessional openness. The secret can hardly be Leggatt's act of murder, since that is known by all on board the *Sephora*. It will ultimately be known to sailors all over that part of the world. The secret must be the narrator's complicity in that murder, his doubling of Leggatt's act by harboring him, and, most hidden secret, the secret behind the secret, the occult ground or obligation that justifies that act in its doubling and makes it the right thing to do.

Conrad repeatedly emphasizes the similarity between the narrator and Leggatt in their propensity to lawless transgression and consequent guilt. This similarity is most overt when the narrator's sense of identity with Leggatt makes him feel guilty too when the captain of the *Sephora* comes seeking Leggatt: "I felt as if I, personally, were being given to understand that I, too, was not the sort that would have done for the chief mate of a ship like the *Sephora*. I had no doubt of it in my mind" (144); "I believe that he [the captain of the *Sephora*] was not a little disconcerted by the reverse side of that weird situation, by something in me that reminded him of the man he was seeking—suggested a mysterious similitude to the young fellow he had distrusted and disliked from the first" (44).

That "mysterious similitude" can be identified, at least in part. Both Leggatt and the narrator have the same social and class background. Both have been trained in the same naval school in preparation for assuming the loneliness of command and the responsibility of independent decision. Such training was an essential part of the formation of those Englishmen who dominated so much of the world during the time of the British Empire. Both have taken the law into their own hands. Both have made an instantaneous decision or a series of decisions that reaffirms the law by transgressing the law. Leggatt has killed an insubordinate crewman in order to save his ship in the storm and in order to maintain the hierarchy of command that is essential on board ship. He has preserved law and order where, according to the narrator, "no means of legal repression" were available. The narrator has, in a spontaneous decision, taken Leggatt on board his ship and has repeated the murderer's crime by hiding him. In doing so he becomes an accessory after the fact, liable to the same punishment as Leggatt himself might receive from the law. Already the narrator has transgressed the ship's normal rules by taking the night-time anchor watch himself. He doubles both of those transgressions again at the end of the story when he shaves the shore dangerously close, risking his ship and horrifying the crew, in order, on his "conscience," to bring Leggatt just as close to shore as he can. These transgressions, the whole force of the story implies, are absolutely necessary to make the narrator worthy of command. Only through those acts can he, at the end of the story, leave Leggatt "to take his punishment, a free man, a proud swimmer striking out for a new destiny." This separation allows the narrator to replace the homosocial relation to Leggatt with the heterosexual relation to his ship that means he is no longer a stranger aboard: "Already the ship was drawing ahead. And I was alone with her. Nothing! no one in the world should stand now between us, throwing a shadow on the way of silent knowledge and mute affection, the perfect communion of a seaman with his first command" (59).

"The Secret Sharer" shows that law and order, the justice that validates command and hierarchy, cannot be maintained by the simple reaffirmation of rules and conventions that are already in place and remain in place. That justice must be periodically interrupted by some decisive act that reaffirms the law by breaking the law. Such an irruptive or disruptive act always has something violent, dangerous, or illicit about it. Its emblems in "The Secret Sharer" are Leggatt's act of murder and the narrator's secret hiding of Leggatt. The ground for such acts remains secret. It is felt only by those on whom it imposes a "pitiless obligation," though that ground is absolutely compelling in the responsibility it lays on the one who receives its commands.

Conrad's name for this command is a traditional one, "conscience," twice repeated as the name for what drives him to go so close to the shore: "It was now a matter of conscience to shave the land as close as possible" (56); hidden in the sail locker Leggatt "was able to hear everything—and perhaps he was able to understand why, on my conscience, it had to be thus close—no less" (58). In a brilliant recent book on Shakespeare, *Daemonic Figures*, Ned Lukacher has shown how the word "conscience" is at the confluence of the two great lines of the Western tradition, the Socratic and Hellenic tradition of the daemon who commands me to act in a certain way and the Judeo-Christian tradition of the still small voice of conscience, the voice of God within the soul that imposes an implacable obligation to act in a certain way in witness of the truth, even if it is against the law. An example of the latter is the appeal to conscience by

English protestants under Catholic rule during the reign of Mary Tudor. They refused in the name of conscience to recant, even when that refusal meant they would be burned at the stake. In their case, as in the case of the narrator's risking of his ship and all aboard, the call of conscience is stronger even than the wish to live, stronger than the appeal of any established law.[26]

The law can be preserved and reaffirmed only by acts that are apparently against the law. The ground for these acts remains private, hidden, secret, apparent only to those who are sensitive to it, who hear its call. It is apparent even then only in not being apparent. It is something that I cannot show to others, something that is, strictly speaking, unpresentable, unrepresentable, just as the narrator cannot find a word for that "sort of feeling, a quality," he senses in Leggatt.

If, however, this secret ground of law-preserving and law-affirming transgression cannot be presented, nevertheless it can be passed on to those who are fit to "understand," as the narrator understands Leggatt. It can be transmitted in a narration like "The Secret Sharer" that makes its demand on the reader for a similar understanding. The ultimate secret of "The Secret Sharer" remains a secret, but that by no means deprives it of power.

Near the beginning of this essay I asked: "Did the narrator do right or wrong in hiding the fugitive murderer Leggatt? On what basis did he make that decision? On what basis should we judge him?" Now I am in a position to answer those questions, after a fashion. Yes, he did right, he acted justly, but we cannot know the ground of that rightness and justice. We can only feel or "understand" its effect in another doubling—or perhaps, on the contrary, not feel it. That cannot be known beforehand or safely predicted for a given reader. The story itself gives the reader a model of an inaugural act that responds to a secret demand. The story is a violent tropological transformation turning "the basic fact of the tale" into a story of testing and testimony. What led Conrad to make this transformation cannot be known. It remains secret. The basis of ethical decision and act, including the act of writing or reading, is the ultimate secret, the most secret secret. This secret cannot be revealed. It is not the object of a possible clear knowledge. Nevertheless, it is a secret I can share, though it remains secret. This secret can only be passed on to me as an obscure but commanding force that comes from something absolutely other. If it cannot be named, it can be made into a story and so transferred to me when I read it. That reading imparts another strong demand for response and taking of responsibility. An example of such a response would be teaching "The Secret Sharer" or writing an essay about it, such as this one.

NOTES

1. Preface to Joseph Conrad, *The Nigger of the "Narcissus"* (London: Penguin, 1989), xlix.

2. Joseph Conrad, "The Secret Sharer," ed. Daniel R. Schwarz (Boston: Bedford Books, 1997), 31. Page numbers henceforth refer to this edition, which is easily available, has useful additional material indicating the multitudinous and somewhat contradictory ways the story has been read, and reprints the 1924 Doubleday edition. "The Secret Sharer" was originally published in 1910.

3. In *Under Western Eyes* (1911), the composition of which Conrad interrupted in order to write "The Secret Sharer," the same situation is presented with a reverse outcome. Whereas the narrator of "The Secret Sharer" hides and protects Leggatt, in *Under Western Eyes* the hardworking, ambitious student, Razumov, turns a revolutionary activist, Victor Haldin, over to the police when the latter comes to his room seeking asylum after having assassinated an official of the repressive czarist regime. It seems as if Conrad were compelled to write the same story twice with opposite choices by the person on whom another person makes a demand.

4. The alert reader will note the doubling of two letters that turns "legate" (meaning emissary, as in "papal legate"; it comes from the Latin *legare*, to depute, commission, charge) into a proper name, Leggatt. The pronunciation would perhaps be the same. The doubling of letters is not only another example of the doubling that is ubiquitous in the story, but by way of the pun on legate also defines Leggatt as an emissary of some sort and the narrator as the recipient or legatee of a charge transmitted to him by Leggatt. This legacy from Leggatt the narrator passes on to the readers of the story or rather to me as a solitary reader who must take sole responsibility for what I make of the story. "Legate," "legacy," and so on are related etymologically to words like "legal" and "legislate" (from Latin *lex*) that have to do with law-making, law-giving. In some obscure way, Leggatt comes to the narrator bearing a legacy that has the force of law.

5. Readers of Conrad's *Lord Jim* (1900) will juxtapose Leggatt's jump to Jim's quite different jump from the *Patna*. Jim abandons the ship with all its passengers, the one thing a ship's officer is not supposed to do. " 'I had jumped . . It seems," says Jim, as if it were an event that was not the result of conscious decision and that he cannot now even remember (Joseph Conrad, *Lord Jim* [London: Penguin, 1989], 125). Nevertheless, he is held accountable for it by the law and disgraced for life as punishment for his act. Should we not hold Leggatt accountable for the determining acts of *his* life?

6. The best account of the factual background of "The Secret Sharer" is in Norman Sherry, " 'The Secret Sharer': The Basic Fact of the Tale," in *Conrad's Eastern World* (Cambridge: Cambridge University Press, 1966), 253–69.

7. See Byron James Caminero-Santangelo, *Failing the Test: Narration and Legitimation in the Work of Joseph Conrad* (Ann Arbor: UMI, 1993).

8. As Norman Sherry tells us Conrad himself did when he had his first command (*Conrad's Eastern World*, 267).

9. It comes from a Greek word *hermeneuein*, to interpret. "Hermeneutics" is

"the science and methodology of interpretation, especially of Scriptural text" (*The American Heritage Dictionary*).

10. Jacques Derrida, "Fourmis," in *Lectures de la différence sexuelle*, ed. Mara Negrón (Paris: Des femmes, 1994), 89, my translation.

11. In a way something like this appearance of the devil when you sneeze, it could be argued, it is not without significance that Leggatt appears just after the narrator-captain has broken the normal rules of good seamanship and sent all the crew to bed so he can take a solitary five-hour anchor watch himself. His law-breaking or rule-breaking has made him vulnerable to the apparition of Leggatt.

12. He did initially intend to swim on in the open sea until he sank from exhaustion, as no doubt the scorpion in the inkwell did, if scorpions can swim.

13. In the "Author's Note" of the 1920 reprint of the volume *'Twixt Land and Sea* of 1912. The latter contained the original book publication of "The Secret Sharer." Its first publication was in serialized form in *Harper's Magazine* in August-September 1910.

14. I cite this from *"The Shadow-Line" and Two Other Tales*, ed. Morton Dauwen Zabel (Garden City, N.Y.: Doubleday Anchor, 1959), 32, 33.

15. "He kept silent for a while, then whispered, 'I understand.'"
'I won't be there to see you go,' I began with an effort. 'The rest . . I only hope I have understood too.'
'You have. From first to last'" (55).

16. (Paris: Galilée, 1991); *Given Time, I: Counterfeit Money*, trans. Peggy Kamuf (Chicago: University of Chicago Press, 1992).

17. (Paris: Galilée, 1993); "Passions," trans. David Wood, in *On the Name*, ed. Thomas Dutoit (Stanford: Stanford University Press, 1995), 2–31.

18. I owe this reading of "secret sharer" to Kevin Yee.

19. See Walter Benjamin's "Critique of Violence" ("Zur Kritik der Gewalt" [1921]) as the most troubling and searching investigation of this problem. See also Jacques Derrida's discussion of Benjamin's essay and related questions of the grounds of justice in *Force de loi* (Paris: Galilée, 1994); "Force of Law: The 'Mystical Foundation of Authority,'" trans. Mary Quaintance, in *Deconstruction and the Possibility of Justice*, ed. Drucilla Cornell, Michel Rosenfeld, and David Gray Carlson (New York: Routledge, 1992), 3–67.

20. Since Conrad wrote this story, partly through colonization of the political or of the economic sort, partly through the work of many busy Western anthropologists, fewer and fewer places on the globe are unsolved secrets to the West in this way.

21. I mean the word "sublime" in the strong, traditional sense of the word, as it is used from Longinus through Kant and Burke up to present-day theorists of the sublime such as Thomas Weiskel, Jean-François Lyotard, or Paul de Man. For all of these philosopher-critics the sublime, in one way or another, is a subjective feeling mingling fear and inordinate pleasure. Strictly speaking, no object is sublime, but the feeling of the sublime may be aroused or represented by some aspect of nature that exceeds human comprehension, something that is terrifying because it is unknown and unknowable. The sublime can only be named in figures that are illegitimate in the sense that they are not proper names and are not commensurate with the frightening unknowability they seek to make apparently

namable. An empty sea under the empty sky is one example Kant gives of the sublime, though, like Conrad, he sees this in architectural terms. It cannot be seen in its sheer materiality. See Paul de Man, "Phenomenality and Materiality in Kant," in *Aesthetic Ideology*, ed. Andrzej Warminski (Minneapolis: University of Minnesota Press, 1996), 70–90.

22. Aristotle, *Poetics*, 22:9, 1459a. William Wordsworth, in the "Preface" of 1815, is true to Aristotle when he sees such metaphorical transformations as prime evidence of the poetic imagination. See William Wordsworth, *Poetical Works*, ed. Thomas Hutchinson and Ernest de Selincourt (London: Oxford University Press, 1966), 754. This passage is cited and discussed in chapter 1. For Wordsworth, as for Conrad, the primary evidence of word power is the ability to use words in personifications of the inanimate and depersonifications of the animate.

23. William Carlos Williams long ago formulated this strange effect of certain word uses apropos of Marianne Moore's poetry, though with emphasis on the making material of words rather than on the uncanny draining away of meaning I am stressing. "Miss Moore," wrote Williams, "gets great pleasure from wiping soiled words or cutting them clean out, removing the aureoles that have been pasted about them or taking them bodily from greasy contexts. For the compositions which Miss Moore intends, each word should first stand crystal clear with no attachments; not even an aroma" (*Selected Essays* [New York: Random House, 1954], 128).

24. Sigmund Freud, "The Uncanny," in *Studies in Parapsychology* (New York: Collier, 1971), 27. Further citations will be to this edition.

25. These definitions are drawn from *The American Heritage Dictionary*.

26. See Ned Lukacher, *Daemonic Figures: Shakespeare and the Question of Conscience* (Ithaca: Cornell University Press, 1994). I owe the example of the protestants' appeal to conscience in sixteenth-century England to an admirable lecture by Steven Mullaney. "Reforming Resistance: Class, Gender, and Legitimacy in Foxe's *Book of Martyrs*."

Chapter Seven

W. B. YEATS:
"THE COLD HEAVEN"

Le poème échoit, bénédiction, venue de l'autre.
(The poem falls, benediction, come from the other,
the coming of the other.)
　　—Jacques Derrida, "Che cos'è la poesia?"

A POEM comes by fate or by chance. It "befalls" the one who receives it, like a benediction, that is, like words that confer a blessing or that invoke a blessing. Benediction means, literally, speaking well, usually of some person, not of some thing. A benediction invokes what comes from the other or is the coming of the other, subjective and objective genitive at once. The "other" in question here is that wholly other about which Derrida writes, tautologically, in *The Gift of Death*: "tout autre est tout autre." This means, among other possibilities, "every other is wholly other."[1] We usually think of the "other" as just somewhat different, for example someone from a different culture. For Derrida the other in question in a poem's benediction is entirely different, "wholly other." The consequences of accepting such a notion are not trivial. Something wholly other is frighteningly alien, inassimilable. Nevertheless, Derrida argues that a poem comes from such a wholly other and speaks for it. Just what that might mean, this chapter will try to show.

I shall be responding to the benediction of a single poem, W. B. Yeats's "The Cold Heaven." The words "poetry," *poésie* (French), *poesia* (both Italian and Spanish), and *Dichtung* (German) are notoriously equivocal. Aristotle used the Greek equivalent, *poiesis*, making, to name the whole field of what today, and for only a little more than two hundred years, we in the West have called "literature," *littérature, letteratura, literatura, Literatur*. "Poetry" is still sometimes used in this extended sense to name in general any special use of language that involves "literarity," whatever *that* is. By "poetry" we usually mean those conglomerations of words marked by rhythmic, semantic, and sonorous repetitions (rhyme, assonance, alliteration, etc.) and printed in odd or conventional ways, line by line, with blank spaces around. You can tell a poem when you see one, on the page, even if it is an abstract from a newspaper or from a telephone book arranged "poetically," as a "found poem":

Blue Angels Youth Ski and Snowboard Program;
Blue Auto Glass;
Blue B;
Blue Beet Cafe The;
Blue Bell Foundation for Cats;
Blue Bell Pools;
Blue Betty PhD;
Blue Bird Motel & Cafe.[2]

That such a fortuitous set of words can be "taken as a poem" indicates that "poetry," in the narrow sense, is both an intrinsic feature of certain words taken together and at the same time the product of a complex set of historical determinations. It is not the case that I am free to take anything I like as poetry. Rather, a large, overdetermined set of collective conventions and rules acts through me to lead me to take a given set of words as a poem and treat it as such. These rules and conventions are historically situated, for example in relation to certain technological regimes. They change from time to time, from country to country, and from language to language. Poetry is a subset of what we have meant by "literature" in the West since the eighteenth century. As such, it is associated, as I mentioned in chapter 5, with democracy and with freedom of speech. Freedom of speech would include the privilege, never of course perfectly realized, to say anything, to put anything in question, and not to be held responsible for it, to disclaim responsibility in the name of another responsibility or a responsibility to the other. I can always say, "That was not me speaking. That was an imaginary or fictive voice speaking in my poem. I wrote out of an obligation to the wholly other."

This excuse, I hasten to add, would not exonerate someone hailed before one or another of the censoring powers that exist even now in democratic countries. Nevertheless, if it is right to historicize literature this way, and I believe it is, it would follow that poetry in "our" sense did not exist prior to the development of Western-style democracies. Poetry could cease to exist and civilization would not come to an end. Insofar as what we mean by poetry belongs to the post-Cartesian epoch of print culture in the West, that is, the period of a particular subject/object dichotomy strongly reinforced or even generated by the technology of the printed book, what we call "poetry" may now be coming to an end. This is happening as print technology is replaced by television, cinema, videocassette recorders, computers and the Internet, in short by the new regime of telecommunications.

Within print culture, poetry as a subcategory of literature depends on the possibility of suspending in a given case the referential force that all language has and attending to the words in themselves, as a benediction from the other, the coming of the wholly other. My telephone book poem exemplifies that. In the real world one might urgently need to order something from the Blue Beet Cafe, or to make a contribution (or send a cat) to the Blue Bell Foundation for Cats, or enlist the services of Dr. Betty Blue. In that case the accuracy of the telephone numbers listed with each entry would be crucial. As Paul de Man observes, an "irresistible motion . . . forces any text beyond its limits and projects it towards an exterior referent."[3] We use the telephone book to make telephone calls. When the extract I have cited (omitting the numbers) is taken as a poem, however, that pragmatic use is not so much abolished (that cannot be) as short-circuited. A poem is like an extract from a fictional telephone book or, rather, like an extract from a telephone book whose truth or fictionality does not determine its literary function or lack of it. As a poem my citation would work just as well even if there were no such thing as the Blue Bell Foundation for Cats or the Blue Beet Cafe. The power of Henry James's *The Wings of the Dove* does not depend on whether or not Kate Croy, Merton Densher, and Milly Theale were "based on" real people, nor does the power of Yeats's "The Cold Heaven" depend on whether or not the "experience" "recorded" in the poem "really happened" to Yeats, though much criticism in both cases and in most other such cases mistakenly assumes that it does.

These assertions must not be misunderstood. "The Cold Heaven," *The Wings of the Dove*, and my telephone book "poem" are all deeply embedded in history, surrounded by complex, overdetermined historical contexts. As I have said, the possibility of taking them as literary works depends on specific historical conditions and expectations. The inalienable referential or mimetic dimension of language, however, is in literature turned or troped to become what I call performative catachreses for the "wholly other" that Derrida names. The catachreses in literature are performative in two senses. They are speech acts in response to the demand made on the poet by the "tout autre." They give names to a wholly other that does not have any given names. The poem or novel whenever it is read then reenters history, intervening not just to mirror history but to alter it performatively, in however minuscule a way. What we call history is generated by innumerable such small performative speech acts.

I turn now to present a reading as exemplification of what is always to some degree sui generis, an example only of itself, a poem as read. I choose W. B. Yeats's "The Cold Heaven." It comes from his 1914 volume, *Responsibilities*. Here is the poem:

THE COLD HEAVEN

Suddenly I saw the cold and rook-delighting heaven
That seemed as though ice burned and was but the more ice,

And thereupon imagination and heart were driven
So wild that every casual thought of that and this
Vanished, and left but memories, that should be out of season
With the hot blood of youth, of love crossed long ago;
And I took the blame out of all sense and reason,
Until I cried and trembled and rocked to and fro,
Riddled with light. Ah! when the ghost begins to quicken,
Confusion of the death-bed over, is it sent
Out naked on the roads, as the books say, and stricken
By the injustice of the skies for punishment?[4]

This poem is characteristic not only of Yeats, but of the Romantic lyric tradition he inherited. Yeats's work is, according to Pater's formula in "Aesthetic Poetry," a "strange second flowering after date" of that tradition.[5] The poem presents itself as the record in the past tense of a powerful subjective event that happened at some indeterminate time in the past. This event was generated by the confrontation of something in nature, the winter sky.[6] The poem is not so much emotion recollected in tranquillity, as Wordsworth said a poem should be, as it is emotion recollected in agitation. Memory, for Yeats, and its expression in words, repeat the emotion, renew it. The speaker is agitated even at the beginning of the poem, not just at its end. "Suddenly," it seems, may name the now of the speaker's speech, or of the writer's writing, as well as the moment in the past when he suddenly saw the cold and rook-delighting heaven. Six times intersect or are superimposed in "suddenly": (1) the moment of the original, perhaps imaginary, event commemorated in the poem, (2) the earlier time, "of love crossed long ago," that was remembered and renewed in that event, (3) the now of the putative speaker's speech, (4) the now of the writing of the poem, (5) the anticipated moment of death, and (6) the reader's repetition of all these in their overlapping when the poem is read or recited. The last of the six may be indicated in the perpetual present of the title. The poem asks how all these are related, after a sudden insight that they *are* related.

"Suddenly" and "sudden" are recurrent words in Yeats's poetry. They are used to name the moment of poetic vision, as in the first words of "Leda and the Swan": "A sudden blow" (VP, 441), or as in climactic lines in "Vacillation": "While on the shop and street I gazed / My body of a sudden blazed" (VP, 501). Like Wordsworth, Yeats focuses on a moment of visionary interruption and breakthrough. In that moment ordinary indifference to one's surroundings is for some reason shattered. Suddenly one *sees*. In Wordsworth this often happens at the moment of breakdown of an expected reciprocity between self and its surroundings, as in "The Boy of Winander" or as in De Quincey's report of Wordsworth listening with his ear to the ground for the expected mail cart and not hearing it.[7] In a more exalted form, the crossing of the Simplon Pass in *The Prelude* is such an abrupt interruption and breakthrough. It is when the expected does not happen that the sudden visionary insight occurs. Paradoxically, you see what is there or you see through what is there when the subject/object mirroring breaks down. Rather than being a mirror in which you see your own excited face, to alter a figure Yeats uses in "The Symbolism of Poetry,"[8] nature now enters into a subjectivity that has been emptied out. Or the naked power of that subjectivity appears when nature no longer reflects and supports it. Consciousness becomes mirror of the nonpersonified, deathly impersonality of nature. This nature, called in this poem the "cold heaven," may delight the rooks, but it delights not the normal "I" that can easily and unselfconsciously appropriate nature, for example by personifying it. In reporting this afterwards you can or must say, "Suddenly I saw." Wordsworth's personification of nature—"And then my heart with pleasure fills / And dances with the daffodils"[9]—is by comparison a relatively tame reciprocity.

"The Cold Heaven" figures the injustice of the skies in the combination of contradictories, ice and fire, that brings visionary insight ("Suddenly I saw"), if one takes the blame out of all sense and reason. This recalls the catharsis of Greek tragedy, for example in those dramas of *Oedipus the King* and *Oedipus at Colonus* that Yeats adapted for modern stage performances. In Sophoclean tragedy the protagonist retains or regains his freedom by taking the blame and punishment for something he has been fated to do but has done without meaning to do it, without knowing he did it, has done without doing it. Oedipus did not mean to kill his father and marry his mother. Nevertheless Jocasta hangs herself and Oedipus blinds himself as self-punishment for crimes they did not knowingly or intentionally commit. In a similar way, the "love crossed long ago" in "The Cold Heaven" was not the speaker's fault, but he takes the blame, out of all sense and reason.

A slightly closer look at "The Cold Heaven" shows that the little word "and," the copula, occurs an amazing number of times—eleven, to be exact—whereas, for example, in the poem just previous in *Responsibilities*, "Friends," the word occurs only twice, though that poem is longer: "The cold and rook-delighting heaven": "as though ice burned and was but the more ice": "And thereupon imagination and heart were driven": "every casual thought of that and this"; "Vanished, and left but memories"; "And I took the blame"; "out of all sense and reason." The "ands" rise to a climax with "Until I cried and trembled and rocked to and fro," three ands in a single line. After the "Ah!" that comes next, only one more "and" appears ["and stricken"]—as though the need for "and" had exhausted itself for some reason in that "Ah!"

Why all these "ands"? Are they the sign of narrative progression or perhaps of nonprogressive metonymic side-by-sideness or contingency? First this and then that. This and that and that and that, one after the other. It might seem so from lines 3, 5, and 7: "And thereupon"; "and left but memories"; "And I took the blame." Or perhaps these "ands" indicate a causal progression. Suddenly he saw the cold and rook-delighting heaven "and thereupon" something happened that was a result of the seeing. Or are the "ands" not rather, in several cases at any rate, the sign of an alternation, a vacillation between what look like extremes, opposites: "this and that"; "to and fro." Does the "and" not join in a copula what only appear to be opposites, so that "x and y" expresses an unfolded or elaborated oxymoron. This heaven is "cold," inhospitable, detached, inhuman, unsympathetic. At the same time it delights the rooks. The cold heaven is the rooks' element. It seems warm to them. The heaven is "cold and rook-delighting." The second line unfolds the implicit oxymoron "fiery ice" in "seemed as though ice burned and was but the more ice." This is no natural heaven. It seems icy cold and at the same time fiery hot. Other nouns paired by the copula "and" seem, however, perhaps mere poetic redundancies. In any case they are not obviously opposites, so the reader's mind puzzles over them. Fire and ice are clearly opposites, but what is the difference between "imagination" and "heart," or between "sense" and "reason"? The first eight lines of the poem seem to exploit all these different uses of "and," alternating from one to another. The "and" of alternation ultimately dominates, as casual thoughts of that and this were transformed, when he took the blame out of all sense and reason, into an oscillation so rapid that it became an incandescent blur that almost reduced all language to "and, and, and, and," as he "cried and trembled and rocked to and fro / Riddled with light." At that moment of taking fire, "and" has been heard so often that it is becoming empty of sense. The word has been taken out of all sense and reason and approaches pure sound. "And" then is transformed into the senseless violence of an involuntary exclamation: "Ah!," the first phoneme of "And" without the second differentiating one that makes it an articulate word: "Say Ah!" "Ah!" is said with *bouche ouverte*, an open mouth to modulate as little as possible the sound of expelled breath from low in the throat. The *American Heritage Dictionary* defines "Ah" as an interjection "used to express various emotions, such as surprise, delight, pain, satisfaction, or dislike." "Ah!" is a double or antithetical word, combining opposites. It can be the expression of extreme physical pleasure but also marks the moment of expiration when the ghost is exhaled at the instant of death. You die a little death every time you say, or are forced to say, "Ah!" All the merely sequential elements in the poem, all the causal followings (this and thereupon that), all the opposites both outside (fire and ice) and inside (imagination and heart), come together in the nonsense of that "Ah!" "Ah!" is the register of a visionary insight beyond all sense and reason. "And" returns like a secret refrain, beneath the overt prosody, punctuating the poem rhythmically in counterpoint until its incandescent transformation into visionary insight happens in a moment of radical caesura or halt in the rhythm, dividing before from after and leading to the proleptic question: "And . . . and . . . and . . . and . . . Ah! Is the soul . . . ?" That "Ah!" marks the moment of a tense shift from past to present, to the present now of the speaker who asks his urgent question about the future moment of death.

"Visionary insight" into what? Just how is the insight achieved or how does it come about? The title names the scene, "The Cold Heaven." In early printings of the poem, "Heaven" was capitalized within the poem, but in most late printings not. It seems as if Yeats had to have his heaven both ways and could not quite decide between the two. He alternated to and fro between them. "Heaven" is of course a double word, as it was conspicuously for Wordsworth, as in "The Boy of Winander." "Cold Heaven" names the actual natural sky on a wintry day. It also names a place of supernatural power and judgment. The word "H/heaven" itself is a place of ambiguous alternation.

That folding of incompatibles in a single word mimes in miniature the way the poem concentrates entire regions from the speaker's life and thought. Each is squeezed in by synecdoche to make an explosive mixture. This is a regular feature of Yeats's work, one of the ways he gets concentration and power, even self-deconstructing violence, in his poems. In "The Cold Heaven" the phrase "love crossed long ago" contains in miniature, it may be (though the poem does not explicitly say so, and though the reader need not know it), the long story of Yeats's failed courtship of Maud Gonne, to whom he formally proposed marriage over and over again, only to be rejected again and again. The reader can learn what he or she needs to know about this from other poems by Yeats, poems that transform autobiography into the impersonality of poetry. "Sent out naked on the roads" is a part standing for the whole of the poet's esoteric ideas about the soul's adventures after death, with "roads" containing all that Yeats writes elsewhere about the circling gyres, the trajectory or journey of the soul, as well as possibly a covert allusion to the Sphinx's riddle, and to the place where three roads intersect, the crossroads where Oedipus killed Laius. One section of Yeats's *Autobiographies* is called "Hodos Cameliontos," the road of the camelion. All this "context" is buried in that one word "roads." The poem exploits these concentrating powers of the synecdochic in enacting a to and fro that builds up to a moment that takes fire "suddenly" when contradictory elements are brought together and fused, like fire and ice, guiltlessness and guilt, freedom and necessity, responsibility and passive suffering, this-worldly experience of a certain weather on a certain imagined day in Ireland and other-worldly experiences of the soul after death.

The poem ends then with an urgent, unanswered and perhaps unanswerable question. Is the newly quickened ghost "sent / Out naked on the roads, as the books say, and stricken / By the injustice of the skies for punishment?" This is not a rhetorical question, as Harold Bloom avers.[10] It is a real question, and a lot hangs on the answer. The poet would like to know. The reader would like to know too. In this climactic question "skies" substitutes for "heaven." If the answer is an affirmative one, then "skies" or "heaven" becomes the emblem of a supernatural unjust judging power. On the other hand a certain notion of the supernatural, what those old esoteric books Yeats read told him, is expressed in a striking natural image. The ghost, confusion of the deathbed over, "quickens" as an embryo is said to "quicken" when it becomes viable, or as a seed quickens when it sprouts. The deathbed becomes figuratively a birthbed, perhaps even a bed of lovemaking leading to conception. The quickened ghost is then, in a powerfully naturalistic image, "sent out naked on the roads," as if it were a naked person or a newborn. There this quasi-person is stricken by the injustice of the skies for punishment, as every mother's son or daughter is born naked into a cold world, or as a naked living person outcast outside the safe enclosure of home might wander homeless on the roads and suffer cruelly from being out in the open, on the roads, in bad weather.

Another way to ask the question that ends the poem would be to ask which takes precedence here, natural image or supernatural emblem (to borrow the terms that organize de Man's reading of Yeats in "Image and Emblem in Yeats").[11] Is the human, natural scene, the imagined speaker looking at a cold sky and imagining what it would be like to wander naked on the roads under such a cold heaven, an emblem of the experience by the "ghost" after death of "the injustice of the skies," or is it the other way around? If "things below are copies" (VP, 556), nevertheless things above can only be named by human beings with the names of things below. "Heaven" is at first the natural sky's name and then by transfer the name of a supernatural place. Which is the literal, which the figurative, heaven or Heaven? There is no way to know, and so the concluding question hovers interminably and unanswerably in the air. How could we know the answer until we are dead?

Dead men, however, tell no tales. The meaning of "The Cold Heaven" is this undecidability, the impossibility of knowing whether the most extreme experiences, triggered by earthly memories, such as memories of love crossed long ago, are copies of things above, immemorial memories, proleptic foretastes of the soul's experience after death, or whether there are certain purely human, bodily experiences that make one tremble and rock to and fro, experiences so extreme that the only adequate expression in language for them is what the old books say, perhaps meretriciously, about what happens to the soul after death.

This uncertainty about which H(h)eaven is the emblem of which is expressed in concentrated form in the marvelous climactic phrase, just before the "Ah!": "riddled with light." The poem reaches that climax by a series of precisely and succinctly enumerated steps, each the necessary presupposition, so it seems, of the next. It is not entirely clear, however, just why the sudden seeing of the cold heaven should make the speaker remember love crossed long ago, unless the sky's coldness and indifference is the emblem of the woman's repudiation, nor why that memory should lead him to take the blame out of all sense and reason. The sequence of events, nevertheless, could not happen in any other order. Each has to happen before the next can happen. Like the sequence of events in a Greek tragedy—*Oedipus the King* or *Oedipus at Colonus*—the series is fortuitous and necessary at once. The speaker sees the cold sky that combines ice with fire, burning ice that is all the colder for burning. This drives his imagination and heart, that is, both his mental power of forming images, of imagining things, and his heart, his power of feeling, including sexual feeling, emotions that tie him to the earth, so "wild" that "every casual thought of that and this" "vanishes" and all his powers of thinking, imagining, and feeling are focused on memories of love crossed long ago. These memories are out of season in the sense that they are appropriate not for an aging man but for the hot blood of youth.

Those memories lead the speaker to a decision, to an act, to a silent and therefore anomalous speech act. Though the "crossing" of his love was not unambiguously his fault, any more than it was Oedipus's fault that he killed his father, married his mother, and begat children who were his own brothers and sisters, nevertheless the speaker "took the blame out of all sense and reason," just as Oedipus took the blame on himself for the parricide and incest he did not mean to do and did not know he was doing. Implicitly the speaker in "The Cold Heaven" says: "I did it, and I accept responsibility," though he does not, apparently, speak aloud, and though no witness attests to his speech act, except you and me as readers of the poem. This taking of the blame is an odd and anomalous speech act. It is private and mute, unless the "Ah!" can be taken as its speaking out. The poem itself articulates for us as readers the taking of blame. The poem records a singular and private imaginary experience. Turning it into poetry, however, makes it infinitely repeatable. The poem may be printed and reprinted, read over and over by thousands of different people all over the world. Does the speech act not reoccur every time the poem is read, happen again not as "mention" but as "use," in the endless iterability of the poem as benediction? The speech act is then transferred to the reader. It becomes through the recitation of the poem the reader's speech act, no longer the speaker's private one.

If the poem is such a speech act, what does it do? How is the poem when I read it a way of doing things with words? Only when the speaker takes the blame does what might be called the apotheosis occur: "Until I cried and trembled and rocked to and fro/Riddled with light. Ah!" The reader must repeat through reading this taking of blame if the poem is to work as benediction, the coming of the wholly other, a riddling of the reader with light. He or she must, like the speaker of the poem, take the blame out of the realm of sense and reason into the realm of unanswerable enigma, in another possible meaning of the phrase.

I call it an apotheosis because the speaker is filled with light, penetrated by it, perforated by it, riddled by it, as in a moment of mystic illumination. It is an apotheosis in the sense of being filled by a god, though in this case an exceedingly dark and ominous god, an impersonal god of injustice, insoluble riddle, and death. The *American Heritage Dictionary* gives three meanings for the first form of "riddle" as a verb: (1) to pierce with numerous holes; perforate, as in *riddle with bullets*. (2) To put through a coarse sieve. A riddle is a coarse sieve for separating or grading materials such as gravel and the like, as in *potato riddle*, a meaning quite likely known to Yeats. (3) To find or show weakness in; disprove or damage. Though Yeats probably did not know it, the root is *skeri*, meaning cut, separate, sift, also the root of words like crime and discriminate, discern, scribble and script, not to speak of crisis and critic, all words naming some act of sifting in the sense of dividing this from that, the sheep from the goats. To be riddled with light means not only to be penetrated, perforated, and filled with light, but also to be judged by it, as the speaker imagines the ghost after death stricken by the injustice of the skies as punishment for a crime he did not commit.

To be riddled with light also no doubt invokes the other, etymologically unrelated, form of "riddle" as "a question or statement requiring thought to answer or understand; a conundrum. Something perplexing; an enigma," for example the Sphinx's riddle: "What walks on four feet in the morning, two feet at noon, and three feet at the end of the day?" As a verb this second form of "riddle" means either "to solve or propound riddles" or "to speak in riddles." To be riddled with light is to have a perhaps unsolvable riddle propounded on one's body, to be riddled with a riddle. All good riddles obscurely or openly involve death, or are deadly to answer, as in the angry question posed by that goddess of crossroads, Hecate, to the three witches in *Macbeth* V.3: "How did you dare / To trade and traffic with Macbeth / In riddles and affairs of death?" or in the way Oedipus, in answering "man" to the Sphinx's riddle, is also unwittingly anticipating his own fate, to wander on the roads, self-blinded as a result of seeing too much, feeling his way with a stick, there-fore walking on three legs, making his way on a journey leading ulti-mately to his death and apotheosis at Colonus.

What the deadly riddle in "The Cold Heaven" is the reader knows. It is propounded in the question of the final lines: "Is the ghost after death sent out naked on the roads, as the books say, and smitten by the injustice of the skies for punishment?" Well, is it, or is it not? The speaker and the reader need urgently to know. No answer to the riddle is given, just as no answers are given to the riddles that end "Among School Children" and "Leda and the Swan." The reader is left at his or her peril to hazard an answer, though to answer may be deadly.

What is that light that riddles the speaker? What is its source? Far from illuminating the speaker, this light puts him, it may be, in a permanent state of unseeing perplexity. It is a blinding light. The climactic cry of "Ah!" that responds to being riddled with light is a strange kind of asemantic oxymoron. The light that riddles the poet is the diffused figure of that sun the wasteful virtues earn.[12] Among the wasteful virtues are being secret and taking defeat out of every brazen throat ("To a Friend Whose Work Has Come to Nothing," VP, 290–91), the desire to destroy the half-imagined, the half-written page, and, in this poem, taking the blame out of all sense and reason. *Responsibilities* sets those reckless, spendthrift ancestors Yeats praises in several poems, or the reckless pa-triotism of Daniel O'Leary and other heroes of the long Irish fight against England, or Major Robert Gregory's sacrifice of his life as an Irish airman fighting for the English in the First World War, that is, fighting for a cause in which he did not believe, against the bourgeois shopkeepers (mostly Catholic) whom Yeats so detested for "fumbling in a greasy till," for "toiling to grow rich."

To say only the wasteful virtues earn the sun looks like saying you gain by throwing away, by spending as a spendthrift. In fact you gain, as poem after poem by Yeats makes clear, nothing but death and the injustice of the cold heaven. This is affirmed overtly in the next poem after "The Cold Heaven," "That the Night Come" (VP, 317), as well as, for example, in "An Irish Airman Foresees His Death" (VP, 328). To put this in the terms of "The Cold Heaven": you gain through taking the blame out of all sense and reason not the sun as gold, as the greatest value, as measure, logos, ratio, ruler, dispenser of justice, but rather the absent sun as abso-lute loss, as injustice, the injustice of the cold heaven. The sky in Yeats's poem is empty. The sun is nowhere overtly mentioned in the poem, though it must somehow be the source of the light that riddles the poet. The absent sun is present only in dispersed figure, as burning ice, or as the "light" with which the speaker is "riddled." Instead of earning the sun as a positive recompense through the wasteful virtue of taking the blame out of all sense and reason, the speaker earns the injustice of the empty skies for punishment. The injustice of the skies is the absence of the sun, a measureless lack of just measure. Yeats's absent sun is a figure for something like Derrida's wholly other, what the latter calls, at the very end of "Aphorism Countertime," "a true sun, the other."[13]

"The Cold Heaven" itself is a mirroring example of the earning of the injustice of the skies the poem names. Rather than achieving the plenitude of accomplished organic form and powerfully expressed meaning, as we have been taught to believe all good lyric poems should do, "The Cold Heaven" violently empties itself out. It wastes itself, spends itself, cancels itself out in that final question and in the impossibility of deciding whether natural image or supernatural emblem takes precedence as the literal referent of which the other is the figure. This self-canceling leaves the reader empty-handed, riddled with light, driven out of all sense and reason by an effort of reading.

Reading is conventionally defined as an accounting for some text or other that brings it back to sense and reason, finds out its sense, in the sense of meaning, and its reason, in the sense of its underlying ground or reason for being. This happens according to the Leibnizian "principle of reason" (*Satz vom Grund*) that says everything has its reason, can have its reason rendered back to it. The research university exists as the place that accounts for everything, renders everything reasonable, including poems and other literary works. Literary history, philology, biography, *Literaturwissenschaft* in general, have this latter task as their charge. Poetry, however, or "the poetic" in language, if there is such a thing, is what cannot be rendered reasonable. It takes the reader out of all sense and reason. The reader will note that my reading of a poem has differed from a New Critical "close reading," which it might seem superficially to resemble in its attention to detail and to figurative language, in three fundamental ways: (1) it overtly uses speech-act theory; (2) it encounters the limits of the assumption that a good poem must be an "organic unity"; (3) it also encounters, within the poem, invoked by the poem, something unintelligible, something "wholly other." The most extreme efforts to preserve sense and reason, those saving virtues of literary studies, must be made, however, as I have sought to make them in this reading, before the reader meets at the border of the intelligible (for example in "The Cold Heaven") the black hole of what is beyond all sense and reason.

NOTES

1. See Jacques Derrida, *Donner la mort* (Paris: Galilée, 1999), 114–57; *The Gift of Death*, trans. David Wills (Chicago: University of Chicago Press, 1995), 82–115. Chapter 11 of this book discusses "Derrida's others" in more detail.

2. From an Orange County Pacific Bell phonebook, with telephone numbers omitted.

3. Paul de Man, "Reading (Proust)," in *Allegories of Reading* (New Haven: Yale University Press, 1979), 70.

4. W. B. Yeats, *The Variorum Edition of the Poems*, ed. Peter Allt and Russell K. Alspach (New York: Macmillan, 1977), 316. Henceforth cited as VP.

5. Walter Pater, *Appreciations* (London: Macmillan 1889), 213.

6. The poem does not say it is winter, but Yeats told Maud Gonne, who asked the meaning of the poem, "that it was an attempt to describe the feelings aroused in him by the cold detached sky in winter" (A. Norman Jeffares, *A Commentary on the Collected Poems of W. B. Yeats* [Stanford: Stanford University Press. 1968], 146).

7. Thomas De Quincey, *Recollections of the Lakes and the Lake Poets* (Harmondsworth: Penguin, 1970), 160.

8. W. B. Yeats, *Essays and Introductions* (London: Macmillan, 1961), 163.

9. William Wordsworth, *Poetical Works*, ed. Thomas Hutchinson and Ernest de Selincourt (London: Oxford University Press, 1966), 149.

10. Harold Bloom, *Yeats* (New York: Oxford University Press, 1970), 175.

11. Paul de Man, *The Rhetoric of Romanticism* (New York: Columbia University Press, 1984), 145–238.

12. Yeats puts it this way in an enigmatic aphorism in the "Introductory Rhymes" of *Responsibilities*: "Only the wasteful virtues earn the sun" (VP, 270).

13. Derrida, *Acts of Literature*, ed. Derek Attridge (New York: Routledge, 1992), 433.

Chapter Eight

E. M. FORSTER:
JUST READING *HOWARDS END*

A place, as well as a person, may catch the glow.
—E. M. Forster, *Howards End*

A JUST READING of *Howards End*[1] all depends on how you take the word "unseen" and its synonyms, "invisible" (5), "unknown" (100), "infinity" (9), "the obscure borderland" (57), "the submerged" (70), "a more inward light" (88), "the inconceivable" (202), "the glow" (335), the "idea of Death" (236), and so on. These words and phrases recur in the novel. An adept reader of *Howards End* soon comes to notice such repetitions and to assume they are probably important. The phrase "panic and emptiness," for example, recurs, as does the phrase "his hands were on all the ropes of life" (129). Both Leonard Bast and Margaret Schlegel, in quite different circumstances, drop a framed photograph of a woman and cut themselves on the broken glass. Does that not assert some obscure connection between the two characters and some special meaning for the doubled event?

Among other such repetitions, the word "unseen" echoes discreetly and unostentatiously through the novel like a musical motif. It occurs repeatedly in different contexts. The word is especially associated with Margaret Schlegel. She, for example, is said to have concluded that "any human being lies nearer to the unseen than any organization" (28). Later she asserts that for the Germans "literature and art have what one might call the kink of the unseen about them" (74). The narrator observes of Mrs. Wilcox's strange decision on her deathbed to leave Howards End to Margaret Schlegel: "The desire for a more inward light had found expression at last. The unseen had impacted on the seen" (97). Margaret writes to her sister Helen: "Don't brood too much . . . on the superiority of the unseen to the seen" (101). Later she thinks, "All vistas close in the unseen—no one doubts it—but Helen closed them rather too quickly for her taste" (192), whereas for Charles Wilcox's shallow wife Dolly " 'spooks' and 'going to church' summarized the unseen" (200). What does the word "unseen" mean in these sentences? To what does it refer? Should we as readers take it seriously, or does it name no more than a personal "kink" ascribed ironically to the characters, especially to Margaret, by a demystified narrator?

By "you" in "all depends on how you take the word 'unseen' " I mean *you*, the reader of these words, the person to whom they are addressed. In the same way the narrator of *Howards End* speaks to you, to me, or to any other reader in a way that seems unique in each case. The narrator is speaking to *me*, and I must respond as best I can. Just who or what that narrator is, what he, she, or it invokes, demands, requests, or obliges me to do is another question, to which I shall return.

One of the many ways in which *Howards End*, like other Edwardian and modernist English novels, is continuous with the great tradition of the English Victorian novel is in its use of a so-called omniscient narrator. Like George Eliot's narrator in *Middlemarch*, for example, or Anthony Trollope's narrator in *Ayala's Angel*,[2] Forster's narrator in *Howards End* not only knows everything and is able to move at will back and forth in time and space as well as in and out of the characters' minds. He (or she or it) is also present as a constant garrulous, ruminative commentator on the persons and their story. The importance of the narrator's "reading" of the story is one of the things that makes a cinematic version of *Howards End* necessarily so different from the book version. The conventions of cinema have little place for anything like a narrator, whereas a novel in words demands a narrative voice, however much it may be depersonalized. Forster's narrator in *Howards End* has in fact a strongly individualized personality.

Another feature of Forster's narration that is both inherited from the Victorian novel and almost impossible to carry over to a cinematic version is indirect discourse. Forster's narrator not only can enter into the characters' minds and report on what is going on there; he can also speak for the characters in that transformation of first-person present-tense interior monologue into the third-person past-tense locution that is called "indirect discourse." An example is the narrator's rephrasing of what Margaret Schlegel is thinking when the Schlegel sisters discover that the Wilcoxes have taken a flat in the building opposite their house in London. Margaret's sister Helen has had a brief and unfortunate romance with Paul, the younger son in the Wilcox family: "Oh yes, it was a nuisance, there was no doubt of it. Helen was proof against a passing encounter, but—Margaret began to lose confidence. Might it reawake the dying nerve if the family were living close against her eyes?" (60). A cinematic version of this would need to do a good bit of translation into some different mode of expression (dialogue, for example, or some awkward kind of voice-over) to convey it to the viewer, whereas it is a conventional procedure for the novel, just as is the presence of a narrator's commentary to guide the reader's interpretation. Film, which has its own strong visual resources, not available to the novel,[3] has no easy equivalent either for the narrator's commentary or for indirect discourse. Two other differences between the novel and the film are that the film is by necessity much briefer, omitting or shortening many episodes, and leaves out many of those repetitions (for example of the word "unseen" or of references to hay and hay fever) that generate so much of the meaning of the novel.

Since my discussion of *Howards End* will be more or less solemn, perhaps this is a good moment to stress its comic aspect. The novel is full of many jokes and comic contretemps, big and little, as when an Italian chauffeur is reported to have said about the anger of the country girl whose cat the Wilcoxes have flattened with their motor car: "She was a very ruda girla" (211), as though her rudeness were inappropriate to the circumstances. Forster, or at any rate his narrator, has a deep distaste for motor cars. They stink, make loud noise, raise dust, and are destroying the English countryside. In this case the cat is the victim of the juggernaut. The wry comedy lies in the discrepancy between Margaret's understanding of this and the indifference of the chauffeur and the Wilcoxes. An example of black humor in the novel is the way a bookcase and its books falls over the distressingly bookish Leonard Bast when he dies. Much of the comedy of *Howards End* lies in the narrator's wry commentary, often made indirectly through accurate reporting of what imaginary people said and did. Even serious aspects of the novel often have something comic about them. Sensitivity to the unseen in *Howards End*, for example, is in inverse proportion to a tendency to hay fever. Mrs. Wilcox and Margaret Schlegel have no problem with hay. Their closeness to the earth is signaled in the wisps or handsful of hay they carry at crucial moments in the novel. The Wilcoxes all suffer badly from hay fever. During haying time they must stay indoors with the windows closed and the blinds drawn. Helen in a letter imitates their sneezing: "a-tissue, a-tissue" (2).

With indirect discourse goes an intrinsic tendency toward irony in the narrator's language. It is impossible to be sure whether the narrator in a given case is speaking for himself (or herself or itself) or repeating in a different mode, with ironic undercutting, what one or more of the characters think. It is not the case, as some theorists of narrative (most notoriously Wayne Booth[4]) have claimed, that some narrators are reliable, some unreliable, and that reliable narrators are best. A penchant for the "unreliability" that is a main feature of irony is intrinsic to the conventions of narration in Victorian and Edwardian fiction. You cannot choose to have it or not to have it. You have it, willy-nilly, by the mere fact of employing indirect discourse and narrational commentary.

Howards End is no exception. A good part of the pleasure of reading this novel is the pleasure, if you happen to enjoy it, of the admirable ironic note in the narrator's discourse. The pleasure of irony, however, is a disquieting one, since it is the experience of an obligation conferred. The narrator will not unequivocally decide. You must decide for yourself, and the ironic suspension demands that you do decide. This is perhaps most intensely present in the narrator's defenses of the Wilcoxes. The Wilcox men, Henry, Charles, and Paul, are appalling people—brutal, smug, sexist, bigoted, xenophobic, insensitive. Margaret ultimately tells Henry so. But the narrator tends to defend the Wilcox men by miming ironically the reasonableness of their beliefs and behavior. An example is what the narrator says about the Wilcox's decision to burn the note in which the dying Mrs. Wilcox left Howards End to Margaret:

> To them Howards End was a house: they could not know that to her it had been a spirit, for which she sought a spiritual heir. And—pushing one step further in these mists—may they not have decided even better than they supposed? Is it credible that the possessions of the spirit can be bequeathed at all? Has the soul offspring? A wych-elm tree, a vine, a wisp of hay with dew on it—can passion for such things be transmitted where there is no bond of blood? No; the Wilcoxes are not to be blamed. The problem is too terrific, and they could not even perceive a problem. No; it is natural and fitting that after due debate they should tear the note up and throw it onto their dining-room fire. The practical moralist may acquit them absolutely. He who strives to look deeper may acquit them—almost. For one hard fact remains. They did neglect a personal appeal. The woman who had died did say to them, "Do this," and they answered, "We will not." (97)

Two attitudes are here contrasted, that of the "practical moralist" and that of the one who "strives to look deeper." The narrator does not openly decide between these. He gives each side its due. The reader is left with the responsibility of choosing for himself or herself. The two sides are presented. It is up to you to take one or the other. The narrator will not make it all that easy for you, since the plausibility of both positions is fairly presented. Far from being a nihilist feature that takes away all firm ground for moral judgment, irony is essential to the way a work of literature may make a demand on the reader for judgment and action. Irony and the ethical dimension of reading literature are inextricably intertwined.

By a "just reading" in my title I mean one that does justice to the text, one that fulfills the demand the novel makes on me when I read it. A just reading does not simply get the novel right, that is, understand it correctly. It also responds in a responsible way and acts rightly on the basis of the reading. A just reading is as much a matter of doing as of knowing. Doing what? This doing might be behaving differently in your daily life as a result of the reading, or it might be bearing witness to other people about your reading, for example in talking, teaching, or even writing about the novel, as for example in this present essay. Just as Jane Austen's novels measure their characters on a scale of intelligence, on their ability to reconcile the claims of both sense and sensibility, and just as Anthony Trollope's novels measure their characters on a scale of faithfulness to the commitment made by falling in love, so *Howards End*, like Forster's other novels, measures the characters by their responses to the unseen. The readers of all these novels are put on trial in relation to the different scale of evaluation set up in each case.

I mention Jane Austen and Anthony Trollope because their novels, like Forster's *Howards End*, deal with courtship and marriage among the middle and upper classes at specific moments in English history. The novels of all three have as central themes the redistribution of money and property through marriage. They place these transactions within a given social context and locate them at a given historical moment. *Howards End*, it could be said, is the story of how possession of a house in the country, Howards End, is passed from the first Mrs. Wilcox to the second. Perhaps it would be better to say "possession *by* the house," since the house is the novel's most material and powerful mediator of the unseen. For Jane Austen the historical moment is the Napoleonic era, the aftermath of the French Revolution, a period of reaction in England. For Trollope it is the high Victorian period, the period of the Albert Memorial and of an imperialism so taken for granted that it is only obliquely a question in his novels.[5] For Forster in *Howards End,* the time is that high moment of English prosperity, at least for the ruling classes,[6] just before the First World War, a time when the British Empire was in its last phase of flourishing, but when the justice or injustice of imperialism was a little more overtly an uneasy question. Henry Wilcox, we are told, has made his fortune first in Cypress and now in African rubber plantations. He is "the man who had carved money out of Greece and Africa, and bought forests from the natives for a few bottles of gin" (280). A map of Africa is on the wall at his firm's offices. The firm is called the Imperial and West African Rubber Company. His son Paul goes out to do his "duty," as Margaret calls it, in Nigeria: "beastly work—dull country, dishonest natives, an eternal fidget over fresh water and food. A nation who can produce men of that sort may well be proud. No wonder England has become an Empire" (109–10). When Henry Wilcox is asked, "Isn't the climate of Nigeria too horrible," he answers: "Someone's got to go. . . . England will never keep up her trade overseas unless she is prepared to make sacrifices. Unless we get firm in West Africa, Ger—untold complications may follow" (128). He stops before completing the word "Germany," out of courtesy to Margaret Schlegel, who is half German, but the reference shows the intimate connection between imperialism and nationalism. If England does not do it, Germany may take over West Africa. In a slightly later scene, Margaret has lunch with Henry Wilcox, his daughter, and her fiancé at the fake Old English restaurant, Simpson's in the Strand ("no more Old English than the works of Kipling" [149]; it still exists today). They eat a good Old English meal of saddle of mutton, cider, and Stilton cheese and overhear scraps of conversation from nearby tables: " 'Right you are! I'll cable out to Uganda this evening,' came from the table behind. 'Their Emperor wants war; well, let him have it,' was the opinion of a clergyman" (150). "Their Emperor" is of course Kaiser Wilhelm of Germany. Once again imperialism and the nationalism are connected. This combination was to lead four years later to the First World War, the war the Emperor is here said to want. Forster is much more overt than Trollope in specifying his complex feelings about the British Empire. Trollope thought it was on the whole a very good thing. Forster is on the whole opposed, though it is hardly the case that *Howards End* is simply anti-imperialist. His narrator quotes Margaret's words and Henry Wilcox's but does not pass overt judgment on them, though the awfulness of the Wilcox men is a kind of indirect judgment. This is what imperialists are like, for better or for worse, the narrator in effect says, but it is up to the reader to pass judgment. Ultimately the narrator does say straightforwardly enough that "the imperialist is not what he thinks or seems. He is a destroyer. He prepares the way for cosmopolitanism, and though his ambitions may be fulfilled the earth that he inherits will be gray" (320). High value is here given, as it often is today, to ethnic difference. Globalization is deplored as destroying cultural specificity. Nevertheless, Henry Wilcox's virtues are consistently praised, in the teeth of the demonstration of his limitations. One difference between the novel and the film, at least in my sense of it, is that Anthony Hopkins's performance as Henry Wilcox in the film makes Wilcox rather more attractive than he is in the novel.

Howards End carries on the long tradition of the English novel in its exact specification of the characters' social placements. Forster tells the reader just how rich or poor the characters are, where their money comes from, what work they do or what professions they follow, what foods they like, what sorts of houses or flats they live in, what servants they have, whether they have country houses as well as houses in London, what their furniture is like, whether or not they have motor cars or travel by underground and train. Trollope's *Ayala's Angel*, for example, assumes that the reader will have the topography of London and the social meaning of various regions of London and England clearly in mind. Trollope can place his characters simply by saying they live in Queens Gate or in Notting Hill. *Howards End* assumes the same knowledge in its readers when it puts the Schlegels in Wickham Place in Chelsea or the Wilcoxes in Howards End in Hertfordshire or in Ducie Street in London, "close to Sloane Street" (133). Though Howards End, Wickham Place, and Ducie Street are fictitious place names, Hertfordshire, Sloane Street, and Chelsea are not. The reader is told enough about the characters' addresses to figure out more or less where they are in London or in the country. *Howards End* is, among other things, an eloquent celebration of the beauties of the English countryside. Forster has an extraordinary ability to convey economically the sense of a setting, as in his descriptions of Howards End, modeled on a house in Hertfordshire, Rooksnest, where Forster himself had lived as a child. Though Forster writes in prose, his name could be added to Wordsworth's and others' as one of England's great topographical "poets."

My mention of Wordsworth is not fortuitous. As for Wordsworth, so for Forster, topographical features—trees, houses, fields, and so on—are chief mediators of the unseen, just as certain persons are valued, like Wordsworth's old leechgatherer or Forster's Mrs. Wilcox, as specially initiated mediators of the unseen that is mediated by the landscape. Toward the end of the novel, long after Mrs. Wilcox's death, she has become, at least in Margaret Schlegel's mind, a ubiquitous, all-knowing, all-encompassing spirit. "I feel," says Margaret, "that you and I and Henry are only fragments of that woman's mind. She knows everything. She is everything. She is the house, and the tree that leans over it" (311).

An admirable and characteristically Forsterian topographical notation is what the narrator says about the railway stations that still today form an inner ring around London leading out in various directions toward the outlying country. Forster, like present-day sociological geographers, or like Martin Heidegger in "Building Dwelling Thinking,"[7] recognizes that for the inhabitants of a city the places of egress already in a sense contain the distant places to which they lead:

> Like many others who have lived long in a great capital, she [Margaret Schlegel] had strong feelings about the various railway termini. They are our gates to the glorious and the unknown. Through them we pass out into adventure and sunshine, to them, alas! we return. In Paddington all Cornwall is latent and the remoter west; down the inclines of Liverpool Street lie fenlands and the illimitable Broads; Scotland is through the pylons of Euston; Wessex behind the poised chaos of Waterloo. (9)

The word "unknown" here, a variant of "unseen," is accentuated a paragraph later when the reader is told that "to Margaret—I hope that it will not set the reader against her—the station of King's Cross had always suggested infinity" (9). The narrator, it can be seen, is a little embarrassed about these notations of the unseen but must make them anyway, in order to tell the truth about the characters.

This topographical specificity and the concomitant assumption that the reader will know the sociological meaning of place names make considerable difficulties for an American reader who does not know London and the English countryside. The topographical notations are a shorthand code for what the characters are. If you do not know the code, the meanings will elude you. Moreover, most Americans are more like the Wilcoxes than like the Schlegels or like the first Mrs. Wilcox. Many Americans are nomads. We move from place to place without ever putting down deep roots in "one dear perpetual place," as Yeats puts it.[8] We are much less inclined than Forster to believe that what a person *is* can be defined by where he or she lives and how long the family has lived there. Forster foresees with strong disapproval the transformation of England into a country of nomads: "The feudal ownership of land did bring dignity, whereas modern ownership of movables is reducing us again to a nomadic horde. We are reverting to the civilization of luggage, and historians of the future will note how the middle classes accreted possessions without taking root in the earth, and may find in this the secret of their imaginative poverty" (146); "London was but a foretaste of this nomadic civilization which is altering human nature so profoundly, and throws upon personal relations a stress greater than they have ever borne before" (258).

This topographical assumption, as it might be called, along with assumptions about gender and class, makes *Howards End* more alien to a late twentieth-century American reader than the fact that it is written in a version of his or her own language might make it appear. One general problem for American readers of English literature is that the sameness of the language masks many deep differences. These might be easier to notice if *Howards End*, for example, were written in another language than English. To a considerable degree the assumptions about gender and class in *Howards End*, as in *Pride and Prejudice* or in *Ayala's Angel*, are so different from our own as to make reading it as much an encounter with otherness as the study of those non-Western cultures whose kinship systems and marriage customs anthropologists explore. To this cultural strangeness may be added the specific distinctiveness of Forster's own special vision of his culture. This strangeness makes a just reading of *Howards End* not all that easy, in spite of the superficial familiarity of the world we Americans enter when we read it.

Readers today are trained to be sensitive to assumptions about class, gender, nation, and race (those four leitmotifs of contemporary cultural studies). These, it is presumed, govern a given literary work and form its presupposed ideology. By "ideology" I mean what both Louis Althusser and Paul de Man mean by the word: unspoken and often unconscious assumptions that are taken to be natural and universal though they are social or linguistic and could be otherwise.[9] Though *Howards End* makes some perhaps unconscious ideological assumptions of its own, it is at the same time, like most great English novels, a critical exposure of the ideologies of its characters and of the community to which they belong. Exposure of ideological assumptions, knowledge of them, does not, however, free one from them, as both Althusser and de Man, in their different ways, stress. For that the "just reading" I began by advocating would be necessary, that is, a "materialist" reading that does something, that leads to action in the real world rather than just to knowledge.[10]

I have said that Forster places his characters in relation to gender, class, nation, and race. I have also said that he measures them by their openness or lack of openness to the "unseen." These two forms of placement are related, but they also conflict. Let me explain how.

Part of the difficulty *Howards End* presents to an American reader is the complexity of social discriminations in the Edwardian England Forster depicts, to which may be added the complexity of the narrator's response to those complexities. The refinement of notation with which *Howards End* presents class, gender, national, and racial difference would merit a lengthy analysis. Forster is wonderfully adept at catching subtle nuances of clashes between sexes or between classes. It is not that present-day United States culture is not complex and finely reticulated, but that the lines go in different places. England was in 1910 still a class society in a way the United States has never been. In the United States we still assume, as a deeply held ideological presupposition, an almost unlimited possibility of social mobility. As a multicultural and multiracial country we are divided more along economic, racial, and ethnic lines than along anything like class lines in the English sense. An American's expectations are defined by being Caucasian, African American, Hispanic, or Asian American, by being male or female, by being rich or poor, not so much by fixed, inherited class placement. England is presented in *Howards End* as a uniracial and unicultural country. Race appears only peripherally in the novel, as in those remarks about the African natives I have quoted. The almost complete omission of racial difference is significant. That all middle-class English men and women are white and that the British Empire rested on the exploitation of Indians and Africans are assumptions so taken for granted that race is hardly an overt issue. In place of racial difference is put national difference, about which I shall have more to say later.

Divisions of class, on the other hand, are in *Howards End* relatively fixed and highly discriminated. It is not all that easy for an American reader to get the hang of these discriminations, particularly since Forster is to some degree putting in question the nominal class distinctions that were assumed in England in his time. Class distinctions in Edwardian England depended on money, but not just on money, though Forster by no means minimizes the difference having money or not having it can make. The Schlegel sisters have less money than the Wilcoxes, but still enough to relieve them of the necessity of working. They are by inheritance members of an emancipated group of intellectuals, whereas the Wilcox men are frozen in the ideological complacencies of the commercial middle class. This puts the Schlegels in a class above the Wilcoxes, according to the subtle discriminations the novel makes. It also deliberately puts in question the class discriminations that members of the new plutocracy like the Wilcoxes make. As Helen says about a moment of insight into this: "I felt for a moment that the whole Wilcox family was a fraud, just a wall of newspapers and motor-cars and golf-clubs, and that if it fell I should find nothing behind it but panic and emptiness" (23). Helen and Margaret Schlegel, on the other hand, "know that personal relations are the real life, for ever and ever" (25). Mrs. Wilcox is in a class above them all, or rather her superiority is not a matter of class but a matter of superior sensitivity to the unseen. Her superiority is beyond class distinctions. Miss Avery, in spite of her low class status, is also superior to the Wilcoxes by virtue of the uncanny awareness of the unseen she shares with Mrs. Wilcox. Mrs. Wilcox has brought to her marriage only the house in which she was born, Howards End, but her attachment to the house and to the immemorial tradition it embodies puts her at the top of the social hierarchy in the novel: "She seemed to belong not to the young people and their motor, but to the house, and to the tree that overshadowed it. One knew that she worshipped the past, and that the instinctive wisdom the past alone can bestow had descended upon her—that wisdom to which we give the clumsy name of aristocracy. High-born she might not be. But assuredly she cared about her ancestors, and let them help her" (19). Much further down in the social hierarchy, so taken for granted as to be almost invisible, are those in the servant class. Whether or not they have any sensitivity to the unseen is impossible to say. As is the case in most nineteenth- and twentieth-century English novels, the servants do all the housework but are invisible, scarcely ever presented from the inside, as having personalities, lives, and loves of their own. All the main characters in the novel but the Basts have servants:

chauffeurs, housemaids, cooks, gardeners, bootcleaners, and so on, but for the most part we learn little about them. Only the Basts cook their own meals, or rather Leonard Bast cooks them. Forster's description of this makes it a sordid and unattractive event (51).

In Forster's England a person tended to remain permanently placed in whatever class he or she was born into. Class, moreover, determined capabilities, an assumption that will seem absurd to most American readers today. Leonard Bast is a clerk in an insurance company, grandson of agricultural laborers. He marries a vulgar woman of loose morals. He is fixed on the thin edge between respectability and depths of poverty that are "unthinkable"[11] and not narratable. He can move only slightly, to one side or the other of that thin edge. However hard Leonard Bast tries to get "culture" by reading books and going to concerts, he will never get it right. All his reading of Ruskin, Borrow, Jefferies, Stevenson, and Thoreau has only put him in "a swamp of books" (118), without raising him one inch above his fixed class status. As the grandson of Virginia farmers myself, I find obnoxious the assumption that Leonard Bast as a result of his heritage and class status is unable to read books right. In America we tend to assume that ability to read depends on an innate intelligence that crosses economic lines and on education, which in principle is open to everyone. In America in the 2000s you cannot blame an inability to read perceptively so easily on class heritage, but in *Howards End* in 1910 you could.

I have said that national difference plays the role in Forster's England that racial and ethnic difference does in the United States today. A further distinction must be made, however. Many races and different ethnic heritages live side by side in the United States. *Howards End* still belongs to the high period of the nationalism that was about to lead to the First World War and subsequently to the Second World War. Nationalism assumes that England is filled with English men and women, Germany with Germans, Russia with Russians, and so on. Minorities do not count. A national heritage is a prime determinant of identity. An Englishman will be—well, like an Englishman. Germans will be Germans. The characteristics of each nationality can be precisely defined.

Howards End dramatizes the ideological assumption that nationality determines personal identity not only in many remarks by the characters but, more centrally, in the way the two chief protagonists, Margaret Schlegel and her sister Helen, are defined as products of a marriage between nationalities. Their father was German, their mother English. The narrator remarks that being half English and half German "was a unique education for the little girls" (27). Their mixed national heritage means that as children they have been exposed to English people, like their Aunt

Julia, who think God has appointed England to govern the world, and to German people, like their cousins who visit their father in England, who think God has appointed Germany to lead the world. The precocious Margaret aged thirteen causes embarrassment all around when she says, "To me one of two things is very clear: either God does not know his own mind about England and Germany, or else these do not know the mind of God" (27–28). The dangerous absurdity of these assumptions is evident, but how many of us can say we are entirely free of such assumptions about fixed national identity and its God-given mission? Which of us does not have some ignoble hankering to live in a country where everyone speaks the same language, shares the same "values," reads the same books, and inhabits the same culture? Do not some Americans still think that God has appointed the United States to govern the world?

If, on the one hand, nationalist assumptions are shown to be ideological delusions, on the other hand, the novel itself seems to some degree to depend on them. In a scene late in the novel that takes place at the estate Henry Wilcox rents in Shropshire, near the Welsh border, Margaret challenges an unseen intruder on her walk on the estate's grounds: "Saxon or Celt?" The estate is said by the narrator to have "suffered in the border warfare between the Anglo-Saxon and the Celt, between things as they are and as they ought to be" (228). The allusion is to racist and nationalist assumptions popular in the nineteenth century (and in our century too) that claim members of the Saxon race are reasonable, practical, down to earth, while Celts are dreamy and otherworldly.[12] This is parallel to the distinction between those who are sensitive to the unseen and those who are not. It parallels also, rather surprisingly, the distinction between English and German nationality traits on which depends the characterization of the Schlegel sisters as divided between two cultural heritages. Since *Howards End* centers on this self-division in the two main protagonists, one could claim that the novel as a whole relies on assumptions about national identity. Margaret, in particular, is torn between her allegiance to the Germanic unseen and her allegiance to the practicality, grit, and manliness she admires in Henry Wilcox. Though her father was a heroic soldier in the German Army in the Franco-Prussian War, though he was "the man who beat the Austrians, and the Danes, and the French," as Margaret says to her sister, he also "beat the Germans that were inside himself." He emigrated to England to escape German chauvinism and ambitions of conquest. "And we're like him," Margaret concludes (156). The father "was not the aggressive German, so dear to the English journalist, nor the domestic German, so dear to the English wit. If one classed him at all it would be as the countryman of Hegel and Kant, as the idealist, inclined to be dreamy, whose Imperialism was the Imperialism of the air" (26).

"Schlegel" is not just a random German-sounding name. It was the name of the two Schlegel brothers, Friedrich and August Wilhelm, countrymen and contemporaries of Hegel and Kant, who were, in their different ways, important spokespersons for the unseen in German romanticism. An earlier manuscript version of the passage about Kant and Hegel confirms this: "Their father, a distant relation of the great critic. . . ."[13] Chapter 1 of this book discusses Friedrich Schlegel. On the question of the reality or the ideological mystification of nationalist assumptions, *Howards End* is somewhat contradictory, as in its attitudes toward imperialism, and as in the way Forster both shows up class assumptions and nevertheless uses them to place the characters. The reader must make a judgment. The book will not clearly decide.

The same thing can be said for the treatment of gender and sexual difference in *Howards End*. This is perhaps the most elaborately refined element in the system of ideological assumptions that the novel both exposes and employs to place the characters. The novel is a powerful exposure and implicit condemnation of what today we would call "patriarchy," as embodied in Henry Wilcox and his two sons. Their insensitivity, their blatant assumption of male superiority, their acceptance of a "double standard" that allows marital infidelity in men, while ostracizing any woman who has sex outside marriage, their unconquerable and insufferable condescension to women—these are shown again and again in wonderfully adroit little touches, as when Henry is described at the wedding of his daughter: "Henry was already installed; he ate slowly and spoke little, and was, in Margaret's eyes, the only member of their party who dodged emotion successfully. . . . he dwelt intact, only issuing orders occasionally—orders that promoted the comfort of his guests. . . . 'Burton,' called Henry, 'serve tea and coffee from the sideboard!' " (217). Women in this society have little choice between marrying, thereby becoming subordinate to their husband, or not marrying, thereby remaining celibate and without a vocation. The possibility that the Schlegel sisters, who are intelligent and well educated, might have a job or a profession is never really considered as an option possible under the then present social conditions, any more than it would have been in the Victorian period. Only men are supposed to work. The Schlegel sisters' younger brother Tibby causes them much trouble because, though he does well at Oxford, he refuses to consider turning his hand to any profession, though his sisters preach to him the Victorian gospel of manly work. The Schlegel sisters are emancipated in their thinking. They believe in "temperance, tolerance and sexual equality" (25). Nevertheless, even though Helen has a child out of wedlock, the lives of these two women are for the most part determined by Edwardian assumptions those around them make about the

place of women. These are admirably encapsulated in a description of the
trip by train from London to Shropshire for Henry's daughter's wedding:

> Nothing could have exceeded the kindness of the two men [Henry and
> Charles Wilcox]. They raised windows for some ladies, and lowered them
> for others, they rang the bell for the servant, they identified the colleges as the
> train slipped past Oxford, they caught books or bag-purses in the act of
> tumbling onto the floor. Yet there was nothing finicking about their polite-
> ness: it had the Public School touch, and, though sedulous, was virile. More
> battles than Waterloo have been won on our playing-fields, and Margaret
> bowed to a charm of which she did not wholly approve, and said nothing
> when the Oxford colleges were identified wrongly. "Male and female cre-
> ated He them"; the journey to Shrewsbury confirmed this questionable state-
> ment, and the long glass saloon, that moved so easily and felt so comfort-
> able, became a forcing-house for the idea of sex. (208)

All the elements are present in *Howards End* for a strong feminist reading of the novel, but, as with the treatment of other ideological elements,
it is not all that easy to figure out just where Forster stands. His narrator
gives the Wilcoxes their due for the efficient exercise of patriarchal power.
He shows Margaret genuinely in love with Henry, while at the same time
displaying abundantly and with evident relish what havoc these "virile"
men wreak all around them, most melodramatically in causing the death
of Leonard Bast. Perhaps the climax of the novel, for many readers, is
the moment when Margaret speaks out at last in fierce condemnation of
Henry Wilcox, now her husband:

> You shall see the connection if it kills you Henry! You have had a mistress—I
> forgave you. My sister has a lover—you drive her from the house. Do you see
> the connection? Stupid, hypocritical, cruel—oh, contemptible!—a man who
> insults his wife when she's alive and cants with her memory when she's dead.
> A man who ruins a woman for his pleasure, and casts her off to ruin other
> men. And gives bad financial advice, and then says he is not responsible. The
> men are you. . . . No one has ever told you what you are—muddled, crimi-
> nally muddled. (305)

The matter of gender treatment is made even more complicated if the
reader knows that Forster became a practicing homosexual and wrote in
1914 an overtly homosexual novel, *Maurice*, published in 1971 after his
death. What difference does this knowledge make to a reading of *Howards End*? Is *Howards End* a covertly homosexual novel? It is not all that
easy to answer those questions. For one thing, "being homosexual" is not
an absolute condition, like having red hair, or even like being biologically
male or female, though the latter has its ambiguities too. An infinite vari-
ety of ways to be gay, as of ways to be straight, exists. Every person is to

some degree bisexual. Homosexual behavior and feelings, moreover, like heterosexual ones, are embedded in each individual case in a complex social, cultural, personal, psychological, and physiological matrix. Saying "Forster was homosexual" does not so much solve problems in the reading of *Howards End* as raise new ones. The social history of homosexuality in England has been quite different from its history in the United States, different in the process of its legalization, in the degree of its acceptance or rejection in different classes, and in the distinctions made between gay and lesbian. Homosexuality between men was always much more tolerated in the English professional and governing class than lesbianism, as feminist interpreters of Virginia Woolf, a contemporary of Forster, have lamented.[14] Though homosexual behavior was still illegal in England when *Howards End* was published, at just this time what has been called a "cult of homosexuality" flourished at Oxford and Cambridge. A special kind of more or less underground poetry, so-called Uranian poetry, expressed the feelings and attitudes of this group. Noel Annan has argued that this secret society of homosexuality among university students and dons depended on the fact that homosexuality was illegal and disappeared when homosexuality was legalized in Britain, which was only in 1967.[15] This special and localized social history is another example of the difficulty an American reader may have in reading *Howards End* right.

Does Forster's "homosexuality," whatever that means exactly, explain the rather cool and distant treatment heterosexual passion gets in this novel, as in others by him, or as in novels by Henry James, another supposedly homosexual novelist? The reader is told that Henry Wilcox's proposal of marriage to Margaret Schlegel "was not to rank among the world's great love scenes" (161). They do not even shake hands to mark the event, much less kiss. The film version deviates significantly from the novel in having Margaret kiss Henry in acknowledgment and acceptance of his proposal, as well as in showing a good bit of overt physical affection later on between them. The sexual encounter between Helen Schlegel and Leonard Bast has been found implausible. Katherine Mansfield wondered in her diary "whether Helen was got with child by Leonard Bast or by his fatal umbrella."[16] The film's interpolations make the seduction of Helen by Leonard (or of Leonard by Helen) more believable. In any case it fits Helen's slightly defiant recklessness as presented in the novel. I find more inexplicable the attraction of Margaret to Henry Wilcox, and I have difficulty imagining them making love, in spite of the care with which Forster builds up Margaret's admiration for conventional domineering males. But Henry is presented as so despicable, so inhabited by "panic and emptiness," so incapable of saying "I," that is, of taking responsibility for a personal commitment or action, that Helen's reaction of dislike and distaste (she says his eyes are like "brandy-balls" [158], a kind of candy) seems more plausible than Margaret's love. Nevertheless, Henry Wilcox, like Leonard Bast, is praised for being a "real man" (144), whereas their brother Tibby is not a real man. Tibby's apparent asexuality is presented as part of his weakness as a person, while Henry's virility is part of his attraction for Margaret, part of his general possession of male mastery. Margaret's marriage to Henry is necessary to put her ultimately in triumphant matriarchal possession of Howards End, firmly in control of her subdued and broken husband, as much so as Jane Eyre is in control of a mutilated and blinded Rochester at the end of Charlotte Brontë's *Jane Eyre*. Perhaps there is some wish-fulfillment in both cases.

Does Forster's "homosexuality" explain why conventional marriages in his novels are generally such disasters, why he has such distaste for "patriarchal males" like Henry and Charles Wilcox, why strong and mysterious older women play such a role in his novels, for example Mrs. Wilcox in this novel and Mrs. Moore in *A Passage to India*? To suppose, however, that we are incapable of understanding the sexual feeling of the other sex or of those with different sexual preferences might involve putting in question the ability of apparently "straight" nineteenth-century male novelists, like Trollope, Thackeray, Meredith, or Hardy to do what they spend much of their time in their novels doing, that is, presenting the feelings and thoughts of female protagonists. In a passage already cited in chapter 4, Henry James said Trollope made the English girl his special province.[17] Many of James's protagonists are also English or American girls, as are those of the other novelists I have mentioned. Forster joins this long tradition in the English novel by centering *Howards End* on the Schlegel sisters and primarily on heterosexual love.

Howards End, in any case, remains very much in the closet. There are only moments here and there of what Eve Sedgwick calls "male homosociality,"[18] for example in the tight bond between Henry Wilcox and his son Charles. It breaks Henry's spirit when his son is sent to prison for manslaughter. One of the warmest moments in the novel, a bright moment in an array of tense and never wholly satisfying relations between the "opposite" sexes, is the episode of Leonard Bast's casual encounter with a male undergraduate on a train. Leonard is shown early in the novel as having extreme distaste for the prospect of sleeping with his mistress, soon to be wife, Jacky. Jacky is "now a massive woman of thirty-three" whose weight hurts Leonard when she sits on his knee and fondles him. Later, Jackie calls from the bedroom, but he puts off coming to bed (52). Her pneumatic blisses hold no attraction for him, whereas: "Perhaps the keenest happiness he had ever known was during a railway journey to Cambridge, where a decent-mannered undergraduate had spoken to him. They had got into conversation, and gradually Leonard had flung reticence aside, told some of his domestic troubles, and hinted at the rest. The undergraduate, supposing they could start a friendship, asked him to 'coffee after hall,' which he accepted, but afterwards grew shy, and took care not to stir from the commercial hotel where he lodged" (120). The warmth of this brief encounter anticipates the more overtly homosexual tenderness between Fielding and Aziz in *A Passage to India*. Nothing matches it for warmth in the novel except the affection and understanding between the two Schlegel sisters and that between Ruth Wilcox and Margaret Schlegel. The latter are powerfully presented examples of female homosociality.

As in the cases of class, race, and nationalism, so the attempt to read *Howards End* rightly on the issue of gender leads the reader into a labyrinth of to some degree conflicting evidence. But the responsible reader will want to be able to give evidence supporting his or her interpretation. The admirably complex presentation in this novel of relations among the sexes in Edwardian England leaves the reader in the end, however, forced to judge for himself or herself on the basis of evidence that allows latitude of interpretation.

That leaves the "unseen." I began by saying that the characters in *Howards End* are measured on a scale of their responsiveness or lack of it to the unseen. Is the unseen, like class, race, nationality, and gender, just one more way of measuring the characters in relation to a prevailing ideology? Well, not exactly. For one thing, it is an absolute, not an ambiguous, yardstick of measurement. Those who are sensitive to the unseen are unequivocally superior to those who are not. Ability to respond to the unseen cuts across all the other measures. Leonard Bast has this ability, but his wife Jacky certainly does not. Margaret Schlegel does, as does her sister Helen, though in a somewhat different way. Mrs. Wilcox has it to a supreme degree. None of the other Wilcoxes have it at all, including Henry's daughter Evie. Nor does the Schlegel sisters' Aunt Julia, nor their cousin Frieda from Germany. Response to the unseen is not a matter of female against male, nor of lower against middle class, nor of Germany against England, since not all women or Germans or members of any class are aware that there is any unseen to respond to. Yet to have this awareness is, for Forster, the one thing needful.

Just what does it mean to have or not to have awareness of the unseen? One word that might be used today for the unseen would be "the other." For Forster, or perhaps it would be better to say, for Forster's narrator in *Howards End*, the otherness of race, nationality, class, and gender can in one way or another, by tolerance and sympathy, be reduced to the same. This is true in spite of Forster's celebration of difference.[19] The national, class, and gender other can be comprehended and so assimilated, at least in principle, into an ideal society such as Margaret and Helen Schlegel imagine as their utopian goal. The happy ending of the novel is a miniature version of this ideal society. Forster's belief in this possibility is what is meant by his "liberal humanism." Though he considers briefly, or has Margaret consider, the possibility, for example, that the two sexes may be radically other to one another, this suggestion is quickly rejected: "Are the sexes really races, each with its own code of morality, and their mutual love a mere device of Nature's to keep things going? Strip human intercourse of the proprieties, and is it reduced to this? Her judgment told her no. She knew that out of Nature's device we have built a magic that will win us immortality" (237–38).

Forster's notion of the "unseen," on the other hand, what he calls the "glow," responsiveness to which leads some few "beyond humanity" (335), puts him outside liberal humanism. The unseen remains just that: unseen. It is therefore unknown, submerged, obscure, invisible. It cannot be returned to the same. It remains heterogeneous to any act of understanding. It is "wholly other." Since the unseen remains invisible, there is no way to adjudicate between those who are aware of it and those who are not. You are either aware of it or you are not aware. The appeal the unseen makes is therefore in principle different from the appeal another person makes, even though the latter appeal may mediate the unseen, as Mrs. Wilcox does for Margaret Schlegel.

Margaret's phrase, uttered when she still hopes to change Henry Wilcox to something nearer her own vision, "Only connect!," by which she means "Only connect the prose and the passion, and both will be exalted" (183), is often taken as the pinnacle of wisdom in *Howards End*. This consoling and optimistic slogan is not, however, compatible with the irreconcilable opposition shown everywhere in the novel between "life's daily gray" (142) and the urgent demand made by the unseen. The latter leads to action that can with difficulty, if at all, be reconciled with the prose of everyday life. The prose and the passion remain in conflict. Attempts to connect them are rarely successful. Margaret conspicuously fails in getting her husband to connect the prose and the passion or to have even a glimpse of the unseen.

The calling that being aware of the unseen makes is the highest vocation, the most demanding, the most absolute, even though it lays on those it calls a responsibility impossible to fulfill. It is impossible to fulfill because it comes from the "infinite" and so puts an infinite obligation on the one who receives the call. It is not a demand to do this or that, but a demand to be and feel in a certain way that then leads spontaneously to right action. That the action is right, however, cannot be verified by any preexisting code of ethics or moral behavior. You can never know for sure that you have responded rightly to the demand the unseen makes.

No voice of commendation comes down from heaven to tell you you have done right, in spite of the narrator's ironic sympathy for those who wish there were "a man of our own sort—not anyone pompous or tearful—. . . caring for us up in the sky" (107).

Helen Schlegel is made the spokesperson for a distinction that will help the reader understand the difference between those who are responsive to the unseen and those who are not. People like the Wilcox men are incapable of taking "personal responsibility" because

> the little thing that says 'I' is missing out of the middle of their heads, and then it's a waste of time to blame them. . . . there are two kinds of people— our kind, who live straight from the middle of their heads, and the other kind who can't, because their heads have no middle[.] They can't say "I." They *aren't* in fact, and so they're supermen. Pierpont Morgan has never said "I" in his life. . . . Never the "I"; and if you could pierce through him you'd find panic and emptiness in the middle. (232)

The paradox is evident. Men of authority and power, like Henry Wilcox, have no authentic center on which action can be based, however egotistical, decisive, and active they seem. They act mechanically, on the basis of conventional codes. They have panic and emptiness at the center. Those who are responsive to the unseen, on the other hand, have an emotional center that gives their actions and choices validity, even though they do not seem to have particularly aggressive or stable egos. Nevertheless, they can say "I." They can take personal responsibility for what they do. Their taking of responsibility is a concomitant of their ability to say "I." Saying "I" is a performative speech act that creates the "I" each time anew in the moment of taking responsibility.

This distinction between those who can say "I" and those who cannot is correlated to two different ways to life in time. Henry Wilcox has no now, just as he has no well-remembered past. He lives in terms of what needs to be done in the immediate future. Helen and Margaret, on the other hand, like Mrs. Wilcox, strive to live in a perpetually recurrent "now" that ties them to nature and to the earth as well as giving them a continuity with a personal and communal past they are linked to by "tradition." The narrator says of Margaret, when she returns to Howards End, in defiance of her husband, to join her sister Helen: "The peace of the country was entering into her. It has no commerce with memory, and little with hope. Least of all is it concerned with the hopes of the next five minutes. It is the peace of the present, which passes understanding. Its murmur came 'now,' and 'now' once more as they trod the gravel, and 'now' as the moonlight fell upon their father's sword" (312).

Examples of right actions in *Howards End* in response to the unseen are Mrs. Wilcox's decision to bequeath Howards End to Margaret

Schlegel, Leonard Bast's taking a night's walk in the woods, Helen's sleeping with Leonard Bast, Margaret's jumping out of the car in sympathy for the flattened cat and its owner, Margaret's taking over of Howards End, in place of the first Mrs. Wilcox, at the end of the novel. This is a heterogeneous list. All these acts, however, are in one way or another acts of transgression. They defy ordinary morals and ordinary rules of behavior. They go against the dictates of those ideological assumptions I have identified.

The Schlegel sisters' German cousin Frieda, of all people, expresses in a sentence a key to understanding what it means to measure people by their sensitivity to the unseen: "One is certain of nothing but the truth of one's own emotions" (167). The narrator comments that this aphorism, though "not an original remark" (it comes from one of Keats's letters), "betrayed that interest in the universal [the manuscript at first had 'unseen' here] which the average Teuton possesses and the average Englishman does not. It was, however illogically, the good, the beautiful, the true, as opposed to the respectable, the pretty, the adequate. It was a landscape of Böcklin's beside a landscape of Leader's, strident and ill-considered, but quivering into supernatural life. It sharpened idealism, stirred the soul" (167). Emotions are the result of a response to the unseen. Reason has little to do with it. The unseen is unknowable, not amenable to reason or understanding. Its truth cannot be spoken rationally. It does, however, generate emotions that have their own kind of truth. It is a truth of corresponding to the unseen. That emotional truth is the only thing of which we can be certain. It carries its own guarantee and validation. The emotions then determine the appropriate action, without reference to ordinary codes of morality or behavior. Mrs. Wilcox leaves her house to someone who is almost a stranger. Margaret jumps out of the motor car. Leonard Bast spends a night walking in the woods. Helen sleeps with Leonard Bast.

The demand made by the unseen on the one who feels it is absolute, exigent, irresistible. Nevertheless, it is impossible to justify what you do in response to the unseen by reference to ordinary laws of behavior. What you do is right, but it is impossible to prove that it is right. The unseen is like a black hole at the center of *Howards End*. The other chief thematic elements, distinctions of class, nation, gender, and so on, could be measured as true or false by comparison with other accounts of Edwardian society. Nothing can measure or validate the black hole of the unseen. It is not even possible to prove that it exists, that is not a subjective fantasy. The Wilcoxes have no understanding of, no possibility of understanding, the actions I have listed, all of which follow in one way or another from an encounter with the unseen. The Wilcoxes have panic and emptiness at the center, not a responsible "I" aware of the unseen.

The reader's right response to *Howards End* is like the actions I have named. Just as Mrs. Wilcox is a mediator of the unseen that is embodied in Howards End, so *Howards End* is a further mediator in this chain of mediation. The novel presents models of correct behavior in response to the obligation laid on those who are sensitive to the unseen, but the reader is by no means supposed to copy these. You are on your own in response to the unseen. Each reader must negotiate his or her own reaction. Might it not be possible, for example, to claim that all the strand of *Howards End* that refers to the unseen is no more than another part of conservative, white, Western, male ideology, something that functions as a bogus absolute keeping the other ideological elements concerning race, gender, and the uneven distribution of privilege and goods firmly in place, the lines of power unchanged? Yes, it would be possible to claim that. You are free to do so. It would also be possible to take the unseen seriously as something that works against the various elements of that conservative ideology in *Howards End*. Then you would have an obligation to respond in some way to the unseen. It is up to you. Or, rather, if Forster is right, it is a matter of the spontaneous truth of your own emotions in response to the unseen as it is mediated by *Howards End*. This is the only truth of which you can be certain. On the basis of that certain truth you must then act rightly.

NOTES

1. E. M. Forster, *Howards End*, ed. Oliver Stallybrass, vol. 4 of the Abinger edition of E. M. Forster (London: Edward Arnold, 1973), 335. Henceforth citations will be to this edition.

2. I mention *Ayala's Angel* (1881) out of all Trollope's nearly fifty novels because, like *Howards End*, it tells the story of two middle-class girls left orphans. This is another example of the continuity of *Howards End* with the conventions and plots of Victorian novels. So many of the latter deal with orphans that it almost seems a great plague must have taken away all the parents. An unmarried woman in English Victorian and Edwardian society is a wild card in the social game, something unpredictable and therefore threatening, at least to the male hegemony. Victorian and Edwardian novels characteristically tell the story of how such a wild card ultimately gets placed and defined by marriage. An orphan girl is even more unpredictable than one merely unmarried, therefore an even better protagonist for such a story than one with parents to control her and discreetly arrange her marriage.

3. Alistair Duckworth, in a letter to me, identifies these succinctly apropos of the film of *Howards End*: "(1) The film is a visual medium that gives imagistic representation to what is a verbal description in the novel, and (2) the film uses sound both mimetically and diegetically and thus either performs or 'underscores' Forster's words."

4. In *The Rhetoric of Fiction* (Chicago: University of Chicago Press, 1961). Booth's chapter on James Joyce's *A Portrait of the Artist as a Young Man* (345–55), for example, condemns Joyce and *A Portrait* for not making absolutely clear and explicit what judgment we should make of the hero of the novel, Stephen Daedalus. It is immoral, Booth implies, to leave the reader in doubt, perhaps because it encourages his or her relativism.

5. Statues of animals at the four corners of the Albert Memorial (finished in 1875), designed by Sir George Gilbert Scott and dedicated to the memory of Queen Victoria's Prince Consort, who died in 1861, celebrate the four continents where England lay or had colonies: Asia (elephant), Africa (camel), America (bison), and Europe (bull). At the angles of the base are also allegorical groups standing for Agriculture, Manufactures, Commerce, and Engineering, those "goddesses of getting on" that Henry Wilcox and his ilk worship. Lucy Dormer, Ayala's sister, in Trollope's *Ayala's Angel*, at one period of her life takes a daily walk in Kensington Park around the Albert Memorial. Though Trollope says nothing about its significance as a monument to British imperialism, most of his English readers would have known it in all its Victorian Gothic grandiosity. For many American readers the reference is invisible.

6. This prosperity for the rich went along with increasing poverty and ill health for the lower classes, especially in the cities. The Basts are the example of this in *Howards End*.

7. M. Heidegger, "Bauen Wohnen Denken," in *Vorträge und Aufsätze* (Pfullingen: Neske, 1954), 2:19; "Building Dwelling Thinking," in *Poetry, Language, Thought*, trans. Albert Hofstadter (New York: Harper & Row, 1971), 145.

8. W. B. Yeats, "A Prayer for My Daughter," l. 48, *The Variorum Edition of the Poems of W. B. Yeats*, ed. Peter Allt and Russell K. Alspach (New York: Macmillan, 1977), 405.

9. For Althusser, see chapter 4, note 2. For de Man on ideology, see chapter 10.

10. "[M]aterialist practice assumes language acts on the real world and . . . continually credits the possibility that literature acts on historical reality" (Elaine Scarry, "Introduction," in *Literature and the Body: Essays on Population and Persons*, ed. Elaine Scarry [Baltimore: The Johns Hopkins University Press, 1988], xxiii).

11. "We are not concerned with the very poor," says the narrator, in a remarkably condescending assertion, an assertion that is hardly redeemed by whatever irony it may have. "They are unthinkable, and only to be approached by the statistician or the poet" (43).

12. A more specific allusion may be to George Meredith's *Celt and Saxon*, left unfinished at his death in 1909 and then published in 1910 in the *Fortnightly Review* in England and in *The Forum* in the United States. See George Meredith, *Celt and Saxon*, *Works*, vol. 20, memorial ed. (London: Constable, 1911). Meredith was a Victorian novelist much influenced by German romanticism. Forster has Leonard Bast in *Howards End* decide to spend a night in the woods partly as a result of remembering a similar scene in Meredith's *The Ordeal of Richard Feverel* (1859).

13. *The Manuscripts of Howards End*, ed. Oliver Stallybrass (London: Ed-

ward Arold, 1973), 26. There is no way to tell whether Forster had in mind Friedrich Schlegel or August Wilhelm Schlegel as the "great critic." August Wilhelm may have had greater importance in Forster's day. Today, Friedrich is more admired by most scholars.

14. There may be a discreet hint of lesbianism is the description of Monica, the woman Helen shares an apartment with in Munich when she has fled England after being got with child by Leonard Bast: "Margaret guessed at Monica's type— 'Italiano inglesiato' they had named it: the crude feminist of the South, whom one respects but avoids. And Helen had turned to it in her need!" (291).

15. Public lecture given some years ago at a conference at the University of South Florida. See also Hugh David, *On Queer Street: A Social History of British Homosexuality: 1895–1995* (London: HarperCollins, 1997).

16. Katherine Mansfield, *Journal*, ed. J. Middleton Murray (London: Constable, 1954), 121.

17. See the discussion of this in chapter 4.

18. In *Between Men: English Literature and Male Homosocial Desire* (New York: Columbia University Press, 1985).

19. Margaret Schlegel makes an eloquent defense of difference in a speech to her sister at the end of the novel: "It is only that people are far more different than is pretended, All over the world men and women are worrying because they cannot develop as they are supposed to develop. . . . And others—others go further still, and move outside humanity altogether. A place, as well as a person, may catch the glow. Don't you see that all this leads to comfort in the end? It is part of the battle against sameness. Differences—eternal differences, planted by God in a single family, so that there may always be colour; sorrow perhaps, but colour in the daily gray" (335–36). This recognition of difference (perhaps even a difference in sexual preference, as is here intimated) is not incompatible in Margaret, however, and in Forster's narrator too, with a confidence that sympathy and tolerance will make the different understandable, even though difference, as the reader can see, is a response to the unseen, the "glow."

Chapter Nine

MARCEL PROUST:
LYING AS A *RECHERCHE* TOOL

THE PECULIARITY of a lying promise, as of lies in general, is that, as Jacques Derrida observed in a recent seminar on lying in Proust's *À la recherche du temps perdu*, no discernible linguistic mark distinguishes a lie from a true statement. Both employ the same syntax, the same grammar, the same semantic resources. The possibility of lying depends on this, as does the possibility of literature or of irony. Lying is like irony. There is no external way to tell that a given sentence is ironic rather than straight. Unlike the situation with other tropes—simile, for example, with its "like" or "as"—nothing intrinsic to its language labels a sentence as ironic or lying. Nevertheless, a lie is perhaps a little more likely to contain the explicit assertion of the testimonial side that is always implicit in any declarative sentence. This testimonial aspect makes every constative sentence contaminated by a performative dimension. When I say, "It is raining outside," I also implicitly say, "I swear to you that this is true," or "I swear that I believe this to be true." Albertine, for example, in Proust's *À la recherche du temps perdu*, when she is (apparently) telling a whole series of lies to cover up what she almost said, or probably almost said, to Marcel (the obscene phrase "me faire casser le pot"), asserts "I swear to you that was all (je vous jure que c'est cela). . . . The words—I don't even know what they mean. I heard them used in the street one day by some very low people—just came into my head without rhyme or reason. It had nothing to do with me or anybody else (Ça ne se rapporte ni à moi ni à personne). I was simply dreaming aloud." Marcel's response is an act of belief, not knowledge: "it was still impossible for me to doubt her sworn word."[1]

The fact that a lie, like an ironic statement, does not signal itself as what it is may explain the rage that is aroused in those who discover that they have been fooled by an irony or a lie. It is the one thing it is most difficult to forgive in another. The whole contractual give-and-take of family relations, political discourse, and commerce between nations depends on the conventional presumption that lies and irony are absent, even though all these regions of language use are haunted by the possibility and perhaps even by the inevitability of lies and irony. It is not being just willfully cynical to wonder how many marriages, or how many peaceful relations between nations, would survive truth telling between the partners. Diplomacy, as Proust demonstrates at length, is a conventional art of lying, often by the time-honored technique of the bluff, the promise to do something that you have no intention of doing. Social and family life would be impossible without lying, as Marcel says.

What I have just said presupposes an intimate and unbreakable connection among a cluster of topics: lies, performative language, death, testimony, diplomacy, secrets, love, jealousy, the other or others, and art in the sense of painting, music, and literature. Well, what about the lie in Proust?

It is in the context of Marcel's misguided attempt to get definite proof that Albertine is or is not lesbian that the question of whether or not Albertine lies to him becomes his obsession. A lie, we presume, is a contrary-to-fact statement made by someone who knows that it is false. To prove that a lie is a lie, so it seems, we need only confront the lie with the truth. Even if being or not being lesbian is not an essence, nevertheless actual lesbian lovemaking is, so it seems, a palpable physical fact about which it ought to be possible to get irrefutable evidence, even if one has not oneself been there to see it, as for example Marcel was present when he saw through the lighted window of the Vinteuil house Mlle Vinteuil and her friend making love—and desecrating her father's photograph to boot.

Though these assumptions about lies seem so reasonable, however, they are in error, as Marcel's experience of Albertine's lies demonstrates. His mistake in his *recherche* into lies is to mistake a performative utterance or an utterance that is always partly performative for a purely constative one. Just what does it mean to say that a lie, if there is such a thing, is a speech act?

The answer to that question is given in a long series of episodes in which Marcel tries unsuccessfully to catch Albertine in a lie, continuing his search even after her death. These episodes manifest fractal self-similarity of the aleatory kind. The same elements are composed and composed anew in them, but always with a slight difference introduced by the chance change of circumstances. What fuels both the written Marcel's engagement in these experiences and the writing Marcel's retrospective attempt to analyze and understand them is the ever-renewed, ever-frustrated attempt to get definite knowledge about Albertine. Did she lie to him? Did she love women? "It is one of the faculties of jealousy," says Marcel,

> to reveal to us the extent to which the reality of external facts and the sentiments of the heart (les sentiments de l'âme) are an unknown element which lends itself to endless suppositions. We imagine that we know exactly what things are and what people think, for the simple reason that we do not care about them. But as soon as we have a desire to know, as the jealous man has,

then it becomes a dizzy kaleidoscope in which we can no longer distinguish
anything. Had Albertine been unfaithful to me? With whom? In what house?
On what day? On the day when she had said this or that to me, when I
remembered that I had in the course of it said this or that? I could not tell (je
n'en savais rien). (F, 4:100; E, 3:529)

The episode, or rather repeated episodes, of the anacoluthon, since Marcel says it happened often, when Albertine habitually starts a sentence in
the first person, so that it might have been going to be an inadvertent
confession, and then ends it in the third person, so it seems she is talking
about someone else (F,3:658–59; E,3:149–50);[2] the episode of her use of
the not quite completed obscene phrase, referring to anal sex, "me faire
casser . . . [le pot]"; the episode of Albertine's presumed lie to Marcel on
the day after Bergotte's death; the episode in which Albertine covers up a
liaison with Andrée in Marcel's own house by claiming she has had an
allergic reaction to syringa; the quarrel after the Verdurins' party that
leads to Albertine's flight; Marcel's attempt after Albertine's death to get
information from the bathhouse keeper where, if the woman is to be believed, Albertine used to go with women friends; the episode of the laundry girl with whom Albertine perhaps took pleasure on the riverbank a
few days before her death; Andrée's final confession, if confession it is, of
"the things she used to do" with Albertine—these are salient moments in
the trajectory of Marcel's unsuccessful research.

The reader who knows the *Recherche* will note how explicitly all these
episodes have to do with language. The jealous man (or woman) is per-
force a reader. This means he or she needs to be a grammarian, a specialist in syntax, have knowledge of slang, and most of all understand tropes.
Nevertheless, all his or her skill as a reader does not get the knowledge
wanted, since the text he or she is trying to read is, strictly speaking,
unreadable. The lover can never verify a reading of the signs. The trajectory of these episodes is not, however, simply a repetitive series. The sequence of little waves makes up a large, wavelike pattern of Marcel's
falling into love and then out of it. This sequence demonstrates the Proustian law that says the deeper the lover's love, the less he can know of the
beloved. The fifth section of this huge novel, "Albertine disparue," is the
story of Marcel's agonized and prolonged mourning after Albertine's departure and then death, as he gradually begins to forget her, no longer to
love her. It is only when he no longer cares, or no longer cares so much,
that Andrée ceases to lie to him and tells him the truth, or perhaps tells him
the truth.

I say "perhaps tells him the truth" because Marcel can never know for
sure. The otherness of the other person remains wholly other. Marcel can
never know for sure because the presumed lies that Albertine and the

others tell him are speech acts, not simply contrary-to-fact constatives. They are a form of bearing witness. A lie is a version of that kind of speech act called testimony. It always has implicitly or explicitly attached to it an oath: "I swear to you that what I say is true." Examples are what Albertine says of "me faire casser le pot": "je vous jure que c'est cela" (F, 3:841; E, 3:343). or what she says when she denies that she ever had relations with Andrée: "'I can swear to you by anything you like, the honour of my aunt, the grave of my poor mother.' I had believed her" (F, 4:191; E, 3:625). A lie, if there is such a thing, is likely to be surrounded with juridical terminology and a whiff of the courtroom, as when Marcel calls in witnesses and wants to pronounce, like a judge, "guilty" or "not guilty" of Albertine's presumed perfidies. Of Andrée's admission, long after Albertine's death, of what she and Albertine did, Marcel says: ". . . if I did not suffer unduly at this revelation, it was because, some time since, the belief in Albertine's innocence that I had fabricated (forgée) for myself had been gradually replaced, without my realising it, by the belief, ever present in my mind, in her guilt" (F, 4:188; E, 3:622–23).

The verdict of guilty or innocent, as this passage makes explicit, is pronounced, as in the courtroom, not on the basis of knowledge but on the basis of belief. The only possible response to a witness's testimony is not the conviction of achieved knowledge but an act of credence. A jury, as I have said in chapter 5, convicts a criminal not because it knows the criminal's guilt, but because a majority believe beyond the shadow of a doubt that he or she is guilty. As Derrida patiently and at length showed in his recent seminars on witnessing and attestation, any act of bearing witness carries its own validation, such as it is. Contrary to what common sense indicates, testimony cannot be verified by further testimony or by further information.

It is true that one cannot appeal to another witness for verification or disproval of what the first witness says (as Marcel tries to do when he appeals to the bathhouse keeper, to the laundry girl, and to Andrée to prove that Albertine was lying), but my belief in the witness's attestation is itself another act of bearing witness. It is, as Marcel says of his conviction of Albertine's innocence, an act of belief born of desire. Love for the other leads me to believe in the beloved's lies, to live in a whole dream-world her lies engender: "Now if I no longer believed in Albertine's innocence, it was because I had already ceased to feel the need, the passionate desire to believe in it. It is desire that engenders belief, and if we are not as a rule aware of this, it is because most belief-creating desires (désirs créateurs)—unlike the desire which had persuaded me that Albertine was innocent—end only with our own life (qu'avec nous-même)" (F, 4:188–89; E, 3:623). Life is here defined as the prolonged living within a lie or set of lies, while truth is death. Lies are a way of holding off death.

A number of special features, however, distinguish the lie as a form of testimony from other kinds of testimony. As I have said, false witness, the lie, bears no linguistic marks discriminating it from true witness. The same forms of language are used in either case. This means that the lie brings into the open features of witnessing in general that are obscured in presumably true testimony. One is the impossibility of ever having direct access to the motives and intentions of the one who lies. It is always possible that the "liar," if there is such a person, may have believed what he or she says was true. You can never know. The otherness of the other person remains unknowably other. It is because you can never know that one has to say about lies what Derrida scrupulously repeats about the secret. If one must say "the secret, if there is such a thing," one must also say "the lie, if there is such a thing." The lie and the secret are, it is easy to see, closely dependent on one another. Albertine's secret is her presumed lesbianism. She lies, if she does indeed lie, in order to keep that secret, if it exists, hidden. That presumed secret is the allegory of her impenetrable otherness.

The lie, moreover, if there is such a thing, brings into the open another aspect of testimony in general, the detachment of its efficacy as a speech act from its constative value, its truth telling. Just as no linguistic mark distinguishes a lie from a truth, so a lie, if it is believed, will do as well as a truth as a way of doing things with words. J. L. Austin himself recognized this in a passing comment about lying in *How to Do Things with Words*: " 'I promise but do not intend' is parallel to 'it is the case but I do not believe it'; to say 'I promise,' without intending, is parallel to saying 'it is the case' without believing."[3] They are parallel because in both cases the locution may function as an efficacious speech act. The lying promise still puts you in the new situation of either fulfilling or not fulfilling the promise. Densher, in Henry James's *The Wings of the Dove*, discovers this about the implicit lying promise he has made to Milly Theale, when he has led her to believe that Kate Croy does not return his love, so he is free to love Milly and be loved by her. To say "it is the case" without believing may have as much power to change the world as a true statement, if others believe the lie. Its power does not depend on its truth, as the realm of politics shows us every day, for example when lying politicians tell us "The American people want . . . so and so" and this eventually brings it about that the American people are hypnotized into wanting so and so, even if it is greatly against their manifest interest.

The lie, finally, has an amazing power to bring into existence just that about which it prevaricates. The performative efficacy of the lie may be measured by the way it has of becoming true. Densher pretends to make love to Milly Theale or allows her to think that he is making love to her,

though he loves Kate Croy instead. He then does come to love Milly, or
rather, after her death, he comes to fall in love with her memory. It is as
though his own lie had power to force him, against his will, to make it
true. Marcel, on the night of his quarrel with Albertine after the Verdurin
party, pretends that he does not love Albertine and says they must part.
What he says is all lies, an extended playacting, or at least he tells us that
this is the case, but the result, as Marcel says, is that all these lies come
true, "for life in its changing course makes realities of our fables" (E,
3:373);[4] "Time passes, and little by little everything we have spoken in
falsehood becomes true (tout ce qu'on disait par mensonge devient vrai)"
(F, 4:44; E, 3:470).

Just why is it that lies seem so often to have something to do with
death? Albertine's lies are validated by an oath on her mother's grave.
One of her most signal and apparently gratuitous lies occurs at the moment of Bergotte's death (though she probably lied to cover up a meeting
about which she did not want Marcel to know). The fulfillment of Densher's lying promise to Milly is made certain by her death. Marcel's lying
separation of himself from Albertine on the night of the Verdurins' party
comes true in her death. His lie anticipates and even in a way helps bring
about her death, for which Marcel bitterly reproaches himself later.

There would be much to say about the relation of lies to death. To
speak too precipitously and too schematically about something that mer-
its a long and careful development, one can say that if death is another
name for the otherness of the other, if a lie in a curious way brings into the
open, in the anguish of our inability to know whether or not the lie is a lie,
the unknowable otherness of the other person, then lies always have
about them a taint of death. To swear on my mother's grave is not only
to endorse what I say by the sacred obligation I had to my mother for
truth telling, but also to swear in relation to someone whose death means
that there is no way I could ever make up for the damage a lie would do
to her, since I would be being unfaithful to her memory, unfaithful to
implicit or explicit promises I made to her while she was alive. In the same
way, in *The Wings of the Dove*, Densher, once Milly is dead, cannot
explain, apologize, offer reparation, or in any other way make up for the
lying promise he has tacitly made to her. He can only, by a kind of irresistible coercion, make the implicit lying promise come true.

When Albertine claims to have had a long conversation with Bergotte
on the day he was already dead, this puts that nonexistent event, fabricated by her lie, in direct relation to death. It suggests the way all lies are
related to death. They hover over death as over their abyssal foundation
or lack of foundation. Since a lying oath involves death by not having
any roots in the solid materiality of history, only a nonfoundation in the

shadowy abyss of death, such an oath is particularly compelling. A lying oath is like a mortgage (mort-gage), in which I put my death on the line as earnest, security, or gage for the fulfillment of my promise. Even if I die, my obligation will continue. I swear on my own death to go on paying.

Nevertheless, an oath sworn on the death of those to whom I have the greatest obligation to be truthful or sworn on my own death ("I wish I may die if I am not telling the truth") is perhaps even more likely to be perjury than one not so extravagantly affirmed. In the sadness of his discovery on the basis of Andrée's testimony, at least so he believes at that moment, that he had interrupted the lovemaking of Albertine and Andrée in his own house on the night Albertine claimed to be allergic to syringa, Marcel asserts this dark law by way of a sentence that contains a double oath, the lying oath and the oath that repudiates that oath as a lie:

> when a married woman says to you of a young man: "Oh! it's perfectly true that I have an immense affection for him, but it's something quite innocent, quite pure, I could swear it on the memory of my parents (je pourrais le jurer sur le souvenir de mes parents)," one ought oneself, instead of feeling any hesitation, to swear to oneself (se jurer à soi-même) that she has probably just come out of the bathroom into which, after every assignation she has with the young man in question, she rushes in order not to have a child. (F, 4:191; E, 3:625)

The careful reader will note an important feature of the two examples I have given. Albertine does not swear she had no relations with Andrée. She says, "I *can* swear." The adulterous wife does not swear, she says, "I *could* swear it on the memory of my parents." In neither case is it a real oath, but rather what speech-acts theorists call the "mention" of one. I could swear, or I can swear, but in saying that I do not really do so. It would be possible to read this as a sign that the speaker is lying, since it is evidence of a reluctance actually to endorse the presumed lie with an oath. The little words "can" and "could" are attempts to have it both ways, to swear without swearing.

Now it might be argued that one important technique for revealing the truth behind a lie is much in evidence in all this part of the *Recherche*. This is the identification of contradictions in what the presumed liar says. When Marcel says, "I had believed her" of Albertine's assertions that she never did anything with Andrée, he goes on to add:

> And yet even if my suspicions had not been aroused (mis en méfiance) by the contradiction between her former partial admissions with regard to certain matters and the vehemence with which she had denied them as soon as she saw that I was not indifferent to them, . . . I ought to have reflected that there are two worlds one behind the other, one consisting of the things that the

best, the sincerest people say, and behind it the world composed of what those same people do. (F, 4:191; E, 3:625)

There are two worlds, one of lying language and the other of what really happens, but lying language sooner or later, we have been taught to believe, gives itself away in contradictions, in two statements that logically contradict one another so that one or the other of them must be false. The truth will always out. It is this presupposition that underlies the courtroom procedure of cross-examining the witness. If the witness is lying, sooner or later, by adroit questioning, the opposing lawyer is supposed to be able to get that witness to contradict himself or herself and so reveal that one or the other of the things the witness has said must be a lie.

A number of things can be said to put in question this assumption. For one thing, if people are really as diverse and heterogeneous as Marcel finds them to be, then it might be the case that the realm of otherness, or of that plural "others," might be a realm contradicting the law of non-contradiction.[5] Two contradictory things might simultaneously be true of that realm of the others. Albertine might both be and not be lesbian: "We would like the truth to be revealed to us by novel signs, not by a sentence similar to those which we have constantly repeated to ourselves. The habit of thinking prevents us at times from experiencing reality, immunises us against it, makes it seem no more than another thought. There is no idea that does not carry in itself its possible refutation, no word that does not imply its opposite (un mot le mot contraire)" (F, 4:181–82; E, 3:615). The mere fact of a contradiction does not prove that either of the assertions is a lie. Both might be true.

One might argue, however, that in certain frequent cases one or the other of two contradictory statements must be a lie and verifiably so, since the statements do not bear on the unique, hidden, secret, unknowable region of otherness down to which or toward which each person reaches but make statements about the material, historical world. Such a statement, one would think, must be either true or false. It ought to be verifiable or able to be proved false. Albertine either did or did not go to Buttes-Chaumont with Andrée. She either did or did not meet women and have relations with them in the bathhouse. She did or did not make love with the young laundress. The problem, as Marcel again and again discovers, is that all he can ever get as evidence proving that these supposed historical events did or did not occur is someone's testimony. This testimony may be true or false. It is up to him to decide whom to believe, Albertine or the bathhouse woman. Repeatedly Marcel thinks he has convincing evidence that Albertine must have been lying and then realizes that the witness to her behavior may herself or himself be lying. He sends Aimé to interview the bathhouse keeper and thinks that at last he knows the truth. Albertine did make love to women there. The bathhouse woman swears that this is so. Then he remembers that his grandmother had asserted that this woman had a great talent for mendacity. She may for one reason or another be lying. This puts Marcel right back where he started and where he permanently remains, unable to know for sure, able only to believe or not believe.

When after Albertine's death Marcel has gradually ceased to love her and to believe in her innocence, what seems to be the definitive proof of her lesbian proclivities in the circumstantial details of their lovemaking Andrée gives leads Marcel first to think that now he knows at last, when he no longer really cares. He then ultimately realizes, in the last sentences of this whole long sequence recounting his mourning for Albertine and the slow death of his love for her, just before the Venice episode, that Andrée may well be lying in order to make him unhappy and in order to make him feel less superior to her. The upshot of all his desire to know is no more than a renewed uncertainty and a renewed recognition that the ultimate wisdom is to know that he cannot know, since what we call knowing is really only a matter of credence: "But why should I believe that it was she [Albertine] rather than Andrée who was lying? Truth and life are very difficult to fathom (bien ardues), and I retained of them, without really having got to know them, an impression in which sadness was perhaps actually eclipsed (dominée) by exhaustion" (F, 4:202; E, 3:637).

"La verité et la vie sont bien ardues"—that has certainly turned out to be the case. In fact truth and life have turned out to be bottomless, unfathomable, at the bottom of a very deep well.

One final common-sense recourse remains. Even if all the witnesses have been suborned, as Marcel says "I" suborned (J'achetai) any number of women from whom I learned nothing (qui ne m'apprirent rien)" (F, 4:92; E, 3:521), one can at least trust the evidence of one's own eyes. Ocular proof is, so it seems, irrefutable evidence, as when Marcel keeps coming back to the certainty he has that Mlle Vinteuil and her friend made love because he saw them doing it with his own eyes through the lighted window of the Vinteuil house. So powerful is the performative effect of a lie, however, that it makes even the evidence of the senses dubious. Marcel makes this clear in analyzing the episode of Albertine's presumed lie to him about her long conversation with Bergotte on the day when he was already dead. Marcel observes, as Jacques Derrida noted and commented on in his seminar on lying in Proust, that Albertine had a "charming skill in lying naturally" (F, 3:694; E, 3:187). What Marcel says is that "je n'appris que bien plus tard l'art charmant qu'elle avait de mentir avec simplicité (in a more literal translation: it was not until much later that I took in the charming art she had of lying with simplicity)." At the time he did not take it in ("appris"), but much later he did. This is a good example of the refrain of "Then I was ignorant. Now I know" that punctuates Marcel's discourse in the *Recherche*.

Lying naturally is for Albertine a skill in storytelling, the sort of skill that makes a good novelist, such as Marcel Proust: "What she said, what she admitted," says Marcel, using the legal terminology that is habitual to him in analyzing Albertine's lies, "had to such a degree the same characteristics as the formal evidence of the case (le formes de l'évidence)—what we see with our own eyes or learn from irrefutable sources—that she sowed thus in the gaps of her life episodes of another life the falsity of which I did not then suspect" (F, 3:694; E, 3:187). The episode itself, however, not to speak of many other episodes in this long sequence telling the story of Marcel's jealous love of Albertine, questions the certainty of what we see with our own eyes and casts doubt on the assumption that there is such a thing as "irrefutable evidence."

As Derrida noted, the word "charming," used twice in this sequence to define Albertine's gift of the lie, means not only "attractive in a feminine way," as when we say, "What a charming girl!" It also names a magical power to create through the charm of words belief in something that has no existence outside the words. That is why I say "gift of the lie" rather than "gift for lying." A lie is a gift. It creates something new or brings something new into the world and therefore is like a donation. A "charm" is a formula, often in poetry, that has a magical potency to cure disease, ward off evil, or disable an enemy. Some of the earliest Old English texts are "charms." The word "charm," in French or in English, is related to the Greek word "carmen," the general name for lyric poetry. Poetry is charming in the potent sense of being able to cast a magical spell. Albertine's charming novelistic power of lying with verisimilitude, "the happy aptitude for a lie that is animated (au mensonge animé), colored with the very hues of life" (F, 3:696; E, 3:190), certainly fools Marcel. It fools him into disbelieving the testimony of the newspapers: "I learned (J'appris), as I have said, that Bergotte had died that day. And I was amazed at the inaccuracy of the newspapers which—each of them reproducing the same paragraph—stated that he had died the day before. For Albertine had met him the day before, as she informed me that very evening, and indeed she had been a little late in coming home, for he had chatted to her for some time. She was probably the last person to whom he had spoken" (F, 3:693; E, 3:186). Marcel has here been charmed by Albertine's lie into repeating as if it were true the details of what must be an entirely fictitious event, since Bergotte was in truth already dead. The narrative is ironic in the sense that the writing Marcel now knows the newspapers had it right and he had been beguiled by a lie. He would have known this if he had been there to see with his own eyes the death of

Bergotte, which he reports with such mendacious accuracy in the episode just prior to this one. It is mendacious because Marcel was not there and because he tells the reader what neither he nor anyone else but the now dead Bergotte could ever know, that is, just what Bergotte was thinking and feeling as he looked in the very moment of his death at the little patch of yellow wall in Vermeer's "View of Delft."

Even had Marcel seen Bergotte die, he could not have trusted the testimony of his own eyes. The charming lie would have had power to countervail even the apparently irrefutable force of ocular evidence. The example Marcel gives for this is a claim by Albertine that she had met such and such a woman in the street and talked briefly to her on a day when Marcel knew that woman could not have been there "for the simple reason that the person had not been in Paris for the last ten months" (F, 3:697; E, 3:187). Suppose, says Marcel, I had happened to be in the street at that time and had seen with my own eyes that Albertine had not encountered the woman:

> I should then have known that Albertine was lying. But is this absolutely certain even then? . . . A strange darkness (Une obscurité sacrée) would have clouded my mind, I should have begun to doubt whether I had seen her alone, I should hardly even have sought to understand by what optical illusion I had failed to perceive the lady, and I should not have been greatly surprised to find myself mistaken, for the stellar universe is not so difficult of comprehension as the real actions of other people, especially of the people we love, fortified as they are against our doubts by fables devised for their protection. (F, 3:694–96; E, 3:188).

As Marcel says, "The evidence of the senses (témoignage des sens) is also an operation of the mind in which conviction creates the facts (la conviction crée l'évidence)" (F, 3:694; E, 3:188).

Albertine's lies have such charming power that they lead Marcel to doubt the witness of his senses and to see what he has not seen or to believe that he has seen what he has not seen or could not have seen because it did not occur. Even the senses give not verified fact but one more form of witness, no more certain than that of external witnesses and just as much requiring to be believed in order to be efficacious. The testimony of the senses is in this analogous to a performative use of language, not analogous, as one would think, to a constative one. We must say "I believe I see so and so," or "I swear I see so and so," not just "I see so and so." Albertine's words become eyes through which Marcel sees an entirely fictive world as if it were real. She has a power like that wielded by the great novelists to open up for us imaginary worlds. Albertine was, says Marcel, "charming (charmante), as I have said, when she invented a story which left no room for doubt, for one saw then in front of one the thing—albeit imaginary—which she was describing, through the eyes, as it were, of her words (en se servant comme vue de sa parole)" (F, 3:695; E, 3:190).

That we are ourselves at that moment reading a fiction that has power to masquerade as eyes through which we see a new reality is momentarily revealed by the fact that the new Pléiade edition does not quite agree, in what is included in this section and in the order of the paragraphs, either with the old Pléiade edition or with the English translation of Moncrieff and Kilmartin. The discrepancy allows the reader for a moment to glimpse the factitiousness of the whole fabric of words, the way we have been fooled by a lie. The new Pléiade edition adds another sentence, a sentence present neither in the old Pléiade nor in the Moncrieff/Kilmartin translation, to the passage I have just quoted: "C'était ma vraie perception (It was my true perception)" (F, 3:696; my trans.). This makes explicit the way Marcel's perception, as if with his own eyes, of the truth of Albertine's lies is a matter for further testimony. It is as if Marcel were in the witness box swearing on oath: "It was my true perception. I swear to you that this is what I really saw."

As I have elsewhere demonstrated,[6] an "unknown world" is for Proust in both art and lying "invented" in the double sense of being made up and discovered. When it has been made up it seems as if what is made up has been there all along waiting to be invented in the sense of discovered. Vinteuil's music offers a glimpse of the unknown homeland that is the source of his music and that is unique to him. It is unique because it is a homeland with a single inhabitant. That homeland preexists Vinteuil's music. It is revealed by the music as something always already there rather than being created by it. Nevertheless, the inventive, performative power of the music is absolutely necessary to release any knowledge, indirect and mediated though it is, of that homeland. In an analogous way, what Proust calls "the lie, the perfect lie" (F, 3:721; E, 3:213) does not create a factitious or fictitious world, wholly imaginary, as might seem to be the case in what Marcel says about Albertine's "charming art of lying with simplicity." Each perfect lie functions rather as an art of invention in the sense of discovery. It opens a window on a new and unknown world that was always latently there, though our sleeping senses were not awake to it. That world would have remained waiting to be discovered even if the appropriate lie had never been uttered to unlock it. It would still remain there if every trace of the lie that "invented" it were to disappear. To each such lie belongs a different universe. Without the charming power of many lies we should never have a chance to know all those different and incommensurate universes. Like the *Recherche* itself, the lie, the perfect lie, can be a means of research, of investigation and discovery, not so much of lost time as of a hitherto unknown realm which only that particular lie can uncover.

NOTES

1. Marcel Proust, *À la recherche du temps perdu*, ed. Jean-Yves Tadié, éd. de la Pléiade (Paris: Gallimard, 1989), 3:841; *Remembrance of Things Past*, trans. C. K. Scott Moncrieff, Terence Kilmartin, and Andreas Mayor (New York: Vintage, 1982), 3:343–44. Henceforth citations will be to F and E.

2. The paragraph about this has great intellectual and comic power. It describes as a comic disability but with admirable intellectual insight limitations of memory that make our inability to integrate all the times of our lives something like the inability of a reader, myself as a reader of Proust, for example, to remember simultaneously every detail of a complex text: "The beginnings of a lie on the part of one's mistress are like the beginnings of one's own love, or of a vocation. They take shape, accumulate, pass unnoticed by oneself. When one wants to remember in what manner one begins to love a woman, one is already in love with her; day-dreaming about her beforehand, one did not say to oneself: 'This is the prelude to love; be careful! (c'est le prélude d'un amour, faisons attention)'" (F, 3:659; E, 3:149–50).

3. J. L. Austin, *How to Do Things with Words*, ed. J. O. Urmson and Marina Sbisà, 2d ed. (Oxford: Oxford University Press, 1980), 50.

4. The paragraph from which this comes is omitted in the new Pléiade edition. It is given as an asterisked footnote in the old Pléiade edition, ed. Pierre Clarac and André Ferré (Paris: Gallimard, 1954), 3:365.

5. Each one of these plural worlds is, according to Proust, some one person's unique homeland, in which he or she participates as in his or her own singular death. See F, 3:721; E, 3:213; F, 3:761; E, 3:258. I have discussed these passages in *Black Holes* (Stanford: Stanford University Press, 1999).

6. This final paragraph is adapted from a longer discussion of the passage containing the phrase "the lie, the perfect lie," in *Black Holes*, 431–39. I have reached here a similar point by a different trajectory from that followed in the discussion of Proust in *Black Holes*.

Chapter Ten

PAUL DE MAN AS ALLERGEN

IT IS DIFFICULT to establish just what Paul de Man's ultimate place will be or to identify with accuracy his legacy. Probably it is still too soon to tell. His work continues to be widely read, perhaps especially at somewhat peripheral (?) places like Aarhus, Amsterdam, Valencia, Beijing, or Irvine, but the profession, as he foresaw, has taken another tack or never really deviated for more than the blink of an eye or the paroxysm of a sneeze from the tack it was already on. De Man's name for that tack was "aesthetic ideology," for which one present incarnation is a certain version of so-called cultural studies.[1] A few days before his death de Man observed dispassionately that he had not changed one iota the university where he had been teaching for over a decade. Why one should want to change one's university is not entirely clear, unless one cares about it and about its students, while thinking it is on a wrong course or embodies a false ideology. Certainly United States universities have now for the most part closed pretty seamlessly over the wound de Man's presence constituted. That closing over, however, has happened for the profession of literary studies in the West generally. It happened even during de Man's lifetime. The "scandal" of de Man's wartime writings has only made it possible to go on doing with a clearer conscience what had been happening for a long time already, that is, the suppression or evasion of de Man's work. Reuben Brower was unsuccessful in his attempt to get de Man a tenure-track post at Harvard in 1960.[2] De Man's long connection with the *New York Review of Books* (which began in 1963) came to an end when they rejected as "too technical for general readership" an essay of 1972, "Roland Barthes and the Limits of Structuralism."[3] De Man's biggest book, the magisterial *Allegories of Reading*, was negatively reviewed by the British reader for Oxford University Press, the first publisher of *Blindness and Insight* and the holder then of an agreement to consider his next book, that is, *Allegories of Reading*. The manuscript had been sent to a British reader because it involved European literature. Such manuscripts were the province of the Oxford Press in England. *Allegories of Reading* was then published (in 1979) by de Man's own university press, that is, Yale University Press.

The opening paragraphs of one of de Man's most important essays, "The Resistance to Theory," give a dryly ironic account of how that essay was commissioned for a collective Modern Language Association volume entitled *Introduction to Scholarship in Modern Languages and Literatures* and then rejected by the MLA committee. De Man was to write the section on literary theory. As he says, he "found it difficult to live up, in minimal good faith, to the requirements of this program." Instead, his essay, de Man asserts, "could only try to explain, as concisely as possible, why the main theoretical interest of literary theory consists in the impossibility of its definition." This was "rightly judged" to be "an inauspicious way to achieve the pedagogical objectives of the volume," and so the MLA committee commissioned another essay. "I thought," says de Man, "their decision altogether justified, as well as interesting in its implications for the teaching of literature."[4] This resistance to de Man's work does not mean that de Man has not received a lot of attention, been published by major presses, had lots of books and essays written about him, and so on, but even the favorable attention has often taken the form of trying to put him in his place, and then going beyond or around him, as I began this essay by saying it is hard to do.

It is easy to see why the institution of literary study in the United States, or, in a different way, in Europe, including journalistic reviewing in both regions, is antipathetical to de Man and needs to suppress him in order to get on with its business. De Man's work is a violent allergen that provokes fits of coughing, sneezing, and burning eyes, perhaps even worse symptoms, unless it can be neutralized or expelled. "Allergen": a substance that causes an allergy. The word "allergy," oddly enough, comes from the German *Allergie*, meaning "altered reaction," a Teutonic formation from the Greek *allo*, other, plus *ergon*, work. The "gen" in "allergen" means generating or causing. De Man's work as allergen is something alien, something other, that works to bring about a reaction of resistance to that otherness. To vary the metaphor, de Man's writings are a monkey wrench in the works, sand in the salad. The best antihistamine might be to forget them altogether and get on with the reproduction of some form or other of aesthetic ideology. The trouble is that once you have read de Man seriously it is difficult to do that without a vague uneasy feeling that you are laying traps for yourself and others, or, to put it more simply, promulgating something false, perhaps dangerously false.

In a remark near the beginning of "Kant and Schiller," which, it should be remembered, is the transcription of an oral performance, Paul de Man observes that though his Cornell audience has been "so kind at the beginning and so hospitable and so benevolent," nevertheless, in this case as in others in his experience, "it doesn't take you too long before you feel that you're getting under people's skin, and that there is a certain reaction which is bound to occur, certain questions that are bound to be asked, which is the interesting moment, when certain issues are bound to come up" (AI, 132–33). My figure of de Man as allergen is a slight transposition of this figure. An allergen causes an allergic reaction. It gets under your skin or into your nose, and "there is a certain reaction which is bound to occur." You sneeze or break out in a rash. This figure is only a figure. It compares what happens to some people in reading de Man to what happens in a certain material reaction to a foreign substance by a living organic body.

The figure is not innocent, however. In comparing something seemingly "abstract," intentional, linguistic, or "spiritual"—reading—to something material, automatic, autonomic, and involuntary, something "bound to happen," that is, an allergic reaction, the question of the relation of language to "materiality" is raised. Does any substantial connection justify the figure? This is one of the central questions in de Man's conception of a "material event." How can a linguistic act, such as the formulations reached by Kant's philosophic rigor, intervene in the "material" world and bring about what de Man calls "the materiality of actual history"?[5] How can writing or reading be a material event? How can speech be an act? As I shall show, de Man's transformation of the usual meaning of "materiality" (the transformation is itself a speech act) goes by way of a new conception of the relation of language to that reconceived materiality.

Almost any page of de Man's work, but especially the beginnings and endings of essays, contains rejections of well-established received ideas about literary study. These rejections can best be characterized as ironically and joyfully insolent or even contemptuous, as well as dismayingly rigorous and plausible.[6] De Man's essays have the structure he identifies in "The Concept of Irony" as "the traditional opposition between *eiron* and *alazon*, as they appear in Greek or Hellenic comedy, the smart guy and the dumb guy" (AI, 165). De Man is of course the *eiron*, the smart guy, and all the previous experts on whatever topic or text he is discussing are the *alazons*, the dumb guys.[7] The received ideas he attacks, often fundamental assumptions of our profession, are characteristically called aberrant, deluded, or simply false. The reader can only hope or assume that "This does not, cannot, mean me! Surely I would not make such stupid mistakes." De Man forestalls that defensive move, however, when he asserts, for example, in "Kant and Schiller," that everyone, including himself, however ironically, in a collective "we," is still bewitched by aesthetic ideology:

> Before you either contest this [what he has been saying about Schiller's distortion of Kant], or before you not contest but agree with it and hold it against Schiller, or think that it is something we are now far beyond and that we would never in our enlightened days do—you would never make this

naive confusion between the practical and the pragmatic on the one hand and the philosophical Kantian enterprise on the other—before you decide that, don't decide too soon that you are beyond Schiller in any sense. I don't think any of us can lay this claim. Whatever writing we do, whatever way we have of talking about art, whatever way we have of teaching, whatever justification we give ourselves for teaching, whatever the standards are and the values by means of which we teach, they are more than ever and profoundly Schillerian. They come from Schiller, and not from Kant. (AI, 142)

De Man goes on to make a warning that certainly applies to what has happened in his own case, in spite of the fact that he was protected by being a Sterling Professor at Yale, which is about as much security as you can get: "And if you ever try to do something in the other direction [in the direction of Kant, that is, rather than Schiller] and touch on it you'll see what will happen to you. Better be very sure, wherever you are, that your tenure is very well-established, and that the institution for which you work has a very well-established reputation. Then you can take some risks without really taking many risks" (AI, 142).

I have said that de Man's work is threatening to "us all" because almost any page contains cheerfully taunting rejections, explicit or implicit, of "our" most basic ideological assumptions, the ones "we" most need to get on with our work, the ones the university most needs to get on with its work. Let me give two salient examples of that, among almost innumerable ones throughout his work. After its rejection by the MLA, de Man retooled "The Resistance to Theory" for an issue of *Yale French Studies* on "The Pedagogical Imperative: Teaching as a Literary Genre."[8] After telling his story about the MLA, de Man goes on in the next paragraph to unravel one by one our usual assumptions about teaching literature or about teaching as a form of literature, leading by rapid steps to the impossibility of teaching what ought (or rather ought not) to be taught, not to speak of the impossibility of his own enterprise in this essay and in his own or others' teaching generally. He thereby undoes the project of that particular *Yale French Studies* issue before it even gets under way.

De Man first dismisses the idea that teaching is an I/thou relation in which the teacher as subject elicits a response from the pupil as another subject in a face-to-face encounter that would have an obvious ethical dimension, as in the maieutic relation of Socrates to the youth of Athens: "Overfacile opinion notwithstanding, teaching is not primarily an intersubjective relationship between people but a cognitive process in which self and other are only tangentially and contiguously involved" (RT, 4). Even worse are sentimental ideas about teaching as theater or as therapy: "analogies between teaching and various aspects of show business or guidance counseling are more often than not excuses for having abdicated the task" (ibid.). What can and should be taught, de Man goes on to say, is scholarship, that is, achieved factual knowledge. What is solidly known can and ought to be taught: "Scholarship has, in principle, to be eminently teachable" (ibid.). That seems clear enough, and the (unwary) reader breathes a sigh of relief. Here is a clear and rational task for the teacher of literature, with nothing about the "impossibility of reading"[9] and other such disquieting "aporias" for which de Man is notorious.

The problems begin, however, as we might have suspected, when de Man goes on. He continues by distinguishing between two kinds of scholarship, "historical and philological facts as the preparatory condition for understanding, and methods of reading or interpretation" (RT, 4). These both seem teachable enough, and de Man allows that they are, along with theory as reflection on method: "As a controlled reflection on the formation of method, theory rightly proves to be entirely compatible with teaching, and one can think of numerous important theoreticians who are or were also prominent scholars" (ibid.). Taken together, historical facts, methods, and theories are the staple of curricula in literature, especially nowadays when courses in the various theories of literature and culture ("Theory 101") are well established in most departments along with courses having titles like "Renaissance Lyric" or "Victorian Novel."

"A question arises," de Man goes on to say, however, "only if a tension develops between methods of understanding and the knowledge which those methods allow one to reach" (ibid.). This small loose thread, in the rest of the paragraph, rapidly unravels the whole fabric. "If there is indeed something about literature, as such, which allows for a discrepancy between truth and method, between *Wahrheit* and *Methode* [the reference is of course to Hans-Georg Gadamer's hermeneutics], then scholarship and theory are no longer necessarily compatible" (ibid.). For one thing, literature can no longer be clearly delimited from nonliterature, nor can the distinction between history and interpretation be taken for granted. De Man means by this, I suppose, first, that in order to get on with the work of teaching literature, one must assume that one knows already what "literature, as such," is. As soon as the question "What is literature?" is seriously asked, immense, endless, difficulties arise. Second, no such thing exists as dispassionate philological or historical "facts." Each, for example periodization, as in "Renaissance Lyric" or "Victorian Novel," is the product of an act of interpretation that turns out to be unwarranted. The discrepancy between method and truth means that methodical teaching inculcates mystification, not enlightenment: "For a method that cannot be made to suit the 'truth' of its object can only teach delusion" (ibid.). De Man sees a symptom of the resistance to this dismaying fact in "the hostility directed at theory in the name of ethical and aesthetic values, as well as recuperative attempts of theoreticians to reassert their own subservience to these values [for example in books with titles like *The Ethics of Reading*]. The most effective of these attacks will denounce theory as an obstacle to scholarship and, consequently, to teaching" (ibid.).

Such attacks will be effective because they will be true. Theory *is* an obstacle to scholarship and teaching. To put this another way, theory cannot be taught. It is impossible to do so. Anyone who tries to do it is bound to fail. The rest of "The Resistance to Theory" shows through an intricate series of steps why this is so, culminating in the assertion, first, that "The resistance to theory . . . is a resistance to reading," and then to the more radical and enigmatic assertion that "Nothing can overcome the resistance to theory since theory *is* itself this resistance" (RT, 17–18, 19). I shall come back again ultimately to these sentences.

The paragraph about teaching I have been examining from the beginning of the essay ends, however, with an equally rigorous, intransigent, and perhaps even almost equally unintelligible sentence: "For if this [the way theory is an obstacle to scholarship and teaching] is indeed so, then it is better to fail in teaching what should not be taught than to succeed in teaching what is not true" (RT, 4). This aphorism, if that is the right word for it, is a good example of the sort of culminating encapsulations in de Man that I have been saying it would be better to forget if we want to get on with our work. In de Man's remorselessly lucid formulation, the cognitive categories of truth and falsehood distressingly do not mesh with the ethical categories of better and worse, nor with the pragmatic categories of success and failure in teaching. Whether one responds to this formulation with a shrug, with a shudder of disgust, or with a sneeze, it is in any case hard to take, perhaps deadly to be exposed to. On the one hand, what can be taught successfully is falsehood, the falsehood of scholarship in either of its modes. De Man has shown persuasively, if elliptically, why it is false. Surely no one would want to teach lies. On the other hand, theory "should not be taught." The "not" here is the surprise, the final twist of the knife. One might have expected that de Man would have said that it is better, ethically more responsible, to try heroically to teach what should be taught, theory, even though one is doomed to fail. No. Not only will you inevitably fail if you try to teach theory, it is also ethically wrong to do so. Theory "should not be taught," but it is nevertheless "better to fail in teaching" it. The two ethical terms here, "better" and "should not," are asymmetrical. Put together, they produce, strictly speaking, a sentence that is incoherent, irrational, that resists the intelligence.

The reader is left to decide how much or how little irony there is in that assertion, or in the paragraph as a whole, for that matter. Theory should not be taught, presumably, because it will put a stop to the whole ethi-

cally admirable institution of teaching literature, including courses presenting a repertoire or potpourri of methods and theories, along with
courses teaching literary works for their positive or negative ethical con-
tent. The ethically admirable, however, though it can be taught, has the
distressing limitation of being "what is not true," therefore not really
ethically admirable, assuming, contra Nietzsche, that ethics can be correlated with truth and lie.[10] It is therefore "better" to try to teach what
"should not be taught" and what you are bound to fail to teach. The
reader will see what I mean by saying that de Man is hard to take, that he
is likely to arouse an allergic reaction. In one short paragraph he has
moved from a rather banal remark ("the only teaching worthy of the
name is scholarly, not personal") to a mind-twisting aphorism that puts
the whole enterprise of teaching in the humanities radically in question
("it is better to fail in teaching what should not be taught").

I turn now to one more example of the sort of thing that is hard to swallow in de Man, in this case a characteristic exuberantly bleak formulation
near the end of an essay. "Shelley Disfigured" is one of de Man's most
luminously intelligent essays. It is an amazing reading of Shelley's "The
Triumph of Life." The essay was produced on commission, so to speak,
as his contribution to the collective volume *Deconstruction and Criticism*.[11] The essay is by no means easy reading, since it stays close to Shelley's difficult poem and moves rapidly and with concentrated intensity
through an intricate series of steps that is like a dance no one has ever
danced before, or perhaps like a violent act of trampling, to draw two
images from the poem itself and from de Man's essay about it. The essay
is also, characteristically, a polemic, in this case a discreet one, directed
against canonical readings of the poem and of romantic poetry generally
by Donald Rieman, Meyer Abrams, and two colleagues in the volume,
Geoffrey Hartman and Harold Bloom. "Shelley Disfigured" is a particularly complex version of a reading strategy familiar to readers of
de Man's other essays: the claim that a text is a tropological system that
is deconstructed by the text itself, with the deconstruction engendering "a
supplementary figural superposition which narrates the unreadability of
the prior narration" (AR, 205). Such supplements de Man calls "allegories," or, more precisely, "allegories of the impossibility of reading—a
sentence in which the genitive 'of' has itself to be 'read' as a metaphor"
(ibid.). Figure that out if you can! I mean figure out how the innocent
"of," whether subjective or objective genitive or both, in either or both of
the "ofs" in the sentence, can by itself be metaphorical. I suppose, or
propose (more about "-pose" later, as present here in de Man's phrase
"supplementary figural superposition"), that de Man means to disarticu-
late the causal, generative, or incorporative force of the "of." The relation

between such allegories and what they are allegories of, or between impossibility and reading, is only figuratively genitive in either of its senses, subjective or objective, the first sense internalizing the impossibility of reading within the allegory, the second sense making the impossibility of reading the object of which the allegory gives knowledge. The formulation is a commentary on the title de Man gave his book: *Allegories of Reading*.

Already in that book, however, at the very end, such magisterial formulations, that promise knowledge, albeit a negative knowledge, that is, knowledge of the impossibility of reading, are undone by an apparently casual tierce de Picardy[12] or just plain concluding discord that introduces irony as a permanent parabasis: "Irony is no longer a trope but the undoing of the deconstructive allegory of all tropological cognitions, the systematic undoing, in other words, of understanding. As such, far from closing off the tropological system, irony enforces the repetition of its aberration" (AR, 301). So much for learning to understand the impossibility of reading through allegories of it!

I shall return later to irony as nonunderstanding, as what Friedrich Schlegel called *Unverständlichkeit*, discussed in chapter 1. Now I want to argue that "Shelley Disfigured," which comes a year or two after the Rousseau essays in *Allegories of Reading* I have been citing, picks up from that conclusion to *Allegories of Reading*. Since it reads Shelley's reading of Rousseau, "Shelley Disfigured" may be considered an appendage to *Allegories of Reading*. It is continuous with the work performed in that volume. The essay takes the opportunity afforded by Shelley's poem to work out the full implications of the phrase about "the systematic undoing . . . of understanding," or, it might be more proper to say, to work through again to the point or frontier where the blank night of nonunderstanding begins, the point beyond which there is nothing more to say because nothing intelligible can be said. "Whereof one cannot speak, thereof one must be silent."[13]

Most of those celebrated defiantly, ironically, exuberantly negative remarks in de Man tend to come at the end of essays or sections of essays, though this is not always the case: "Conceptual language, the foundation of civil society, is also, it appears, a lie superimposed upon an error" (AR, 135); "One sees from this that the impossibility of reading should not be taken too lightly" (AR, 245); "The error is not within the reader; language itself dissociates the cognition from the act. *Die Sprache verspricht (sich)*; to the extent that is necessarily misleading, language just as necessarily conveys the promise of its own truth. This is also why allegories on this level of rhetorical complexity generate history" (AR, 277); "it is better to fail in teaching what should not be taught" (RT, 4). Beyond the edge of such sentences lies an echoing silence that is often represented by the blank space at the end of an essay or by the extra line spacing at the end of a section within an essay. Coherent language cannot cross that border, but a certain hallucinatory incoherence has already infected these sentences themselves, coming from across the border, like the ripple of approaching madness distorting syntax within the order of logical discourse. "To the extent that is necessarily misleading": that is certainly an odd locution! I use the word "madness" deliberately, not only because de Man borrows it from Friedrich Schlegel in "The Concept of Irony" to define the source, effect, and goal of irony, but also because de Man uses it on his own in "Shelley Disfigured": "No degree of knowledge can stop this madness, for it is the madness of words" (RR, 122).

Of course it is always possible to start over again with new materials and to move by a different path back to that border of nonunderstanding. "Shelley Disfigured" does this by (correctly) finding "The Triumph of Life" to be a poem made of a discontinuous series of repetitive episodes each both started and stopped by an interruption that de Man calls a positing followed by a forgetting and erasure or, more accurately, following more closely Shelley's actual language in the poem, half erasure. De Man's detailed reading of the poem leads up to the general statement that the whole intricate sequence has earned him the right to say and that I cite as my second example of a statement in de Man that is violently allergenic, that causes an allergic reaction to it as to something "allo," something wholly other to what we normally think and in terms of which we do our work in scholarship and teaching: "*The Triumph of Life* warns us that nothing, whether deed, word, thought, or text, ever happens in relation, positive or negative, to anything that precedes, follows, or exists elsewhere, but only as a random event whose power, like the power of death, is due to the randomness of its occurrence. It also warns us why and how these events then have to be reintegrated in a historical and aesthetic system of recuperation that repeats itself regardless of the exposure of its fallacy" (RR, 122). The repetition of "random" by "randomness" is the tinge of word-madness here. What is random randomness?

In any case, these are strong words, hard to take. The reader says to himself or herself that de Man must have got it wrong, since so much is at stake in believing the opposite of what he says, namely, that in one way or another things hang together, make sense, can be known and ethically evaluated, that literary works can and should be understood in terms of their relation to their cultural contexts, and so on. What he says must be, to put it delicately, "bull." The two sentences are, strictly speaking, as the reader will have noted, speech acts. A warning is one of the examples given by J. L. Austin in *How to Do Things with Words* of the way the first person singular pronoun and an active verb in the present tense (as in "I promise") are not always necessary for a felicitous speech act. In Austin's example, there is not time to say, "I respectfully warn you that there is a ferocious bull in that field charging toward you." You just say, "Bull!" and hope your auditor does not take this as a tame constative statement conveying neutral information: "Let me inform you of an interesting fact. There is a bull in that field."[14]

Strictly speaking, de Man's sentences are not themselves a warning. They only report the double warning said to be given by Shelley's poem. Moreover, if Austin was right, which he was not on this point, a poem could never be a felicitous speech act, for example a warning. In this case, however, and in most other cases too, no one can doubt that the report of the warning iterates the warning, that the warning is Paul de Man's own: "Watch out. Nothing, whether deed, word, thought, or text . . . etc." It is dangerous to cite a speech act, for example a curse, since citation always carries with it at least some of the performative force of the original utterance. This is because the original utterance was already an iteration. The distinction between "use" and "mention" cannot be rigorously maintained.

Unfortunately, in addition, in a way that is entirely characteristic of such climactic formulations in de Man, the warning warns us that we shall be unable, however hard we try, to heed the warning. The bull is bound to gore us even if we have been warned against him. We cannot help recuperating events that are as random and senseless as death, Shelley's death by drowning, say, or de Man's own death by cancer, into an aesthetic and historical sequence, to make a story out of them. We cannot help committing another aberrant version of aesthetic ideology.

Nor can we legitimately make value judgments for or against this "madness of words." "No degree of knowledge can stop this madness, for it is the madness of words." Words are not, strictly speaking, mad. People are mad. The phrase is a prosopopoeia. I have discussed elsewhere the role of prosopopoeia in de Man's work.[15] It is the one trope that he cannot or will not expunge from his own work. "What *would* be naive," says de Man of the madness of words that is the strategy whereby "to read is to understand, to question, to know, to forget, to erase, to deface, to repeat," "is to believe that this strategy, which is not *our* strategy as subjects, since we are its product rather than its agent, can be a source of value and has to be celebrated or denounced accordingly" (RR, 122). No ethical evaluation for or against this deplorable fate can be made. The subject is not its agent but is generated by it, automatically, by a mechanical process. This process makes us not so much talking heads as reading heads that then talk or write on the basis of their (mis)reading. No one can be blamed for this process, nor can we judge as good or bad the bearer of such bad news, though my words "deplorable" and "bad" do just that, as, more covertly, do de Man's terms "madness" and "strat-

egy," the first ascribed to words in another of those shimmering subjec-
tive/objective genitives: "the madness of words." The strategy of recuperation just happens because it has to happen, according to the law de Man,
in the preface to Carol Jacobs's *The Dissimulating Harmony*, establishes
by paraphrasing Hölderlin's "es ereignet sich aber das Wahre." This, says
de Man, "can be freely translated, 'What is true is what is bound to take
place'" (CW, 221).

On what grounds, in the name of what authority, does Paul de Man say
such dark things and so cheerfully inform us that we are bound to be in
error? I propose to answer this question, or at least to understand better
why it cannot be answered or is wrongly posed, by investigating two
topics in his work: his concept of irony, and the strange use he made of
the term "materiality." These have been touched on already, but much
more remains to say about them. Though the sequence I have put these
two in corresponds to some degree to changes in terminology in de Man's
work, much overlapping exists. It would be a big mistake to see these
terms as forming a progression, or a regression for that matter. My order
is, as Proust puts it, "pour la commodité du récit," but the reader should
remember what de Man says about the falsehood involved in making a
story or "récit" out of what is in no way a causal, dialectical, or historical series, neither an advance nor a degradation, but a running in place,
or a stuttering iteration, like random randomness, though no doubt with
differences as the terms substitute for one another. That I make a narrative out of what is not really a narrative is an example of that destiny of
recuperation to which de Man says we are all predictably and implac-
ably subject. My essay is another, no doubt unsuccessful, attempt to put
de Man in his place. Whether or not my failure is a good thing or a bad
thing, happy or unhappy, I must leave my readers to decide. It depends on
whether your allegiance is to the true or to what is teachable, namely,
delusion.

"The Concept of Irony" (AI, 163–84) is a transcription from the tape of
a lecture given at Ohio State University on April 4, 1977. It has the advantage (or disadvantage) of reflecting what de Man's seminar presentations
were like. The essay compresses into one lecture what was spread over a
whole semester in the graduate seminar on irony de Man gave at Yale in
the spring of 1976. The lecture (and the seminar) pick up notions about
irony from the second half of a much earlier essay, "The Rhetoric of
Temporality."[16] De Man himself, in "The Concept of Irony," "puts in
question," as he says, the reduction of irony, in the earlier essay, "to a
dialectic of the self as a reflexive structure": "It is in that way, to the
extent that I have written about the subject, that I have dealt with it

myself, so what I have to say today is in the nature of an *autocritique*, since I want to put in question this possibility" (AI, 170). Once more, however, it would be a mistake to stress too much the differences or to hypothesize on the basis of de Man's autocritique here some grand development in de Man's thought. "Irony" in "The Rhetoric of Temporality" also takes from Friedrich Schlegel the definition of irony as permanent parabasis, pays much attention to linguistic structures, and, like the later essay, the earlier essay, by way of a reading of Baudelaire's "L'essence du rire," as well as of Schlegel, defines irony as a kind of vertiginous madness, "folie lucide," "le vertige de l'hyperbole": "Irony is unrelieved *vertige*, dizziness to the point of madness" (BI, 215–16). Nevertheless, dizziness and madness are subjective properties. The later essay makes even clearer the way these are cover-names, displaced figures for properties of language.

One feature of irony is the way it is catching, so that it is extremely difficult if not impossible to talk about irony without being ironic. This is confirmed not only by the irony in de Man's own essay or in the great book on irony, Søren Kierkegaard's *The Concept of Irony*, that is being ironically alluded to in de Man's title, but also by such evidence as the way de Man began his seminar on irony by confronting the seminar room full of students and auditors, an audience made up of both students and faculty, and saying with a small smile, as well as I can remember it, something like this: "I must begin by telling you that this seminar will not help you at all in preparing for your qualifying orals, or in any other professional way. In fact it might be positively detrimental. I suggest you drop the course." No one left.

"The Concept of Irony" is even more openly polemical than de Man's essays usually are. It is overtly directed against the whole tradition of interpreting irony, especially so-called romantic irony. His targets include such dignitaries as Wayne Booth, Peter Szondi, Kierkegaard himself, Hegel, Walter Benjamin, Ingrid Strohschneider-Kohrs,[17] and the entire discipline of German studies: "It would hardly be hyperbolic to say (and I could defend the affirmation) that the whole tradition of *Germanistik* has developed for the single reason of dodging Friedrich Schlegel, of getting around the challenge that Schlegel and that *Lucinde* offer to the whole notion of an academic discipline that would deal with German literature—seriously" (AI, 168). These are formidable opponents. De Man says they were all wrong about Friedrich Schlegel in particular and about irony in general. This is another example of the way de Man works as an allergen to the entire enterprise of literary study as it has been institutionalized. Either he is right or they are. If he is right, then a whole tradition of scholarship and erudition has been barking up the wrong tree. How can he justify and make cogent such a sweeping denunciation?

I work toward an answer by way of the two enigmatic references to preformative utterances and speech-act theory in "The Concept of Irony." These elliptical passages are strange, puzzling, counterintuitive. They come at the beginning and end of the essay and so bracket its main business, which is to read some ironic passages on irony by Friedrich Schlegel in the light of Schlegel's productive misreading of Fichte. De Man's account of Fichte also depends on speech-act theory, but his use will not be at all enigmatic to readers of "Rhetoric of Persuasion (Nietzsche)" and "Shelley Disfigured," since all three use the (correct) notion that "positing" is a speech act. The other two references to speech acts are more puzzling. Understanding why de Man said them will get us a good way toward understanding "The Concept of Irony."

The first comes in rather casually apropos of de Man's argument that getting a good definition of irony turns out to be "uncannily difficult" (AI, 164). It is in fact impossible, even though it ought to be possible enough to define irony if irony is really a "concept." A little later, de Man asserts in passing, as ancillary to that, that we can be sure of one thing, even if we cannot define irony, namely, that it is performatively effective, felicitous: "Irony also very clearly has a performative function. Irony consoles and it promises and it excuses. It allows us to perform all kinds of performative linguistic functions which seem to fall out of the tropological field, but also to be very closely connected with it. In short, it is very difficult, impossible indeed, to get to a conceptualization by means of definition" (AI, 165). De Man has just been saying that irony seems to be a trope and yet not a trope, though it may be "the trope of tropes" (AI, 165). What does it mean to fall out of the tropological field and yet be closely connected to it? Connected in what way? By mere adjacency, or in some other more intimate fashion? I suppose de Man means that since irony is a "turning away" it must be a trope of sorts. Nevertheless, as he asserts elsewhere, it is an exceedingly peculiar kind of trope, since it can pervade an entire discourse and has no overt distinguishing linguistic signs, such as the "like" or "as" that identify a simile. That is one reason why people can disagree distressingly about whether a given text is ironic or not.

The real puzzle, however, is what de Man could mean by saying that irony is performatively efficacious, that it promises, consoles, or excuses. If we take seriously de Man's claim later in the essay that irony is a permanent parabasis that radically suspends meaning by the incursion of chaos, madness, and stupidity into language, then it would seem radically counterintuitive to say that irony has a successful performative function. To be more concrete, if I make an ironic promise ("You have my promise, and *of course* I never make a promise I don't intend to keep"), or ironically console someone ("Poor thing, I feel for you"), or ironically excuse oneself ("I'm so sorry. Did I really step on your toe?"), it would seem that the irony would suspend altogether the felicity of the promise, the consolation, or the excuse. It would be, so it seems, be a big mistake to expect someone who has ironically promised to keep an appointment to be there at the promised time.

The reference to speech-act theory at the end of the essay is equally puzzling and elliptical. De Man must have known what he was saying, we assume, but it is not at all clear just what he meant to say or what he meant by what he said. De Man has been demonstrating that Szondi, Benjamin, and Kierkegaard get irony wrong. They do this by attempting to recuperate what resists any recuperation because it is radical *Unverständlichkeit*. This recuperation, de Man says, takes the form, in all these misunderstanders of irony, of an "invoc[ation] of history as hypostasis as a means of defense against this irony" (AI, 184). The two other related forms of recuperation mentioned earlier in the essay, making three along with the appeal to history, are seeing irony as aesthetic adornment, *Kunstmittel*, in an essentially serious work whose meaning can be identified,[18] and seeing irony as a moment in a dialectic of self-reflexivity. The third illegitimate way to recuperate irony, really another version of the first two, is, as already mentioned, "to insert ironic moments into a dialectic of history" (AI, 170). Hegel, as I mentioned in chapter 1, reproached his immediate predecessor and colleague Solger for having got as far as defining irony as "infinite absolute negativity" without being able to take the third step in a dialectical Aufhebung or synthesis of the affirmation and its negation by irony. For Kierkegaard, Socratic irony is a moment in the historical progression from Hellenic to Christian cultures.

De Man concludes from the way irony is so often recuperated by an appeal to the irresistible march of history that "Irony and history seem to be curiously linked to one another" (AI, 184). The link, however "curious," that he has shown is a more or less totally negative one. The appeal to a hypostasized history, that is, to history objectified, made substantial and knowable, is an aberrant way to avoid the radical threat of irony. This does not keep de Man from concluding his essay by the puzzling claim that the relation between irony and history is the next topic that should be taken up, though it can only be "mastered" by first mastering the way speech acts work: "This [the relations of irony and history] would the topic to which they would lead, but this can only be tackled when the complexities of what we could call performative rhetoric have been more thoroughly mastered" (AI, 184). What can this mean? If irony and history are antipathetical, why is there anything more to say about their "curious" relation than he has already said, and why in the world would mastering performative rhetoric be necessary to understanding

this (non)relational relation? It can only be because irony in some mysterious way generates history, just as he says at the end of "Promises (*Social
Contract*)," also with enigmatic abruptness, that "This [the fact that 'Die
Sprache verspricht (sich),' which means 'Language promises' and also
'Language makes a slip of the tongue'] is also why textual allegories on
this level of rhetorical complexity generate history" (AR, 277). The concluding enigma of "The Concept of Irony" is, the reader can see, more or
less the same as the earlier puzzle about how irony can promise, console,
or excuse, that is, be performatively efficacious. Understanding the intervening essay, if nonunderstanding can be said to be understood, may help
understand these curious claims about irony.

Speech-act theory is an integral part of de Man's theory of irony, or
of the theory of irony he finds in Friedrich Schlegel and in Schlegel's
(mis)appropriation of Fichte. It would not be going too far to say that
de Man's "concept of irony" is a special case, a particularly important
special case, to be sure, of his more general "concept" of performative
utterances as I have identified it elsewhere.[19] You cannot "understand"
the one without understanding the other. How does this work?

De Man begins by showing that an important "fragment" by Schlegel,
Lyceum Fragment 37, is steeped in Fichtean language about *Selbstschöp-
fung*, *Selbstvernichtung*, and *Selbstbeschränkung* (self-creation, self-
destruction, and self-restraint) and can only be understood by way of
Fichte's *Grundlage der gesammten Wissenschaftslehre* (1794). The latter
Schlegel called, along with the French Revolution and Goethe's *Wilhelm
Meister*, one of the three main events of the century. This admiration of
Schlegel for Fichte justifies the brilliantly condensed and clear account of
the *Wissenschaftslehre* that follows in de Man's lecture. De Man's account of Fichte's system stresses the way it begins with acts of positing,
Setzungen, that is, speech acts, that are performed by language itself, not
by any self-conscious ego or subjectivity. The latter is the result of the
positing done by language, not its origin. Once more the stress is on the
radical and counterintuitive claim that language can act and does act performatively on its own. What is posited by language at one and the same
time is the self and the not-self. De Man stresses the simultaneity of these
two acts for Fichte and the way the second does not grow dialectically out
of the first:

> Language posits radically and absolutely the self, the subject, as such. . . . It
> is the ability of language to posit, the ability of language to *setzen*, in Ger-
> man. It is the catachresis, the ability of language catachrestically to name
> anything, by false usage, but to name and thus to posit anything language is
> willing to posit. . . . The I, language, posits A and posits minus-A at the same

time, and this is not a thesis and antithesis, because the negation is not an antithetic negation, as it would be in Hegel. It is different. It is itself posited and it has nothing to do, for example, with a consciousness. (AI, 172–73)

This act of positing is a catachresis because it gives a borrowed name to something that has no proper name. In de Man's account, however, this catachrestic naming is fundamentally creative. What is named, the self and the nonself, comes into existence through the act of naming. What is most radical, however, is the ascription to language of an ability to posit on its own, without any help from the enunciator of the language. Just how, when, where, or why this happens, whether it happens in more or less any language or just in German,[20] are impenetrable mysteries. This is another case of the unknowable and unintelligible in de Man's thinking, in this case what is at the "origin" of the everyday, ideology-dominated world in which we all live. It is unknowable in principle, not just because neither Fichte nor de Man bothers to explain it to us. Nothing at all can be said by the self, known by it, or performed by it until it exists. Since that is done by language acting on its own, it has always already happened by the time any self exists to ask questions about its origin. This is like wanting to have been present at the moment of one's own conception—or wanting to be present at the moment of one's death, for that matter.

Once the self and the not-self are posited, then Fichte's system is in business, so to speak. An enormous network of entities is developed by synthetic and analytic acts of judgment, judgments of similarity and dissimilarity. The somewhat daring novelty of de Man's reading is to see this structure, "the isolation and the circulation of properties, the way in which properties can be exchanged between entities when they are being compared with each other in any act of judgment," as nothing more nor less than the system of figurative exchanges the reader of de Man has already encountered in so many of his essays about the "epistemology of tropes": "This system is structured like metaphors—the figures in general, metaphors in particular" (AI, 174).

The final stage in Fichte's system, a system that is also, as de Man notes, a narrative, therefore an allegory, is the definition of man within this system as free or as moving toward a state of infinite freedom, as a line moves toward the asymptote it will touch only at infinity. This freedom, says de Man, is like the negative capability Keats ascribed to Shakespeare, the ability to "take on all selves and stand above all of them without being anything specific himself, a self that is infinitely elastic, infinitely mobile, an infinitely active and agile subject that stands above any of its experiences" (AI, 175).

The peculiarity of Fichte's system, as de Man describes it, is that it is at one and the same time two things said elsewhere in de Man to be incom-

patible. It is "a performative system" and at the same time it is "tropological system in its most systematic and general form. . . . It is an allegory, the narrative of the interaction between trope on the one hand and
performance as positing on the other" (AI, 176). What is remarkable
about de Man's conclusions from this is that although he recognizes that
"the self is never capable of knowing what it is, can never be identified as
such, and the judgments emitted by the self about itself, reflexive judgments, are not stable judgments," nevertheless "the fundamental intelligibility of the system is not in question because it can always be reduced
to a system of tropes" (AI, 176). In this case the tropological, that is, the
cognitive, the knowable, dominates the performative, which is the unknowable. De Man wants and needs to able to say this, to assert the
fundamental intelligibility of the Fichtean system, in order to be able to
argue that Schegelian irony is the radical interruption, disruption, of
Fichte's narrative and tropological system. In this little drama, Fichte
plays the role of the *alazon*, the dumb guy, whereas Schlegel and de Man
are *eirons*, smart guys who know about irony. It is the case that Fichte's
Wissenschaftslehre is not what you would call ironical. Fichte was a
pretty solemn writer.

The way Schlegelian irony radically disrupts or "brutally interrupt[s]"
(AI, 179) this solemnity and intelligibility is what de Man means by going
one step beyond Schlegel's definition of irony as permanent parabasis and
calling it "the permanent parabasis of the allegory of tropes" (AI, 179). A
parabasis is a breaking of the dramatic illusion when a character steps
forward to comment on the action. A permanent parabasis is an ironic
contradiction in terms, an unintelligible formulation, since a parabasis
needs something to suspend, whereas a permanent one would be all on
the same level of suspension, a suspension with nothing to suspend. In an
elliptical comparison of Pascal's zero to Schlegel's irony in "Pascal's Allegory of Persuasion" (AI, 51–69), de Man says as much, though he also
says that what he is saying is unintelligible:

> The anacoluthon is omnipresent [in the "interruption of a semantic contin-
> uum in a manner that lies beyond the power of reintegration" that occurs in
> Pascal], or, in temporal terms and in Friedrich Schlegel's deliberately unin-
> telligible formulation, the parabasis is permanent. Calling this structure
> ironic can be more misleading than helpful, since *irony*, like *zero*, is a term
> that is not susceptible to nominal or real definition [a reference to Pascal's
> two forms of definition; de Man is saying that irony is radically indefinable,
> as "The Concept of Irony" iterates]. To say then, as we are actually saying,[21]
> that allegory (as sequential narration) is the trope of irony (as the one is the
> trope of zero) is to say something that is true enough but not intelligible,
> which also implies that it cannot be put to work as a device of textual analy-
> sis." (AI, 61)

Here is another one of those defiant moments in de Man's writing, a place where he asserts that what he is saying is true (enough) but not teachable, or at least not of any use in one of the main activities of teaching in the humanities, that is, textual analysis.

A permanent parabasis suspends meaning and intelligibility all along the narrative line that tells the allegory of tropes. Irony is the incursion of "chaos" (Schlegel's term) into human language and therefore into the workings of the human mind. It is illegitimate, de Man says, to interpret this "chaos" is a positive and idealist sense, since Schlegel, in the revision of a crucial passage on *reele Sprache* (authentic language) in the "Rede über die Mythologie (Talk on Mythology)," from the *Gespräch über die Poesie (Dialogue on Poetry)*, changed the words "the strange [das Sonderbare], even the absurd [das Widersinnige], as well as childlike and yet sophisticated naïveté [geistreiche naïveté]" in the first version to the much more radically negative terms that, for de Man (and I think he is right in this), characterize what irony allows to "shine through" as a pervasive element into human discourse: "error, madness, and simpleminded stupidity." I discussed this Schlegel passage in chapter 1. De Man does not cite the German original at this point. Schlegel wrote in the final version: "wo der naive Tiefsinn den Schein des Verkehrten und Verrückten oder des Einfältigen und Dummen durchshimmern läßt." Behler and Struc translate this as "where the naive profundity permits the semblance of the absurd and of madness, of simplicity and foolishness, to shimmer through."[22] "Dummen" sounds to me a little more like de Man's "stupidity" than like Behler and Struc's milder "foolishness."

The astute reader will note that the stuttering iteration of words beginning in "*Ver-*," picking up from *Verwirrung* (confusion) a little earlier in the paragraph, is an example of that play of the signifier de Man stresses as an example of the way for Schlegel and *in* Schlegel's own writing words get away from the author's control and act on their own:

> Words have a way of saying things which are not at all what you want them to say. You are writing a splendid and coherent philosophical argument but, lo and behold, you are describing sexual intercourse [the reference is to "Eine Reflexion" in Schlegel's *Lucinde*, discussed by de Man earlier in the essay]. Or you are writing a fine complement for somebody and without your knowledge, just because words have a way of doing things, it's sheer insult and obscenity that you are really saying. There is a machine there, a text machine, an implacable determination and a total arbitrariness . . . which inhabits words on the level of the play of the signifier, which undoes any narrative consistency of lines, and which undoes the reflexive and dialectical model, both of which are, as you know, the basis of any narration. (AI, 181)

"As you know?" I do not suppose most of us know that at all. The reader wishes de Man had explained more fully here just what he means by "the reflexive and dialectical model" and just how that model is "the basis of any narration." "Reflexive" might mean, I suppose, either "self-referential," as the words, figures, or episodes of a narrative may refer back and forth to one another, in a chain of repetitions, or "having to do with consciousness of consciousness," as in de Man's phrase in "The Concept of Irony," already quoted: "a dialectic of the self as a reflexive structure" (AI, 169), or in Hegel's "wenn ich sage: 'Ich,' *meine* ich mich," to be discussed below, or in de Man's own "Die Sprache verspricht (sich)," in which language is personified as being able to make promises or to turn back on itself in slips of the tongue, which is one meaning of the German reflexive verb *versprechen sich*. "Dialectical," I suppose, here names one of the chief ways a narrative sequence can hang together by an apparently ineluctable necessity, like the chain of events, for example, that makes up the narration of Sophocles's *Oedipus the King*, or like Hegel's and Kierkegaard's dialectical recuperation of irony into a necessary historical progression. Irony radically interrupts this reflexive and dialectical model, all along the narrative line.

Words, for Schlegel and for de Man, have a way of doing things, and this doing is a radical undoing—of knowledge, of control, even of morality and decency. This is de Man's version of J. L. Austin's notion that words do things, though for Austin it is things that can be controlled and predicted, so that it makes sense to write a manual or instruction book called *How to Do Things with Words*, however ironic that title is. For de Man, on the contrary, no "how to" manual will help you to control or understand what words do. What happens through words just happens, like a machine gone wild, a text machine, like "say," "saying," "say" in the passage quoted above from "Pascal's Allegory of Persuasion." As in the case of de Man's speech-act theory generally, his concept of irony, a branch of his speech-act theory, ends up once more at the borders of unintelligibility. Or rather, the unsettling fact that any piece of language may be undermined by irony, just as any performative utterance, for Derrida, may be contaminated by literature (perhaps no more than another name for irony), shows that the darkness of error, madness, and simpleminded stupidity, Dummen, from beyond the border of rationality, has always already entered into human language to suspend its intelligibility.

It is no wonder that admirably perceptive critics like Peter Szondi and Walter Benjamin, who recognize Friedrich Schlegel's importance and admire his work, have gone out of their way to make Schlegel say something quite other and more positive than what he did say. They have tried to recuperate Schlegelian irony in one way or another into an aesthetic or historical dialectic, in Szondi's case by incorporating it into a theory of romantic comedy, in Benjamin's case by making irony a stage on the work's dialectical way toward the absolute (AI, 182–83). It is also no surprise that de Man's theory of irony should be one of the most allergenic aspects of his work, more or less ignored by most commentaries on that work. What I have said, however, though true enough to what de Man says, still leaves hanging in the air the questions about why irony can make promises and execute other performatives, and why irony and history "seem to be curiously linked." Grasping what de Man meant by "materiality" may help glimpse an answer to those questions, out of the corner of the eye, so to speak.

I turn now to de Man's materialism. The " 's" in this phrase too is a double genitive, both objective and subjective. It names both de Man's theory of materiality and the way his own writings may show materiality at work or may be examples of materiality at work. De Man's materiality is one of most difficult and obscure parts of his work, but what has been said already about his "concept" of irony may help at least to approach what he may have meant by materiality. Confronting the latter may also help answer two unanswered questions still left hanging: How does irony promise, console, and excuse? What does irony have to do with history?

De Man's use of the terms "materiality" and "materialism" poses several special problems, resistances to comprehension. One or the other word is most often introduced as a term only briefly and elliptically. If the reader does not keep a sharp eye out for it, it appears in a given essay for an instant, for the blink of an eye, like a meteor, and then vanishes. Moreover, in these passages de Man seems to be saying exceedingly strange things, such as the assertion that materiality is not "phenomenal." Second, unlike "performative" and "irony," which are not terms on everyone's lips and that clearly need some explaining, we tend to think we already know what materiality is. It is the property possessed by these hard objects right in front of me now, impassive, impassible, resistant, not dependent on my perception for their continued existence, like that stone Samuel Johnson kicked to refute Berkeley's idealism: "I refute him thus" (kicking the stone). Third, the term "materialism" is extremely difficult to extricate from its associations with modern empirical science or with vulgar understandings of Marxism. Is not Marxism to be defined as "dialectical materialism"? De Man is supposed to be in one way or another a linguistic formalist, someone who believed, as all so-called deconstructionists are supposed to believe, that it is "all language," though the reader might remember that de Man began his higher education as a science, mathematics, and engineering student at the École Polytechnique of the University of Brussels (1936). His professional interest in language came later. Nevertheless, for de Man to call himself a materialist, or for us to call him one, seems as absurd and counterintuitive as for de Man to call Kant and Hegel materialists or to find crucial materialist moments in their work, since everybody knows (without necessarily having read them) that they are "idealists." Equally absurd would be to think one might find any kinship between de Man's thinking and Marxism, though the truth is that a deep kinship exists between de Man's work and Marx's thought in *The German Ideology* and in *Capital*, as Andrzej Warminski has been demonstrating in his seminars.[23] To show this it is necessary actually to go back and read Marx, as well as de Man, no easy tasks.

The term materiality or its cognates appear at crucial moments in de Man's work as early as a citation from Proust in "Reading (Proust)" in *Allegories of Reading*. What Proust calls the "symbols," in Giotto's *Allegory of the Virtues and Vices* at the Arena in Padua, meaning representations like the Charity that looks like a kitchen maid, are "something real, actually experienced or materially handled" (AR, 78). That this passage was important to de Man is indicated by the way he cites it again at a crucial moment when he is discussing the symbol in Hegel just at the end of one of his late essays, "Sign and Symbol in Hegel's *Aesthetics*." This time de Man translates the phrases himself somewhat differently from the standard Scott Moncrieff translation, and he cites the French original: "the symbol represented as real, as inflicted or materially handled (. . . [le symbole représenté] comme réel, comme effectivement subi ou matériellement manié)" (AI, 103).

The terms "material," "materiality," and the like then appear with increasing frequency in de Man's later work. It is as though de Man had discovered in such words a way to "call" more accurately something he wanted performatively to name, perhaps even to invoke; that is, to "call forth": "The only word that comes to mind is that of a *material* vision" ("Phenomenality and Materiality in Kant," AI, 82). What Michael Riffaterre misses or evades in Hugo's "Écrit sur la vitre d'une fenêtre flamande" is just what the title indicates or names, namely, what de Man calls "the materiality of an inscription" (RT, 51). A climactic passage in Shelley's "The Triumph of Life" is said to stress "the literal and material aspects of language" (RR, 113). "Anthropomorphism and Trope in the Lyric" ends, in a phrase I have already cited, with an appeal to "the materiality of actual history" (RR, 262). A cascade of such terms punctuates the essays in *Aesthetic Ideology*, not only in "Phenomenality and Materiality in Kant" and in "Kant's Materialism," where "a materialism that Kant's posterity has not yet begun to face up to" (AI, 89) is the focus of the argument in both essays, but also in "Sign and Symbol in Hegel's *Aesthetics*," where we read that "The idea, in other words, makes its sensory appearance, in Hegel, as the material inscription of names" and also in the way Hegel's "theory of the sign manifests itself materially"

(AI, 102, 103), and in "Kant and Schiller," where we read of the irreversible progression "from states of cognition, to something which is no longer a cognition but which is to some extent an *occurrence*, which has the materiality of something that actually happens, that actually occurs" and of "the materiality of the inscribed signifier in Kant" (AI, 132, 133).

The reader will have seen that the term "materiality" and its cognates occur in three related, ultimately more or less identical, registers in de Man: the materiality of history, the materiality of inscription, and the materiality of what the eye sees prior to perception and cognition. In all three of these registers, as I shall show, materiality is associated with notions of performative power and with what seems materiality's opposite, formalism. In all three modes of materialism, the ultimate paradox, allergenic idea, or unintelligibility is the claim or insinuation that materiality is not phenomenal, not open to the senses. Just what in the world could that mean?

The phrase "materiality of history" seems the easiest to understand and accept as commonsensical. Of course history is material. It means what really happened, especially as a result of human intervention (though we speak, for example, of the history of the mollusks, or of geological history). History, people may be inclined to think, is wars, battles, the building of the pyramids, the invention of the steam engine, migrations of peoples, the clearing of forests, global warming, that sort of thing. De Man's materiality of history, however, is not like that. For him the materiality of history, properly speaking, results from acts of power that are punctual and momentary, since they are atemporal, noncognitive and noncognizable performative utterances. History is caused by language or other signs that make something materially happen, and such happenings do not happen all that often. The most radical, and allergenic, counterintuitive, scandalous formulation of this is in "Kant and Schiller." There de Man asserts that Kant's *Critique of Judgment* was an irreversible historical event brought about by the shift from cognitive to efficaciously performative discourse in Kant's own words, whereas Schiller's ideological misreading of Kant and its long progeny in the nineteenth and twentieth centuries was a nonevent, certainly not an irreversible material event.

In "Phenomenality and Materiality in Kant," de Man speaks of the crucial shift to a "formal materialism" in Kant's *Critique of Judgment* as "a shift from trope to performance" that is "a deep, perhaps fatal, break or discontinuity" (AI, 83, 89, 79). This is the place, as he puts it in "Kant and Schiller," at which Kant "found himself by the rigor of his own discourse [the project of aesthetics as articulation of pure reason and practical reason or ethics] to break down under the power of his own critical epistemological discourse" (AI, 134). This was an event, strictly speaking an irreversible historical event, "to some extent an *occurrence*, which has the materiality of something that actually happens, that actually occurs. And there, the thought of material occurrence, something that occurs materially, that leaves a trace on the world, that does something to the world as such—that notion of occurrence is not opposed in any sense to the notion of writing" (AI, 132). Since the event of Kant's materialism is punctual and instantaneous, it is in a curious sense not within time, though it has a permanent and irreversible effect on what we usually (mistakenly) think of as the temporality of history: "history is not thought of as a progression or regression, but is thought of as an event, as an occurrence. There is history from the moment that words such as 'power' and 'battle' and so on emerge in the scene. At that moment things *happen*, there is *occurrence*, there is *event*. History is therefore not a temporal notion, it has nothing to do with temporality [there's allergenic assertion for you!], but is the emergence of a language of power out of a language of cognition" (AI, 133). I do not think de Man meant that the words "power" and "battle" are in themselves always historical events in the sense de Man is defining such events, but that he means the uses of such words in effective performative utterances are historical events.

As opposed to the moment of Kant's self-undoing materialism in the third *Critique*, Schiller's recuperation of Kant within aesthetic ideology and its long progeny, the procedures of which are identified in the main body of "Kant and Schiller," did not happen, were not historical events:

> One could say, for example, that in the reception of Kant, in the way Kant has been read, since the third *Critique*—and that was an occurrence, something happened there, something occurred [de Man's stuttering iterations here mime the punctualities of historical events; the reader will remember that this is the transcript of an oral presentation that was not written down as such]—that in the whole reception of Kant from then until now, nothing has happened, only regression, nothing has happened at all. Which is another way of saying there is no history ... that reception is not historical. ... The event, the occurrence, is resisted by reinscribing it in the cognition of tropes, and that is itself a tropological, cognitive, and not a historical move. (AI, 134)[24]

These sternly recalcitrant statements may be more understandable and perhaps even more acceptable if we remember that Althusser, and de Man in his own way, define ideology as having no history, as being outside history, as having no purchase on history, since ideology is precisely an illusory misunderstanding of the "material conditions of our existence," as Althusser put it in "Ideology and State Apparatuses," or, as de Man puts this in "The Resistance to Theory": "What we call ideology is precisely the confusion of linguistic with natural reality, of reference with phenomenalism" (RT, 11).[25] The reception of Kant by Schiller and his followers, including you and me as inheritors of aesthetic ideology, is ideological, therefore not historical.

We are (I am) now in a position at last to answer those puzzling questions about what de Man says in "The Concept of Irony." Irony, as we have seen, is perhaps the most radical example of the rupture between cognitive and performative discourses. Insofar as an utterance is performative it is unknowable. Irony suspends cognition. It is just because irony is error, madness, and simpleminded stupidity that it can be performatively felicitous. Promises, excuses, consolations can be done by irony, or can be especially done by ironic utterance, just because irony is the radical suspension of cognition. Another way to put this is to say that even the most solemn performative utterances are contaminated by being possibly ironic. The reader will perhaps remember that Derrida in "Limited Inc a b c . . ." includes irony along with literature among the parasitical presences that are present within any performative as a result of its intrinsic iterability.[26]

What I have just said will also indicate the surprising and "curious" connection of irony with history. Since the materiality of history as event is generated by acts of linguistic power, that is performative speech acts, though by no means necessarily intentional ones, irony as a form of such power or as an ingredient of any such act of power, against all our instinctive assumptions, can be said not only to promise, console, and excuse, but also to generate the events that make up the materiality of history. Just as, for Derrida, the possibility of felicitous speech acts depends on the possibility that they may be "literature," so for de Man the efficacy of performative utterances, including those that generate history, depends on the possibility that they may be ironical. They may be. You cannot tell for sure.

If speech acts generating history are, strangely enough, one form of materiality or are the places where language touches materiality, leaves a mark on it, materially handles it, the materiality of what the eye sees appears more obvious but turns out to be more difficult to grasp. Of course, we say, what the eye sees is material. That received opinion or doxa turns out, however, once again not to be quite what de Man means. What he does mean is the central argument of the two essays on Kant, "Phenomenality and Materiality in Kant" and "Kant's Materialism." For received opinion, what we take for granted, phenomenality and materiality are the same thing or are two aspects of the same thing. Because something is material it is phenomenal, open to the senses. For de Man, following Kant, phenomenality and materiality are not conjoined but opposed. How can this be?

De Man sees in Kant's theory of the dynamic sublime two radically contradictory notions. On the one hand, the sublime is the moment when the imagination triumphs over fear and puts all the elements of the sublime scene together, articulates them in a grand aesthetic synthesis, as tropes articulate, or as the body's limbs are articulated: "The imagination overcomes suffering, becomes apathetic, and sheds the pain of natural shock. It reconciles pleasure with pain and in so doing it articulates, as mediator, the movement of the affects with the legal, codified, formalized, and stable order of reason" (AI, 86). In so doing the imagination of the sublime or the sublime itself accomplishes the goal of the third *Critique*, which was to find a "bridge" between the first and second *Critiques*, between pure reason and the practical reason of moral obligation and choice. On the other hand, Kant's analysis of the dynamic sublime contains a moment that radically disrupts, interrupts, and suspends this happy articulation. Kant reaches this moment through the very rigor of his critical thinking. He proposes that the paradigmatic example of the dynamic sublime is when the overarching vault of the sky and the outstretched mirror of the sea are seen just as the eye sees them, or as the poets see them, without thought for their meaning. Seeing them as meaningful would occur, for example, when we view the sea as a reservoir of edible fish, or the sky as a producer of life-giving rain. De Man quotes section 28 of Kant's *The Critique of Judgment*: "we must regard it [the starry heaven], just as we see it [*wie man ihn sieht*], as a distant, all-embracing vault [*ein weites Gewölbe*]. . . . To find the ocean nevertheless sublime we must regard it as poets do [*wie die Dichter es tun*], merely by what the eye reveals [*was der Augenschein ziegt*]" (AI, 80). De Man goes on to argue that this way of seeing is radically nonphenomenal. It does not involve the mind that in its activity of perception would make sense of what is seen. It just sees what it sees, in an activity of the eye operating by itself, wholly detached, disarticulated, from thinking and interpreting: "No mind is involved in the Kantian vision of ocean and heaven. . . . That is how things are to the eyes, in the redundancy of their appearance to the eye and not to the mind, as in the redundant word *Augenschein*, . . . in which the eye, tautologically, is named twice, as eye itself and as what appears to the eye" (AI, 82).

De Man's name for this way of seeing is "material vision": "The only word that comes to mind is that of a *material* vision" (ibid.), which is another way of saying, performatively, "I call this '*material* vision.'" The word material then appears in a cascade of phrases in the subsequent pages: "the vision is purely material"; "what we call the material aspect"; "a materialism that, in the tradition of the reception of the third *Critique*, is seldom or never perceived"; "If the architectonic then appears, very near the end of the analytics of the aesthetic, at the conclusion of the section on the sublime, as the material disarticulation not only of nature but of the body [traditional examples of the beautiful or the sublime], then this moment marks the undoing of the aesthetic as a valid category. The critical power of a transcendental philosophy undoes the very project of such a philosophy leaving us, certainly not with an ideology—for transcendental and ideological (metaphysical) principles are part of the same system—but with a materialism that Kant's posterity has not yet begun to face up to" (AI, 83, 88, 89).

How could we "face up to" something that we can see but not face up to in the sense of clearly confronting it and making it intelligible to ourselves? The idea of a way of seeing that is performed by the eye alone, wholly dissociated from the mind, is, strictly speaking, unintelligible, since any sense we give to this "Augenschein" is an illicit, ideological imposition: "To the extent that any mind, that any judgment, intervenes, it is in error" (AI, 82). That is what I mean by saying that de Man's materiality is nonphenomenal, since phenomenality always involves, instantly, making sense or trying to make sense of what we see. It is a "materiality without materialism."[27] This "material vision" would be pure seeing prior to any seeing as the sort of understanding that we name when we say, "I see it all now." It would be a preseeing seeing, that is, something unthinkable, unknowable, unintelligible, a tautological eye eyeing: "Realism postulates a phenomenalism of experience which is here being denied or ignored. Kant's looking at the world just as one sees it ('wie man ihn sieht') is an absolute, radical formalism that entertains no notion of reference or semiosis" (AI, 128).

This idea of a materiality that would not be phenomenal does not make sense. Nevertheless, that is just what de Man affirms, most overtly and in so many words at the end of the essay on Michael Riffaterre, "Hypogram and Inscription," where he speaks of the way "the materiality (as distinct from the phenomenality) that is thus revealed [when we remember that Hugo's poem was supposed to have been written on a window pane], the unseen 'cristal' whose existence thus becomes a certain *there* and a certain *then* which can become a *here* and a *now* in the reading 'now' taking place, is not the materiality of the mind or of time or of the carillon—none of which exist, except in the figure of prosopopeia,—but the materiality of an inscription" (RT, 51). The paradox is that the window glass, figure here for the materiality of inscription, is not what the eye sees but what the eye sees through. In the Kant essays, as in "Hypogram and Inscription," the rigor of de Man's own critical thinking brings him, by different routes, across the border of the intelligible and into the realm of the allergenic. In these essays this takes the form of recognizing a materialism in Kant that has seldom or never been recognized in the whole distinguished tradition of Kant scholarship and so is anathema to it, just as de Man's reading of somewhat similar material moments in Hegel was anathema to the distinguished Hegel specialist Raymond Geuss.[28]

The third version of materiality in de Man is the "prosaic materiality of the letter" (AI, 90). Just what does de Man mean by that? No one doubts that writing (and speaking too) have a material base, marks on paper or modulated waves in the air. This materiality is the benign base of the meaning, permanence, and transmissibility of language. No problem. De Man of course does not mean anything so in agreement with common sense and received opinion. When de Man calls Kant's sublime Augenschein of sky and sea a "*material* vision" he goes on to raise a further question that is not answered until the end of essay: "how this materiality is then to be understood in linguistic terms is not, as yet, clearly intelligible" (AI, 82). The answer is the materiality of the letter, but just what does that mean? The essay ends with an explanation that, if not clearly intelligible, at least indicates why these "linguistic terms" must be unintelligible. The reader is given intelligence of unintelligibility, new news of the unknowable.

The prosaic materiality of the letter, linguistic "equivalent" of a materialism of vision, has two main features. One is a disarticulation of language equaling the disarticulations of nature and the human body de Man has found in Kant's dynamic sublime: "To the dismemberment of the body corresponds a dismemberment of language, as meaning-producing tropes are replaced by the fragmentation of sentences and propositions into discrete words, or the fragmentation of words into syllables or finally letters" (AI, 89). Strictly speaking, as linguists, not to speak of language philosophers like Wittgenstein, have shown, words do not have meaning by themselves. They have meaning only when they are used, incorporated into sentences. To detach them from their sentences and leave them hanging there in the air or on the page, surrounded by blank paper, is the first stage in a progressive disarticulation of meaning that goes then to syllables and finally to letters. It is extremely difficult to see words, syllables, or letters, for example on a printed page, in this way, just as it is extremely hard to see as the eye sees. One has to be a poet, as Kant says, to do it. The mind instantly interprets what the eye sees, "perceives it," and gives meaning to it, just as the mind projects meaning into those mute letters on the page. It is almost impossible to see letters as just the material marks they are. Even words in a language we do not know are seen as language and not as sheer materiality. We tend to see random marks on a rock as possibly writing in an unknown language.

The other feature of the materiality of the letter stressed by de Man makes it more likely to be glimpsed, in the wink of the eye, before the mind starts "reading." This is repetition of words and word parts that calls attention to the absurd and unmotivated echoes among them at the level of syllable and letter—puns, rhymes, alliterations, assonances, and so on, that is, precisely those features of language poets especially use, "the play of the letter and of the syllable, the way of saying . . . as opposed to what is being said" (AI, 89). The "persuasiveness" of the passage in Kant about the recovery of the imagination's tranquillity through material vision depends, de Man says, "on the proximity between the German words for surprise and admiration, *Verwunderung* and *Bewunderung*" (AI, 89). The reader, furthermore, is led to assent to the incompatibility or aporia between the imagination's failure and its success by "a constant, and finally bewildering alternation of the two terms, *Angemessen(heit)* and *Unangemessen(heit)*, to the point where one can no longer tell them apart?" (AI, 90). One additional example of this in de Man's essays, besides what he says about Verwunderung and Bewunderung, Angemessen(heit) and Unangemessen(heit), is the cascade of words in "fall" that he finds in a passage by Kleist: Fall, Beifall, Sündenfall. Rückfall, Einfall, Zurückfall, Fälle: "As we know from another narrative text of Kleist ['On the Gradual Formation of Thoughts While Speaking'], the memorable tropes that have the most success (*Beifall*) occur as mere random improvisation (*Einfall*) at the moment when the author has completely relinquished control over his meaning and has relapsed (*Zurückfall*) into the extreme formalization, the mechanical predictability of grammatical declensions (*Fälle*)" (RR, 290). By the time the reader gets to the end of this, the root "fall" is fast becoming a mere surd, a sound emptied of meaning: "fall, fall, fall, fall."

The reader will see that "formalism" or "formalization" names for de Man not the beautiful aesthetic formalization of the artwork, but a principle of mechanical senselessness in language that he associates with the arbitrariness of grammar, of declensions, Fälle. De Man goes on to make a pun of his own. Since "Falle" means also trap in German, he can say that everyone falls into "the trap of an aesthetic education which inevitably confuses dismemberment of language by the power of the letter with the gracefulness of a dance" (ibid.). That trap, however, is not a benign aestheticizing of the random formalizations of language in grammar and paronomasia such as poets are known to play with. It is a mortal danger, a pericolo de morte, according to the last words of the last essay in *The Rhetoric of Romanticism*, "the ultimate trap, as unavoidable as it is deadly" (RR, 290). The reader will note that this aspect of the materiality of the letter tends to disappear in translation. It depends on the unique idiom, idiolect, or even "idiocy," in the etymological sense, of a certain language. Ultimately this repetition of words and bits of words empties language of meaning and makes it mere unintelligible sound, as when the poet Tennyson used as a child to repeat his own name over and over, "Alfred, Alfred, Alfred," until it ceased to mean anything at all and he melted into a kind of oceanic trance. Try it with your own name as I do here with mine: "Hillis, Hillis, Hillis, Hillis."

De Man's formulation of this in one notable place is more prosaic. As he shows, Hegel's theory of memory as Gedächtnis, in opposition to Erinnerung, is that it memorizes by emptying words of meaning and repeating them by rote, as pure arbitrary signs that might be in a foreign language or in no language at all: " 'It is well known,' says Hegel, 'that one knows a text by heart [or by rote] only when one no longer associates any meaning with the words; in reciting what one thus knows by heart one necessarily drops all accentuation.' [I suppose Hegel means that one repeats the words mindlessly, like a schoolchild or a robot.] . . . The idea, in other words, makes its sensory appearance, in Hegel, as the material inscription of names" (AI, 101–102).

Speaking in "Hegel on the Sublime" of Hegel's "Gesetz der Äußerlichkeit (law of exteriority)," de Man says, "Like a stutter, or a broken record, it makes what it keeps repeating worthless and meaningless" (AI, 116). This had already been exemplified in a truly vertiginous couple of paragraphs in "Sign and Symbol in Hegel's *Aesthetics*." There de Man takes two at first innocent enough looking, but in fact "quite astonishing," sentences in Hegel's *Encyclopedia*: "Since language states only what is general, I cannot say what is only my opinion [so kann ich nicht sagen was ich nur meine]," and "When I say 'I,' I *mean* myself as *this* I to the exclusion of all others; but what I say, I, is precisely anyone; any I, as that which excludes all others from itself [ebenso, wenn ich sage: 'Ich,' *meine* ich mich *als* diesen alle anderen Ausschließenden; aber was ich sage, Ich, ist eben jeder]." The sentences themselves are bad enough, though worse in German (e.g., wenn Ich sage, Ich, *meine* ich mich), but by the time de Man gets through with them the reader is dizzied by the repetitions, like Tennyson repeating his own first name, or as if he had been caught in a revolving door.[29]

Through this dizziness the reader reaches in the emptying out of meaning a glimpse of the materiality of the letter. In commenting on the first sentence de Man plays with *mein* and *meinen* as mine and mean and generates a sentence in which the cascade of "sinces," and sinces within sinces, produces its own stuttering repetition, like a broken record: " 'Ich kann nicht sagen was ich (nur) meine' then means 'I cannot say what I make mine' or, since to think is to make mine, 'I cannot say what I think,' and, since to think is fully contained in and defined by the I, since Hegel's *ego cogito* defines itself as mere *ego*, what the sentence actually says is 'I cannot say I'—a disturbing proposition in Hegel's own terms since the very possibility of thought depends on the possibility of saying 'I'" (AI, 98).

The other sentence, with its a repetitions of *ich* and the ich in *mich*, is already "astonishing" enough itself, as de Man says, in the sense of numbing the mind, turning it to stone (to play on a false etymology; the word really means, etymologically, "to strike with thunder"). The sentence shows the impossibility not only of the deictics "here," "now," "this," as when I say, "This sentence which I am here and now writing on my computer at 8:51 a.m. on November 4, 1997," or, in Hegel's example, this piece of paper on which I am now writing, but also of the deictic use of "I" to point to me myself alone as a unique I. These words are "shifters," placeholders. Instantly, as soon as they are uttered, the words assume the utmost generality and can be shifted to any I, any here, now, and this.[30] However hard you try, you cannot say this I here and now or this keyboard, processor, and computer screen at this moment that are prostheses of my body and by means of which I think. "I cannot say I." "Aber was ich sage, Ich, ist eben jeder (but what I say, I, is precisely anyone)." De Man takes the otherness of "jeder" not to refer to another I, "the mirror image of the I," but to name "*n'importe qui* or even *n'importe quoi*," that is, anybody at all or even anything at all, just as the name Marion, in de Man's reading of Rousseau's *Julie*, is ultimately just a random sound, not even a proper name: "Rousseau was making whatever noise happened to come into his head; he was saying nothing at all, least of all someone's name" (AR, 292).

As de Man says of Rousseau's excuse in *Julie* for what he had done to Marion, "When everything fails, one can always plead insanity" (AR, 289). A certain madness, the madness of words, the reader can see, often infects de Man's own language. He mimes in what he says the materiality of the letter he is naming. At this point his own work becomes a performative utterance working to lead the reader to the edge of unintelligibility once again, this time by the route of the materiality of the letter, and once more in a way that is counterintuitive, since it is a materiality that is nonphenomenal, unable to be seen, like the "invisible crystal" of that Flemish windowpane on which Hugo's poem was scratched.

The back cover of de Man's *Aesthetic Ideology* speaks of the "ironic good humor that is unique to him." I find de Man's irony, especially when it expresses itself in wordplay, much more threatening than this phrase implies, and so have many of de Man's readers or listeners. Such passages as I have been discussing, where the madness of words has

crossed over into de Man's own language, are places that readers or auditors have found especially allergenic, that they have especially resisted.
The audience of de Man's "Semiology and Rhetoric," for example, when
it was presented as a sort of inaugural lecture after de Man took up his
professorship at Yale, was more than a little scandalized or even offended
by the elaborate pun de Man develops based on the Archie Bunker television show. This pun depends on the difference between lacing your shoes
over or under. ("What's the difference?" asks Archie Bunker.) This leads
to the punch line of calling Jacques Derrida an "archie Debunker" (AR,
9–10). The audience did not find that wholly appropriate for such a solemn occasion. The complex double talk that de Man, in an exuberant
reading, finds in Proust's phrase *torrent d'activité* (AR, 64) has seemed to
some readers just going too far. Raymond Geuss especially resisted what
de Man says about *mein* and *meinen* in Hegel. De Man's "Reply to Raymond Geuss" patiently laces over and under, that is, explains what he
meant and why he is right and Geuss wrong, guilty of "misplaced timid-
ity," an unwillingness to face up to the "difficulties and discontinuities"
in Hegel's text (AI, 189–92).

The resistance to de Man, what I have called an allergic reaction to his
writings, is not a resistance to theory in the etymological sense of the
word "theory," a generalizable "clear-seeing," but a resistance to what in
his work precisely cannot be seen clearly, the penumbra of the unknowable, the unintelligible, the nonphenomenal that is everywhere in his
work. This is perhaps most threateningly present not in the radical incompatibility of the cognitive and performative dimensions of language,
and not even in the madness and stupidity, *Dummen*, of irony as permanent parabasis, nor even in Kant's materiality of vision, but in the prosaic
materiality of the letter. The latter is present at every moment, though for
the most part it is invisible, suppressed, covered over, in all those words
that surround us all the time and that generate the reassuring ideologies
in terms of which we live our lives. What is most threatening, most allergenic, most truly frightening about de Man's writings is the way they
force their readers to confront a darkness of unknowability that is not
just out there somewhere, beyond the circle of light cast by the desk's
reading lamp. That would be bad enough, but this darkness has woven
itself into the light of reason itself and into the "instrument" by which it
expresses itself, language. No degree of knowledge can ever stop this
madness, for it is the madness of words.

I conclude by asking about de Man's authority. Another double genitive there: the authority Paul de Man exerts and the authority in whose
name he speaks. This chapter began by exemplifying what is insolent or

outrageous about de Man's writings, namely, his calm, laconic assertions that all the basic assumptions of literary studies as a discipline, all the greatest authorities in that discipline, are just plain wrong. I then asked where de Man got his authority to say such things. In the light of my investigation of what he says about irony and materiality, I propose now in conclusion three braided answers to the question of what justifies de Man to say what he says. All these can be inferred from de Man's own writing.

First, he might be imagined as replying that what he says, allergenic as it is, is not his own willful desire to cause trouble, but something that just happens, through reading. De Man's work is all reading of some text or other, primarily canonical texts that are among the most revered and cherished in our tradition. Therefore all these outrageous statements are not de Man speaking, but him speaking in indirect discourse for what his authors say. It is Shelley, not de Man, who says that nothing is connected to anything else. Hegel or Kleist, not de Man, repeats the same words or syllables until they become senseless. It is not I, Paul de Man, speaking, but I speaking in the name of, with the authority, of my authors. As Chaucer says, "My auctor wol I folwen if I konne."[31] In the "Reply to Raymond Geuss," de Man says, "The move from the theory of the sign to the theory of the subject has nothing to do with my being overconcerned with the Romantic tradition, or narcissistic, or ('c'est la même chose') too influenced by the French. It has, in fact, nothing to do with me at all but corresponds to an inexorable and altogether Hegelian move of the text" (AI, 189).

Or, second appeal to authority, what I, Paul de Man, say happens through the rigor of critical reading. This rigor is something that produces the generalizations of theory, something that is wholly rational, logical, transmissible, the product of rigorous thinking that might have been done by anyone with de Man's intelligence and learning. Theory grows out of reading and is authorized by it, though it is in a different register and even though theory and reading, as "The Resistance to Theory" shows, are not symmetrical. Though "the resistance to theory is in fact a resistance to reading," nevertheless "rhetorical readings, like the other kinds, still avoid and resist the reading they advocate. Nothing can overcome the resistance to theory since theory *is* itself this resistance" (RT, 15, 19). In the "Reply to Raymond Geuss," de Man asserts that the commentator should accept the "canonical reading" up to the point where something is encountered in the text that makes it impossible to go on accepting the canonical interpretation. De Man's formulations are couched in the language of ethical obligation and inevitability: "should," "could," and "necessity." The necessity arises from the reader's encounter with the text. What happens in reading happens, and it imposes implacable obligations on the reader that exceed the presuppositions both of the canonical reading and of "theory":

> The commentator should persist as long as possible in the canonical reading and should begin to swerve away from it only when he encounters difficulties which the methodological and substantial assertions of the system are no longer able to master. Whether or not such a point has been reached should be left open as part of an ongoing critical investigation. But it would be naive to believe that such an investigation could be avoided, even for the best of reasons. The necessity to revise the canon arises from resistances encountered in the text itself (extensively conceived) and not from preoccupations imported from elsewhere. (AI, 186)

Third source of de Man's authority, deepest and most serious: the scandalous, counterintuitive things he says come into language through the encounter, at the limits of the most exigent theoretical rigor and obedient close reading, of the unintelligible. De Man takes the rational to the edge of irrationality, or identifies the unintelligible as that which has always already infected the pursuit of rational knowledge: "after Nietzsche (and, indeed, after any 'text'), we can no longer hope ever 'to know' in peace" (AR, 126). Wherever de Man starts, whatever texts he reads, whatever vocabulary he uses leads ultimately beyond itself to its limits at a border of a dark unintelligibility, *Unverständlichkeit*, madness, *Dummen*. Three names de Man gives this unintelligibility are performative language, irony, and materiality. Kant may be taken as the paradigmatic model here. Kant's rigor of critical thinking itself led him to what undid his enterprise of architectonic articulation, disarticulated it. The same thing can be said of de Man's writing, except that de Man's writing is throughout a long meditation on what happens when thinking encounters that momentary event when the unintelligible, error, madness, or stupidity undoes the rational enterprise of critical thinking, or turns out to have been undoing it all along.

De Man speaks in the name of, on the grounds of, these three quite incompatible but nevertheless inextricably intertwined justifications for the allergens that he generates in words. This authority is, however, no authority in the ordinary sense. It is an authority without authority, or the authority that undoes all grounds for speaking with authority. How can one speak intelligibly on the grounds of the unintelligible? At the limit, and indeed all along the way, de Man's writings are allergenic because they pass on to the reader an allergen, a radical otherness, with which they have been infected and that is quite other to the smiling, calm, implacable, rational, maddeningly difficult to refute[32] rigor of de Man's argumentation. Or rather the latter turns out to be the same as the former, reason to be other to itself.

NOTES

1. De Man presciently outlined the project of cultural studies, as well as the ideology cultural studies tries to contest, in a paragraph in "Kant and Schiller." Paraphrasing Schiller's *On the Aesthetic Education of Man*, de Man says:

> The human is determined by this possibility of free play. . . . Hence the need, which follows, for a free and humanistic—because the notion of free and humanity go together—education, which is called an aesthetic education, and which is still the basis of our liberal system of humanistic education. Also the basis of concepts such as "culture," and the thought that it is possible to move from individual works of art to a collective, massive notion of art, which would be, for example, one of national characteristics, and which would be like the culture of a nation, of a general, social dimension called "cultural." And hence, as a logical conclusion of that, the concept in Schiller of an aesthetic state, which is the political order that would follow, as a result of that education, and which would be the political institution resulting from such a conception. (*Aesthetic Ideology* [Minneapolis: University of Minnesota Press, 1996], 150, henceforth AI)

I say cultural studies also tries to contest this set of assumptions. The contestation is often, however, done with tools borrowed from the ideology that is being contested, thereby inadvertently reaffirming it, for example mimeticist, referential, organicist, subject/object assumptions, the assumption that "culture" forms a global whole within a given nation or ethnic group, including, along with elitist forms, popular forms, all the media available at a given time, and such cultural expressions as sports, cuisine, and fashion; and, finally, the assumption that the individual artist and his or her work are to be more or less completely defined by membership in some ethnic, national, or sexual community. Cultural studies nevertheless also often makes use of concepts of hybridity and other notions of differentiations within a given culture. Those in cultural studies who are interested in reflecting on the latent assumptions of their enterprise would do well to read carefully not only Schiller's *On the Aesthetic Education of Man* and de Man's "Kant and Schiller," but also de Man's wartime writings. The later, taken as a whole, are a more or less full-fledged expression of the aesthetic ideology de Man's later work is most concerned to put in question, to "deconstruct," if you will, though hints of the later rejection of aesthetic ideology are also present in the wartime writings. They are not entirely homogeneous, woven in one whole cloth. All the urgency of de Man's postwar writing work derives from that "concern to put in question."

2. See Brower's letter to Harry Levin and Renato Poggioli, printed in Lindsay Waters's introductory essay to Paul de Man, *Critical Writings: 1953–1978* (Minneapolis: University of Minnesota Press, 1989), xiii–xiv, henceforth CW.

3. The essay is now printed in *Romanticism and Contemporary Criticism*, ed. E. S. Burt, Kevin Newmark, and Andrzej Warminski (Baltimore: The Johns Hopkins University Press, 1993), 164–77, henceforth RCC. The quoted phrase is from the editors' notes, 209. It is more likely that the essay was actually rejected because it radically put in question the ideological commitments of *The New York*

Review of Books. "The main point to be learned from Barthes," says de Man in this essay, "is not that literature has no referential function but that no 'ultimate' referent can ever be reached and that therefore the rationality of the critical meta-language is constantly threatened and problematic" (RCC, 176). This sentence is by no means too "technical" to be understood, but it is, one can imagine, something the editors of the journal did not want said in their pages. The sentence is a miniature example of that encounter through rational analysis of the nonrational-izable, the unintelligible, that is the main movement of de Man's work through-out. I shall return to unintelligibility in de Man.

4. Paul de Man, "The Resistance to Theory," *The Resistance to Theory* (Min-neapolis: University of Minnesota Press, 1986), 3, henceforth RT.

5. Paul de Man, *The Rhetoric of Romanticism* (New York: Columbia Univer-sity Press, 1984), 262, henceforth RR.

6. I use the word "joyfully" as an allusion to Nietzsche's "joyful wisdom" or *fröhliche Wissenschaft.* Anyone who fails to see the exuberant or even comic joy in de Man's writings, anyone who sees him as a "gloomy existentialist," as one commentator calls him, simply lacks an ear. The ironic comedy sometimes sur-faces openly, as when he says, apropos of Kant's assertion that the Dutch are all phlegmatic, "interested only in money and totally devoid of any feeling for beauty or sublimity whatsoever": "I have never felt more grateful for the hundred or so kilometers that separate Antwerp [de Man's home city] from Rotterdam" (AI, 125). Another example is what he says as part of an assertion that the self-undoing of Kant's critical enterprise through "the rigor of his own discourse" was not felt as a subjective, affective shudder: "I don't think that Kant, when he wrote about the heavens and the sea there, that he was shuddering in mind. Any literal-ism there would not be called for. It is terrifying in a way which we don't know. What do we know about the nightmares of Immanuel Kant? I'm sure they were . . . very interesting . . . Königsberg there in the winter—I shudder to think" (AI, 134). This joy is no doubt one of the things that is held against de Man, as Der-rida's exuberant hijinks, in format for example, are held against him. Both make ironic jokes about deadly serious matters. There is no room, some people seem to think, for comedy, or for joy either, in philosophy and theory. They are solemn matters for which you should, if you are a man, always wear a shirt and tie.

7. De Man goes on to recognize that the final twist of irony in Greek or Hel-lenic comedy is that the smart guy is "always being set up by the person he thinks of as being the dumb guy, the *alazon.* In this case the *alazon* (and I recognize this makes me the real *alazon* of this discourse) is American criticism of irony, and the smart guy is going to be German criticism of irony, which I of course understand" (AI, 165). This seems to be a rare example of an overt admission by de Man that he is bound to be caught in the traps he sets for others, that what is sauce for the goose is sauce for the gander. In the rest of "The Concept of Irony," however, de Man allows precious little in the way of smart-guy attributes either to Ameri-can criticism of irony, represented by Wayne Booth, presented as a dumb guy through and through, or to German and Danish criticism of irony either, with the exception of Friedrich Schlegel. Hegel, Kierkegaard, Benjamin, Szondi, etc., are all as dumb as Booth, though in different ways. In the vibrating irony of the passage I have quoted from de Man, it is ironic for him to claim he represents

American criticism of irony, though of course he is not German either. In any case, for him to say he is "the real *alazon* of this discourse" is at the same time to say he is the real *eiron*, since the *alazon* always turns out to be the disguised *eiron*, the smartest smart guy, or the only smart guy around.

8. *Yale French Studies*, no. 63 (1982).

9. Paul de Man, *Allegories of Reading* (New Haven: Yale University Press, 1979), 245, henceforth AR.

10. The reference of course is to Nietzsche's "On Truth and Lie in an Extramoral Sense," commented on by de Man in several essays, most cogently at the beginning of "Anthropomorphism and Trope in the Lyric" in RR, 239–43.

11. (New York: Seabury, 1979).

12. Tierce de Picardie or Picardy third: "The major third as used for the final chord of a composition in a minor key" (Willi Apel, *Harvard Dictionary of Music*, 2d ed. [Cambridge: Belknap Press of Harvard University Press, 1973], 677).

13. "Woven man nicht sprechen kann, daruber muss man schweigen," the last sentence of Ludwig Wittgenstein's *Tractatus Logico-Philosophicus*, 2d imp. (London: Routledge & Kegan Paul, 1933), 188.

14. J. L. Austin, *How to Do Things with Words*, ed. J. O. Urmson and Marina Sbisà, 2d ed. (Oxford: Oxford University Press, 1980), 55, 59. That bull, or another one, Irish or French, shows up in de Man's own writing by way of a reference at the beginning of "Excuses (*Confessions*)" to Michel Leiris's "De la littérature considérée comme une tauromachie": "the deadly 'horn of the bull' referred to by Michel Leiris in a text that is indeed as political as it is autobiographical" (AR, 278).

15. In *Speech Acts in Literature* (Stanford: Stanford University Press, 2001).

16. Reprinted in *Blindness and Insight*, 2d ed. (Minneapolis: University of Minnesota Press, 1983), 208–28, henceforth BI.

17. Author of *Die Romantische Ironie in Theorie und Gestaltung* (Tübingen: Max Niemeyer Verlag, 1960).

18. "Thus irony allows one to say dreadful things because it says them by means of aesthetic devices, achieving a distance, a playful aesthetic distance, in relation to what is being said" (AI, 169).

19. In *Speech Acts in Literature*.

20. Fichte is notorious, to me at least, for having said that anyone anywhere, within any nation or culture, can think philosophically, so long as they do it in the German language. As I have argued in *Black Holes* (Stanford: Stanford University Press, 1999), 503, to put it this way is a schematic summary of the complex argument made in the seventh of Fichte's *Reden an die Deutsche Nation*, "Noch tiefere Erfassung der Ursprünglichkeit, und Deutschheit eines Volkes (A Closer Study of the Originality and Germanness of a People)." See Johann Gottlieb Fichte, *Reden an die Deutsche Nation* (Hamburg: Felix Meiner, 1955; originally published in Berlin: In der Realschulbuchhandlung, 1808), 106–24 and, for a translation, *Addresses to the German Nation*, ed. George Armstrong Kelley (New York: Harper and Row, 1968), 92–110. For a discussion of Fichte's views on Germanness, see Jacques Derrida, "Privilège," in *Du droit à la philosophie* (Paris: Galilée, 1990), 51–53, and "La main de Heidegger (*Geschlect* II)," in *Psyché: Inventions de l'autre* (Paris: Galilée, 1987), 416–20.

21. See Andrzej Warminski's admirably exuberant commentary on the temporally contradictory iterations or stutters ("then" and "actually," "say," "saying," "say") in de Man's own parabasis here, "To say then, as we are actually saying, . . . is to say," in "Introduction: Allegories of Reference" (AI, 31–32).

22. Friedrich Schlegel, *Kritische Schriften* (Munich: Carl Hanser, 1964), 501–502; Schlegel, *Dialogue on Poetry and Literary Aphorisms*, trans. Ernst Behler and Roman Struc (University Park: The Pennsylvania State University Press, 1968), 86.

23. And as I have argued in "Promises, Promises: Speech Act Theory, Literary Theory, and Politico-Economic Theory in Marx and de Man," forthcoming in a Chinese periodical, *The Journal of Marxist Aesthetics*.

24. The anonymous reader of the part of this chapter in *Material Events: Paul de Man and the Afterlife of Theory*, ed. Tom Cohen et al. (Minneapolis: University of Minnesota Press, 2001), strongly resisted this account of de Man's concept of historical events in their materiality. "Miller's idea of history, moreover" the reader said, "is of little merit and has, as far as I can tell, very little to do with de Man." This is a good example of what I mean by an allergic reaction. My own idea of history is not expressed anywhere here, only de Man's. Perhaps the reader missed the irony, as well as the covert reference to George Eliot's *Middlemarch*, in my sentence about history as wars, migrations of peoples, etc. That is not my idea of history, but an attempt at an ironic formulation of what some people may take for granted history is. As for the reference to *Middlemarch*, when Will Ladislaw tells Dorothea, in an admirably ironic interchange, that his painting of "Marlowe's Tamburlaine Driving the Conquered Kings in his Chariot" represents "the tremendous course of the world's physical history lashing on the harnessed dynasties," she asks if that includes "earthquakes and volcanoes." "O yes," he answers, "and migrations of races and clearings of forests—and America and the steam-engine. Everything you can imagine!" To which Dorothea responds: "What a difficult kind of shorthand! . . . It would require all your knowledge to be able to read it" (George Eliot, *Middlemarch*, ed. W. J. Harvey [Harmondsworth: Penguin, 1974], 245–46). In any case, after a careful rereading of my essay, I claim that the citations from de Man I make support what I say about his concept of history. It is de Man's concept, not mine, that scandalizes the reader, makes him (or her) sneeze and cough. I have, however, altered one phrase that apparently misled the reader into thinking I understand de Man to be saying that history is caused by "intentional" uses of language and that might therefore mislead you, dear reader. As any careful reader of de Man knows, his theory of the performative "use" of language (as opposed to its mention) is detached from any conscious intention in the user. Language works performatively, on its own, most often against the intentions or knowledge of the speaker or writer. As he says, in the conclusion to "Promises (*Social Contract*)," "The error is not within the reader; language itself dissociates the cognition from the act. *Die Sprache verspricht (sich)*" (AR, 277), which means, as I have said, "Language promises" and also "Language makes a slip of the tongue." I have thought it worthwhile to refer directly to the comments of the Minnesota reader in order to try to forestall similar errors on the part of readers of this chapter.

25. In an equally important, though much less well-known, definition of ideologies near the beginning of "Phenomenality and Materiality in Kant," de Man

asserted that ideologies are on the side of what Kant called "metaphysics," that is, in Kant's use of the term, precritical empirical knowledge of the world. Only critical analysis of ideologies will keep ideologies from becoming mere illusion and critical philosophy from becoming idealism cut off from the empirical world (AI, 72). One reader of the section on de Man's materialism challenged my understanding in this note of Kant's use of the term "metaphysics." This is another allergic reaction, one that demonstrates just the point I am making about de Man. Surely Kant cannot have meant something so strange as this by "metaphysics"! At the risk of making this note tediously long for those who have read Kant and de Man's commentary on Kant, here is the relevant passage from Kant, followed by de Man's comment on it. I think my reader is mystified through having accepted received opinion about what Kant must be saying because everyone knows that is what he says. That received opinion is, precisely, a species of "ideology," even of "aesthetic ideology." Kant says:

> A transcendental principle is one through which we represent *a priori* the universal condition under which alone things can become Objects of our cognition generally. A principle, on the other hand, is called metaphysical (Dagegen heißt ein Prinzip metaphysisch), where it represents *a priori* the condition under which alone Objects whose concept has to be given empirically (empirisch), may become further determined (bestimmt) *a priori*. Thus the principle of the cognition of bodies (der Erkenntnis der Körper) as substances, and as changeable substances, is transcendental where the statement is that their change must have a cause (Ursache): but it is metaphysical where it asserts that their change must have an *external* cause (eine äußere Ursache). For in the first case bodies need only be thought through ontological predicates (pure concepts of understanding [reine Verstandesbegriffe]), e.g. as substance, to enable the proposition to be cognized *a priori*; whereas, in the second case, the empirical concept of a body (as a movable thing in space) must be introduced to support the proposition (diesem Satze zum Grunde gelegt werden), although, once this is done, it may be seen (eingesehen) quite *a priori* that the latter predicate (movement only by means of an external cause) applies to body. (Immanuel Kant, *Kritik der Urteilskraft*, ed. Wilhelm Wieschedel [Frankfurt am Main: Suhrkamp, 1979], 90; Kant, *The Critique of Judgement*, trans. James Creed Meredith [Oxford: Oxford University Press, 1982], 20–21)

De Man comments, in "Phenomenality and Materiality in Kant":

> The condition of existence of bodies is called substance; to state that substance is the cause of the motion of bodies (as Kant does in the passage quoted) is to examine critically the possibility of their existence. Metaphysical principles, on the other hand, take the existence of their object for granted as empirical fact. They contain knowledge of the world, but this knowledge is precritical. Transcendental principles contain no knowledge of the world or anything else, except for the knowledge that metaphysical principles that take them for their object are themselves in need of critical analysis, since they take for granted an objectivity that, for the transcendental principles, is not a priori available. Thus the objects of transcendental principles are al-

ways critical *judgments* that take metaphysical knowledge for their target. Transcendental philosophy is always the critical philosophy of metaphysics. (AI, 71)

De Man goes on to associate ideology with metaphysics as Kant defines it. The passage is an important gloss on de Man's definition, or, more properly, "calling," of ideology in "The Resistance to Theory," cited above. In the sentences that follow just after the ones already quoted from "Phenomenality and Materiality in Kant," de Man associates ideology with Kantian "metaphysics" and argues for an intricate interdependence of critical thought on ideology and of ideology itself, if it is to other than "mere error," on critical thought. If metaphysics or ideology needs critical thought, critical thought also needs ideology, as its link to epistemological questions. The link is "causal." The "passage" is a good example of that almost imperceptible crossing, in de Man's formulations, of the border between rigorous reading of passages in the author being discussed and statements that are de Man's own, authorized by his own rigor of thought, as it extrapolates from what the author in question says:

> Ideologies, to the extent that they necessarily contain empirical moments and are directed toward what lies outside the realm of pure concepts, are on the side of metaphysics rather than critical philosophy. The conditions and modalities of their occurrence are determined by critical analyses to which they have no access. The object of these analyses, on the other hand, can only be ideologies. Ideologies and critical thought are interdependent and any attempt to separate them collapses ideology into mere error and critical thought into idealism. The possibility of maintaining the causal link between them is the controlling principle of rigorous philosophical discourse: philosophies that succumb to ideology lose their epistemological sense, whereas philosophies that try to by-pass or repress ideology lose all critical thrust and risk being repossessed by what they foreclose. (72)

The only responsible way to challenge de Man's reading of Kant would be to go back to Kant for oneself and read him with scrupulous care, trying not to be mislead by ideological presuppositions about what Kant must be saying. This is extremely difficult, not just because Kant is difficult, but because those ideological presuppositions are so powerful and are unconscious to boot, as Althusser says of ideology in general, that is, a taken for granted assumption that something really linguistic is phenomenal.

26. See Jacques Derrida, *Limited Inc* (Evanston: Northwestern University Press, 1988), 48.

27. Derrida's phrase in "Typewriter Ribbon: Limited Ink (2): ('within such limits')," in *Material Events*. Derrida's full characterization of de Man's materiality is: "machinistic materiality without materialism and even perhaps without matter." For an astute discussion of de Man on Kant's material vision, see Andrzej Warminski, "As the Poets Do It: On the Material Sublime," in *Material Events*, 3–31.

28. See de Man's "Reply to Raymond Geuss" (AI, 183–92), first published in *Critical Inquiry* 10, 2 (December 1983), a rejoinder to Geuss's "A Response to Paul de Man," in the same issue of *Critical Inquiry*.

29. Speaking in "Autobiography as De-Facement," of what Gérard Genette says about the undecidable alternation between fiction and autobiography in Proust's *Recherche*, de Man says: "As anyone who has ever been caught in a revolving door or on a revolving wheel can testify, it is certainly most uncomfortable, and all the more so in this case since this whirligig is capable of infinite acceleration and is, in fact, not successive but simultaneous" (RR, 70).

30. Jacques Derrida approaches this problematic from another direction in his second essay on Lévinas, "En ce moment même dans cet ouvrage me voici," *Psyché: Inventions de l'autre* (Paris: Galilée, 1987), 159–202.

31. Geoffrey Chaucer, *Troilus & Criseyde: A New Edition of "The Book of Troilus,"* ed. B. A. Windeatt (London: Longman, 1984), bk. 2, p. 154, l. 49.

32. I do not mean that it is impossible to disagree with what de Man says or to challenge his positions, as I have done elsewhere (by way of calling attention to the way de Man cannot expunge one trope, prosopopoeia, from his own language, though he rejects prosopopoeia as a false projection), or as I am in a sense doing here in stressing what is "unintelligible" in what de Man says, or as Jacques Derrida does with exemplary care and delicacy in "Typewriter Ribbon," apropos of de Man's sense of the relation of Rousseau's *Confessions* to literary history. I mean that challenging de Man persuasively and responsibly is not all that easy. De Man will most often have foreseen and effectively forestalled the objections that occur to a skeptical or antagonistic reader to make. As de Man himself says in "The Resistance to Theory," "Technically correct rhetorical readings may be boring, monotonous, predictable and unpleasant, but they are irrefutable" (RT, 19). The reader should remember, however, that de Man goes on, in a series of intricate formulations, to say that to the extent that such readings are totalizing, potentially totalitarian, and generalizable or universalizable, that is, theoretical, they are a resistance to reading, not its apotheosis, and therefore are a resistance to the theory that is supposed to arise from reading. Let me quote again sentences from "The Resistance to Theory" already quoted, coming at them now from a slightly different angle: "to the extent however that they are theory, that is to say teachable, generalizable and highly responsive to systematization, rhetorical readings, like the other kinds, still avoid and resist the reading they advocate. Nothing can overcome the resistance to theory, since theory *is* itself this resistance" (RT, 19). The clearer and more irrefutable a rhetorical reading is, the more generalizable it is, that is, the more theoretical it is, the more incapable it is of accounting for what is unique, particular, singular, ungeneralizable about a given text. Since theory is supposed to account for the unique, particular, and singular, its success in achieving generalizations, such as those generalizations about tropes or allegories de Man makes, is at the same moment its failure to achieve the goal of theory. It is in this sense, I suppose, that de Man means theory is the resistance to theory.

Chapter Eleven

JACQUES DERRIDA'S OTHERS

L'autre appelle à venir et celà n'arrive qu'à
plusieurs voix.
　　　—Jacques Derrida, "Psyché:
　　　　Invention de l'autre"

"L'AUTRE" has long been a key word in Jacques Derrida's vocabulary. Just what does he mean by "the other"? My goal is "plainly to propound"[1] what Derrida means by "l'autre," for example in the sentence I have quoted as an epigraph, repeating it from its citation as the epigraph for the "Introduction," thereby bringing this book full circle. The word or the concept of "the other" is used in many different and by no means compatible ways in current humanistic discourse. I have described these elsewhere.[2]

Jacques Derrida's reflections on the other take their place in the context of the melange of contradictory assumptions about otherness in current critical thought. As opposed to Lacan, for example, for whom, in spite of the fact that the unconscious is the discourse of the other, the letter always reaches its destination, for Derrida, as he says, the letter never gets to its destination. This is true even when, as in a postcard, the letter is exposed where all can read it, including even the one to whom it is apparently addressed. The letter, for Derrida, is condemned to wander interminably in "destinerrance," not so much in its plurisignificance as in its aporetic indeterminacy of meaning and addressee. For Derrida, as he says, "Tout autre est tout autre," one meaning of which is "Every other is completely other."[3] This means, among other things, that the lines of communication are down between me and the other.

The notion of otherness has fundamental importance from one end of Derrida's work to the other, even when it is given other names, or is glimpsed in different ways, for example in the reference of "la différance" to a past that never occurred, or in the exploration in "Fors" of what it means to speak of an event that took place without ever having taken place and that has brought it about that the Wolfman is haunted by the dead-alive body of the radically other in a crypt in his unconscious. Derrida's recent work on the gift, on the secret, and on testimony all presuppose a notion of otherness. The other, however, is always already there (or rather not there, but elsewhere), as an effaced presupposition of even Derrida's earliest work.

It would be a long trek to track the Protean other through all the diversity of Derrida's work. Many recent essays confront the question of the other more or less directly: an interview with Jean-Luc Nancy called " 'Il faut bein manger' ou le calcul du sujet" (" 'Eating Well,' or the Calculation of the Subject");[4] the title essay in *Psyché: Inventions de l'autre*;[5] Derrida's book on death, *Apories*; the chapter entitled "Tout Autre Est Tout Autre" in *Donner la mort*;[6] "Fourmis," the essay on Hélène Cixous in *Lectures de la différence sexuelle*;[7] an essay published in English in a Norwegian journal, "The Monolingualism of the Other or the Prosthesis of Origin" and then in a much longer French version as *Le Monolinguisme de l'autre ou la prothèse d'origine*.[8]

If every other is wholly other, then any thought of the other is certain to lead to paradoxes, catachreses, and aporias. In *Apories*, for example, Derrida patiently demonstrates that Heidegger's thought about death in its relation to Dasein is undermined by an aporia. If the otherness of death is wholly other, it cannot be used as a distinguishing feature of Dasein. If death is the possibility of an impossibility, then it is impossible to say anything more about it than that. Even to say that is too much, since as an aporia it is an impasse in speech and thought, marking all the way in thought that has been traversed to get to it with the sign not of a "Holzweg" but of a "Dead End." The fact that the other cannot be thought directly by no means, however, forbids thinking or speaking about it, as Derrida's work abundantly shows.

Richard Kearney asked Derrida in an interview in 1981: "What then of the question of language as reference? Can language as mutation or monstrosity refer to anything other than itself?" To this Derrida answered:

It is totally false to suggest that deconstruction is a suspension of reference. Deconstruction is always deeply concerned with the "other" of language. I never cease to be surprised by critics who see my work as a declaration that there is nothing beyond language, that we are imprisoned in language; it is, in fact, saying the opposite. The critique of logocentrisim is above all else the search for the "other" and the "other of language." . . . Certainly deconstruction tries to show that the question of reference is much more complex and problematic than traditional theories supposed. It even asks whether our term "reference" is entirely adequate for designating the "other." The other, which is beyond language and which summons language, is perhaps not a "referent" in the normal sense which linguists have attached to this term. But to distance oneself thus from the habitual structure of reference, to challenge or complicate our common assumptions about it, does not amount to saying that there is *nothing* beyond language. . . . I totally refuse the label of nihilism which has been ascribed to me and my American colleagues. Deconstruction is not an enclosure in nothingness, but an openness towards the other.[9]

Just what notion of "the other" is being invoked in these sentences? What does Derrida mean when he says the other is "beyond language and summons language"? What does he mean by "an openness towards the other"? The first thing to stress in answering these questions is that exploration of what Derrida means by "l'autre" is a good way to see how wrong are the journalistic (and academic) accounts of his work that say for Derrida we are all immured in a prison-house of language, that Derrida is a nihilist, that he denies the referential dimension of language, and so on, in a familiar litany of denunciation and incomprehension. Derrida, in the interview with Kearney, invokes the other as a means of countering those false but deeply rooted mistakes about his thought and about so-called deconstruction. Much is at stake, therefore, in understanding just what Derrida means by "the other." It is a crucial aspect of his thinking that has for the most part been ignored not only by falsifying journalists but sometimes even in friendly accounts of his work. Getting right what Derrida means by "l'autre" is essential to understanding what he says about ethics, selfhood, responsibility, literature, law, psychoanalysis, sexual difference, politics, religion, translation, and the university. "L'autre" is by no means just one perhaps peripheral element that could be safely omitted in accounting for what he says about any one of these practical domains or domains of praxis.

In all his important uses of the word "autre," Derrida clearly names by it something that is completely other, something that cannot be returned to the same by any form of dialectical sublation or *Aufhebung*. What is somewhat less easy to think or see is the relation of the other to a special and paradoxical kind of speech act. I present below four citations from Derrida that use the word "autre." One of them has already been cited as my epigraph. If we can understand them, if they are indeed understandable in the ordinary sense of the word, if we can understand them both in themselves and as they grow out of the contexts that justified their utterance, we shall be on the way toward understanding what Derrida means by "l'autre." The four extracts are not arranged in any hierarchy, or logical progression, though their sequence helps me to make my own argument. Nor do they follow some presumed chronological development in Derrida's writings. Each one is sui generis. I do not claim that, taken singly or together, they are "representative," nor even especially salient. Many other citations might have done as well. A different result, however, would have followed from choosing others rather than these. The citations do not form the outline of stages in a dialectic, getting closer and closer to the heart of the other. They represent rather a kind of movement in place, each one a gesture toward "l'autre" that withdraws in the moment it is proffered as a response to the call of the other. Each one is as close and as distant as the others from the other. That means they are at once proximate and infinitely distant, both from one another and from the other, since, as Derrida says, the other that is in question for him is the other of any language for it. Nor should this chapter be thought of as the climax of this book, getting finally to the truth about the other. All the other chapters have equal validity and authority in what they say about the other(s).

The four citations, abstracted from their original contexts, are turned by my act of citation into aphorisms. "Aphorism"—the word means "a short, pithy sentence, stating a general doctrine or truth" (*Webster's Collegiate Dictionary*). Etymologically, "aphorism" means "from the horizon." The word comes from the Greek word *aphorizein*, to define, from *apo* (from, away from; detached, separate) + *horizein* (to bound or separate), taking "horizon" as a border, boundary, or bourne that separates or defines, gives borders or edges. If Derrida's "autre" is the other of all language, this means that any aphoristic definition of it incorporates the other within the sentence. It does this, however, without doing it, that is, by stating anew, in yet another way, the impossibility of incorporating the other within any form of language. Derrida's "autre" is beyond the horizon of any linguistic formula. It keeps its secret from any way of speaking in any natural language. These aphorisms must therefore not be thought of as passwords allowing the knowing reader of them to cross some border to a direct confrontation with the other. No direct confrontation with the other is possible, for reasons the aphorisms directly or indirectly give. An aphorism about the other is a perturbation around the horizon or "event horizon" bordering the black hole[10] of the other, which is another way of saying it is a peculiar form of catachresis. The perturbation of the language is evidence of an other that is always the other of language, summoned by it, summoning it.

As the reader will see, each of the citations I am about to make is, strictly speaking, untranslatable, though of course it has been translated well enough. Each exploits, however, as Derrida so often does, the idiomatic and idiosyncratic properties of the French language: word play of various kinds, puns, homonyms, plays on families of words with the same roots, the powerful resources of the French reflexive, the particular structure of French pronouns (the words for "it" are, for example, gendered in French, as is not the case in English), disguised allusion, and so on. I shall try to account later for just why this particularly needs to be the case when Derrida speaks about the other, though I have already hinted at the answer.

Though I can understand the passages I shall cite and their contexts well enough, my relation to the French language is still a little like that of a jealous lover. I want to penetrate within the language, to identify myself with its secret essence, to feel at home there, to know it from the inside. But I cannot. I can only know it from the outside, as a "foreign language." Even study of *Littré* or *Robert* gives me only an external and objective knowledge of the nuances of French, whereas the *Oxford English Dictionary* in a way only tells me what I already know through already possessing (more or less) mastery of my mother tongue. This is true only "in a way," however, since my own mother tongue contains many secrets and surprises even for a "native speaker," not only in its history but also in the novel possibilities that a great writer may invent or discover, wresting them from that secret reservoir of otherness that even one's own language harbors. Nevertheless, the fascination of the French language, for me, is the fascination of the alien, the other. Strangely enough, the pleasure of knowing another language is almost an erotic pleasure. It is a form of exogamy, like entering, or thinking you enter, into the intimacy of another person, another home. Nevertheless, the French language, as used by Derrida, for example, keeps its secret from me. It hides in its otherness. I remain a guest or ghost or stranger haunting a place where I do not really belong. Here are the four citations. In the first, the French word "autre" is represented by its Latin equivalent, "alter," though the word "autre" appears in closely adjacent sentences:

> L'*alter ego* ne peut pas se présenter, devenir une présence originaire pour l'*ego*. (The *alter ego* cannot present itself, cannot become an originary presence for the *ego*.)[11]

> Tout autre est tout autre.

> (L'autre est déjà là, irréductiblement.) (The other is already there, irreducibly.)[12]

> L'autre appelle à venir et cela n'arrive qu'à plusieurs voix. (The other calls [something] to come, and that does not happen except in many voices.)[13]

The first aphorism emerges in an interview with Jean-Luc Nancy conducted in lieu of a written contribution to a collection of essays solicited by Nancy apropos of a series of questions asking "Who comes after the subject?" and presupposing the recent "simple liquidation" of the subject. Derrida sharply took issue with some of Nancy's formulations, especially the notion of "liquidation." Derrida argued forcefully that the subject has been no doubt problematized but by no means liquidated in current discourse—not in Lacan, nor in Lacoue-Labarthe, Foucault, Althusser, Freud, Marx, Nietzsche, nor even in Heidegger. Later on in the interview the sentence I have turned into an aphorism appears in a place where Derrida associates the new problematizing of the subject in the 1960s with a rereading of Husserl by many people then. In Derrida's own work, *La voix et la phénomène* most notably testified to this.[14] Derrida is no more a Husserlian than he is a Heideggerian, but his work remains rooted in a deconstructive (if I may dare to use that word) reading of both. In the interview with Nancy he asserts that in the 1960s "people began to become interested in those places in Husserl's discourse where the egological and more generally the subjective form of the transcendental experience appeared to be more *constituted* than *constitutive*—in sum, as much grounded as precarious. The question of time and of the other became linked to this transcendental passive genesis" (F, 278; E, 263).

I shall return later to the question of what is at stake in this shift to a "constituted" status from a "constitutive" one for the subject. What is important here is the way the imperial mastery by subjectivity, the subject, the ego, of all that it thinks, so that the transcendental ego seems for Husserl constitutive of everything else, turns out to be constituted by something that it cannot experience directly, something that is radically other to it. To that other Derrida here gives the Husserlian name, *alter ego*, meaning by that not just something other than the ego, but the other ego, the ego of the other. What is peculiar about the *alter ego*, in Derrida's reading of Husserl, is that it marks the *ego*, that is, to a degree constitutes it, without being present to it as such. This is the case in spite of the fact that the sovereignty of the *ego* is defined by the fact that everything that is, is present to it. The power of the *ego* to constitute everything by thinking of it is here broken by a nonpresence that constitutes the ego, that is, moreover, inside it without being present to it.

A crucial word in Derrida's formulation is "marked" (*marqué*). To be "marked" here means to be inscribed in a way that is originarily constitutive by something that is nevertheless not present. It is originating without being part of the given of originary presence. It is a feature of "marks" that they are the signs of something nonpresent. In this case that nonpresent is not just something that does not happen to be present, but something that is irreducibly nonpresent, therefore a scandal to the withinness of the living present as the ego experiences it.

This means that the *alter ego*, what we might call, somewhat riskily, the subjectivity of the other person, can only be presented indirectly, by what Derrida calls, following Husserl's own language, "an analogical a-presentation (apprésentation) of the *alter ego*" (F, 278; E, 263). *Appré-*

sentation is not an English word. It is not easily translatable, since it adds to "presentation" the same mark of distance and privation that is incorporated into the beginning of "aphorism": *apo*, meaning in Greek, as I have said, from, away from, detached, separate. An *apprésentation* is presentation without presentation, that is, it is presentation in an indirect form of something unpresentable by way of something that seems analogous. Since the *alter ego* cannot be known directly, such a presentation would necessarily take the form of what in rhetoric is called a catachresis, a name displaced from something known to stand for something unknown, unknowable; nameless and unnamable except by a blind and abusive transfer of a word whose referent is known. For Derrida, following what Husserl saw without wanting to see it, since it contradicted his basic premises, the other, at least in the form of the other subject, is wholly other, tout autre, but that does not deprive the other of the power to enter in, to "effract," the safe home of my own subjectivity and in a manner of speaking to constitute it, at least in the sense of fundamentally dislocating it.

Here is the whole passage from which I have extracted and so created my first aphorism, taking it by an act of violence from its context into my own ego and into my own discourse on Derrida's others. I give the aphorism itself in boldface:

> It is within (à l'intérieure), one might say (but it is precisely a question of the effraction of the within) the living present, that *Urform* of the transcendental experience, that the subject conjoins (compose) with the nonsubject or that the *ego* is marked (que l'*ego* se trouve marqué), without being able to have the originary and presentative experience of it, by the non-*ego* and especially by the *alter ego*. **The *alter ego* cannot present itself, cannot become an originary presence for the *ego*.** There is only an analogical a-presentation (*apprésentation*) of the *alter ego*. The *alter ego* can never be given "in person," it resists the principle of principles of phenomenology—namely, the intuitive given of originary presence. This dislocation of the absolute subject from the other and from time (depuis l'autre et depuis le temps) neither comes about, nor leads *beyond* phenomenology, but rather, if not in it, then at least on its border, on the very limit of its possibility. (F, 278; E, 263–64)

The second aphorism appears in *Apories*, and then, echoing in many repetitions through the early chapters of *Donner la mort*, it serves as the title of the last chapter of the latter. In one place, *Donner la mort* picks up and repeats almost word for word what is said about the *alter ego* in the interview with Jean-Luc Nancy. A new stress is placed, however, on the completeness of the otherness of the other, on what might be called the pathos of the wholly other, and on the consequences of this for religious and ethical obligation:

> And since each of us, everyone else, each other is infinitely other in its absolute singularity (chaque autre, tout autre est infiniment autre dans sa singularité absolue), inaccessible, solitary, transcendent, nonmanifest, originarily nonpresent to my *ego* (as Husserl would say of the *alter ego* that can never be originarily present to my consciousness and that I can apprehend only through what he calls *appresentation* and analogy), then what can be said about Abraham's relation to God can be said about my relation without relation (mon rapport sans rapport) to *every other (one) as every (bit) other (tout autre comme tout autre)*, in particular my relation to my neighbor or my loved ones who are as inaccessible to me, as secret and transcendent as Jahweh. (F, 110; E, 78)

Donner la mort is a meditation on death and responsibility by way of discussions of the Czech philosopher Ján Patocka, as well as of Lévinas, Heidegger, Kierkegaard, Melville's "Bartleby the Scrivener," and the story of Abraham and Isaac in *Genesis*. "L'autre" in *Donner la mort*, as can be seen from the citation I have already made, has an association with death, with ethics, and with religious thought. The formula, which Derrida says just came to him out of the blue, as a gift—"Tout autre est tout autre"—becomes a crux or pivot of Derrida's thinking through of the conflicted relation between our obligation to our neighbor and our obligation to God. The formula in itself, however, in its enigmatically smiling self-enclosure and in its all or nothing generality, exceeds the contexts in which it is used in this book. Its meaning, even more than is the case with most sentences, depends on what we a little too complacently call its "context," on the uses to which it is put.

Derrida opens the chapter named with this formula with a meditation on the formula itself. The problem lies in its shimmering or trembling with various possible meanings. This is easiest to see if you try to translate it. As Derrida observes, it is in a certain sense untranslatable:

> The essential and abyssal equivocality, that is, the play of the several senses of *tout autre est tout autre* or *Dieu est tout autre*, is not, in its literality (that of French or Italian, for example), universally translatable according to a traditional concept of translation (si on se fie au concept courant de la traduction). The sense of the play can no doubt be translated by a paraphrase in other languages; but not the formal economy of the slippage (l'économie formalisante du glissement) between two homonyms in the language that can here be called singularly my own, that is, the use of *tout* as an indefinite pronominal adjective and as an adverb, and *autre* as indefinite pronominal adjective and noun. We have here a kind of *shibboleth*, a secret formula such

as can be uttered only in a certain way in a certain language (qui ne peut se dire que d'une certaine façon dans telle ou telle langue). A chance or aleatory effect (En tant que chance ou aléa), the untranslatability of this formal economy functions like a secret within one's so-called natural or mother tongue. (F, 121–22; E, 87–88)

I have translated the phrase as "Every other is wholly other." David Wills, in the English translation of *Donner la mort*, translates it as "Every other (one) is every (bit) other," which, in its awkward parentheses, has the virtue of calling attention to the problem of meaning and translation. Both translations, however, choose one meaning out of the indefinite array of possible ones implicit in the French original. As Derrida observes, the phrase trembles with several contradictory meanings.

It could be an empty tautology, saying more or less nothing at all: "Every other is every other," or "The wholly other is the wholly other." Yes, we knew that already.

Even if the two "touts" and the two "autres" are taken as having each a different meaning, adjective and then adverb for "tout," noun and then adjective for "autre," the phrase could still name what Derrida calls "a hetero-tautological speculation" that would enclose otherness within a Hegelian dialectical *Aufhebung*. As Derrida says, "the speculative always requires a hetero-tautological position. That is its definition according to Hegel's speculative idealism, and it is the impetus (moteur) for the dialectic within the horizon of absolute knowledge" (F, 116; E, 83). To say "Tout autre est tout autre" would then be a way of returning the other ultimately to the same, or at least promising such a return out at that horizon of absolute knowledge.

Finally, the phrase could name a principle of alterity that would be "totally, absolutely, radically, infinitely other," that could in no way be recuperated or negotiated with, that could in no way be sublated in a dialectical progression, but that would remain stubbornly, irreducibly, infinitely other.

The three meanings cannot be reconciled or synthesized. The sentence vibrates within itself with these possibilities, possibilities that seem to harbor a secret expressible only in French or in closely related Romance languages.

If the phrase, taken in the final way, as Derrida of course wants us (also) to do, is understood to name the absolute singularity of my neighbor or of God, then, as Derrida demonstrates, important and troubling consequences follow for ethics, religion, economic, political, and legal affairs. For one thing, the limit between religion and ethics, so important in different ways for Kierkegaard and for Lévinas, would be impossible to determine. If *"tout autre est tout autre* signifies that every other is singular, that every one is a singularity," then it is impossible to distinguish between our obligation to God as singular and our obligation to every one of our neighbors, each an absolute singularity. Moreover, since our obligation to each one of these singularities, each of those who are wholly other, is infinite, no way can be found to fulfill all of those obligations; each of them equally exigent. As Derrida says, this aporia "applies all the more to political or legal matters (la chose politique ou juridique). The concept of responsibility, like that of decision, would thus be found to lack coherence or consequence, even lacking identity with respect to itself, paralyzed by what can be called an aporia or an antinomy (ce qu'on aussi bien appeler une aporie qu'une antinomie)" (F, 117; E, 84).

Earlier, in the previous chapter of *Donner la mort*, Derrida gives moving expression to the affective consequence of this aporia by comparing it to the situation of Abraham about to sacrifice Isaac on Mount Moriah:

> *Every other (one) is every (bit) other [tout autre est tout autre]*, every one else is completely or wholly other. The simple concepts of alterity and of singularity constitute the concept of duty as much as that of responsibility. As a result, the concepts of responsibility, of decision, or of duty, are condemned a priori to paradox, scandal, and aporia. Paradox, scandal, and aporia are themselves nothing other than sacrifice (ne sont autres, eux-mêmes, que le sacrifice), the revelation (exposition) of conceptual thinking at its limit, at its death and finitude. As soon as I enter into a relation with the other, with the gaze, look, request, love, command, or call of the other (avec le regard, la demande, l'amour, l'ordre, l'appel de l'autre), I know that I can respond only by sacrificing ethics, that is, by sacrificing whatever obliges me also to respond, in the same way, in the same instant, to all the others. I offer a gift of death, I betray (Je donne la mort, je parjure), I don't need to raise my knife over my son on Mount Moriah for that. Day and night, at every instant, on all the Mount Moriahs of this world, I am doing that, raising my knife over what I love and must love, over those to whom I owe absolute fidelity, incommensurably (sur l'autre, tel ou telle autre à qui je dois fidélité absolue, incommensurablement). (F, 98; E, 68)

As the reader can see, Derrida's *Donner la mort*, as it meditates on the aphoristic "tout autre est tout autre," in all its idiomatic otherness, shows that the consequences of taking seriously the otherness and singularity of the other are by no means trivial. In fact the consequences may be intolerable, the intolerable as such, something that no one can bear to see face to face. All the civilized conventions of law, ethics, family life, politics, institutionalized religion, international diplomacy, and institutionalized pedagogy may have as one of their main functions to obscure the otherness and singularity of the other, to sidestep the aporia or antinomy that puts each one of us in Abraham's place on Mount Moriah every moment of every day, unable to fulfill our obligation to all the singularities to whom we owe absolute fidelity. The scandalized resistance to Derrida and to so-called deconstruction may be, in part at least, a resistance to confronting the wholly other otherness of the other as it enters his work not just as a theme but also as a perturbation in his language.

The third aphorism I have fabricated by extraction is drawn from "Fourmis (Ants)," an essay paying homage to the fictional work of Hélène Cixous. It has been published in a volume of essays called *Lectures de la différence sexuelle*. Measuring the density or hijinks of Derrida's styles on a scale of one to nine, from more academic or traditional to less so, this essay may join *Glas*, *Signéponge*, *La carte postale*, or *Feu la cendre* in meriting a nine. The careful reader will, however, be wary of such distinctions, since the most academic-looking of Derrida's writings often hide puns, make hidden allusions, and exploit the secret resources of the French language as much as do the more openly wild of his writings. In the case of my extract from "Fourmis" and its immediate context, the play is on pronouns, *il* and *tu*, as well as perhaps on the homonymic relation between *tu* as a pronoun and *tu* as one form of *tuer* (kill) and as the past participle of *taire*, meaning "keep silent or hide," and on the untranslatable give-and-take among French words using the -*pell* of appellation or calling, whether with or without the reflexive: *appeler*, *rappeler*, *se rapeller*, and so on.

This aphorism also affirms the crucial role of an anomalous speech act, anomalous in its difference from the Austinian one, in Derrida's thought of the other. Commenting on Cixous's narrator's commentary on what a character named Tatiana in one of her stories writes to a male friend, "Je suis à toi (I am yours)," Derrida confirms Cixous's assertion that such a statement ordains the other to be in his sexual difference from the speaker. The "Be who you are" calls the other into being as a "he," in a way that in its performative power recalls Augustine's "volo ut sis (I want you to be)," spoken by God to his creatures but also by any human creature speaking his or her love for another. "Tout cela," says Derrida, "*semble* instituer la différence sexuelle dans l'*acte* de lecture/écriture le plus pragmatique, le plus performatif, ici l'expérience d'une apostrophe originaire rappelant aussi l'origine de l'apostrophe, le 'tu' qui, interrompant le silence de ce qui est tu, fait naître, engendre et provoque, convovoque, appelle mais en vérité *rappelle* le 'il' à l'être." (All that *seems* to institute sexual difference in the most pragmatic, the most performative *act* of reading/writing, here the experience of an originary apostrophe, the 'thou' which, interrupting the silence of what is silenced, brings to birth, engenders and provokes, convokes, calls but in truth *recalls* the 'he' into being.) ("Fourmis," 89, my trans.). The "sois qui tu es (be who you are)" seems, but only seems, to institute sexual difference in an autonomous speech act that is like an originary apostrophe because an apostrophe is spoken to the absent, inanimate, or dead and brings them to life and proximity, as in P. B. Shelley's "Be thou me, impetuous one!" spoken to the West Wind in his "Ode to the West Wind" (l. 62). An apostrophe always calls (*appelle*) the "thou" into being by saying "thou," but this only *seems* a free and unsponsored act. Actually the calling is a recalling, the "thou" as the "he" that Tatiana loves is always already there, waiting to be recalled. The seeming in Derrida's word *semble* does not mean that the "Be who you are" is powerless or empty. As Derrida makes clear in the last two sentences of this paragraph, the sentences I have cited as an aphorism, the calling reverses into an experience of being called. The sovereign act of writing, as in Tatiana's letter, becomes an act of reading, a deciphering or citing of writing already there as much as it is an originating inscription.

Derrida here plays on the word "act," as in "speech act," but also on its presence in an untranslatable French idiom, *prendre acte*, meaning something like "take place," "occur," but with a stress on the violence of the event. This event does not just happen. It is an act. Derrida here describes a magic calling that becomes an experience of being called by the other. What begins as a free speech act turns into an act of memory. Finally, as the thou is called back into being, recalled (the *rappelant* in "en te rappelant" means called anew, called back, but also brought back into memory), the act *se rappelle*, that is, it remembers. It calls something back into consciousness that was already there but forgotten, waiting to be remembered. The French reflexive determines a nuance of meaning. The closest to *se rappeller* in English is the reflexive version of "remind," as in "That reminds me." It is as if in English one could distinguish between "I remember" and "I remember me of so and so." The second locution would mean an act of memory that returns the "me" to itself in an event of anamnesia. This remembering brings back to the "me" something that it had lost of itself by forgetting it, as one says in English: "I returned to myself." The "something" in question is the other that is already there, irreducibly:

> Lisant autant qu'il écrit, déchiffrant ou citant autant qu'il inscrit, cet acte est aussi un acte de mémoire (l'autre est déjà la, irréductiblement), cet acte prend acte. En te rappelant, il se rappelle. (Reading as much as it writes, deciphering or citing as much as it inscribes, this act is also an act of memory [the other is already there, irreducibly], this act enacts itself. In recalling you, it remembers, it reminds itself, it recalls itself to itself.) (Ibid., my trans.)

My fourth and final aphorism is the last sentence of "Psyché: Invention de l'autre": "L'autre appelle à venir et cela n'arrive qu'à plusieurs voix (The other calls [something] to come and that does not arrive except in many voices)." Those who know French will see how much my translation misses, for example the pun on *avenir* (future) in "à venir" (to come) which makes *cela* (that) refer to the future as well as to what the other calls to come: "the future does not arrive except in many voices." This aphoristic sentence holds in compact or "pithy" form what has been said in the previous dense and complex four pages that end the essay. These pages are perhaps the most important, detailed, and explicit of all those places where Derrida speaks about the other or uses the word *autre* in a charged context. They also represent an extravagant example of the sort of more or less untranslatable wordplay I have identified in "Fourmis."

The pages at the end of "Psyché" would merit a long and detailed commentary. These pages, in turn, are the climax of an extended essay that, among other things, reads at length a short poem by Francis Ponge, "Fable." The poem is exemplary of invention, in Derrida's reading, because it turns back on itself ("Par le mot *par* commence donc ce texte [By the word *by* this text thus begins]"), in a species of unthinkable torsion, and because it names what the words of the poem at the same time bring about. The reading of this poem, in turn, has as its context Derrida's book on Ponge, *Signéponge*, in a characteristic widening of the circle of resonances that come to mind when one tries to explain a given single sentence in Derrida. The last page of the essay, for example, contains a phrase, "la différance de l'autre," that connects this essay with one of Derrida's best known early works, "La différance."[15] What is differed, or differentiated, and at the same time deferred in the spacing of time Derrida calls, in a famous neologism, "la différance," is, precisely, "l'autre." "La différance de l'autre" names the differing and deferring of the other. This self-citation or allusion is further evidence that a thought of the other is at work from Derrida's earliest writing down to the present.

The concluding pages of "Psyché: Invention de l'autre" distinguish between two forms of invention that are nevertheless always involved with one another. "Invention" is taken in its everyday sense of technological invention as well as in its traditional rhetorical or poetic sense as the name for innovation in speaking or in writing poetry. "Invention" in the rhetorical context (Latin *inventio*) means both innovation and finding. The art of *inventio* is finding the appropriate material for a given purpose (an argument or a poem), taking it from what is already there in the storehouse of commonplaces or common places, places we all hold in common as members of Graeco-Latin-Judeo-Christian culture. As Derrida argues, basing what he says on a reading of passages in Schelling, powerful institutional assumptions in art, technology, science, law, theology, and philosophy urge us to think of invention as the discovery of something that fits into the program of what is already known and already institutionalized, something that is possible on the basis of what we already know. Such a possible invention supplements what is already there but is congruent with it, preprogrammed by it. Such an invention "revient au même (returns to the same)." It returns the other to the same. It does not bring anything of the wholly other: "elle ne déploie que la dynamis de ce qui déjà *se trouvait là*, ensemble de possibles compréhensibles qui se manifestent comme verité ontologique ou théologique, programme d'une politique culturelle ou techno-scientifique (civile et militaire), etc. (it does not deploy anything other than the force of what is to be found already there, an ensemble of comprehensible possibilities that manifest themselves as ontological or theological truth, the program of a cultural or techno-scientific (civil and military) politics, etc.)" (*Psyché*, 58, my trans.).

Such an invention, however, would not be of the truly other at all. The invention of the other is impossible because it must be invention of the impossible, that is, of what appears to be impossible from the perspective of what we already have, technologically, legally, and poetically. The invention of the wholly other would be a noncalculable, aleatory irruption or interruption, the chance appearance of the truly monstrous or unheard of: "La venue aléatoire du tout autre, au-delà de l'incalculable comme calcul encore possible, au-delà de l'ordre même du calcul, voilà la 'vraie' invention. (The chance coming of the wholly other, beyond the incalculable as still possible calculation, beyond the very order of calculation, that is 'true' invention.)" (ibid., 59, my trans.).

It will not do to define the invention of the completely other as a performative speech act in the ordinary sense. The event of an invention of the other, as Derrida says, will occur "non seulement par l'invention singulière d'un performatif, car tout performatif suppose des conventions et des règles institutionnelles; mais en tournant ces règles dans le respect de ces règles mêmes afin de laisser l'autre venir ou s'annoncer dans l'ouverture de cette déhiscence (not only by the singular invention of a performative, because every performative presupposes institutional conventions and rules; but in turning these rules out of respect for these very rules in order to let the other come or announce itself in the opening of this dehiscence" (ibid., 58–59, my trans.).

"Dehiscence": the word names the bursting open of a seed pod to disseminate its contents. If the invention of the other does not occur by way of a regular performative, since the institutionalized context presupposed for any felicitous performative means that nothing unforeseen is supposed to occur, neither does it occur in some performative of a second or third kind that would say "Come" to the wholly other, outside of any institutionalized program, in a kind of magic originality of originating. All the invention of the other can do is to make possible the coming of the other, by an act that Derrida here names "deconstruction." This act consists "à ouvrir, déclôturer, destabiliser des structures de forclusion (in opening, disenclosing, destabilizing the structures of foreclosure)" (ibid., 60, my trans.). We do not say "Come!" to the other. The other says "Come" to us, to which we respond with another "Come!," but a "Come!" that is secondary, responsive, not initiatory or inaugural.[16] We let the other come, and the other comes or does not come, unpredictably.

The "we," finally, does not even preexist the "Come!" spoken by the other, but is brought into existence by it, invented by it. The "nous" "ne peut être inventé que par l'autre, depuis la venue de l'autre qui dit 'viens' et auquel la réponse d'un autre 'viens' paraît être la seule invention désirable et digne d'intérêt. ([The 'we'] cannot be invented except by the other, from the coming of the other who says 'come' and to which the response of another 'come' appears to be the only invention that is desirable and worthy of interest" (ibid., my trans.).

It is now possible to see, as a conclusion to this gesture toward Derrida's "autres," what justifies or necessitates the wordplay all my aphorisms contain, for example "L'autre appelle à venir et cela n'arrive qu'à plusieurs voix." The linguistic play is necessary to break up or destabilize ways of thinking, speaking, and writing that are already programmed and in place. This destabilization is performed in order to give a chance to the secret other that is hidden in language to come by way of the interstices or dark, untranslatable places in a given set of words. These are those places where the words shimmer with contradictory meanings that return the language used to the density of a single language's idiom and, beneath that, to a level of nonmeaning that might be called the materiality of language, though Derrida would not be likely to use that de Manian phrase for it.

It is also possible now to see why it is that the other never comes except in multiple voices. To ascribe to it a single voice is to circumscribe it within the logical, the ontological, the monological, almost to personify it as the One or as God, Jaweh. To all these circumscriptions the "tout autre" is alien. As in Derrida's aphorisms themselves, or as in those various essays by him that are "polylogues" uttered by an indeterminate number of voices speaking in turn (for example "Restitutions"[17]), the wholly other always comes in a simultaneous speaking of many contradictory voices. "Psyché: Invention de l'autre" itself ends with two unidentifiable voices speaking in a question-and-answer sequence in which the final voice denies that "l'autre" can ever be invented and says that rather the other calls (something) to come, or calls forth, names, the future. This other calling on us to respond, this future that comes into being by way of the response, can only get here, arrive on this shore,[18] speaking in tongues, in a multitude of overlapping and contradictory voices. That is why we must speak not of "the other in Derrida's work," but of "Derrida's others":

L'autre appelle à venir et cela n'arrive qu'à plusieurs voix.

NOTES

1. Wallace Stevens's phrase, in "Notes toward a Supreme Fiction," in *Collected Poems* (New York: Knopf, 1954), 389. Stevens says our goal is "not to console/Nor sanctify, but plainly to propound."

2. In *Black Holes* (Stanford: Stanford University Press, 1999), 155–69.

3. Jacques Derrida, *Apories* (Paris: Galilée, 1996), 49; *Aporias*, trans. Thomas Dutoit (Stanford: Stanford University Press, 1993), 22. The sentence also appears repeatedly in *Donner la mort*, as I shall show below.

4. Jacques Derrida, *Points de suspension: Entretiens*, ed. Elisabeth Weber (Paris: Galilée, 1992), 269–301; " 'Eating Well,' or the Calculation of the Subject," trans. Peter Conner and Avital Ronell, in *Points . . . : Interviews, 1974–1994*, ed. Elisabeth Weber (Stanford: Stanford University Press, 1995), 255–87. Henceforth references to these and other works by Derrida will be cited as letters (F for French; E for English).

5. (Paris: Galilée, 1987).

6. (Paris: Galilée, 1999), 114–57.

7. Ed. Mara Negrón (Paris: Des femmes, 1994), 69–102.

8. English: *Est XI: Gåter: Grunnlagsproblemer i Estetisk Forskning*, ed. Karin Gundersen and Ståle Wikshåland (Oslo: NFR/EST, 1995), 7–23; French: (Paris: Galilée, 1996).

9. Jacques Derrida, "Deconstruction and the Other," in Richard Kearney, *Dialogues with Contemporary Continental Thinkers: The Phenomenological Heritage* (Manchester: Manchester University Press, 1984), 123–24.

10. For a recent essay on black holes, see Jean-Pierre Lasota, "Unmasking Black Holes," *Scientific American* 280 (May 1999): 40–47. The table of contents summarizes this essay as follows: "Evidence for black holes was until recently all circumstantial. Distinguishing them at a distance from other highly compact, gravitationally massive bodies is inherently problematic. Now astronomers may have direct proof: energy is vanishing from volumes of space without a trace" (ibid., 5). The reader will remember that my reference to "black holes" is only a figure, a figure moreover with no more authority than any other as a catachresis for the "tout autre."

11. *Points de suspension*, 278. The translation is in *Points*, 263.

12. "Fourmis," in *Lectures de la différence sexuelle*, 89, my translation. No translation, so far as I know, has yet been published.

13. "Psyché: Invention de l'autre," in *Psyché: Inventions de l'autre*, 61. For an English translation, see "Psyche: Inventions of the Other," trans. Catherine Porter, in *Reading de Man Reading*, ed. Lindsay Waters and Wlad Godzich (Minneapolis: University of Minnesota Press, 1989), 25–65. I have preferred, however, to

cite the French and to make my own translations here and in the discussion below, as evidence of a more intimate negotiation with the original.

14. (Paris: Presses Universitaires de France, 1967); *Speech and Phenomena and Other Essays on Husserl's Theory of Signs*, trans. David B. Allison (Evanston: Northwestern University Press, 1973).

15. In *Marges—de la philosophie* (Paris: Minuit, 1972), 3–29; *Margins of Philosophy*, trans. Alan Bass (Chicago: University of Chicago Press, 1982), 1–27.

16. The context for these two "comes" is another work by Derrida, the meditation on apocalypse and on the Book of Revelation in *D'un ton apocalyptique adopté naguère en philosophie* (Paris: Galilée, 1983); "Of an Apocalyptic Tone Recently Adopted in Philosophy," trans. John P. Leavey Jr., *Oxford Literary Review* 6, 2 (1984): 3–37.

17. In *La Verité en peinture* (Paris: Flammarion, 1978), 291–436; "Restitutions," trans. Geoff Bennington and Ian McLeod, in *The Truth in Painting* (Chicago: University of Chicago Press, 1987), 255–382.

18. *Rive*, enclosed in *arriver*, means "shore."

CODA

THIS BOOK has exemplified the law that says the other does not arrive except in different voices. This law is evident in the diversity of all the voices that I have invoked in citation and commentary. I have called or been called by Friedrich Schlegel, Dickens, George Eliot, Anthony Trollope, Conrad, Yeats, Forster, Proust, de Man, and Derrida, Or rather I have responded to whatever voices of otherness are called forth to speak through the words they wrote. Responding to these demands, I have allowed each hetero-otherness, as one might call it, to speak again as I quote each work or let each work speak through my words of interpretation. In doing this I have been instigated by the demand all these works make on me to read them in both the passive and active senses of that word—to let the words take on meaning in my mind and feelings and to intervene actively in the work of reading, in a wrestling with the angel that is both appropriation and being appropriated. It would be a grave mistake to think a single concept of the "other" speaks in all these works. The other calls to come and that does not arrive except in multiple voices. I have attempted to be faithful to the multiplicity of those voices and have signaled this multiplicity by calling this book *Others*.

INDEX

Abraham, 93–94, 95, 97, 266, 268
Abrams, Meyer, 225
Absalom, Absalom! (Faulkner), 88
Achebe, Chinua, 108, 111
Acts, 95
"Aesthetic Poetry" (Pater), 173
Albert, Georgia, 13
Albert, Prince, 204n5
Alcmaeon, 6
Allegory of the Virtues and Vices (Giotto), 18, 239
Althusser, Louis, 83–84, 85, 87, 90, 100n2, 191, 241, 257n25, 264
Anatomy of Criticism (Frye), 7, 63n10
Apocalypse Now, 117
Apollo, 6, 16, 98, 103n19
Ariadne, 77, 81n11
Aristotle, 5–6, 21, 27, 158
Ästhetik (Hegel), 10, 11, 21–22
Athenaeum, 99
Athenäum, 7, 8, 34
A to Z Atlas of London and Suburbs, 44
Augustine, St., 139, 269
Austen, Jane, 67, 187
Austin, J. L., 102–3n17, 108, 136n6, 210, 227–28, 237

Bacchus, 7
Balzac, Honoré de, 84
Barthes, Roland, 7, 253n3
"Bartleby the Scrivener" (Melville), 266
Baudelaire, Charles, 46, 59, 61, 230
Behler, Ernst, 9, 23, 29, 236
Benjamin, Walter, 36, 230, 232, 237–38, 253n7
Berkeley, George, 238
Bible, 71
Billy Budd (Melville), 154
Black Holes (Miller), 218n6
Blanchot, Maurice, 3
Bloom, Harold, 177, 225
Blütenstaub (Pollen) (Novalis), 9
Bon, Charles, in *Absalom, Absalom!*, 88
Booth, Wayne, 185, 204n4, 230, 253n7
Borrow, George Henry, 193

"Boy of Winander, The" (Wordsworth), 173, 176
"Building Dwelling Thinking" (Heidegger), 189
Bunker, Archie, 249
Burke, Edmund, 23, 168n21

Capital (Marx), 85, 101n7, 239
Cassell's German Dictionary, 31
Celan, Paul, 104
Celt and Saxon (Meredith), 204n12
Cervantes (Miguel Cervantes Saavedra), 16, 17, 19, 27
Chaucer, Geoffrey, 250
Christ, Jesus, 11, 70, 94, 118, 125, 142–43
Cixous, Hélène, 269
Clinton, Bill, 40n18, 95
"Comedian as the Letter C, The" (Stevens), 1
Concept of Irony, The (Kierkegaard), 10, 230
Confessions (Augustine), 139
Confessions (Rousseau), 258n32
Conrad, Joseph, 3, 79, 104–69, 276
Conrad, Joseph, works and characters: "Author's Note" of 1920, 149–50; Donkin, in *The Nigger of the "Narcissus"*, 154; "End of the Tether, The," 115–16; Gould, Charles, in *Nostromo*, 129; Haldin, Victor, in *Under Western Eyes*, 167n3; *Heart of Darkness*, 76, 104–36, 139, 147; Jim, in *Lord Jim*, 129, 167n5; Lingard, in *The Rescue*, 129; *Lord Jim*, 129, 139, 167n5; *Mirror of the Sea, The*, 111; *Nigger of the "Narcissus", The*, 124, 136n10, 141, 153–54; *Nostromo*, 129; *Notes on Life and Letters*, 111; *Personal Record, A*, 111; Razumov, in *Under Western Eyes*, 167n3; *Rescue, The*, 129; "Secret Sharer, The," 116, 135n2, 137–69; "Shadow Line, The," 141; "Typhoon," 141; *Under Western Eyes*, 167n3; *Youth*, 115–16; "Youth," 115. See also *Heart of Darkness*, characters in; "The Secret Sharer," characters in